*Special Edition*

# Using
# Enterprise
# Java

*Special Edition*

# USING
# ENTERPRISE
# JAVA

*Written by Jeff Schneider and Rajeev Arora*

# Special Edition Using Enterprise Java

Library of Congress Catalog No.: 97-66494

ISBN: 0-7897-0887-6

99 98 97    6 5 4 3 2 1

Interpretation of the printing code: the rightmost double-digit number is the year of the book's printing; the rightmost single-digit number, the number of the book's printing. For example, a printing code of 97-1 shows that the first printing of the book occurred in 1997.

All terms mentioned in this book that are known to be trademarks or service marks have been appropriately capitalized. Que cannot attest to the accuracy of this information. Use of a term in this book should not be regarded as affecting the validity of any trademark or service mark.

Screen reproductions in this book were created using Collage Plus from Inner Media, Inc., Hollis, NH.

# Credits

**PRESIDENT**
Roland Elgey

**SENIOR VICE PRESIDENT/PUBLISHING**
Don Fowley

**PUBLISHER**
Stacy Hiquet

**DIRECTOR OF MARKETING**
Lynn E. Zingraf

**PUBLISHING MANAGER**
Tim Ryan

**GENERAL MANAGER**
Joe Muldoon

**EDITORIAL SERVICES DIRECTOR**
Elizabeth Keaffaber

**MANAGING EDITOR**
Patrick Kanouse

**ACQUISITIONS DIRECTOR**
Cheryl D. Willoughby

**ACQUISITIONS EDITOR**
Jeff Riley

**PRODUCT DIRECTORS**
Erik Dafforn
Stephen L. Miller

**SENIOR EDITOR**
Elizabeth A. Bruns

**PRODUCTION EDITOR**
Aaron Gordon

**EDITORS**
Matthew B. Cox
Tonya Maddox
Jade Williams

**STRATEGIC MARKETING MANAGER**
Barry Pruett

**WEBMASTER**
Thomas H. Bennett

**PRODUCT MARKETING MANAGER**
Kristine R. Ankney

**ASSISTANT PRODUCT MARKETING MANAGER/ DESIGN**
Christy M. Miller

**ASSISTANT PRODUCT MARKETING MANAGER/ SALES**
Karen Hagen

**TECHNICAL EDITORS**
Sundar Rajan
Steve Tallon

**MEDIA DEVELOPMENT SPECIALIST**
Brandon Penticuff

**TECHNICAL SUPPORT SPECIALIST**
Nadeem Muhammed

**SOFTWARE RELATIONS COORDINATOR**
Susan D. Gallagher

**EDITORIAL ASSISTANT**
Andrea Duvall

**BOOK DESIGNER**
Ruth Harvey

**COVER DESIGNER**
Dan Armstrong

**PRODUCTION TEAM**
Maribeth Echard
DiMonique Ford

**INDEXER**
Tim Tate

Composed in *Century Old Style* and *ITC Franklin Gothic* by Que Corporation.

*This book is dedicated to my parents, Ray & Rosemary Schneider, for encouraging me to always reach for my dreams.*

*-Jeff Schneider*


*To my late father, Shri Ram Krishan Kumar, who taught me the art of learning and self-improvement.*

*-Rajeev Arora*

# About the Authors

**Jeff Schneider** is a software consultant of six years. He is employed as the Java Practice Manager for Delphi Consultants L.L.C., a company that specializes in developing large-scale Java applications for Fortune 500 clients. Jeff has written articles for **Javology** and the **Java Developers Journal**. He attended the Computer Science program of Illinois State University.

**Rajeev Arora** is Founder and Principal of his company Systemsmiths (**http://www.systemsmiths.com.au**), based in Melbourne, Australia. Systemsmiths is currently focusing on training and consulting in distributed application architectures, distributed SDLC, WWW Application Development, and Web site development. Rajeev, in 16 years in the industry, has developed technical and application architectures for a number of large and small companies in Australia, New Zealand, and India.

He has a Bachelor's degree in Electrical Engineering from the Birla Institute of Technology and Science, Pilani, in India. He is currently working on distributed computing research at the Royal Melbourne Institute of Technology, Melbourne, Australia.

Rajeev enjoys spending time with his family, bush walking, and is the DJ of a weekly radio program in Melbourne.

He can be reached at **rajeev@systemsmiths.com.au**.

# Acknowledgments

I would like to acknowledge Giueseppe Ferrigno and Saul Arizpe for providing feedback on the chapters. Kurt Schmidt and John Pask (my bosses) were a tremendous help, allowing me to have a flexible enough schedule to keep the work flowing. James Higginbotham and Rajeev Arora must be complimented on their crusade to construct some great material, when literally no material existed on many of the subjects covered.

A special thanks goes to Jonathan Robie of Poet Software who created many of the examples in the object database chapter and helped me through several issues. In addition, I must thank Poet Software for allowing me to work with early versions of their Java/ODMG software.

I must also recognize some of the pioneers whose work has been essential in the creation of this book: Marianne Meuller, David Brownell, and Rick Cattell from JavaSoft, and David Taylor, C.J. Date, Mary Loomis, and Jim Melton for creating some superb technical material.

-Jeff Schneider

Special thanks to my wife, Seema, and kids, Chavy and Vidip, who supported me through the unforeseen events between starting and finishing this book. Also, to Dr. Bhuvan Unhelkar for his ongoing encouragement and advice regarding publishing and research in general, and OO Software Engineering in specific. Thanks are also due to Distributed Computing faculty members at the Royal Melbourne Institute of Technology (Drs. Peter Bertok, George Fernandez, and Zahir Tari) for helping build a solid conceptual foundation in Distributed Computing.

-Rajeev Arora

# We'd Like to Hear from You!

As part of our continuing effort to produce books of the highest possible quality, Que would like to hear your comments. To stay competitive, we *really* want you, as a computer book reader and user, to let us know what you like or dislike most about this book or other Que products.

You can mail comments, ideas, or suggestions for improving future editions to the address below, or send us a fax at (317) 581-4663. For the online inclined, Macmillan Computer Publishing has a forum on CompuServe (type **GO QUEBOOKS** at any prompt) through which our staff and authors are available for questions and comments. The address of our Internet site is **http://www.quecorp.com** (World Wide Web).

In addition to exploring our forum, please feel free to contact me personally to discuss your opinions of this book: I'm **76103,1334** on CompuServe, and I'm **smiller@que.mcp.com** on the Internet.

Thanks in advance—your comments will help us to continue publishing the best books available on computer topics in today's market.

Stephen L. Miller
Product Development Specialist
Que Corporation
201 W. 103rd Street
Indianapolis, Indiana 46290
USA

# Contents at a Glance

# Table of Contents

## 13 Object Serialization   247

## III | CORBA

# Appendixes

# Database Access Using JDBC

# An Introduction to Enterprise Computing and Java

Java is the COBOL of the twenty-first century. It will change business computing more dramatically than any other programming language has done. A new way of computing is here; networks dominate, distributed computing is commonplace, and objects are everywhere. Software has always been used as a business weapon, and Java is no exception. For those organizations that believe that information and technology can give them an edge over their competition, Java might be the stealth weapon that they have been looking for. ■

# Who Should Read This Book?

Developers, project managers, architects, and other professionals who are developing large-scale applications in the Java language should read this book. The first 100 or so books on the Java language focused on introductory programming practices. This book focuses on the professional developer who is responsible for delivering mission-critical applications in the Java language. The book looks at database connectivity from Java, scaling applications through distributed computing, security issues, and other issues related to developing large-scale applications. Although the content emphasis is toward information technology shops, developers of commercial grade software will find some valuable information. This book does not cover the introductory Java topics, instead targeting the needs of the professional Java developer.

# Java in the Corporate World

Sun Microsystems is no stranger to the corporate computing world. Its servers and workstations have been a fixture in corporate environments for many years. So it shouldn't come as a surprise to anyone that the Sun R & D group created a language that fits in the corporate world. Many saw Sun's first Java as a "cute applet" running inside a Web browser. This image hampered Java as an industrial-strength programming language. The early days of Java touted its ability to run cross-platform and secure a distributed environment. In overcoming the misconceptions that Java was "just for the Internet," a series of components, later called the "Enterprise Packages," were introduced. This book explores in detail several of these packages, and answers how you can use Java in the corporate environment.

**N O T E**  Only time will tell if people will look back at the early days of Java with remarks of a well-constructed, object-oriented language, or if they take note of the virtual machine that could sit on top of any operating system. ▩

# Why Java?

Many companies have already made significant investments in retraining their mainframe developers in client/server technology. The late '80s and early '90s brought the era of Rapid Application Tools. Visual Basic, PowerBuilder, and Delphi are a few of the tools that proved valuable to I.T.(Information Technology) shops. Now many I.T. shops are asking: Why move out of their existing environment and into Java? There are several reasons why corporations are moving into the Java environment:

- A rapidly changing business environment
- A general movement toward open systems
- An increased emphasis on objects, security, and global connectivity

## Corporate Reengineering

Perhaps one of the most significant factors in enterprise computing in the late '80s and early '90s was the push to reengineer the corporation. The TQM (Total Quality Management) and process improvement movements were displaced by the notion that companies should completely rethink their processes. Gradual improvement efforts were replaced with the bulldoze and rebuild philosophy. Although several reengineering projects were huge successes, many failed. Several reasons were noted for failure, including lack of management support, internal politics, and so on. I.T. shops were pulled into the heart of the reengineering efforts.

The initiatives that would enable new processes required new software to control the process. Developers were thrown into a role of being half programmers and half business reengineering analysts, a role that was new to many of them. The software development programs were usually done by using client/server tools and the users were internal clients. The limitations of client/server software were evidence that it could not support many of the tasks necessary to build the inter-company commerce applications that the reengineered processes required. This was a prime example of how a tool can act as a process disabler instead of an enabler.

## Technology as an Enabler

Java is one of those technologies that comes around every decade. Not only does it change the way in which software is written, it changes the way in which work is done. Java is a process enabler. Perhaps the biggest technology enabler that we have seen in recent years is the rise of the Internet and the World Wide Web, a new delivery paradigm for static information that was created and embraced by virtually all Fortune 1000 companies. Java promises to move more than just static HTML between companies. The transaction systems that typically require a "relay person" to enter the data on behalf of another company will quickly go the way of Java. Positions such as customer service representatives, data-entry clerks, forms administrators, and others that require heavy interaction with business partners for entering data into systems will be the first impacted. Information departments are beginning to redirect their efforts. Instead of delivering systems to internal employees, the trend is to deliver the system to the true "client." The true client is usually an external group such as customers and business partners. The future depicts a Web of highly interactive-transactional systems whose response time (aided by higher bandwidth communication lines) will turn the old-fashioned batch EDI systems into just another legacy concept.

The challenge that the developer community must overcome is to successfully use this technology, not as a replacement for the last technology, but to leverage its unique capabilities to produce software that enables new business processes. The ability to massively deploy a Java system across multiple companies and heterogeneous environments will bring down many of the traditional barriers that I.T. shops once faced.

## The Microsoft Kingdom

In looking at the success of Java, many industry analysts look to the quick rise of the Microsoft kingdom. Businesses have long known that competition is healthy. When the operating system wars ended in the early '90s, the beginning of a monopoly was in the works. The Microsoft pricing polices were reminiscent of the robber barons from a century earlier. The ability for small software companies to compete with the great giant was at an all-time low. Since the majority of the Microsoft technologies were based on proprietary technologies, it was difficult for other vendors to bring products to the market as quickly as the company that owned the operating system. This fear of having one extremely dominant company in the software market has made many skeptical of their reliance on Microsoft. Java seemed to offer the perfect solution. Developers can create their software in Java and run it in Windows or another platform that offers a Java Virtual Machine. Just the idea of not being too dependent on the company that created one of the richest men in the world alleviates fear in many people's hearts.

## The Netscape Factor

Obviously, much of the Java success must be attributed to Netscape. Netscape's decision to include a Java Virtual Machine inside the Netscape Navigator product forced Java into the limelight. Although its Java implementation was perhaps one of the poorest in performance, millions of people saw "bouncing heads" and other silly applets. The real story lies behind the attention the press gave Java and Netscape. Traditional I.T. magazines featured Java-related stories on the front page for weeks. Eventually, enough people would learn the technology and make software development in the language practical based purely on the number of developers that were hypnotized by the media blitz in "catching the next wave."

## JavaBeans

For years software developers have realized the need to reuse code. Many projects have significant overlap in design, yet little or no code is shared between the applications. The creative nature of developers has led to a continuous reinventing of the wheel. The software industry is moving away from this arcane model into a component-based model, very similar to that used in the electronics industry. If an electronic engineer is tasked with designing a new motherboard for a computer, the engineer will first identify all the "off-the-shelf" components that can be used. If the engineer takes the time to construct every semiconductor, resistor, and capacitor on a motherboard from scratch each time, electronic products would never make it to market. Yet in the software industry, we continue to build the majority of our components from scratch. The JavaBean initiative is a standard for creating objects that have expected and documented behavior. Software that adheres to the JavaBean specification will publish information about itself onto an Integrated Development Environment (IDE). IDEs usually consist of a compiler, debugger, and a graphical development environment (Symantec Café and Java Workshop are examples of IDEs). The IDE can then present the developer with the object's attributes as well as notify the developer of events that the object will respond to.

Microsoft Windows has a similar effort called ActiveX, formerly known as OLE. The OLE/ActiveX initiative attempts to solve the reuse problem. ActiveX controls are developed by using C++ and the Microsoft Foundation Class library. Currently, a limited number of programmers are intimately familiar with developing these controls. The users of ActiveX controls are typically programmers who use Rapid Application Development environments such as

PowerBuilder and Visual Basic. Notice that the ActiveX control is programmed by using one language while the output is used in another language. This is not the case with Java; JavaBeans are programmed by using Java and are used in Java IDEs. The one-language model will facilitate the development of a plethora of components. Although the OLE technology has been available for quite some time, it has been plagued by the complexity associated with developing controls. Both the ActiveX and JavaBeans efforts are pushing the software engineering community to a new level of reuse.

# Building Software Better, Faster, and Cheaper

Perhaps the most sound reason why people are switching to Java is that the tool just does the job better, faster, and cheaper. The cheaper attribute comes in a couple of flavors. JavaSoft started the revolution by giving its software away, which helped to reduce the price of other vendors' tools. But most I.T. managers know that the real costs are not associated with the one-time purchase of a development environment, but in the labor costs associated with the project. The object-oriented nature of Java will push reusable components not only within companies, but within the entire development community. Thousands of pre-built objects are already available on the Internet. In addition, several universities have begun teaching Java to business and computer students. As these students graduate from college, the market will see the supply and demand for Java developers swing to a buyers' market. The costs associated with paying developers could soon be the most affordable. The ability to build systems faster in Java will probably not be seen until Java developers become more seasoned, JavaBean components mature, class libraries grow, and integrated development environments and screen painting tools mature.

The open nature of Java entices many I.T. shops that have been burned by closed and proprietary systems. Instead of relying on a single vendor to create the next version of a tool, I.T. shops can now choose from hundreds of companies that are creating Java compilers, class libraries, components, and integration tools. The competition in the Java tool area is fierce. Many Java tool companies will not survive the battle for marketplace dominance. Increased competition has raised the bar on the delivery of high-grade software.

## The Java Virtual Machine

Another attractive aspect of Java is its use of a Virtual Machine. The Java Virtual Machine is a piece of software that abstracts applications from the operating system. This facilitates developing cross-platform systems. There is never a need to recompile an application for different operating systems. For corporations that have a variety of client platforms, this enables one version to run on all systems that have a Java Virtual Machine. In addition, Java is supported on many of the traditional server-side hardware platforms. This means that a programmer can use one language to program client software for Microsoft Windows and server software for IBM's largest mainframes. It is no longer necessary to cross-train programmers in a variety of languages based on the hardware environment or operating system.

The Java Virtual Machine interprets software at runtime. This is different from most languages that compile software to machine-specific code. Interpretation at runtime usually causes the application to slow down, although it is the key to facilitating cross-platform delivery. Java applications are stored in a platform- and character-independent format known as byte code. The byte code on a UNIX box looks the same as the byte code files stored on Windows and Macintosh. This means that different platforms can use Java to communicate with messages, passing objects between them at runtime without concern for data and object conversions.

## Network-Enabled Applications

The Java language has extensive support for networking, specifically through support of the TCP/IP, the Internet protocol. TCP/IP support allows Java applications to easily interact with services that have been deployed on the Internet. It also facilitates the publishing of information to the Internet. As inter-company commerce increases and value chains are made more cohesive, the need to move data between companies will rise to an all-time high. Increasing this momentum establishes a common backbone, the Internet.

## Security as an Enabler

By using the Internet as a common backbone, companies can utilize the inexpensive communication lines to reach a growing population of network-enabled businesses and individuals. Unfortunately, the public nature of the Internet is also a breeding ground for hackers, crackers, and information thieves. The Java language is one of the first languages designed to work in this environment. The designers spent a considerable amount of time creating various levels of constraints that Java applications can be created with. For instance, a special kind of Java application called an applet cannot write to the hard drive of a computer. If it could write to the hard drive, a hacker could write Java code that would erase people's hard drives. Since it is necessary to write data to hard drives, JavaSoft has introduced digital signatures that tie an applet back to a responsible party. Thus, if the applet does destroy information on a client machine, the publisher of the software can be traced and prosecuted.

Another aspect of security is the moving of confidential information over the Internet. Several cryptography techniques can be used to enforce data security in the Java environment. Generally, either packets of data or complete data files are encrypted by a sender and decrypted by the receiver. The Java Developers Kit (JDK) version 1.1 introduced several new utilities for ensuring secured communications.

# Overview of API Families

JavaSoft has created several families of related technology that focus on an aspect of the language. Several partnering companies and industry standards groups have been essential in the creation of these families. JavaSoft has encouraged industry specialists to bring their talents to the table. Instead of writing all the specifications themselves, much of the work has been done by groups such as OMG, IBM, Adobe, and others. This fashion of developing Java standards has forced vendors that have historically competed against one another to come together for the creation of standards. Java programmers can now switch out vendor offering without concern for rewriting significant pieces of code. Since the vendors must meet a specification, much of the software is now looked at as a commodity. Vendors must now compete on price and performance and less on proprietary extensions. If this strategy works, information shops will see a buyers' market for products that adhere to JavaSoft standards.

# Core

The core packages are the heart of the Java language. These are written by the JavaSoft group and are packaged with the Java Developers Kit free of charge. The core packages perform basic GUI operations, implement data structures, facilitate input and output, and provide a mechanism for network-enabling a Java application. Within the core family, JavaSoft defines an inner core that must be implemented by all Java Virtual Machines (Java interpreters). The inner core is composed of the basic syntax and constructs of the Java language. Several of the packages were intentionally removed from the inner core to facilitate development across platforms. Thus, computers such as mainframes that traditionally do not have graphical user interfaces can still implement the inner core to perform intensive processing.

# Enterprise

The Enterprise family is the concentration of the book. It consists of a set of APIs that are commonly needed in corporate information shops. The APIs that are defined include:

> **JDBC**—Java Database Connectivity (relational databases)
>
> **RMI**—Remote Method Invocation (Java-specific distributed services)
>
> **CORBA IDL**—Common Object Request Broker Architecture, Interface Definition Language (Platform/language-independent distributed services)
>
> **Transaction Services**—Online Transaction Processing API (OLTP)
>
> **Object Serialization**— A low-level mechanism used primarily for the moving of objects between distributed systems
>
> **ODBMS**—An API for communicating with Object Database Management Systems

# Media

The Media family consists of several packages that focus on publishing, graphics, sound, animation, and so on. As with the Enterprise packages, JavaSoft has relied heavily on partner programs to define the following Media APIs:

> **Media Framework**—Audio, Video, and MIDI players; the framework consists of Java Media Player, Java Media Capture, and Java Media Conference
>
> **2-D Graphics**—Simple graphics and printing operations
>
> **3-D Graphics**—Rendering engines, animation, and so on
>
> **Telephony**—Telephone-enabled applications
>
> **SRAPI**—Speech Recognition API
>
> **VRML**—Some work has been done in creating a standard Virtual Reality Modeling Language API for Java, mostly by Silicon Graphics

## JavaBeans

The JavaBeans initiative is a family of specifications as well as some basic classes that facilitate writing Java Components. Creation of Beans is done with a package called java.beans and a Beans Developer Toolkit, both available for free from the JavaSoft Web site at **www. javasoft.com**.

## Commerce

The Commerce family is part of a larger initiative known as the Java Electronic Commerce Framework (JECF). JECF attempts to address several of the issues in creating a standard means for performing basic commerce operations through the Java language. The Commerce API looks directly at the implementation details of several of the initiatives:

**JavaWallet™**—A purchaser management and GUI API

**Payment and Service**—APIs that offer payment processing

**Merchant APIs**—Provide shopping cart and billing capabilities

**Java Card**—An API for interfacing with Smart Cards

## Embedded

The Embedded family provides the essential, minimal interfaces for applications that target small footprint devices. Since embedded devices generally have a minimal amount of memory available and limited interface capabilities (graphical and networking), the embedded API is a slimmed-down version used to perform basic operations.

## Management

The Management family provides a set of packages for monitoring and maintaining items on a network. The goal is to create a means for viewing the status of all enterprise devices from a single location. The Management architecture builds on preceding efforts such as SNMP.

**JMAPI**—Java Management API; JMPAI defines several APIs to ensure a common look and feel between management services.

## Security

The Security family is an evolving set of packages that provide many features necessary in deploying applications over the Internet in a secured form. Although not in the core security package, JavaSoft has a Secure Sockets Layer for encrypting streamed data.

**ACL**—Access Control Lists

**Core Security**—The core security package includes cryptography, key management, hashing routines, digital signatures, and more.

## Server

JavaSoft has also created a family of products for developing server-based products. These are primarily designed for developing Java-powered Internet and intranet online services. The goal is to create a standard API for developers to use in their custom creation of common services. As part of this development effort, the term "servlet" was introduced. The servlet is an executable program that users upload to run on networks or servers.

**Java Server Toolkit**—A framework for developing server applications

**Java Web Server**—A fully functional Web server in Java

**Java Servlet Engine**—An add-on for Web servers to give servlet capabilities

**Java NC Server**—Server for network computers

# Corporate Databases and JDBC

Business applications of the late twentieth century will be known for the first mass accumulation of data into database management systems. Although simulation software, artificial intelligence, rule-based systems, and other types of applications have emerged, none has had the steam behind it like databases. For Java to be considered a viable tool in the enterprise market, it was essential to create a set of APIs to interact with the millions of data stores created in corporations worldwide.

Realizing the need to interact with databases, the next question became, "What kind of databases should we design the API for?" Undoubtedly, the majority of data in corporations is relational data, but other object-oriented languages have shown that there is not a tight fit between relational databases and object-oriented systems. Perhaps object-database management systems should be put in the forefront, with their ability to interact with object-based programming languages like Java. These were the questions that were presented to the JavaSoft group. The answer was the most practical. If the majority of the data is stored in relational databases, the first API will support this need. Additional work would later be considered regarding Java's ability to interface with object-database systems. The immediate need was to answer the call for access to relational databases. This call was answered with the JDBC, the Java Database Connectivity package.

## JDBC Overview

The JDBC package is a set of Java classes that can be used by applications to make database calls. It is designed for use by programmers for performing low-level access to a database.

Why do we need the JDBC? Before the release of the JDBC, programmers were writing native calls to vendor-specific database libraries to perform basic SQL calls. This created a problem for crossing platforms as well as for switching to different database engines. Some of this was eased by writing native methods directly to ODBC drivers, but this required the Java application and the driver to reside on the same machine. This scenario would not work for Java applets that were delivered through the Internet. A mechanism for making a SQL call in a robust manner was needed. These requirements are as follows:

- The API must support distributed calls to remote systems.
- The solution must be pure Java, or at least pure Java on the client machine.
- The solution must be able to handle the majority of SQL calls according to the current standards.
- The solution should support the object-oriented nature of Java.

The specification for the JDBC is controlled by the JavaSoft group. The JavaSoft group always takes developers' suggestions for changes and enhancements to the API. The group can be reached at **JDBC@Wombat.Eng.Sun.Com**. The JavaSoft group is considering moving the control of Java and other packages to a third party.

## JDBC Architecture

The JavaSoft group decided not to write the software that facilitated database access in favor of writing a template for a JDBC driver. Most of the JDBC classes are interfaces that third-party vendors have implemented. Only a handful of these classes have implementation behind them, and where there is implementation, it is usually minimal.

By specifying an architecture for other vendors to implement, JavaSoft has created a framework that ensures that JDBC drivers can be swapped out, while also leaving the implementation details in the hands of database and networking companies where they may apply their specific skills to the problem.

## Outline of Major Classes

The creators of the JDBC have done a good job of breaking the functionality of the SQL language into a series of objects. Each major class takes on a portion of the problem of handling database calls. Only by using several of the objects together can one create a full functioning database application. The new code that was introduced was the "java.sql" package. The major classes in this package are as follows:

**DriverManager**    The DriverManager object is used to facilitate the use of multiple database drivers in a single application. Each JDBC driver can be used to connect to a different data source. Thus, knowing when to use a specific driver to connect to a given source is an important task.

**Connection**    After a vendor's driver has been registered with the DriverManager, a data source, user ID, password, or other pertinent information can be specified to create a connection to a database. This Connection object is used in later calls to specify against which database the call should be placed. JDBC supports having multiple Connection objects open at any given time.

**Statement**    The `Statement` object mimics the `SQL` statement that the application wants to apply against a database. Three flavors of the `Statement` option are available. `CallableStatement` is used for invoking stored procedures, `PreparedStatement` is used to call pre-bound `SQL` statements and the normal `Statement` object is used when `CallableStatement` and `PreparedStatement` are not an option. The `Statement` object (and its related classes) does not embrace the result set that may pass back to the application. Instead this is dealt with by the `ResultSet` object.

**ResultSet**    After a call is made by a `Statement` object (or `CallableStatement` or `PreparedStatement`), the results of the query are put into a `ResultSet` object. This object can then be traversed to retrieve multiple rows as well as multiple columns.

**ResultSetMetaData**    Often an application will issue a query that is dynamic in nature. That is, the application will not know about the result set return. In these cases, the `ResultSetMetaData` object can be used to inquire about the contents of a `ResultSet` object.

**DatabaseMetaData**    Although many databases fulfill some organizations' standards (such as ANSI), almost every database has offered additional features to make it stand out from its competitors. The `DatabaseMetaData` object can be used to query the support options for a given database. This will include database limitations, nuances, extra features, and so on.

**SQLException**    The JDBC introduces a new exception, the `SQLException`. This exception is used to capture most problems that are returned from database systems. In addition, the JDBC offers a `SQLWarning` class that returns information that is not as severe as the `SQLException` class.

## JDBC versus ODBC

The authors of the JDBC credit much of the design to the ODBC group. Indeed, with similar goals, the JDBC and ODBC have a great similarity. The two major differences are:

1. The ODBC was designed for use in structured programs, thus it wasn't broken into distinct objects.

2. The ODBC has been around for a while, thus maturing into the current product.

Currently, the JDBC has the minimal feature set to support database activity. Where ODBC has significant support for forward and backward cursors and usage of bookmarks to quickly return to a row, the JDBC has virtually nothing. One can expect the feature set of the JDBC to slowly catch up to the ODBC. For now, many applications that rely on the sophisticated calls available in the ODBC may be forced to use native method calls directly to ODBC drivers.

## Current State of SQL (ANSI Level 2)

The JDBC is challenged to keep up with the ever-changing SQL standards. Since the SQL-86 standard, relational-database vendors have committed support to SQL-89 and most recently to the SQL-92 standard. As modern programming languages move from procedural to object-based, the database vendors will be pushed to incorporate more object-based concepts. Two views are emerging on this subject. The relational-database vendors are concentrating on extending the very structured, mathematically firm models, supported by relational databases, to incorporate objects as an "add-on." Many of the object-database vendors support relational queries but only as an afterthought. The ISO/ANSI group is continuing its quest to grow relational databases while the Object Database Management Group is continuing to support many of the relational concepts. The merging of ideas between these organizations is inevitable as the marketplace demands a common language for working with data.

## Two-Tiered Access

The early 1990s saw perhaps the rise and fall of two-tiered computing. To many people, the term "server" in "client/server" computing meant a database server. This model of having a client access data on a physically separate machine will be carried over into the network computing model that Java supports. Many of the first applications that have been built by corporations were developed as client/server utilities. The primary reason for this is purely based on developers doing what they are most familiar with. Although many applications need a server and a few clients, developers in the late 1990s will be plagued with managers who are not familiar with multi-tiered computing. Thus, it will be imperative to transfer the benefits of distributed computing to these individuals. (More on this subject appears in Chapter 12, "Introduction to Distributed Computing.")

## Three-Tiered Access

Taking one step at a time, three-tiered computing is the natural evolution of two-tiered computing. Most developers now recognize the importance of abstracting an application from the data. This understanding is what has propelled database servers forward. The next step is to understand the notion of abstracting common business functions and rules from the client that the user interacts with and the data stored in various databases. Only after writing several applications that share resources on a middle-tier will you see the advantage of abstracting business logic and rules from the rest of the application.

The benefits of Java Applets (rather than applications) in corporate computing are yet to be determined. The original deployment of these applications through Web servers that were not tweaked for delivering full-scale applications can be considered a breakthrough, and at the same time, a failure. The amount of time to deliver an application via a Web browser was considered unacceptable. New delivery mechanisms have since rolled out that overcame many of the original problems; however, the importance of writing "thin clients" has not diminished. By breaking the business logic out of the GUI client, the code moved to a sharable location and the size of the application is reduced, thus decreasing the load time and the burden placed on the client's physical memory limitations.

# Distributed Computing in the Enterprise

Most large organizations have multiple machines hosting their diverse range of applications. Over time, these applications have fed data to one another by using overnight (or other periodic) file transfers. Increased emphasis on employee empowerment and providing a single point of contact for the customer have required a close integration of these applications. Current real-time integration of these applications has been carried out by using remote procedure calls.

Remote procedure calls may help you communicate to another process running on a different machine, but they are a low-level facility lacking the robustness required of mission-critical applications. Distributed computing frameworks are required to provide an integrated view of all the resources of the enterprise-computing environment. These frameworks, among a large number of things, help an application view all the files stored on the network as part of a single directory tree. Such a facility is commonly known as directory service. Examples of other similar integrated services are database access, security, time, and file services.

A number of distributed computing frameworks have evolved over the last ten years. The most significant of these are DCE (Distributed Computing Environment) of X/Open and Object Management Architecture (OMA) of the Object Management Group. You learn more about these computing frameworks, which are covered later in Chapter 12, "Introduction to Distributed Computing."

Besides the key business needs of employee enablement and single-contact point for customers, there are a number of other factors driving the push to distributed computing. The development of multi-tier client/server applications, including applications deployed by using the intranet or Internet, requires a robust distributed applications architecture. Advantages and challenges of distributed computing are also covered in detail in Chapter 12. An overview of various techniques of distributed applications development, including RPC, sockets, DCE, CORBA, and RMI, is also provided in Chapter 12.

## CORBA, IIOP, and Object Management Architecture

Object Management Architecture is the distributed computing framework published by the Object Management Group (OMG). It provides mechanisms and facilities to develop distributed object-oriented applications that can be written in a multitude of programming languages, run on heterogeneous operating platforms, and interoperate transparently. Common Object Request Broker Architecture (CORBA) is the core functionality that permits objects on one machine to invoke the methods of remote objects. Besides CORBA, OMA provides a large number of services and facilities for distributed object applications. Inter-ORB Interoperability Protocol (IIOP) is the actual protocol used by distributed objects to communicate with one another. CORBA products are already available for various operating platforms.

Arrival of the Java platforms has provided the universal client platform, in which the client application can be downloaded and used practically anywhere in the world. CORBA provides the only industry standard object-oriented framework for building distributed applications. Since Java is a good object-oriented programming language (with its added benefits for network and Internet/intranet programming), developing distributed applications by using Java and CORBA provides the best flexibility for the client and server ends.

Java Enterprise API provides a number of mechanisms of communicating with legacy applications and servers. Java RMI and JavaBeans are the other key mechanisms. It also provides Java-IDL API for communicating with CORBA servers by using IIOP.

There is currently a huge investment in the existing applications in organizations around the world. It is on multiple operating platforms and programming languages. CORBA provides the richest mechanism for integrating these applications in a multi-tier client/server environment within the enterprise. By developing Java client applications to access these applications, companies can easily use the same architecture for internal, as well as external, enablement of distributed applications without discarding their investment in current applications.

## Object Serialization

With the inclusion of streams in the 1.0.2 release of Java, many Java applications use streams to store and retrieve object data from a local file or server socket. This gives a developer flexibility when sharing various forms of object data. As Java begins to mature, developers are demanding even more powerful tools for their toolbelt. To meet these demands, the new JDK 1.1 includes a few new classes in the java.io package for Object Serialization.

Object Serialization provides a mechanism for converting objects into byte representations for transportation through a stream. By using serialization, objects may be transported through socket connections, allowing object representations to be transported to other machines on the Internet. Additionally, object serialization provides a mechanism for object persistence. Object persistence is a concept that defines storing an object with its state, and all its members, fully intact. Finally, object serialization includes a concept called versioning, which allows a class to evolve and change without losing compatibility with previously stored versions.

## RMI

Remote Procedure Calls (RPC) have allowed developers to design applications that could span several machines. This brought powerful applications, intended for mainframes, down to the personal computer level. Networks could be used to increase the computational abilities of an application with each computer assigned to a specific set of tasks.

With the addition of the Internet in the 1990s, distributed architecture may now be taken to a new level. A common protocol, TCP/IP, is used to connect one computer to millions of others, regardless of the operating system that exists on each computer. Combining this idea with the powerful, cross-platform nature of Java, Remote Method Invocation (RMI) was formed.

RMI brings a distributed object architecture to JDK 1.1. RMI allows objects to be created as remote objects, providing methods that may be invoked from another object. The objects may exist on the same machine or on another machine; this means that the objects may be located in different Java Virtual Machines.

# From Here...

Java is quickly moving into enterprise computing. The business drivers are pushing Java as a solution for the masses. The technical advantages of Java are making it a language of choice amongst software developers. This combination, along with a growing set of APIs from JavaSoft, are ensuring it as a contender for the tool of choice for developing enterprise applications.

- Chapter 2, "JDBC Data Types," introduces the types of data that can be stored in a relational database via the JDBC interface.
- Chapter 3, "A Simple JDBC Application," will cover the basic connections, drivers, and driver management associated with the JDBC, and introduce a framework for the rest of Part I.
- Chapter 4, "Executing SQL Statements," discusses how to query a SQL database and use getXXX methods to retrieve results.

# CHAPTER 2

# JDBC Data Types

**S**ince we have provided an overview of the JDBC, we're now going to examine how SQL data types and Java data types overcome their differences. Different tools have been developed to make these conversions possible and flexible. These tools include getXXX and setXXX methods in the ResultSet class, the registerOutParameter method in the Callable Statement class, and the Types class. Each of these tools will be explained and evaluated in this chapter. ■

### Review common SQL data types

A review of the common SQL data types will be presented with help in choosing the correct data type when designing new databases.

### Understand mapping SQL data types to Java

Fully understand the Java equivalents to common SQL data types and possible pitfalls to avoid.

### Use advanced data conversion techniques

Utilize built-in Java classes for converting custom and specialized SQL data types, such as binary image data, to Java objects.

# A Review of Common SQL Types

For anyone familiar with SQL data types, this section may be a simple review. However, to familiarize those who are new to SQL, the following section will explain the most common SQL data types and key points that must be understood when building or examining SQL tables.

## Strings

Character data can consist of any combination of letters, numbers, and symbols. If numbers are stored in character data types, these numbers must be converted before mathematical functions may be executed on them. When choosing to store character data, the most common options available for SQL databases are the following:

CHAR[$n$]—Stores an array of characters $n$ characters long. All array elements not used to store a string are padded with spaces and therefore occupy a constant space throughout all of the columns in a table. CHAR data types may contain no characters, represented by a NULL, otherwise they must be between 1–$n$ characters long. When CHAR data is returned from a query, the string is returned with the padded spaces to achieve the correct length chosen in the definition. The maximum length for CHAR data is 255 characters.

VARCHAR[$n$]—Stores character data in a variable-length array $n$ characters long. Any array elements not used when storing a particular string *are not* padded with spaces and therefore return only the string when returned from a query. VARCHAR data types are generally chosen when the length of the data stored will vary greatly. The maximum length of a VARCHAR data type is 255 characters.

**N O T E**   When choosing between CHAR and VARCHAR, note that CHAR will achieve a slight performance boost since the SQL server will know that the length of the data will be approximately the same. VARCHAR is often used when the length of the data being stored will vary greatly, while CHAR is used when data will be mostly the same length. ▪

LONGVARCHAR[$n$]—Stores character data with a minimum array length of 256 and a maximum length of 65,535. LONGVARCHAR, like VARCHAR, does not include padded spaces, but is used for string data that will require storage larger than 255 characters.

**N O T E**   It is important to note that a NULL value and an empty string are not the same. When a string is given the value (''), an empty string, the string is actually assigned a space character. A NULL value indicates that the string has not been assigned a value and is treated differently when comparisons are made.

Also, when a CHAR data type is defined as NULL when using CREATE_TABLE or ALTER_TABLE, the data type is treated as a VARCHAR. This is due to the inability of the database to pad spaces for a NULL value. ▪

> **NOTE** When entering string data into the CHAR types, understand that strings longer than the defined column length will be truncated. When comparing VARCHAR and CHAR data, the operator LIKE will produce different results. This is due to the space padding associated with the CHAR data type. The = operator will behave correctly because it will pad the shortest string with spaces before the comparison is made. ■

## Exact *NUMERIC* Data Types

When storing numeric data that requires a great amount of precision, two data types are provided—DECIMAL and NUMERIC. DECIMAL data types are synonyms to the NUMERIC data types, and are both defined for ANSI compatibility. Exact NUMERIC data types provide numeric precision to the least significant digit. The data types are defined in the following manner:

```
DECIMAL [p[,s]]
or
NUMERIC [p[,s]]
```

These define an exact NUMERIC data type with a precision $p$, specifying the number of digits that can be stored, including the digits to the left and right of the decimal. An optional scale parameter, $s$, specifies the maximum number of digits that may be stored to the right of the decimal place. This parameter must be less than or equal to the value $p$. Storage requirements for these data types may vary from 2 bytes to 17 bytes, depending on the required precision of the data.

## Approximate *NUMERIC* Data Types

Approximate NUMERIC data types store decimal numbers in a binary format, preserving precision as much as the binary system allows. Since the binary system cannot accurately represent all numbers with correct precision, numbers are rounded using the IEEE 754 specification. This specification allows four different rounding methods to be used, and may vary for each SQL DBMS. Since all numbers are not represented with the correct precision required, it is recommended to avoid using these data types in WHERE clauses since the outcome may not be constant or predictable. The data types are described as follows:

**FLOAT**—Data type that holds floating point numbers, which may be positive or negative. The binary precision is specified as $n$ and requires a valid number from 1 to 15. If 1 to 7 is chosen, it is treated as a REAL (see the following data type). If 8 to 15 is chosen, it is treated as a FLOAT. FLOAT data types occupy 8 bytes of storage and represent numbers from $1.7^{-308}$ to $1.7^{+308}$.

**REAL**—Data type similar to a FLOAT, but requires only 4 bytes of storage. REAL may store values from $3.4^{-38}$ to $3.4^{+38}$ and has a precision of 7 digits.

> **NOTE** When trying to determine which to use, exact or approximate NUMERIC data types, consideration must be taken regarding the required precision of the data. Data that must retain its original value without rounding must use the exact data types. Approximate data types are generally chosen when space, instead of precision, is an issue. ■

## *BINARY* Data Types

BINARY data types store hexadecimal values for such uses as bit patterns, and have a maximum length of 255 values. The values are stored in a two-character set, such as "AA". It is important to note that conversions or calculations based on BINARY data types do not always produce reliable results. Please consult the CONVERT function in the proper DBMS reference manual for further information related to the SQL DBMS used.

The available data types for binary data are:

*BINARY[n]*—A binary data type that has a definable length of 1 to 255 values. Like the CHAR data type, BINARY is padded with space holders in any unused array spaces. BINARY data types produce slightly faster results than VARBINARY because the size is always the specified limit, *n*.

*VARBINARY[n]*—A binary data type related to BINARY but that does not get filled with spaceholders as does the BINARY type. VARBINARY types are generally used when the length of the data being stored will vary greatly.

## *BIT* Data Type

The BIT data type stores a value of 0 or 1, and usually represents true/false or yes/no. Bits require a storage size of 1 byte, but multiple bits may occupy 1 byte until the byte is full and another is required. Note that bits cannot be NULL and any other values entered other than 0 or 1 are interpreted as a 1. The usage is straightforward and defined as BIT.

## *INTEGER* Data Types

INTEGER data types represent numeric data with precision to the nearest whole number. There are four INTEGER data types that control the minimum and maximum values:

**INTEGER**—Data type that stores whole numbers from –2,147,483,648 to +2,147,483,647 and requires 4 bytes for storage

**SMALLINT**—Data type that stores whole numbers from –32,768 to +32,767 and requires 2 bytes for storage

**TINYINT**—Data type that stores whole numbers from 0 to 255 and requires 1 byte for storage

**BIGINT**—Data type that stores whole numbers from $-2^{63}$ to $2^{63}-1$ and requires 8 bytes for storage

## *TIME* and *DATE* Data Types

The representation of time and date vary from different SQL databases, so only the most common will be discussed here. The following are different data types that represent date and time storage:

**DATE**—Data types that represent a date, based on the number of days passed from a base date, which may vary for each DBMS implementation. DATE data types require 4 bytes of storage and may be used in LIKE statements for comparisons.

**TIME**—Data types that represent a time based on the number of minutes passed from a base date, which may vary for each DBMS implementation. TIME data types require 4 bytes of storage and may be used in LIKE statements for comparisons.

**TIMESTAMP**—TIMESTAMP is a data type that is automatically updated every time an INSERT or UPDATE statement is executed on a row. TIMESTAMP does not represent the system time, but is simply a counter that is unique to the database. The TIMESTAMP data type is represented as a BINARY(8) data type if it is declared NULL, or a VARBINARY(8) if it is declared NOT NULL.

# Mapping SQL Types to Java Types

Since this portion of the chapter is mostly used as a reference tool and guide during application development, this section will present the discussion of mapping Java types to SQL types in a reference form. Table 2.1 shows an overview of the type mapping, followed by a detailed discussion of Java types that are commonly mapped to the SQL type(s).

**Table 2.1    Overview of Mapping Java Types to SQL Types**

| Java Type | SQL Type |
| --- | --- |
| String | VARCHAR/LONGVARCHAR |
| byte | TINYINT |
| byte[] | VARBINARY/LONGVARBINARY |
| short | SMALLINT |
| long | BIGINT |
| int | INTEGER |
| float | REAL |
| double | FLOAT |
| boolean | BIT |
| java.lang.BigNum | NUMERIC |
| java.sql.Date | DATE |
| java.sql.Time | TIME |
| java.sql.TimeStamp | TIMESTAMP |

## *CHAR, VARCHAR,* and *LONGVARCHAR*

Determining specific storage and performance needs is very important when using CHAR, VARCHAR, and LONGVARCHAR as strings in SQL. Java, however, doesn't require the programmer to know which of these SQL types are used. All CHAR SQL types are easily represented as a Java

String or a char[]. As a general rule, the String class is the preferred method of storage and can easily be used for conversion to char[] if necessary.

The method suggested for most string data retrieval is the Result.getString method, which generates a String object and assigns it the value of the result. In the case of the CHAR data type, it also contains the necessary number of spaces to create a CHAR of $n$ length. The getString method can be used for CHAR and VARCHAR, but for LONGVARCHAR, the length of the result could reach into the megabytes. For this reason, the JDBC API includes a method to retrieve the data using an input stream. The methods are getAsciiStream and getUnicodeStream and are chosen based on the data expected.

## TINYINT, SMALLINT, INTEGER, and BIGINT

All SQL integer types may be mapped to Java types that are very much the same. Unlike strings, the size of the integer must be known during the design process. If the size cannot be determined at design time, it is suggested that you retrieve any results in question with the largest possible representation available. The following table summarizes the relationships between the SQL types and Java types, and also provides the necessary method to retrieve the result.

### Table 2.2   Mapping Integers from SQL to Java

| SQL Type | Bit Size | Java Type | Result Method |
| --- | --- | --- | --- |
| TINYINT | 8 | byte | ResultSet.getByte |
| SMALLINT | 16 | short | ResultSet.getShort |
| INTEGER | 32 | int | ResultSet.getInt |
| BIGINT | 64 | long | ResultSet.getLong |

## BINARY, VARBINARY, and LONGVARBINARY

Just as a Java programmer doesn't need to know the length of the string data that will be stored in SQL, the same principles apply to the BINARY data types. BINARY data types may be expressed as byte arrays in Java.

The method ResultSet.getByte is recommended for retrieving binary data. The only exception is when LONGVARBINARY is used. This type of data may exceed megabytes in size, so a method was developed to allow the data to be read from a stream. The method ResultSet.getBinaryStream can be used to retrieve data in chunks to match the needs of the developer.

## REAL and FLOAT

Java data types that express floating-point numbers in binary format, float and double, may be directly mapped to the SQL types REAL and FLOAT. The REAL SQL type requires seven digits of precision and may be mapped to the Java type float. When retrieving results for REAL data types, it is recommended to use the `ResultSet.getFloat` method. The `FLOAT` SQL data type requires 15 digits of precision and directly maps to the `double` Java type. The general method for retrieving `FLOAT` results is `ResultSet.getDouble`.

## BIT

The SQL `BIT` data type is directly mapped to the Java `boolean` type, and uses the method `ResultSet.getBoolean` for data retrieval. No special needs are required for this data.

## NUMERIC and DECIMAL

As discussed earlier, the SQL data types `NUMERIC` and `DECIMAL` are synonyms for each other and are usually included together for ANSI compatibility. These data types may be mapped to the `java.lang.BigNum` data type. Use of the `BigNum` data type is usually restricted to rare occurrences; it was designed for floating-point numbers that require absolute precision. The `BigNum` class includes methods for basic mathematical functions and may be performed with other `BigNum` values, integers, and floating-point types. The method recommended for data retrieval is `ResultSet.getBigNum`. The JDBC also allows these SQL data types to be retrieved using Java `String`, `char[]`, and other numeric types. When using the `String` class for retrieval, the values can be easily manipulated, but it is difficult for mathematical functions to be performed with them. It is highly recommended that you retrieve them using the `BigNum` class, perform any necessary math, and convert them to `Strings` for final manipulation. Other numeric types such as `float` and `double` may also be used for data retrieval, but precision may be lost.

> **N O T E**  Due to an upgrade of the JDBC package from 1.0 to 1.1, the `ResultSet.getNumeric` method was renamed `ResultSet.getBigNum`. The name was changed to conform with the naming convention associated with the other `getXXX` methods and may require modification to existing code developed under the 1.0 JDBC version. ■

## DATE, TIME, and TIMESTAMP

Since there are no Java classes that truly reflect the architecture of the SQL `DATE` and `TIME` types, the JDBC package includes three new Java classes: `java.sql.Date`, `java.sql.Time`, and `java.sql.TimeStamp`. These new classes extend `java.util.Date` and provide extended capabilities for handling the storage of SQL data types. The first class, `java.sql.Date`, stores the month, day, and year of a particular SQL `DATE` result while zeroing out the other time fields that are inherited from `java.util.Date`. Next, the `java.sql.Time` classes zero out the month, day, and year, concentrating on storing the `TIME` result that is returned from the SQL result set. The beginning time initially set when the class is instantiated is January 1, 1970. The final class included is `java.sql.TimeStamp`, which uses everything from `java.util.Date`, and also adds a new nanosecond field.

Since all three of these classes are subclasses of `java.util.Date`, they may be used where instances of `java.util.Date` are expected. It is important to note that when using the `TimeStamp` class when `java.util.Date` classes are expected, the nanosecond field is lost, but the class still retains its precision to one millisecond.

# A Review of SQL Custom Types

In the relational database model, domains are a set of values and definitions from which a column may inherit. Most relational databases have included a simple version of the domain in their databases and are usually called user-defined data types. These types enable a user to choose a particular SQL data type and assign it a label. Along with the data type, a user-defined data type may also dictate the length, default rules, default null state, and a default value. Once defined, this data type is included in the databases list and can be referenced when creating tables.

User-defined data types are both an asset and a hindrance. They allow a specific data definition to be reused throughout a database, saving the amount of typing and wasted setup time. They also provide the ability to change the definition of the data type without being forced to change each column individually, saving a tremendous amount of time if changes are required to the default value or a rule. The last noticeable advantage is the ability to put more information into the meta-data for better reference.

As stated, user-defined data types have some disadvantages as well. First, the real benefits of a domain, such as strict type checking, are not available. If two user-defined types, such as a Social Security number and phone number, are defined in a database, the two types may be included in the same mathematical calculation without being explicitly converted. Also, the nullability may be overwritten when creating a table, deviating from the definition. Another problem is the lack of extra type-checking for user-defined data types. For instance, if a name, CHAR(25), is put into a field of CHAR(10), the data is truncated without an error or warning. This is a common problem with standard SQL data manipulation, but it has never been strictly enforced when dealing with user-defined data types. Finally, there are many restrictions when creating a custom data type that reduce its robustness. User-defined data types may only choose from the standard data types available, thus, not allowing the creation of more elaborate and useful data types.

# Storing and Retrieving HTML, Images, and Audio

Some implementations of SQL allow databases to contain large binary or text data types, such as images and text. These data types are often provided by SQL implementations for storing large amounts of data, often called the Binary Large Object (BLOB). These data types may be difficult to map directly to Java object types by using the methods mentioned earlier. This section will describe the custom SQL data types and user-defined types, as well as cover mapping these complex data types to Java objects.

## SQL *TEXT* and *IMAGE* Data Types

Most SQL DBMSs provide a data type that allows large text or binary data to be stored and retrieved. These data types, TEXT and IMAGE, provide a maximum of 2,147,483,647 bytes (2M) to store character or binary data. It is important to note that when these data types are initialized with an update, even if the update sets the data to NULL, the minimum 2,048 bytes (2K) is allocated.

TEXT data is a character data type that is used for storage of large documents that may exceed the limits of the basic character types. The LIKE operator works properly with the TEXT data type and produces the same effect as the standard character data types. The TEXT data type may be converted to CHAR or VARCHAR data types but is still limited to the 255-character limit of the CHAR types.

IMAGE data is a BINARY data type that may be used to store images and large binary data for later retrieval. Any data inserted into an IMAGE data type that is less than 255 bytes and of an odd length will be padded with a leading zero. Data that is larger than 255 bytes may not be inserted with an odd byte length. IMAGE data may be converted to BINARY or VARBINARY data types with the CONVERT function, but is limited to the 255 bytes length of the BINARY data types.

Part
I
Ch
2

## Using SQL to Store HTML, Images, and Audio

Manipulating text and image data may be accomplished in several ways. First, SELECT, INSERT, and UPDATE statements may be used to manipulate text and image data. It is important to use these statements for initializing the storage space and it is necessary before using any other method of moving data into TEXT data types. Note, when inserting or updating data, text data must be surrounded by a single quote. Next, the use of the WRITETEXT, READTEXT, and UPDATETEXT statements may be used to move the data into the SQL database. Refer to the proper DBMS reference manual for the availability of these statements. Finally, the use of a bulk-copy program may be used to push data into the database and can usually be found as a supplemental program to the database server.

When retrieving text and image data from a SQL database, the maximum amount of data retrieved may be truncated. This is due to a setting that has been implemented in some DBMSs. This setting, sometimes referred to as the TEXTSIZE setting, may need to be altered to prevent data truncation when retrieving the data stored in these data types.

## Implementations in Java

To demonstrate how to use a SQL database to store image data, Listing 2.1 presents three classes that retrieve an IMAGE BLOB, convert the data into the proper image format, and, finally, create an IMAGE instance containing the image.

### Listing 2.1   Converting SQL Image Types to Java Image Objects

```
/*
    A basic extension of the java.awt.Frame class
 */

import java.awt.*;

public class DBImage extends Frame {

    public DBImage() {
```

*continues*

**Listing 2.1    Continued**

```java
            setLayout(new GridLayout(1,1,5,5));
            addNotify();
            resize(insets().left + insets().right + 430,insets().top +
            ➥insets().bottom + 270);
            setTitle("Untitled");

            MemImage mimage=new MemImage();
            add (mimage);
            mimage.displayImage();

    }
    public boolean handleEvent(Event event) {
        if (event.id == Event.WINDOW_DESTROY) {
          System.exit (0);
        }
          return super.handleEvent(event);
    }

    public static void main (String args[]) {
      DBImage frame=new DBImage();
      frame.resize (600,400);
      frame.show();
    }
}
import sun.awt.image.URLImageSource;

import java.io.ByteArrayInputStream;
import java.net.URL;

public class ArrayImageSource extends URLImageSource {
    ByteArrayInputStream bis;
    URL                   hack;

    public ArrayImageSource(byte buf[], int offset, int len, URL u) {
        super(u);
        bis = new ByteArrayInputStream(buf, offset, len);
    }

    protected sun.awt.image.ImageDecoder getDecoder() {
        return new sun.awt.image.JPEGImageDecoder(this, bis);
    }
}

import java.awt.*;
import java.net.*;
import java.io.*;
import jet.connect.*;
import java.awt.image.*;

public class MemImage extends Canvas {
```

```
//Jet Connect Version
private DbEnv dbenv = null;
private DbDbc dbcon = null;
private DbStmt dbstmt = null;
private Image image;
final private int WIDTH = 250;
final private int HEIGHT = 300;
private URL jpgURL;
private ArrayImageSource foo;

public boolean handleEvent(Event evt){
     if (evt.id == Event.WINDOW_DESTROY) System.exit(0);
   return false;
 }

 public MemImage() {
     System.out.println("In MemImage constructor");

     setBackground(Color.darkGray);
     this.resize(WIDTH,HEIGHT);
     System.out.println("About to link to connection");

             //Create a DbEnv (enviroment) object.
         try {
             dbenv  = DbEnv.SQLAllocEnv( "DUAL90" );

             //Create a DbDbc (database connection) object
             dbcon  = dbenv.SQLAllocConnect();

             //Connect to a database.
             dbcon.SQLConnect("enterprise","sa","");

             //Create a DbStmt object.
             dbstmt = dbcon.SQLAllocStmt();
         } catch (Exception e) {System.out.println ("Error connecting: "+e);}

     System.out.println("Finished linking to connection");
 }

 public void displayImage() {;
     try {
         this.dbstmt.SQLFreeStmt(Db.SQL_CLOSE);
         System.out.println("In display image method");
         System.out.println("about to execute second sql statement");
         this.dbstmt.SQLExecDirect("Select * from blob2");
         System.out.println("Finished sql statements");
         DbInteger bsize = new DbInteger();
         int blobsize;
         InputStream is;
         System.out.println("About to fetch");
         this.dbstmt.SQLFetch();
         System.out.println("Finished fetching");
         DbRetCode returnvalue;
         returnvalue = this.dbstmt.getRetCode();
         System.out.println("Value returned:" + returnvalue.toString());
```

*continues*

**Listing 2.1 Continued**

```
            if (returnvalue.equals(DbRetCode.SQL_SUCCESS)) {
                blobsize=802;
                //System.out.println("Blob size" + blobsize);
                System.out.println("about to get binary stream");
                is = this.dbstmt.SQLGetBinaryStream(1);
                System.out.println("finished binary stream");
                byte[] gifbytes = new byte[blobsize];
                is.read(gifbytes);

                try {
                        jpgURL = new URL("http://www.delphis.com");
                        foo = new ArrayImageSource(gifbytes, 0, blobsize,
                        ➥jpgURL);
                        image = createImage(foo);
                }
                catch (Exception e) {
                    System.out.println("Exception:" + e.toString());
                }
            }
            else {
                System.out.println("Setting image to null");
                image = null;
            }
            this.dbstmt.SQLFreeStmt(Db.SQL_CLOSE);
            System.out.println("Statement closed");

        }
        catch (Exception e) {
            System.out.println(e.toString());
            this.dbstmt.SQLFreeStmt(Db.SQL_CLOSE);
        }
    }


    public boolean imageUpdate(Image image, int flags, int x, int y, int w, int
    ➥h) {
        if ((flags & ALLBITS) != 0) {
            this.repaint();
        }
        return true;
    }
    public void update(Graphics g) {
        System.out.println("In update graphics method");
        paint(g);
    }
    public void paint(Graphics g) {
        System.out.println("In paint graphics method");
        System.out.println("Drawing image");
        try {
            g.drawImage(image, 0, 0, this);
        }
```

```
      catch (NullPointerException np) {
          System.out.println("Null pointer exception caught");
          this.resize(WIDTH, HEIGHT);
          g.drawString("Photo Not Available", 60, 280);
      }
  }

}
```

# From Here...

We have introduced the data types that can be used to map Java data types to SQL data types. We have also reviewed the SQL data type definitions for those who are unfamiliar with the inner workings of SQL data types. The next steps include generating Java code that uses the JDBC to communicate with SQL databases, and advanced topics that help programmers develop scalable Java applications for corporate environments.

- Chapter 3, "A Simple JDBC Application," covers the basic connections, drivers, and driver management associated with the JDBC, and introduces a framework for the rest of Part I.

- Chapter 4, "Executing SQL Statements," discusses how to query a SQL database and use getXXX methods to retrieve results.

- Chapter 10, "Delivering the Application," covers the considerations that need to be understood when delivering a large Java JDBC application, and how to plan for optimizations when building SQL tables and applications.

# CHAPTER 3

# A Simple JDBC Application

**N**ow that we have discussed the basic principles behind ODBC drivers, the ODBC to JDBC bridge, and the essential data types used, we are now going to cover the steps required to develop a basic JDBC application. For any scalable application to be successful, a beginning framework must be developed. The framework usually contains necessary elements, such as a user interface, an event handler, and a central point from which all actions branch. The Enterprise Java framework will be used as a common point for merging each chapter's module into a complete JDBC demonstration. ■

**The Framework**

Learn the JDBC Application Framework from which the modules are launched.

**How to create a database URL**

Learn the method of creating an URL that specifies the driver needed and the server to connect to.

**What JDBC drivers are and how they work**

Discover what a JDBC driver is and how it is handled.

**How the *DriverManager* works**

Understand the DriverManager and how to use it to customize your application.

**Making the JDBC connection**

Discover how to make a JDBC connection.

**Using JDBC exceptions**

Manage and maximize JDBC exceptions for controlling your application.

**Building the first module**

Create the first module for the framework that demonstrates connecting to a database and controlling application-specific settings.

# Understanding the Application Framework

Our framework will begin with a simple application consisting of a primary frame. This frame will contain a menu bar that will divide the application into segments by creating a menu item for each concept. Subsequent chapters will be separate modules that link to the application but can be individual applications themselves. This will allow you to see a complete application in each chapter, while creating a robust demonstration of the JDBC interface. Figure 3.1 shows a view of the framework skeleton. Listing 3.1 shows the basic framework that we will build upon for the rest of Part I.

**Listing 3.1   Enterprise Java Application Framework**

```
import java.awt.*;
import module1.*;
    /**
     * An application that will demonstrate advanced database management
➥concepts.
     *
     * @author James Higginbotham
     * @version 1.00
     */
public class enterprise extends Frame {
    /**
     * Initialize all variables and setup Framework layout
     *
     *
     */
    public enterprise () {
        super ("Enterprise Java");
        MenuBar mbar = new MenuBar ();
        Menu m= new Menu ("File");
        m.add (new MenuItem ("Quit") );
        mbar.add (m);
        Menu m2=new Menu ("Module 1");
        m2.add (new MenuItem ("Start") );
        mbar.add (m2);
        setMenuBar (mbar);
    }
    /**
     * Override action to catch Menu options
     *
     *
     */
    public boolean action (Event evt, Object arg) {
        if (evt.target instanceof MenuItem) {
            if (arg.equals ("Quit")) {
                System.exit (0);
            }
            else
            if (arg.equals ("Start")) {
                Frame f=new module1 ();
```

```
                    f.resize (600,400);
                    f.show ();
                }
        }
        return false;
    }
    /**
     * Override handleEvent to catch destroy and other events
     *
     *
     */
    public boolean handleEvent (Event evt) {
        // catch window destroy
        if (evt.id == Event.WINDOW_DESTROY) System.exit (0);
        return super.handleEvent (evt);
    }
    /**
     * Spawn this frame
     *
     *
     */
    public static void main (String args[]) {
        Frame f=new enterprise ();
        f.resize (640,480);
        f.show ();
    }
}
```

**Part**

**I**

**Ch**

**3**

**FIG. 3.1**
Examining the
Application Framework
for Enterprise Java.

# Introducing Modules and Concepts

Table 3.1 is a brief summary of the modules that we will create, the chapter they are in, and the concepts they will cover.

**Table 3.1    Modules and the Concepts Covered**

| Module | Chapter | Concepts Covered |
|---|---|---|
| Module 1 | Chapter 3 | Basic Framework<br>Drivers<br>Connections<br>`DriverManager` |
| Module 2 | Chapter 4 | Statements Results |
| Module 3 | Chapter 5 | `Prepared` Statements<br>Stored Procedures<br>`Callable` Statement |
| Module 4 | Chapter 6 | Database Information<br>Database Accessors |
| Module 5 | Chapter 7 | Dynamic Data Access<br>Result Set Column Information |
| Module 6 | Chapter 8 | Threads<br>Using multiple threads for efficiency |
| Module 7 | Chapter 9 | Offline Applications<br>Using Flat-Files<br>Persistence |

# Connecting to a Database

Connecting to a database using the JDBC can be divided into three basic tasks. These tasks are:

1. Create a new `driver` instance, or add an entry in the properties file for the driver.

2. Generate the correct URL for the driver being used.

3. Establish a connection using the `DriverManager.getConnection()` method.

# Using Database URLs

The term URL is an acronym for Universal Resource Locator, and is the scheme used to address Internet services on the World Wide Web. An URL specifies the protocol, domain name or IP address, an optional port number, path, and any arguments needed. Whenever you decide to go to a Web site, you have to construct an URL for your Web browser to take you there. It usually looks like this: **http://www.sun.com**. To retrieve a file using the FTP protocol, you would construct an URL similar to the following: **ftp://ftp.sun.com/somefilename.zip**. The protocol specifies what Internet service to use, such as http for the World Wide Web, or ftp for the File Transfer Protocol.

## The Database URL

The JDBC utilizes the same URL specification system to enable an application to specify a particular database source and a JDBC driver. The JDBC format for a database URL is modeled after the Internet URL format, but must be constructed specifically for the particular driver being used. It was chosen due to the varying needs of the drivers. The URL format is standardized, making it easy to parse and determine if it should be accepted or rejected.

## Creating a JDBC URL

To create a general JDBC URL, the following format is used:

```
jdbc:<subprotocol>:<subname>
```

The subprotocol is driver-specific and will likely be the DBMS name and possibly a version number. For example, when using mSQL, a SQL-compliant database distributed as shareware, a format similar to `jdbc:msql://hostname:port/database` would be correct.

# Examining the *DriverManager*

The `DriverManager` is the central object on which the JDBC depends. It is responsible for keeping track of the different drivers used in an application and also manages the loading and unloading of the database drivers. Although the functions are generally hidden to the programmer, it is the key to how connections are established and maintained, and is important to understand.

## Determining Which Driver to Use

The `DriverManager` determines which driver to use based on the URL sent to the `getConnection` method. All known drivers are registered to the `DriverManager` in a vector. The URL is then compared to each registered driver and chosen accordingly. Drivers can register with the `DriverManager` in several ways. One way is by entering a reference to driver(s) in the `HotJava.properties` file. For example:

```
jdbc.drivers=another.new.Driver:newone.sql.Driver:yet.another.Driver
```

Another option is to use a command line argument to inform the `DriverManager` that drivers are to be registered. The format is:

```
java -Djdbc.drivers=another.new.Driver:newone.sql.Driver:yet.another.Driver
myApplication
```

Also, the system property may be set with the key of `jdbc.drivers` and a value of `another.new.Driver:newone.sql.Driver:yet.another.Driver`

Finally, you may instantiate a new driver using the `Class.forName().newInstance()` method. This will explicitly load and register the driver with the `DriverManager`. Listings 3.2, 3.3, and 3.4 show the code that is required to use this method. Note that the Instantiation Exception must be caught.

Part

I

Ch

3

**Listing 3.2   Instantiating a New Driver Option 1 (Using XDB Driver)**

```
try {
        // instantiate a new driver that matches the given Driver
      Class.forName("jet.bridge.JetDriver").newInstance();
    }
    catch (InstantiationException e) {
    System.out.println ("Problem instantiating driver: "+e);
    }
```

**Listing 3.3   Establishing a Connection to a Database Option 2 (Using Intersolv Driver)**

```
try {
   // instantiate a new driver that matches the given Driver
      new jdbc.odbc.JdbcOdbcDriver();
   }
      catch (Exception e) {
      ex=e;
      }
```

**Listing 3.4   Establishing a Connection to a Database Option 3 (Using Imaginary mSQL Driver)**

```
try {
   // instantiate a new driver that matches the given Driver
   Class.forName("imaginary.sql.iMsqlDriver");
    }
      catch (Exception e) {
      ex=e;
      }
}
```

# DriverManager.getConnection()

The DriverManager.getConnection() method is used to request a connection to a database. This method is overloaded and accepts a number of parameters. DriverManager then looks through its known drivers and queries each driver to find if the particular URL can be handled. If a match is found, a connection is attempted. If the connection was successful, a Connection object is returned from the database driver. If no drivers were found, an exception is thrown specifying the problem encountered.

**getConnection (String url, java.util.Properties info) throws SQLException**

attempts to establish a connection to the specified URL.

**Parameters:**

> url String containing a JDBC URL
>
> info Properties object containing name, key values for user ID, password and anything else required by the driver.

`getConnection(String url, String user, String password) throws SQLException`

attempts to establish a connection to the specified URL.

**Parameters:**

> url String containing a JDBC URL
>
> user String containing the user ID to log in as
>
> password String containing the password to log in with

`getConnection(String url) throws SQLException`

attempts to establish a connection to the specified URL.

**Parameters:**

> url String containing a JDBC URL

Listing 3.5 uses the DriverManager.getConnection() method to establish a database connection.

**Part**

**I**

**Ch**

**3**

---

**Listing 3.5   Establishing a Connection to a Database**

```
try {
  connection = DriverManager.getConnection("jdbc:jet:enterprise","sa","");
}
  catch (java.sql.SQLException e) {

      }
```

---

Typical exceptions that can be encountered include:

- java.sql.SQLException: No suitable driver.
- No drivers could be found in the Java Properties file or the CLASSPATH. Check your environment settings or your URL syntax.
- java.sql.SQLException: [Microsoft][ODBC Driver Manager] Data source name not found and no default driver specified.
- No data source was provided or the data source name is incorrect. Check the syntax or your data source driver setup.
- java.sql.SQLException: [Microsoft][ODBC SQL Server Driver][SQL Server] Login failed.

Check the database server's permissions or the user ID and password spelling.

## Vector of Drivers

As we discussed, the DriverManager stores the driver information it collects from the HotJava.properties, drivers registered by the registerDriver method, and drivers in the classpath referenced during the getConnection call. The information about registered drivers is kept in a vector of Driverinfo classes. The Driverinfo class is defined in Listing 3.6.

**Listing 3.6   Structure of the *DriverInfo* Class**

```
class DriverInfo {
    Driver        driver;
    Object        securityContext;
    String        className;
}
```

As you can see, the DriverInfo class contains several key items, including the className, a copy of the driver itself, and the Driver security context. Whenever the DriverManager opens or queries a driver, the security context of the Driver is compared to the security context of the application, and can refuse to load the driver if there is a question of security. The DriverInfo class is private and only used within the Java.sql package for tracking registered drivers.

# Understanding Drivers

We have discussed the registration of the drivers and using the DriverManager to locate the appropriate driver according to the URL provided. Now we are going to discuss the driver itself. It is the software that actually communicates with the database, either directly or by using other software, and can vary depending on the database, platform, and implementation. It is the driver's responsibility to register with the DriverManager. Once registered, it is effectively used as a factory and determines if the URL passed to it can be supported. If so, a Connection object will be returned to the DriverManager for communication. Since the driver is only referenced indirectly, most programmers rarely utilize the driver other than through the DriverManager.

---

### Factories: An Overview

One of the most undocumented yet powerful features of Java is its use of factories. Factory objects allow a Java application to determine the actual type of Java objects to be determined at runtime. This ability allows applications to be dynamically extended by introducing new classes it may create without rebuilding the original application.

To understand factories better, examine this situation: The URL class that Java uses will not know what kind of data is being read from a particular URL until the connection is opened at runtime. Once the data starts to be read, the factory object determines the type of data it is and dynamically creates an object that can handle the data. If new types of data need to be handled in the future, the URL class doesn't have to be modified directly, just informed of the new classes that it may cast. The only requirement that needs to be met is that the objects that are to be cast either derive from the same superclass or implement the same interface. Factories can be thought of as a large switch structure that doesn't have to be modified if new classes are introduced in the future.

## Instantiating a Driver

As we discussed earlier, drivers can be instantiated in two different ways. The first is by referencing it in the HotJava properties file. The second is by using the Class.forName() method to load and register the driver if it is found in the CLASSPATH.

## *Driver.getPropertyInfo()*

When designing applications that may need to connect to various databases determined at run-time, a method of determining enough information to make the connection is necessary. One such method is the Driver.getPropertyInfo method. When supplied with the URL of the database to connect to and a proposed list of tag/value pairs that will be sent once the connection is open, the method will return an array of DriverPropertyinfo objects. This array will describe possible properties needed, or an empty array if none are required. Depending on the values supplied so far, additional values may become necessary and may require several calls to complete the list.

```
DriverPropertyInfo[] getPropertyInfo(String url, java.util.Properties info)
throws SQLException
```

returns an array of DriverPropertyInfo objects containing possible properties needed for a connection to a particular URL.

**Parameters:**

> url String containing URL in question
>
> info Properties object containing name, key pairs specifying information already known

Listing 3.7 shows a method that will return a string containing all of the DriverPropertyInfo elements.

**Listing 3.7   Retrieving *DriverPropertyInfo***

```
public String driverProperties (Driver d, String url) {
      StringBuffer text=new StringBuffer();
      text.append ("\n");
      text.append ("Starting Properties Query");
      text.append ("\n");
      text.append ("\n");
      try {
        DriverPropertyInfo[] di= d.getPropertyInfo (url, new Properties ());
        int l=di.length;
```

*continues*

**Listing 3.7    Continued**

```
            if (l==0) text.append ("No More\nProperties Needed\n");
            else
              for (int i=0;i<l;i++) {
                text.append (di[i].name+" "+di[i].description+" "+di[i].required+"
  "+di[i].value+"\n");
                }
        } catch (java.sql.SQLException e) {
            text.append ("Exception : "+e);
        }
        text.append ("\n");
        text.append ("Done with Properties");
        return text.toString ();
    }
```

In this method, a StringBuffer named text is instantiated and given some leading
text for cosmetic purposes. Inside of the try/catch block is the heart of the method. A
DriverPropertyInfo array is declared which will reference the results of the getPropertyInfo
method. If the length of the returned array is 0, no more properties need to be specified.
If there are any elements in the array, the method then appends the information to the
StringBuffer. Note that the DriverPropertyInfo fields are public and therefore have no
accessor methods to retrieve their values.

# Types of Drivers

JDBC drivers have been broken into four different categories. These categories define the
methods by which the driver communicates with the database server.

Here is a summary of the levels and their definitions as related to JDBC drivers:

**Level 1 Drivers**    Level 1 drivers are a JDBC-ODBC bridge that utilizes most ODBC drivers to
connect to the database. The driver is not written in Java, which means a .dll or .os file will be
required on each client. Currently, major browsers do not allow the use of binary libraries,
which restricts applets from using this style of driver. Level 1 drivers tend to be less efficient
due to the required conversion from JDBC to ODBC and finally to the database API. This
driver is appropriate mostly for an application server written in Java that is part of a three-tier
architecture. Figure 3.2 shows a diagram of a level 1 driver.

**Level 2 Drivers**    Level 2 drivers, shown in Figure 3.3, are developed for a specific DBMS such
as Oracle, Sybase, or Informix, and convert JDBC calls to the proper API calls for the database.
The driver is partly Java, but still requires a binary driver on the part of the client. Drivers of
this nature tend to be more efficient than level 1 drivers since they need to be converted only
from JDBC to the database API.

**FIG. 3.2**
A diagram of level 1 drivers.

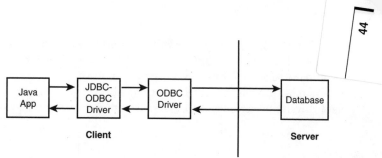

**Level 1 JDBC Driver**

**FIG. 3.3**
A diagram of level 2 drivers for the JDBC package.

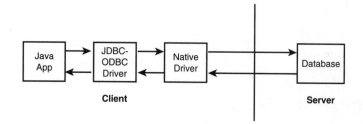

**Level 2 JDBC Driver**

**Level 3 Drivers**  Level 3 drivers are written fully in Java and translate JDBC calls into an independent Internet protocol, which is then translated into the proper DBMS protocol by the server. This method usually requires a server-side proxy or interpreter for the Internet protocol. The proxy may be specifically designed or purchased from a third-party vendor. Security is usually not a priority for vendor solutions and may require extra measures for Internet uses. Figure 3.4 presents a diagram of a level 3 driver scenario.

**FIG. 3.4**
Level 3 drivers use a proxy to allow applets/ applications to connect to a database.

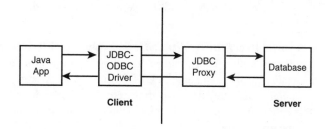

**Level 3 JDBC Driver**

**Level 4 Drivers**    Level 4 drivers are written purely by a DBMS manufacturer and are designed fully in Java. They translate JDBC calls into a DBMS-specific library and are communicated directly to the database's native library. Drivers in this category are generally used to connect a small number of users efficiently or large numbers of users to a large capacity database. Level 4 Drivers, shown in Figure 3.5, are currently very rare but are expected to emerge soon.

**FIG. 3.5**
Level 4 drivers are the most efficient, but are also rare.

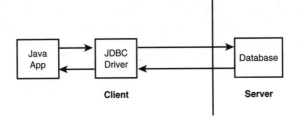

**Level 4 JDBC Driver**

# Which Driver Should I Use?

When deciding on which driver to use, it is important to consider the following factors:

- Is it feasible to provide and maintain a binary driver on each client?
- Is it feasible to provide and configure an ODBC driver on each client?
- Could the cost of a third-party proxy be less than maintaining ODBC drivers and binary drivers on each client?
- Could the cost of purchasing a third-party proxy be less than the cost of developing a custom proxy?
- Can the server handle a large number of concurrent connections if direct access is used?
- How many users will be using the database simultaneously?

With these questions in mind, let's examine several scenarios and determine what options are best suited for our needs.

***Scenario 1—A Single-User JDBC Application***    Suppose an application is required that would be used on only one machine. How could you develop it and what are the costs? It is easily feasible to maintain a binary driver and/or ODBC driver on just one machine, so we can consider this option. It definitely is not worth the cost of a proxy server for just one user, so we will ignore this option. A final option might be to directly connect to the database if a driver is available from the manufacturer. The final decision is a toss-up—a level 1 driver using ODBC, or a level 2 driver using just a binary driver. Most likely, if a level 2 driver is available, it is the best choice because a slight performance boost is gained from this driver.

***Scenario 2—Seven Users, Mixed Platform***    Because this scenario contains mixed platforms, the first two options are not available due to the fact that binary drivers are not always available for a particular platform. The primary decision to be made is if the cost of a third-party proxy is higher than the cost to develop a custom proxy. In most cases, the third-party proxy will be the likely choice. This scenario doesn't allow many choices to be made.

***Scenario 3—300-User Network Application***   To meet the needs of a large network such as this scenario, the first two options are not available. When designing large-scale applications such as this, it is important to reduce the overall client configuration and maintenance. If either of the first two options were chosen, the company would be forced to install and configure binary drivers and ODBC settings for 300 clients! A primary consideration is whether the server can handle 300 connections, possibly simultaneously. If not, the only option that is available is to use a proxy server. Possible options when using the proxy server are either to develop a custom proxy that can do pre-processing for the clients and put the heavy burden on the application server or to purchase a third-party proxy that can handle a minimum of 300 connections.

***Scenario 4—7,000-User Corporate Environment***   Generally, corporate networks have one or more database servers that are designed to provide vast amounts of resources to large amounts of connections. The options are similar to scenario 3, except that the corporation may be able to sustain a large number of connections, so a direct connection is possible. Also, when developing on such a large scale, a custom proxy may be more cost effective than purchasing a third-party solution because the proxy may be optimized for the particular tasks and network loads. Also, keep in mind that hardware considerations must be taken into account when designing for larger-scale applications.

## The Jet Connect Driver

The package we will be using in our examples is the Jet Connect package from XDB Systems, Inc. It contains two drivers: Jet Bridge and Jet Port. Jet Bridge is a level 1 driver which allows the JDBC to communicate with ODBC drivers. Jet Port is a level 3 proxy system which allows applets/applications to communicate with the database without any ODBC or binary drivers loaded on the client.

## Multiple Drivers for the Same URL

Often, multiple drivers will be capable of connecting to the same URL. When this happens, the `DriverManager` will use the first correct driver as its selection. What is the order in which `DriverManager` makes it choice? It first begins to query any driver specified in the `Properties` file. If no match is found, it then proceeds to query each driver registered, in the order it was registered. Keep this order in mind when registering multiple drivers for an application.

## Determining Driver Information

The `DriverManager` provides a method for retrieving an enumeration of drivers that are currently registered. As the elements are traversed, information such as name, version, and JDBC compliance can be determined. The next page contains a method that demonstrates enumerating through the list of drivers returned from the `DriverManager` and displaying all of the information about it. Notice that a call to the previously created `driverProperties()` method is wrapped inside of the enumeration for obtaining a complete list of driver information.

Part

I

Ch

3

The `java.sql.DriverManager` Method:

**`public static java.util.Enumeration getDrivers()`**

returns an enumeration containing a list of drivers registered with the `DriverManager`.

**Parameters:** none

The `java.sql.Driver` Method:

**`boolean acceptsURL(String url) throws SQLException`**

returns `true` if the driver can connect to the URL.

**Parameters:**
> `url` String containing URL to be tested

**`int getMajorVersion()`**

returns an `int` representing the primary version number of the driver, usually 1.

**Parameters:** none

**`int getMinorVersion()`**

returns an `int` representing the secondary version number, i.e., `01`, `15`, `50`.

When combined with `getMajorVersion()`, a complete version number is created. Examples 1 and 15 would be 1.15.

**Parameters:** none

**`boolean jdbcCompliant()`**

returns `true` if the driver is fully JDBC-compliant.

**Parameters:** none

Listing 3.8 shows how to retrieve driver information.

### Listing 3.8   Retrieving Driver Information

```
public void viewDrivers () {
        textDialog text=new textDialog (this,"Enumerate Drivers");
        text.append ("Starting enum");
        text.append ("\n");
        text.append ("\n");
        Enumeration e = DriverManager.getDrivers ();
        while (e.hasMoreElements () ) {
                java.sql.Driver d = (java.sql.Driver)e.nextElement ();
                text.append ("Driver name:   "+d.getClass().getName());
                text.append ("\n");
                text.append ("Major Version: "+d.getMajorVersion());
                text.append ("\n");
```

```
                    text.append ("Minor Version: "+d.getMinorVersion());
                    text.append ("\n");
                    text.append ("JDBC Compliant? "+d.jdbcCompliant());
                    text.append ("\n");
                    text.append (driverProperties (d,"jdbc:jet:enterprise"));
          }
                    text.append ("\n");
                    text.append ("\n");
          text.append ("Done with  enum");
          text.resize (350,200);
          text.show ();
          text.move (100,100);
     }
```

## JDBC-Compliant Drivers

As you may have noticed in the previous example, a driver can be flagged as JDBC-compliant. To be compliant, a JDBC driver must support the full JDBC API and fully support the SQL-92 Entry Level. JavaSoft notes that the `jdbcCompliant()` method "is not intended to encourage the development of non-JDBC-compliant drivers, but is a recognition of the fact that some vendors are interested in using the JDBC API and framework for lightweight databases…" These lightweight databases may not need a SQL implementation, or require all of the JDBC API, and may be designed for special databases such as document retrieval.

# Using the JDBC *Connection* Class

The `Connection` class is an interface to the database connection with common methods needed for communication and database information. The `Connection` class contains methods to control the type of transaction committing, read or read/write mode, and transaction isolation levels.

## How They Are Created

As discussed earlier, the `DriverManager` traverses through its list of drivers and attempts to locate a driver capable of connecting to a particular URL. Since you've now been introduced to the essential ideas behind establishing a connection, it is important to understand the principles behind what actually happens during the `DriverManager`'s attempt at choosing a driver. Listing 3.9 illustrates this.

**Listing 3.9    *java.sql.DriverManager getConnection* Method**

```
public static synchronized Connection getConnection(String url,
          java.util.Properties info) throws SQLException {
    if(url == null) {
        throw new SQLException("The url cannot be null", "08001");
    }
        println("DriverManager.getConnection(\"" + url + "\")");
        if (!initialized) {
```

*continues*

**Listing 3.9    Continued**

```
        initialize();
    }
    // Figure out the current security context.
    Object currentSecurityContext = getSecurityContext();
    // Walk through the loaded drivers attempting to make a connection.
    // Remember the first exception that gets raised so we can reraise it.
    SQLException reason = null;
    for (int i = 0; i < drivers.size(); i++) {
        DriverInfo di = (DriverInfo)drivers.elementAt(i);
        // if the driver isn't part of the base system and doesn't come
        // from the same security context as the current caller, skip it.
        if (di.securityContext != null &&
                    di.securityContext != currentSecurityContext) {
            println("    skipping: " + di);
            continue;
        }
        try {
            println("    trying " + di);
            Connection result = di.driver.connect(url, info);
            if (result != null) {
                // Success!
                println("getConnection returning " + di);
                return (result);
            }
        } catch (SQLException ex) {
            if (reason == null) {
                reason = ex;
            }
        }
    }
    // if we got here nobody could connect.
    if (reason != null)     {
        println("getConnection failed: " + reason);
        throw reason;
    }
    println("getConnection: no suitable driver");
    throw new SQLException("No suitable driver", "08001");
}
```

Once the initial checks have been completed, the DriverManager's vector of drivers is traversed. As we learned earlier, the vector consists of DriverInfo objects containing essential driver information, as well as a reference to the driver itself. The security context is checked, and if it passes, the DriverManager attempts to call the driver's connect() method. If a connection reference is returned from the connect() method, the driver has successfully established a connection and the reference is returned to the application. If no driver is found, the first exception encountered is thrown. Otherwise, a new exception is created and thrown stating that a suitable driver was not found.

# *Connection* Methods

The Connection class has several methods related to database connection states. They control settings such as Connection's read only, auto commit, and auto close modes. Understanding their implications is important and directly reflects your application's actions and results.

**Read Only Mode**   When a connection is set to read/write mode (default), the connection is providing resources for both queries and result sets. To gain a performance boost when only performing queries, set the connection mode to read only. This will cause the connection to be optimized for queries only.

```
void setReadOnly(boolean readOnly) throws SQLException
```

sets the read/write or read only (optimized) mode for the connection

Note: This method cannot be called in the middle of a transaction.

**Parameters:**

> readOnly true for read-only mode, false for read/write mode

```
boolean isReadOnly() throws SQLException
```

returns true if the connection is read only, false if it is in read/write mode.

**Parameters:** none

**Auto Commit**   The Connection class allows statements to be treated as individual committed transactions. This is accomplished by turning on auto commit (default) with the setAutoCommit() method. If auto commit is turned off, SQL statements are grouped into transactions and are finished when either the commit() or rollback() methods are called. The commit actually occurs either whenever the statement completes or the next execute occurs, whichever comes first. Complex cases, such as multiple result sets, define statement completion when all results have been retrieved. To determine the current auto commit state, the getAutoCommit() method is used. Application performance will increase if auto commit is turned off; however, transaction log files will increase until transactions are committed.

```
boolean getAutoCommit() throws SQLException
```

returns true if auto commit is on, false if it is turned off.

**Parameters:** none

```
void setAutoCommit(boolean autoCommit) throws SQLException
```

turns the auto commit on or off.

**Parameters:**

> autoCommit true to turn auto commit on, false to turn it off.

Part

I

Ch

3

**Auto Close**   Depending on the database being used, some support keeping statements and result sets open over multiple commits/rollbacks. To support the databases that have this feature, the Connection class contains an auto close mode, which can be toggled on or off. If the mode is turned on, PreparedStatements, CallableStatements, and ResultSets are closed when a transaction is committed (default). If turned off, the objects will remain open after the transaction has been committed.

```
boolean getAutoClose() throws SQLException
```

returns true if auto close is on, false if it is turned off.

**Parameters:** none

```
void setAutoClose(boolean autoClose) throws SQLException
```

turns the auto close on or off.

**Parameters:**

autoClose true to turn auto close on, false to turn it off.

# Handling Multiple Connections

Designing a large-scale application for intranet or Internet use may require using multiple datasources, or making multiple connections to the same database. Multiple connections may be made using the JDBC and only require that a new connection be established and maintained by the application. This can allow an application to retrieve data from multiple databases across a range of servers. Data can then be manipulated and/or merged for large data analysis or updating. Consideration must be taken into account when using multiple drivers to create multiple connections. Most vendors that provide JDBC drivers provide their own java.sql package. When using multiple drivers within the same application, a problem may arise trying to resolve the proper class to use if the packages contain the same class names and/or methods. Fully qualified class names may be required to avoid such problems. Plan your applications with care when using multiple drivers in the same application.

# Closing It Up

Once the application is finished, the connection must be closed. To close a connection, use the close() method, catching any SQLExceptions. It is recommended to verify that the connection is not null, which would indicate that the connection was never established. It is also good practice to verify that the connection hasn't been closed previously by using the isClosed() method. If a close() method is called on a connection that has already been closed, a SQLException will be thrown.

```
void close() throws SQLException
```

closes a connection—throws SQLException if a connection doesn't exist or a problem has occurred.

**Parameters:** none

```
boolean isClosed() throws SQLException
```

returns `true` if the connection is closed, `false` if it is still open.

**Parameters:** none

Listing 3.10 shows how to close the connection.

### Listing 3.10   Closing the Connection

```
public void closeConnection () {
      SQLException ex=null;
try {
        // try to close the connection
  if (connection != null && !connection.isClosed() ) //verify connection ini-
tialized and open
            connection.close ();
      }
      catch (java.sql.SQLException e) {
        ex=e;
        }
```

It is highly recommended to call the `close()` method from the `dispose()` method to ensure that the connection is cleanly closed whenever the application closes. If `close()` is called only under normal circumstances, the connection may not get closed because the application may terminate abnormally and not even reach the `close()` statement. To make sure that the connection is always closed upon program termination, override the `dispose()` method and insert a call to the method that is responsible for closing the connection.

Listing 3.11 illustrates this technique.

### Listing 3.11   Closing the Connection by Overriding the *dispose()* Method

```
public void dispose () {
      super.dispose ();
      closeConnection();
    }
```

# Using the Standard *SQLException*

Whenever SQL statements are executed, or result sets are being obtained (see Table 3.2), `Java.Sql.SQLException` must be caught. `SQLException` will report any problems during a database access attempt and the current `SQLState`. `SQLState` is an error code identifying the reason the exception was thrown.

Part

I

Ch

3

**Where SQL States Come From**

SQLState errors returned by the SQLException getSQLState() method are based on the 1992 X/Open and SQL Access Group SQL CAE specification. The string returned by this method consists of a two-character class value followed by a three-character subclass value. A class value of 01 indicates a warning, while all other classes except IM indicate an error has occurred. The IM classes are specific warnings and errors derived from the implementation of ODBC drivers. A subclass value of 000 is reserved for custom class conditions. Class and subclass values other than those previously mentioned are defined by the SQL-92 standard. Most SQL-92 DBMS reference manuals contain a list of the SQLState codes and their meanings.

# The Structure of the *SQLException* Class

**Table 3.2** *java.sql.SQLException* **Class**

| Field | Accessor | Description |
| --- | --- | --- |
| SQLState | public String getSQLState() | Returns the SQLState code relating to the error |
| VendorCode | public int getErrorCode () | Returns the vendor-specific error code |

# What *SQLExceptions* Mean to a JDBC Application

A JDBC application can use the fields of the SQLException to determine what may have happened to cause the SQLException, and then determine a course of action. For example, suppose a robust JDBC application was developed for a large corporation. To make trouble-shooting easier for the information department, our application will be smarter. Instead of just reporting what errors have occurred, a class will determine the problem based on the exception thrown. The fields of the exception will then be checked against known problems and solutions. A nice dialog box could appear to alert the user of the problem, and the corrective action, if any are known, that may be necessary. The text displayed can be specific, determined by the SQLState and VendorCode fields of the exception that occurred. This is just one example of how useful SQLExceptions are.

With the implementation of Remote Method Invocation, a Java application becomes very powerful when taking corrective action. A remote server may reside on a computer in the information department that monitors client/server activity. When a Java client encounters an exception, it can take corrective action to alert the department of what error occurred by remotely invoking the proper method on the server. The method can be determined at runtime according to the nature of the problem and can include specific information related to the error. The department then determines the primary cause and plots the correct course to solve the problem. The department can even contact the user within seconds with questions concerning the problem! This sets Java apart from many other languages. Figure 3.6 shows the hierarchy of the SQLException tree.

**FIG. 3.6**
The SQL Exception Hierarchy begins from the Exception class.

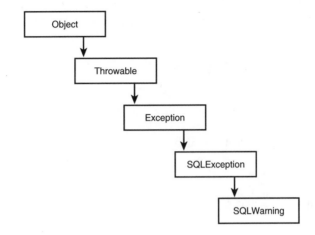

## SQLWarnings

To register problems with a JDBC statement, connection, or result set access, two situations may occur. The first may involve a SQLException being thrown. This will halt an application, or cause a break in the code if the exception is in a try/catch block. The second involves SQLWarnings. To prevent a non-fatal error from disturbing the flow of code, SQLWarnings are instantiated and attached to the object that generated the error. The attachments are silent, and unless specifically detected in the code, will remain until either the object's warning list is reset by a new method call, or the warnings are pulled from the list by an accessor method. In most instances, SQLWarnings are sent to the DriverManager logging device, if specified (see more about logging in the next section).

```
SQL Warning getWarnings() throws SQLException
```

retrieves the objects SQLWarning, returns null if none exist.

**Parameters:** none

```
void clearWarnings() throws SQLException
```

resets the SQLWarning chain to null.

**Parameters:** none

Listing 3.12 determines if a SQLWarning was created while connecting to a database.

Part
I

Ch
3

### Listing 3.12   *SQLWarning* Detection

```
//determine if any warnings occurred
      try {
        SQLWarning sw=connection.getWarnings();
        if (sw !=null) {
          System.out.println ("Warning thrown: "+sw);
          connection.clearWarnings ();
        }
      } catch (java.sql.SQLException e) {
        System.out.println ("ERROR! :"+e);
        }
```

**Chained Warnings**   As SQLWarnings are encountered, they become chained together to the first warning of the object that caused them. To determine if there is another warning chained, a call must be made to getNextWarning(). If another warning is chained, the method will return a reference to the next SQLWarning instance. A value of null indicates the warning chain is complete. Warning chains are essentially linked lists, beginning with the oldest warning and ending with the newest (see Figure 3.7).

**FIG. 3.7**
How warnings are chained.

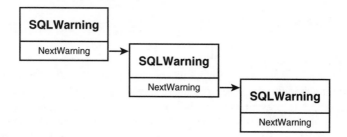

```
public SQLWarning getNextWarning()
```

returns a reference to the next warning in the chain, or null if the warning is the last.

**Parameters:** none

**Creating Warnings and Warning Chains**   Warnings are constructed in the same fashion as SQLExceptions, and vary only by how they are handled. To instantiate a new SQLWarning, call one of the overloaded constructors with any parameter such as reason, SQLState, or vendorCode. In most cases, the SQLWarning will not be thrown, but instead be attached to the object. The next step is to set the object's warning reference to the new warning. If a warning already exists for the object, the new warning should be placed into the object's chain at the end using the setNextWarning() method. Note that the java.sql package classes that support warnings do not allow external warnings to be chained. However, warnings may be used for custom classes within an application, or an application itself.

`public SQLWarning(String reason, String SQLstate, int vendorCode)`

constructs a new warning with a `description`, `SQLstate`, and `vendorCode`.

**Parameters:**

reason: `String` containing a description of the warning

`SQLstate int` representing the current error state

`vendorCode int` representing a vendor error code

`public SQLWarning(String reason, String SQLstate)`

constructs a new warning with only a description and `SQLstate`.

**Parameters:**

reason: `String` containing a description of the warning

`SQLstate int` representing the current error state

`public SQLWarning(String reason)`

constructs a new warning with only a description.

**Parameters:**

reason: `String` containing a description of the warning

`public SQLWarning()`

constructs a new warning without a description.

**Parameters:** none

`public void setNextWarning(SQLWarning w)`

assigns a new warning into the end of the chain.

**Parameters:**

*w*: The new `SQLWarning` to be inserted.

## *DataTruncation*

When data is being read from a database after a query, there may be an instance when the data will be truncated. This may be due to size differences between the data being retrieved and the object on which it is being stored. When this happens, the `DataTruncationException` is handled as a `SQLWarning`, being silently attached to the object that made the conversion. However, when a write to a database is attempted and the data is truncated, a `DataTruncationException` is thrown. This occurs when the data stored in an object is larger than the database column.

It is important to understand the dual-mode of this exception, since data truncations that occur from reading a result set are important to catch. `DataTruncation` will be demonstrated in future chapters, when data access and manipulation are discussed.

# Customizing Your Connection

The JDBC package includes several methods of customizing the connection to a database. In addition, correctly managing the connection using these tools can reduce debugging time, and enable an IS department to report errors with additional runtime information.

## Managing the Connection as a Thread

JDBC applications tend to be robust and may require more than modest initialization routines. If a getConnection() method is called for a database outside of the current domain, a noticeable delay may develop. This delay may inhibit specific initialization routines from executing until the connection is either established or determined not available. For application efficiency, a thread can be developed to eliminate this effect and become solely responsible for establishing the connection. This method allows the application to continue in its initialization routines and is especially useful in Internet applications. Since the Internet can have large delays during peak times or due to slow connections, this is often a necessary strategy. For smaller development, or development when connections may be established quickly on most occasions, this method may demand more time coding with less net gain.

## *DriverManager* Logging

DriverManager has a facility for entering all tracing and logging messages into a PrintStream for debugging and moderation. This stream will record all statements, errors, and warnings issued by any of the drivers. The stream is initially disabled, and requires that a PrintStream be established before being enabled. To register the stream as the log stream, call the DriverManager's setLogStream() method. To retrieve the current log stream, assign a PrintStream to the result of the getLogStream() method. An additional method of the DriverManager, println(), will send a message to be sent to the logStream. As shown in Listing 3.13, this method can be used to mark the beginning of a test function, or just comment on the log.

### Listing 3.13  Logging *DriverManager* Messages to a *PrintStream*

```
try {
        FileOutputStream fout = new FileOutputStream ("log.dat");
        PrintStream pout=new PrintStream (fout);
        DriverManager.setLogStream (pout);
        DriverManager.println ("Testing...");
    } catch (IOException i) {
     System.out.println ("PROBLEM: "+i);
    }
```

It is important to note that an applet is unable to utilize this feature since its security context will not allow file input or output to the local client. Options for proper logging and tracing within an applet include logging to a special server application on another socket, tracking errors using another reliable database connection, or the use of Remote Method Invocation. These options are discussed later.

Output resulting from the code:

```
DriverManager.initialize: jdbc.drivers = null
```

JDBC DriverManager initialized

```
registerDriver:
driver[className=jet.bridge.JetDriver,context=null,jet.bridge.JetDriver@a60a58]
```

```
DriverManager.getConnection("jdbc:jet:enterprise")
```

trying
```
driver[className=jet.bridge.JetDriver,context=null,jet.bridge.JetDriver@a60a58]
```

```
SQLWarning: reason([Microsoft][ODBC SQL Server Driver][SQL Server] Changed
database context to 'master'.) SQLstate(01000) vendor code(5701)
```

getConnection returning
```
driver[className=jet.bridge.JetDriver,context=null,jet.bridge.JetDriver@a60a58]
```

Testing...

# The Login Timeout

When an application cannot connect to a database due to slow connect times or a down server, the application may hang indefinitely. Maybe you would like your application to behave faster, knowing that a connection can always be made quickly. DriverManager has two methods that can be used to alter or retrieve the time, setLoginTimeout() and getLoginTimeout(). The setLoginTimeout() method requires an integer to indicate the number of seconds to wait for all connections to be established. GetLoginTimeout() returns an integer representing the current setting. The default setting is 0, which means there is no maximum time to stop a connection attempt.

Determining the best value for the LoginTimeout requires some consideration and testing. For intranet or Internet applications that will consist of a large number of connections, a larger value will be required. When applications will have a smaller number of connections, or connections that will be closed after a small processing time, a smaller value may be used. It is important to emphasize that the default value of 0 is not recommended since applications may remain suspended for an indefinite amount of time (see Listing 3.14).

**public static int getLoginTimeout()**

retrieves the number of seconds all connection attempts will wait for a connection to be established

**Parameters:** none

**public static void setLoginTimeout(int seconds)**

sets the number of seconds all connections will wait for a connection to be established.

**Parameters:**

> seconds: number of seconds to wait.

---

**Listing 3.14   Setting and Getting the *LoginTimeout* from the *DriverManager***

```
System.out.println ("Starting LoginTime methods...");
    System.out.println ("Initial LoginTimeout :
"+DriverManager.getLoginTimeout ());
    System.out.println ("Set LoginTimeout to 10 seconds...");
    DriverManager.setLoginTimeout (10);
    System.out.println ("New LoginTimeout : "+DriverManager.getLoginTimeout
());
```

---

# Creating SQL Exceptions

Earlier, we touched on the subject of SQL exceptions and what they meant to our application. Now, we will build a basic template for creating SQL exceptions of your own, and a custom SQL exception that can be used for better debugging. First, let's start by examining some of the SQLException code.

The fully qualified constructor uses three parameters to construct the exception. The reason parameter is a verbose string describing the problem that was encountered. The SQLState parameter is a string representing an XOPEN code meeting the XOPEN specifications. The VendorCode parameter is a vendor-specific exception code. The constructor calls its parent constructor, java.lang.Exception() with the string containing the reason. The next significant step is to determine if the class is actually an instance of SQLWarning, and if so, skip the rest of the constructor. If it isn't and there is a reference to a PrintStream, then send the text and a stack trace to the stream. Listing 3.15 illustrates a constructor.

---

**Listing 3.15   A *SQLException* Constructor**

```
public SQLException(String reason, String SQLState, int vendorCode) {
    super(reason);
    this.SQLState = SQLState;
    this.vendorCode = vendorCode;
    if (!(this instanceof SQLWarning)) {
        if (DriverManager.getLogStream() != null) {
     DriverManager.println("SQLException: SQLState(" + SQLState +
    ") vendor code(" + vendorCode + ")");
    printStackTrace(DriverManager.getLogStream());
    }
    }
    }
```

---

```
public SQLException(String reason, String SQLState, int vendorCode)
```

constructs a SQLException with all three fields set.

### Parameters:

reason: String containing an explanation/detail about why the exception was thrown

SQLState: String referring to an XOPEN code related to the error

vendorCodeinteger referring to the vendor code that specifies the error that occurred

```
public SQLException(String reason, String SQLState)
```

constructs a SQLException with only a reason and SQLState.

### Parameters:

reason: String containing an explanation/detail about why the exception was thrown

SQLState: String referring to an XOPEN code related to the error

```
public SQLException(String reason)
```

constructs a SQLException with only a reason.

### Parameters:

reasonString containing an explanation/detail about why the exception was thrown

```
public SQLException()
```

constructs a SQLException with no fields set.

### Parameters: none

For our template, we will concern ourselves with overriding only the last two, since we will have no need to specify XOPEN states or vendor codes. Here is a sample template for creating exceptions that extend SQLException. It will simply override SQLException and call its parent constructors. Listing 3.16 shows the template.

### Listing 3.16   A Simple *SQLException* Template

```
class SQLExceptionTemplate extends java.sql.SQLException {
  public SQLExceptionTemplate () {
    super ();
  }
  public SQLExceptionTemplate (String reason) {
    super(reason);
  }
```

Using this template, we will now create a custom SQLException that can be used to record specific application-debug information (see Listing 3.17). The information can later be viewed to determine the time at which the exception was thrown and any other causes.

Part
I

Ch
3

---

**Listing 3.17    A Custom *SQLException* Class**

```
class EnterpriseException extends java.sql.SQLException {
 public EnterpriseException (String debugInfo) {
    super ();
    addInfo (debugInfo);
 }
 public EnterpriseException (String reason,String debugInfo) {
    super (reason);
    addInfo (debugInfo);
 }
 public void addInfo (String debugInfo) {
    DriverManager.println ("Debug state: "+debugInfo);
 }
}
```

---

# Inserting the Module into the Framework

Now that we have the complete code to module 1, we now need to link it into the framework. To do this, a new menu needs to be added:

```
Menu m2=new Menu ("Module 1");
m2.add (new MenuItem ("Start") );
mbar.add (m2);
```

The new menu action needs to be caught and the module 1 frame instantiated as shown:

```
if (evt.target instanceof MenuItem) {
      if (arg.equals ("Quit")) {
         System.exit (0);
      }
else
      if (arg.equals ("Start")) {
         Frame f=new module1 ();
         f.resize (600,400);
         f.show ();
      return true;
      }
```

Finally, the classpath needs to be updated, and the module 1 package needs to be imported:

```
import module1.*;
```

Figure 3.8 shows a screen shot of the completed Module 1.

**FIG. 3.8**

Showing the completed view of Module 1.

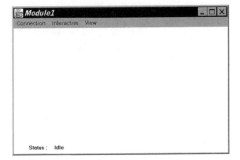

# From Here...

Once you understand how a connection is made using the JDBC, a multitude of opportunities will emerge. This chapter has presented an in-depth explanation of how the `DriverManager`, `Driver`, and `Connection` classes operate, and how to fully use their power. The following chapters will expand upon this base and allow you to discover the power of incorporating the JDBC API into your Java applications for powerful intranet or Internet clients and servers:

- Chapter 4, "Executing SQL Statements," discusses in detail how to execute SQL statements and retrieve results.

- Chapter 5, "Prepared Statements and Stored Procedures," demonstrates incorporating stored procedures for efficiency.

- Chapter 6, "Retrieving Database Information," discusses developing runtime database access applications for complex development.

# Executing SQL Statements

Now that we have looked at the JDBC from a 10,000-foot level and are familiar with its purpose, it is time to get into the meat of the subject—executing SQL statements. Database applications usually have some basic requirements; they need to quickly store, retrieve, and process information. Traditionally, the SQL language has been divided into two primary sections to perform these feats:

**DDL**—The Data Definition Language:

    Create Table, Create View, and so on
    Drop Table, Drop View, etc.

**DML**—The Data Manipulation Language:

    Select, Insert, Update, Delete

Most relational databases have an API (applications programming interface) that is used to relay SQL statements to the Database Management System (DBMS). Sybase has CT-Lib, Microsoft's SQL/Server uses DB-Lib, and Oracle uses ODS (Open Data Services). These interfaces to the DBMS were not specifically designed to work with object-oriented programming languages. Thus, they implemented a procedure-oriented mechanism for sending calls and retrieving result sets. The designers of the JDBC were challenged with the problem of creating an object wrapper that could be wrapped around structured/procedure-style API calls. As part of the design of JDBC, extra attention was paid to abstracting functionality between classes and promoting encapsulation. The result was a set of classes that were able to wholly contain data and perform operations on that data through standard object-oriented method calls. Obviously, the designers could have created one class and presented a massive list of calls, all inside one object, but that approach would not lend itself to the object-oriented nature of Java, nor would it lend itself to the dynamic loading of small self-contained classes. Thus, we are given a robust set of self-contained classes that are engineered to bridge the gap between structured API calls and object-oriented programming. ■

# Preparing to Use the Primary JDBC Classes

The primary classes that the JDBC uses to perform database calls are the `Statement` class and the `ResultSet` class. Before we look at how each of these classes works, let's review the steps that must precede the usage of these classes:

1. A JDBC Driver must be instantiated.

2. A `Connection` object must be created that is pointed at a DBMS or a DBMS proxy server.

After a `Connection` object is created, a SQL statement can be issued. This is done by returning a `Statement` object from the current connection. The `Connection` object has a special method that returns the `Statement` object, declared in `java.sql.Connection`:

```
public abstract Statement createStatement() throws SQLException
```

Notice in Listing 4.1 that the `createStatement()` method returns an object of type `Statement`. This new instance of the `Statement` object will be used in subsequent commands to issue your specific request.

## Listing 4.1   Creating a *SQLStatement* Object

```
Connection  conn;   // Declare a Connection object.
Statement  query_Statement;  // Declare a Statement object
//Create the connection....
try {
    new jet.bridge.JetDriver(); // Instantiate a Driver...
//Connect to the data source
conn = DriverManager.getConnection( "jdbc:jet.jettp://www.delphis.com/crawler",
"Jeff","Mypassword");
    query_Statement = conn.createStatement();
} catch (SQLException se) {
System.out.println(se);}
```

The methods of the `Statement` object are used to execute most DDL and DML commands. The `Statement` object has two sister classes that perform similar duties: `CallableStatement` and `PreparedStatement`. The `CallableStatement` is used to invoke stored procedures while `PreparedStatement` is used on drivers that have the ability to precompile a SQL statement. We will explore both of these options in the next chapter, but first, let's take a closer look at the power of the `Statement` class.

# The *Statement* and *ResultSet* Classes

The following sections explain the Statement and ResultSet classes. These explanations will include the features of each class as well as helpful insights into their functions. Before we discuss the features of the Statement class, the reader should be aware of the tendency to misuse the command. From a software engineering standpoint, the Statement class presents a challenge due to the lack of communication between the Java compiler and the DBMS.

Many of the features necessary in database applications are available as simple method calls, where variables are passed into a JDBC method and a return code and/or result set is returned. This type of call is considered a good programming practice since most of the potential syntax errors can be caught at compile time. In other cases, we are forced to embed a language inside of a language (SQL inside of Java). In this case, only the Java syntax is checked at compile time. The compiler has no knowledge of the database to which the program is connecting, so it is unable to warn the programmer of potential dangers. The current lack of communication between the compiler and the DBMS is unfortunate. In order to minimize the dangers associated with embedding a language inside another language, it is recommended that this feature be used as little as possible. The more SQL that is put in the client code (or middleware), the more likely that runtime errors will occur.

The obvious means to bypass using long SQL strings in Java code is to implement as much as possible through stored procedures (see CallableStatement). Calling a stored procedure will force the majority of the SQL code to the DBMS and save it in a precompiled format. The potential of incorrectly calling a stored procedure still exists. The syntax used in invoking a stored procedure is neither parsed nor verified at compile time, just like in embedded SQL. Only in this case, the majority of the SQL will be moved to the DBMS where its syntax will be verified. Many database management systems now have features that automatically update references to fields, tables, and views as they are changed. Thus, if a field name were changed and we used stored procedures, the DBMS would automatically change all of the places where it was referenced. If all of the SQL were embedded in the application, it would be necessary to make all of the changes by hand in the Java code and then recompile all applications that were affected by the change—a time-consuming and error-prone task.

Certain instances exist when the developer must use embedded SQL. Some database management systems do not support stored procedures. In this case, you may be stuck embedding strings of SQL calls directly into the code.

Part

I

Ch

4

## Executing Commands

The Statement class has three methods that are used to issue SQL statements.

- execute—Executes all types of SQL statements
- executeQuery—Executes SQL queries with a single result set
- executeUpdate—Executes Insert, Update, and Delete statements

At first glance, it would appear that the `execute` statement performs all of the necessary functionality. This assumption is correct. So why do we have the `executeQuery` and `executeUpdate` methods? Convenience. The `executeQuery` and `executeUpdate` combine the functionality of executing statements with the retrieval of the results and/or return codes.

**The *execute* Method**   The `execute` method issues all types of SQL statements to a database server. It can be used in any scenario where `executeQuery` or `executeUpdate` can be used. In addition, it can be used in the following scenarios:

- Creating or dropping structures (tables, views, etc.)
- Executing stored procedures (where parameters are not bound)
- Issuing commands that return multiple result sets
- Performing pass-through SQL commands

The `execute` method (see Listing 4.2) takes a `String` as an argument. The `String` is the SQL command that will be executed. The method returns a Boolean value that states whether the first logical call produced a result set. (Some commands do not return a result set; they may return nothing, or a return code.) Since a SQL command can execute multiple statements in a single command, the JDBC handles them one at a time:

```
public abstract boolean execute(String sql) throws SQLException
```

**Parameters:**

> sql      A string that contains the SQL command to execute.

returns a `boolean`; `true` if the first result is a `ResultSet`; `false` if it is not.

An additional method is used to return an object that contains the result set of the SQL call. The `getResultSet` method is used to return an object of type `ResultSet`. This is a special object that is used to manipulate the data inside of a result set:

```
public abstract ResultSet getResultSet() throws SQLException
```

returns a `ResultSet` object containing the data retrieved in the query.

---

**Listing 4.2   An Example of the *execute()* Method**

```
// This example builds on the code presented in Listing 4.1
boolean rc;  // return code
String SQL_Command = "select name, id from employee";
ResultSet RS;
try {
 query_Statement = conn.createStatement();
 rc = query_Statement.execute(SQL_Command);
 if (rc==true) {
 RS = query_Statement.getResultSet();
 } else {
    System.out.println("The command did not return a ResultSet");
 }
} catch (SQLException se) {
System.out.println(se);}
```

---

**Update Counts**    Several SQL commands return an "update count." The update count states the number of rows that were affected by the SQL command. Update counts are returned by `Insert`, `Update`, and `Delete` statements or stored procedures that contain the aforementioned statements. Often we know the exact number of rows that are affected by a statement, such as:

"`Insert into xyz Values (1,2,3)`"

will affect one row. In other cases, the number of rows is unknown:

"`Update person set income = (income *1.1) where income <25000`"

The number of rows where the income is less than 25,000 is not known to the application. By querying the update count, we could return to the user the number of rows that were affected and translate it into the appropriate business context:

"`17 people whose incomes were less than 25,000 were given a 10 percent raise`"

The update count query `public abstract int getUpdateCount() throws SQLException`

returns an integer specifying the number of rows that were affected by the previous `execute` method.

**The *executeQuery* Method**    The `executeQuery` method (see Listing 4.3) is a convenience method that is used to perform queries. A query in this context is any SQL command that may return a `ResultSet`. The `executeQuery` method provides a simple means to quickly issue queries:

`public abstract ResultSet executeQuery(String sql) throws SQLException`

Part

I

Ch

4

**Listing 4.3    *executeQuery* Example**

```
try {
   Statement st_Jobs = conn.createStatement();
   ResultSet rs_Jobs = st_Jobs.executeQuery("Select job_id,job_desc from
pubs..jobs");
   while (rs_Jobs.next()==true){
       System.out.println(rs_Jobs.getInt(1) + " : " + rs_Jobs.getString(2));
   }
} catch (SQLException se) { // handle problems }
```

The `executeQuery` is actually performing two statements at once:

> `execute()`
>
> `getResultSet()`

**The *executeUpdate* Method**    The `executeUpdate` method (see Listing 4.4) is also a convenience method. Although the name implies it is used for updates, the `executeUpdate` method is used for any DML statement that does not return a result set such as `Insert`, `Update`, or `Delete`.

`public abstract int executeUpdate(String sql) throws SQLException`

returns an integer specifying the number of rows that were affected, or `0` for SQL statements that do not directly modify rows.

---

**Listing 4.4  Example of *executeUpdate()***

```
try {
    Statement st_Jobs = conn.createStatement();
int cnt = st_Jobs.executeUpdate("insert into pubs..jobs
(job_desc,min_lvl,max_lvl) values ('Programmer',10,100)");
    System.out.println(cnt);
} catch (SQLException se) { // handle problems }
```

---

# Manipulating *ResultSet* Objects

The JDBC uses a container class called ResultSet to hold the results from SQL queries. This class acts as an interim holding ground for data. Each result set will vary in the number of rows and columns, the names of fields, as well as their type. The ResultSet class is tasked with being able to dynamically discover information about the result set that was received and fluidly move the data into the application's appropriate containers. This process is known as binding columns.

**Binding Columns to Variables**   The primary mechanism for extracting the data is by "binding" variables to columns in the result set. The ResultSet class defines several methods to peform binding based on the field type:

| | | |
|---|---|---|
| getAsciiStream | getDouble | getShort |
| getBinaryStream | getFloat | getString |
| getBoolean | getInt | getTime |
| getByte | getLong | getTimestamp |
| getBytes | getBignum | getUnicodeStream |
| getDate | getObject | |

The column-binding process is used to direct the information from a column into a variable. Only one bind is necessary for each column (or field) in a result set. The columns may be referred to by their name or by their position. Their position will depend on the order in which the fields were placed in the Select statement. If a "Select *" was used, the order will usually be the same order as the fields were placed in the "Create Table/View" statement, but the JDBC does not define this as part of the standard. The column names that are used as input to get methods are not case-sensitive.

**Problem Column Names**   When issuing a get method using a column name, and several columns have the same name, the value of the first matching column will be returned. Often it is necessary to use functions on data. When these functions are issued, the DBMS will create a new name for the column. The names that are returned will vary by DBMS. A simple solution to this problem is to create an alias name to the column in the Select statement (see Listing 4.5). The column alias can then be referenced by name in the binding process.

### Listing 4.5    Problem Column Names in *Select* Statements

```
String SQL_Select =" Select Last_Name,
    First_Name,
    Middle_Name,
    Substring(Middle_Name,1,1) as 'Middle_Init'
    From Person";
```

**Retrieving the Data**    The actual movement of data from the ResultSet object into your bound variables is initiated by calling the next() method of the ResultSet class. When a ResultSet object is returned, a row pointer exists, but does not point at an actual row. Upon calling the next() method for the first time, the row pointer will point at the first row of the result set. Subsequent calls to the next() method will move the row pointer down through the results. All calls to the next() method return a boolean value. A value of true states that the row pointer was able to successfully move to the next row. A value of false states that the entire result set was processed and the end of the set was reached. Errors and exceptions are thrown to a SQLException object:

```
public abstract boolean next() throws SQLException
```

Listing 4.6 shows an example of the execute() method.

### Listing 4.6    An Example of the *execute()* Method

```
// This example builds on the code presented in Listing 4.1
boolean rc;  // return code
String SQL_Command = "select name, id from employee";
ResultSet RS;
String s_Name;
int i_Id;
try {
 query_Statement = conn.createStatement();
 rc = query_Statement.execute(SQL_Command);
 if (rc==true) {
RS = query_Statement.getResultSet();
while (rs.next() {
 s_Name = getString(1);
 i_ID = getInt(2);
 System.out.println("Name=" + s_Name+" ID=" + i_ID);
} // end while loop
 } else {
    System.out.println("The command did not return a ResultSet");
 }
} catch (SQLException se) {
System.out.println(se);}}
```

**Working with Multiple Result Sets**    Typically, a SQL query will return a single result set; that is, a two-dimensional set of data (rows, columns). In some instances, several result sets can be returned for a given SQL command. This is true for stored procedures, where a series of Select statements might be strung together (see Listing 4.7).

---

**Listing 4.7    Stored Procedure with Multiple Result Sets**

```
Create Procedure SouthWestData as
    Select * from sales where state = "Texas"
    Select * from sales where state = "New Mexico"
    Select * from sales where state = "Oklahoma"
```

---

Note that this stored procedure has three distinct `Select` commands, thus creating three separate result sets. Listing 4.8 shows an example that has multiple `Select` statements that are logically joined with the `union` clause, thus JDBC considers it to be a single result set rather than three distinct results.

---

**Listing 4.8    Unioning Multiple Result Sets**

```
Create View SouthWestData as
    Select * from sales where state = "Texas"
    union all
    Select * from sales where state = "New Mexico"
    union all
    Select * from sales where state = "Oklahoma"
```

---

The `getResultSet` command, when initially called, returns the `ResultSet` object for the first query executed. In order to retrieve information from subsequent queries, the `getMoreResults()` method must be invoked:

```
public abstract boolean getMoreResults() throws SQLException
```

returns a `boolean` value of `true` if the statement object is pointing at a valid `ResultSet`; `false` is returned if the next result was an update count or if there are no more results to be traversed (see Listing 4.9).

---

**Listing 4.9    Example Using *getMoreResults***

```
public void executeQuery() {
        try {
            String Query = Query_TextArea.getText();
            Query = Query.replace('\"','\'');
            Result_TextArea.setText("");
            stmt = conn.createStatement();
            stmt.execute(Query);
            rs = stmt.getResultSet();
            int updt_cnt = stmt.getUpdateCount();
            if (updt_cnt != -1) {
                printResultSet("Rows Affected :"+updt_cnt);}
            else {
                rs = stmt.getResultSet();
                printResultSet(rs);
            }
```

```
        while (stmt.getMoreResults()){
            updt_cnt = stmt.getUpdateCount();
            if (updt_cnt != -1) {
                printResultSet("Rows Affected :"+updt_cnt);}
            else {
                rs= stmt.getResultSet();
                printResultSet(rs);
            }
        }
    } catch(SQLException se) {
        se.printStackTrace();
        printResultSet(se.getMessage());}
}
```

**Return Codes and Update Statistics**   Several of the SQL commands produce update statistics that deliver information on the success or failure of the command. Issuing Insert, Update, and Delete statements all produce a return value. The JDBC uses the getUpdateCount method to retrieve the result:

```
public abstract int getUpdateCount() throws SQLException
```

returns an integer value. Normally the value will state the number of rows inserted, deleted, or updated in the last statement. A value of -1 is returned if the last command issued returned a ResultSet rather than an update count or if the last command issued did not return any information at all (see Listing 4.10).

Part

I

Ch

4

---

**Listing 4.10   Example of Returning Update Statistics**

```
// This example builds on the code presented in Listing 4.1
boolean rc; // return code
ResultSet RS;
try {
 Statement SQL_Statement = conn.createStatement();
 rc = SQL_Statement.execute("Insert into Employee values('Saul Arispe',77) ");
 cnt = SQL_Statement.getUpdateCount();
 if (cnt!= -1) {
System.out.println("The number of rows inserted was :"+cnt);
 }
} catch (SQLException se) {
 System.out.println(se);
 }
```

---

# Run-Away Queries

The Statement class offers several options for controlling the environment in which a SQL call is executed. The most common of these is the ability to halt queries. In some cases, it would be nice if the system would stop "run-away queries" on its own. JDBC provides this functionality through two methods of the Statement class:

```
public abstract void setQueryTimeout(int seconds) throws SQLException
public abstract int getQueryTimeout() throws SQLException
```

By calling the `setQueryTimeout()` method, you tell a database driver to release control of the statement after a certain period of time. This feature is often used in ad hoc report-writing utilities to avoid queries that seem to never return. Caution must be used in setting the time-out period. If the amount is too low, the query will always be canceled by the application before adequate time is given for the command to return. If the amount is too high, the user of the application may find it unacceptable, and instead of waiting, turn the application (or the computer) completely off. This unfortunate scenario will often cause additional problems in the DBMS, where it believes the connection is still intact, and the resources that it has allocated for the connection are never released. Most database management systems now have the capability to measure the amount of time that it takes for a command to run. These utilities can be very helpful in tweaking timeout periods.

The implementation of this feature is done differently by the JDBC vendors. Many of the JDBC drivers leave the responsibility of performing query time-outs to a native driver, and many native drivers do not have this feature. It is strongly recommended that you test this feature on your particular driver by forcing a query to time-out, rather than assuming that your driver/DBMS will handle this feat as expected.

The default value for the query time-out is zero, which means that the query will never time-out due to your application. It is possible that your database system has a default time-out set that is not specific to an application. In this case, the DBMS time-out period usually remains intact, but can be overridden on a connection-by-connection basis. The time-out parameter is often changed throughout the life cycle of an application. As the number of users on an application grows, the amount of traffic, as well as the amount of processing on the database server, increases. Thus, the amount of time that will be required to return a statement will vary throughout the application's life cycle. It is recommended that the value for the time-out be stored in an external file; in most compiled languages (C, C++, etc.), this setting would be dynamically loaded from the client's initialization file. If the program is a Java application, the aforementioned dynamic loading scenario will continue to work, but if the program is an applet, it may be necessary to load the setting from another source such as a table in the DBMS.

## Canceling Queries

In addition to specifying a maximum amount of time that a query should run via the `setQueryTimeout` method, the `Statement` object allows an application to cancel a query at runtime. This is performed by using the `cancel()` method:

```
public abstract void cancel() throws SQLException
```

The cancel method of the `Statement` class allows an application to cancel the execution of a running SQL statement. There are two different scenarios where users need to cancel statements. The distinguishing factor is which of the following two stages the SQL command is in:

1. The command is running on the DBMS and no results have returned to the application.
2. The DBMS has returned the result set and the application is processing the result set.

The `cancel` method deals with the former problem. In order to understand how the `cancel` method can be used, it is necessary to understand the basics of multiple-threaded applications.

A single-threaded application requires that all processing occurs in a sequential manner. The only exceptions are when flow-of-control statements (if/then/else, loops, calls, etc.) alter the flow within the same procedure. The multiple-threaded application simulates the running of different sections of code in parallel. For example, we may issue a long-running query on one thread while opening a data-entry screen on a different thread. Java will maintain the state of both threads and alternate the computer's processing power between the two threads. This allows two completely distinct pieces of code to be executed in parallel. Obviously, this is a nice feature for the end-user who doesn't have to wait for the long-running process to end before starting work with the data entry screen. (Multithreaded applications are covered in detail in Chapter 8, "Multithreaded Database Applications.")

In a single-threaded application, if a long-running query is executed, the execution of code will stop at the offending command until the DBMS returns the results. A multithreaded application could be designed to issue all potential "offending statements" in its own thread. This variation facilitates one thread having the authority to cancel the processing in a second thread. It is absolutely essential to have separate threads executing to perform the dynamic (user-defined) canceling of long-running commands.

## Limiting *ResultSet* Size

The demand that is placed on applications to perform at peak capability is perhaps the one universal truth in writing database applications. Vendors are constantly upgrading their database management system as hardware vendors increase the performance of their machines; yet it never seems to be enough. The requirement to constantly improve application performance continues to rest in the hands of the developer. The JDBC offers several features to verify that outrageously large result sets are not being passed around the network, but the burden of turning on these features remains on the developer.

In addition to relying on the JDBC API to aid in producing compact results, it is the duty of the programmer to ensure that only the necessary information is returned. Some rules of thumb include:

- Return only the rows that are required, no more!
- Return only the columns that are required, no more! Use of Select * is the first sign that you may be issuing careless queries.
- Be very careful in retrieving columns that contain large amounts of data (BLObs, text fields, memos, etc.)

**Limiting Rows Returned**   It is often desirable to limit the size of a result set. This is especially true during the programming and debugging of an application. One missing join, or a where clause that is slightly off, could turn into a projection of the tables queried (X * Y rows). It has happened to the best of us; we expect 50 rows to be returned and instead receive 50,000. This usually means that we end up rebooting our machine, or at least ending the entire process. The limiting of rows returned offers an easy, efficient alternative. Other common uses for limiting the result set size include the need to reduce network traffic or to sample result set data. Do not expect the processing of a query to be expedited by limiting the number of rows returned. The DBMS must still execute the entire query and generate the entire result set. Only after the entire result set is created will the DBMS return the number of rows that you have specified. The length of time that a query takes will be reduced only by the amount of time that is taken to move the data from the database server to your application. By default, JDBC uses a value of zero to denote that the database should always return all rows:

```
public abstract int getMaxRows() throws SQLException
public abstract void setMaxRows(int max) throws SQLException
```

**Parameters:**

> max: The number of rows to return, or 0 for all rows.

**Limiting Column Length**  Several data types exist in relational databases that are used to hold very large chunks of data. The data may be pictures, documents, audio files, or other complex information. Since these fields could contain megabytes worth of data, it is often necessary to limit the amount of information to return. For example, many file formats have a header that specifies proprietary information on the file. Rather than reading in the whole file (five mega-bytes), you decide to read in only the first 50 bytes where the header information tells you all you need to know. Obviously, this feature can significantly expedite the retrieval of the first portion of a large column. Remember that this command is applied to all fields in the SQL statement; thus, limiting the size of one field will limit the size for the other fields:

```
public abstract int getMaxFieldSize() throws SQLException
```

**Parameters:**

> max: The maximum number of bytes to be returned for any one column. A value of zero means that an unlimited size can be returned. The command only applies to columns of the following data types:
>
> BINARY, VARBINARY, LONGVARBINARY, CHAR, VARCHAR, and LONGVARCHAR

```
public abstract void setMaxFieldSize(int max) throws SQLException
```

**Parameters:**

> max: The maximum number of bytes to be returned for any one column. A value of zero means that an unlimited size can be returned. The command only applies to columns of the following data types:
>
> BINARY, VARBINARY, LONGVARBINARY, CHAR, VARCHAR, and LONGVARCHAR

# Escape Clauses

As a result of a loosely defined SQL specification, several DBMS vendors have implemented features in proprietary ways. The ODBC effort realized that this was a problem and was burdened with the task of cleaning up the mess. As a solution, the ODBC defined several "standard" calls that would handle typical requests for features that were implemented in "non-standard" ways. These included the use of extended scalar functions (Date, Money, etc.), wild card characters ( _, %, *, etc.) used in Like statements, and other "non-standard" operations. An ODBC driver that implements Escape clauses accepts requests using the appropriate ODBC syntax. It then changes the syntax to that expected by the database driver and passes it along. From the JDBC perspective, controlling the EscapeProcessing flag is a means to implement SQL pass-thru for ODBC drivers. This enables SQL syntax to be passed to the back end without concern for a driver first parsing, and potentially substituting, the syntax that the application specified. Note that by using SQL pass-thru, you may be writing vendor-specific commands and may void the portability that the JDBC offers:

```
public abstract void setEscapeProcessing(boolean enable) throws SQLException
```

**Parameters:**

> enable—true, enables escape processing; false, disables escape processing

## Simple Cursors

Most of us are familiar with the term *cursor*. In a word processor or a text editor, it indicates the current line you are typing. This concept can easily be transferred to the database world. In a DBMS, a cursor is simply a pointer to the current record in a record set.

Typically, cursors will go through several stages:

1. Declaration   A Select statement defines a result set; the result set is then assigned a cursor name.
2. Open   The declared cursor is opened; the result set is retrieved and the cursor is pointed at the first record in the result set.
3. Fetch   The data to which the cursor is pointing is retrieved; the cursor pointer is then incremented to point at the next record.
4. Manipulate   The data is manipulated; often this includes positioned updates and deletes.
5. Close   The named cursor is destroyed, and the resources that it had allocated are freed.

The JDBC has a limited ability to work with cursors. According to the JDBC 1.10 specification, "Currently, we do not propose to provide support for either scrollable cursors or ODBC-style bookmarks as part of JDBC." The current lack of support for scrollable cursors is unfortunate. These are powerful tools that are required in enterprise-level applications. Hopefully, this functionality will be added to the specification. Currently, two methods are available to work with cursors.

1. The ResultSet class

```
public abstract String getCursorName() throws SQLException
```

returns the name of the cursor being used to traverse a ResultSet object.

2. The Statement class

```
public abstract void setCursorName(String name) throws SQLException
```

sets the name of a cursor for a Statement object.

## Closing the *Statement* Object

The Statement object can be reused to issue several commands all using the same Statement handle. After all commands have been issued, the Statement object should release the memory resources that it has used. This can be accomplished by using the close method of the Statement object:

```
public abstract void close() throws SQLException
```

The close method will be executed when the Java Virtual Machine's garbage collection facility collects the class in which the Statement object was created. It is generally a good idea to explicitly issue the close statement and not rely on garbage collection facilities. Each JVM garbage collector has a proprietary method for determining when a class is no longer reachable. Thus, as a programmer, you may not be able to predict when the Statement object would be closed.

When SQL statements are issued, some kind of feedback is expected. In some cases, the application expects a return code stating the success or failure of the statement. In other cases, it is an answer to a query in the form of a result set. Whatever the scenario, JDBC provides methods for capturing information after issuing SQL statements. The following sections illustrate some common examples.

## Quotation Marks in the Data

Many SQL statements require that parameters be passed into a method. The SQL functions that require strings as parameters often have a hard time inside of JDBC drivers. The problem can usually be overcome by replacing all occurrences of the quotation mark with the single quote (also called a tick mark). The replace method of the String class performs this operation:

```
Query = Query.replace('\"','\'');
```

Notice that the parameters to the replace method are both of type char. This means that the parameter must be specified by using single quote marks.

## Dynamic Data Access

In most scenarios, an application is aware ahead of time of the contents of the database that it will access. That is, the program is hard-coded to return data from a predetermined table, view, or stored procedure. Yet certain applications by nature cannot be hard-coded to return pre-specified tables. This category is usually reserved for report writers and database development tools. In this category of applications, a user or programmer chooses information to be displayed at runtime. Unfortunately, the program is not aware of the metadata (information that describes other information) of the ResultSet object. Programs that perform dynamic data access do not know:

- The number of columns in the result set
- The column name and label
- The data type for each column
- The precision of the data returned

It is expected that applications requiring dynamic data discovery will arise in corporate information shops as distributed applications become commonplace. In this scenario, a client (or middleware) queries a database and then passes the ResultSet object on to other clients (or other middleware). Java Reflection APIs present similar functionality, in that objects other than the ResultSet can have their properties and operations interrogated at runtime.

Dynamic, or runtime queries, are executed in a manner similar to static queries. The difference is in working with the result set that is returned. As with precompiled JDBC queries, a ResultSet object is returned with all of the data. Consider the following scenario:

1. A program asks a user for a SQL statement.
2. The user responds with: "Select * from Authors".
3. The database returns a result set with 150 rows of data, each row containing six columns of information. Each column has different names, column types, precisions.
4. The program could create a series of HUGE exception clauses and guess at what type each column was... but that would be the hard way!

It is for this reason that the JDBC introduced the ResultSetMetaData object. It presents several method calls that can be used to interrogate a ResultSet object. Table 4.1 summarizes the most commonly used methods.

### Table 4.1  *ResultSetMetaData* Calls

| Call | What It Asks |
| --- | --- |
| getCatalogName(int) | What's a column's table catalog name? |
| getColumnCount() | What's the number of columns in the ResultSet? |
| getColumnDisplaySize(int) | What's the column's normal maximum width in characters? |
| getColumnLabel(int) | What's the suggested column title for use in printouts and displays? |
| getColumnName(int) | What's a column's name? |
| getColumnType(int) | What's a column's SQL type? |
| getColumnTypeName(int) | What's a column's data source-specific type name? |
| getPrecision(int) | What's a column's number of decimal digits? |
| getScale(int) | What's a column's number of digits to right of decimal? |
| getSchemaName(int) | What's a column's table schema? |
| getTableName(int) | What's a column's table name? |
| isAutoIncrement(int) | Is the column automatically numbered, thus read-only? |
| isCaseSensitive(int) | Does a column's case matter? |

*continues*

### Table 4.1   Continued

| Call | What It Asks |
|------|--------------|
| isCurrency(int) | Is the column a cash value? |
| isDefinitelyWritable(int) | Will a write on the column definitely succeed? |
| isNullable(int) | Can you put a NULL in this column? |
| isReadOnly(int) | Is a column definitely not writable? |
| isSearchable(int) | Can the column be used in a where clause? |
| isSigned(int) | Is the column a signed number? |
| isWritable(int) | Is it possible for a write on the column to succeed? |

Each ResultSet object has the ability to describe its internal data structures through the getMetaData() method of the ResultSet object:

```
public abstract ResultSetMetaData getMetaData() throws SQLException
```

returns a ResultSetMetaData object that contains information describing the associated ResultSet object (see Listing 4.11).

### Listing 4.11   Example of *ResultSetMetaData*

```
public void showResultSet (ResultSet re) {
              // Obtain the result set meta data object
  try {
       ResultSetMetaData metaData = re.getMetaData();
       // Get column count
       int nresultcols = metaData.getColumnCount();
       System.out.println("Total of " + nresultcols + " columns in the result
➥set");
       int collen = new int[nresultcols];
       data = new String[nresultcols];
       for (int i = 0; i < nresultcols; i++) {
           collen[i] = metaData.getColumnDisplaySize(i+1);
           colname = metaData.getColumnLabel(i+1);
           String coltype = metaData.getColumnTypeName(i+1);
           System.out.println(colname+ " ; "+ collen[i]+" : "+coltype);
           System.out.println(metaData.getPrecision(i+1));
           System.out.println(metaData.getScale(i+1));
           System.out.println(metaData.getColumnType(i+1));
       }
       System.out.println();
     } catch (SQLException se) {System.out.println(se);}
  } // end of showResultSet()
```

The code in Listing 4.11 shows a procedure for extracting information about a `ResultSet`. JDBC relies on the `ResultSetMetaData` object to interrogate the properties of a `ResultSet` object. The code presented previously will loop through all of the columns in the `ResultSet`, printing the metadata for each item.

# From Here...

■ Chapter 5, "Prepared Statements and Stored Procedures," covers JDBC's use of the `PreparedStatement` and the `CallableStatement`.

■ Chapter 10, "Delivering the Application," covers the considerations that need to be understood when delivering a large Java JDBC application, and how to plan for optimizations when building SQL tables and applications.

Part

I

Ch

4

# 5

# Prepared Statements and Stored Procedures

**S**o far, using the JDBC Statement class to gather data has provided a Java developer with the tools to gather information from a database by using a number of different drivers. With the tools presented up to this point, a Java developer may connect to a database and gather data for use in the application. However, using many Statement classes throughout an application can have an impact on application performance. This chapter presents two new Statement classes: PreparedStatement and CallableStatement. These classes provide specialized uses when designing JDBC applications, including precompilation and reusability. ■

**Understand prepared statements and callable statements**

Understand the definitions of, and differences between, PreparedStatement and CallableStatement.

**Review stored procedures in SQL**

Review and fully understand what stored procedures are and how they should be used.

**Dealing with large parameters**

How to deal with large parameters that need to be passed to prepared or callable statements.

**When to use prepared and callable statements**

Understand the advantages and disadvantages of using prepared and callable statements, and how to choose the correct one for the task.

# Prepared Statements

PreparedStatement is an interface that extends java.sql.Statement but adds an extra level of functionality: precompiling a statement. The PreparedStatement class has two primary differences from the Statement class. First, it "prepares" a statement by registering the statement with the database driver so that it may be precompiled and increase efficiency. Second, it allows a statement to contain parameters that may be described and the values linked after the statement is created. Prepared statements are designed to be optimized and used for multiple queries that rely on the same statement. The statements may contain different parameters for each query but may not be altered in any other fashion unless a new PreparedStatement object is created.

## Creating Prepared Statements

Creating a PreparedStatement is similar to a creating a standard java.sql.Statement object, but includes the ability to insert a "?" where a parameter will be inserted later. For example, to create a PreparedStatement using a Connection object named connection, the following code would be required:

```
PreparedStatement pstatement;
pstatement = connection.prepareStatement ("SELECT * from employee where name =
➡?");
```

As demonstrated, the new PreparedStatement object that was created contains a standard SQL statement but also includes a placeholder where a value may be specified before the statement is executed. The java.sql.Connection method:

**PreparedStatement prepareStatement(String sql) throws SQLException**

creates and returns a PreparedStatement object handle to a new precompiled statement.

**Parameters:**

> sql     String containing the SQL Statement

## Understanding How Prepared Statements Work

Understanding the PreparedStatement object is important to understanding why it becomes optimized and how it can increase the efficiency of an application. When the prepareStatement() method is called, the statement is sent to the driver where it is checked for errors. Once it passes the error checks, it then is optimized by the DBMS by evaluating the cost of each execution plan created. The most efficient plan is then prepared, compiled, and stored. Once the call to execute the statement is made, the compiled code generated by the DBMS is used to generate the result set. The final step is to return a handle to the compiled code, which is wrapped into a Java PreparedStatement object.

These steps are common to any SQL statement, but the Statement object doesn't allow these steps to occur until the statement is explicitly executed. Also, the Statement object discards any compiled code after the statement is executed. The PreparedStatement retains a handle to the compiled code for reuse and allows the optimizations to occur before the statement is executed, creating a faster response for the result set.

# Using Prepared Statements

Once the PreparedStatement object has been created, the parameters that have been specified by the question mark ("?") placeholder must be passed. This is accomplished by using the setXXX methods in the PreparedStatement object. The XXX represents a specific SQL data type for the parameter to be passed. The setXXX methods require two arguments: the position of the parameter and the value to be passed. The position is the position number of the placeholder in the statement, and begins numbering at 1. For example, to bind a String value of "Davis" to the previous example, the following code would be used:

```
pstatement.setString (1,"Davis");
```

After all of the parameters have been passed, the last thing to do is to execute the PreparedStatement. Multiple executions of the statement will use the same values until the clearParameters method is called. Once this method is called, all of the parameters must be passed again for the statement to be re-executed. Note that the clearParameters need not be called to make changes to any or all of the parameters during the course of multiple executions. It is just a convenience method that allows all values to be reset quickly and prevents early execution of the statement until all parameters are passed once again. The following are the *java.sql.PreparedStatement* methods:

**void clearParameters() throws SQLException**

clears all parameters that are currently linked to placeholders in a prepared statement.

**Parameters:** None

**void setBoolean(int parameterIndex, boolean x) throws SQLException**

sets a parameter to a boolean value, which is converted to a SQL BIT data type.

**Parameters:**

| | |
|---|---|
| parameterIndex | int referencing the ordinal number of the parameter's position |
| x | boolean value to be stored |

**void setByte(int parameterIndex, byte x) throws SQLException**

sets a parameter to a byte value, which is converted to a SQL TINYINT data type.

**Parameters:**

| | |
|---|---|
| parameterIndex | int referencing the ordinal number of the parameter's position |
| x | byte value to be stored |

**void setShort(int parameterIndex, short x) throws SQLException**

sets a parameter to a short value, which is converted to a SQL SMALLINT data type.

**Parameters:**

| | |
|---|---|
| parameterIndex | int referencing the ordinal number of the parameter's position |
| x | short value to be stored |

**void setInt(int parameterIndex, int x) throws SQLException**

sets a parameter to an integer value, which is converted to a SQL INTEGER data type.

**Parameters:**

| | |
|---|---|
| parameterIndex | int referencing the ordinal number of the parameter's position |
| x | integer value to be stored |

**void setLong(int parameterIndex, long x) throws SQLException**

sets a parameter to a long value, which is converted to a SQL BIGINT data type.

**Parameters:**

| | |
|---|---|
| parameterIndex | int referencing the ordinal number of the parameter's position |
| x | long value to be stored |

**void setFloat(int parameterIndex, float x) throws SQLException**

sets a parameter to a float value, which is converted to a SQL FLOAT data type.

**Parameters:**

| | |
|---|---|
| parameterIndex | int referencing the ordinal number of the parameter's position |
| x | float value to be stored |

**void setDouble(int parameterIndex, double x) throws SQLException**

sets a parameter to a double value, which is converted to a SQL DOUBLE data type.

**Parameters:**

| | |
|---|---|
| parameterIndex | int referencing the ordinal number of the parameter's position |
| x | double value to be stored |

**void setNumeric(int parameterIndex, Numeric x) throws SQLException**

sets a parameter to a numeric value, which is converted to a SQL NUMERIC data type.

**Parameters:**

| | |
|---|---|
| parameterIndex | int referencing the ordinal number of the parameter's position |
| x | numeric value to be stored |

**void setString(int parameterIndex, String x) throws SQLException**

sets a parameter to a string value, which is converted to a SQL VARCHAR or LONGVARCHAR data type.

**Parameters:**

| | |
|---|---|
| parameterIndex | int referencing the ordinal number of the parameter's position |
| x | string value to be stored |

**void setBytes(int parameterIndex, byte x[]) throws SQLException**

sets a parameter to an array of bytes, which is converted to a SQL VARBINARY or LONGVARBINARY data type.

**Parameters:**

| | |
|---|---|
| parameterIndex | int referencing the ordinal number of the parameter's position |
| x | boolean value to be stored |

**void setDate(int parameterIndex, Date x) throws SQLException**

sets a parameter to a date value, which is converted to a SQL DATE data type.

**Parameters:**

| | |
|---|---|
| parameterIndex | int referencing the ordinal number of the parameter's position |
| x | date value to be stored |

**void setTime(int parameterIndex, Time x) throws SQLException**

sets a parameter to a time value, which is converted to a SQL TIME data type.

**Parameters:**

| | |
|---|---|
| parameterIndex | int referencing the ordinal number of the parameter's position |
| x | time value to be stored |

**void setTimestamp(int parameterIndex, Timestamp x) throws SQLException**

sets a parameter to a timestamp value, which is converted to a SQL TIMESTAMP data type.

**Parameters:**

| | |
|---|---|
| parameterIndex | int referencing the ordinal number of the parameter's position |
| x | timestamp value to be stored |

Part

I

Ch

5

# Data Type Mapping with Prepared Statements

When using the setXXX methods to bind parameters to a PreparedStatement, it is important to understand the data conversions that will be made. Table 5.1 shows how the setXXX methods map Java data types to SQL data types.

**Table 5.1  Mapping Java Data Types to SQL Data Types**

| Java Data Type | SQL Data Type |
| --- | --- |
| Boolean | BIT |
| Integer | INTEGER |
| Long | BIGINT |
| Float | REAL |
| Double | DOUBLE |
| Bignum | NUMERIC |
| String | VARCHAR or LONGVARCHAR* |
| byte[] | VARBINARY or LONGVARBINARY* |
| java.sql.Date | DATE |
| java.sql.Time | TIME |
| java.sql.Timestamp | TIMESTAMP |

*\* LONGVARCHAR and LONGVARBINARY are used when the data exceeds the size of the VARCHAR and VARBINARY data types.*

# Using the *setObject* Methods

The setObject methods are often used when a specific Java-to-SQL data type conversion is required. The setObject method has been overloaded to offer several levels of conversions, depending on the needs of the application. The most robust method allows the programmer to specify the parameter index, the object to be converted, the target SQL type as defined by java.sql.Types, and a scale for DECIMAL or NUMERIC types. The simplest method requires only the parameter index and the object to convert.

The ability of a Java programmer to explicitly convert a Java data type to a specific SQL data type allows prepared statements to be adapted to fit the needs of any database configuration. It also allows statements to be generated for data types that may not be known at compile time. Finally, database-specific data types may be passed using the java.sql.Types.OTHER reference and a driver-defined data type.

**void setObject(int parameterIndex, Object x, int targetSqlType, int scale) throws ➥SQLException**

specifies a Java object to be directly converted to a SQL type, with a specific precision (scale) if it is of type NUMERIC or DECIMAL.

**Parameters:**

| | |
| --- | --- |
| parameterIndex | int referencing the ordinal number of the parameter's position |
| x | timestamp value to be stored |

| targetSqlType | int representing SQL type for conversion— see java.sql.Types |
| scale | number of digits for precision (ignored if not NUMERIC or DECIMAL) |

**void setObject(int parameterIndex, Object x, int targetSqlType) throws
➥SQLException**

specifies a Java object to be directly converted to a SQL type.

**Parameters:**

| parameterIndex | int referencing the ordinal number of the parameter's position |
| x | timestamp value to be stored |
| targetSqlType | int representing SQL type for conversion—see java.sql.Types |
| scale | number of digits for precision (ignored if not NUMERIC or DECIMAL) |

**void setObject(int parameterIndex, Object x) throws SQLException**

specifies a Java object to be directly converted to the default SQL type.

**Parameters:**

| parameterIndex | int referencing the ordinal number of the parameter's position |
| x | timestamp value to be stored |

# Representing SQL *NULL* Using Prepared Statements

There are several ways that a programmer may represent the SQL NULL value when using prepared statements. First, the setNull() method may be used, specifying the position number of the parameter and the java.sql.Types data type number as arguments. Second, a SQL NULL may be sent by passing a Java null when using a setXXX method. Finally, the setObject() method may be used, provided that a java.sql.Types reference is specified.

**void setNull(int parameterIndex, int sqlType) throws SQLException**

sets a parameter to SQL NULL.

**Parameters:**

| parameterIndex | int referencing the ordinal number of the parameter's position |
| sqlType | java.sql.Types data type code |

# Sending Large Prepared Statements

Although setXXX methods are available to send large amounts of data, programmers also have the option of sending BLObs of data in smaller chunks by using the setAsciiStream, setUnicodeStream, and setBinaryStream methods. These methods require a total length field for databases that require the length of the data to be known and will be ignored if not needed. Once the prepared statement is executed, the JDBC driver will make repeated calls to the stream to retrieve the data for insertion.

Part

I

Ch

5

The following code demonstrates the use of a `setXXXStream` method:

```
void setUnicodeStream(int parameterIndex, InputStream x, int length) throws
➥SQLException
```

specifies a stream to read a large `Unicode` value, to be used for a `LONGVARCHAR` parameter.

**Parameters:**

| | |
|---|---|
| parameterIndex | int referencing the ordinal number of the parameter's position |
| x | reference to a Java stream or custom stream that implements the common interface |
| length | length of the stream in bytes |

```
void setAsciiStream(int parameterIndex, InputStream x, int length) throws
➥SQLException
```

specifies a stream to read a large ASCII value, to be used for a `LONGVARCHAR` parameter.

**Parameters:**

| | |
|---|---|
| parameterIndex | int referencing the ordinal number of the parameter's position |
| x | reference to a Java stream or custom stream that implements the common interface |
| length | length of the stream in bytes |

```
void setBinaryStream(int parameterIndex, InputStream x, int length) throws
➥SQLException
```

specifies a stream to read a large binary value, to be used for a `LONGVARBINARY` parameter.

**Parameters:**

| | |
|---|---|
| parameterIndex | int referencing the ordinal number of the parameter's position |
| x | reference to a Java stream or custom stream that implements the common interface |
| length | length of the stream in bytes |

# Executing Prepared Statements

Executing a prepared statement is a little different than executing a standard statement. Since the statement has already been declared, there are no arguments to be sent to the `executeupdate()` and `executeQuery()` methods. To execute the statement that we created earlier, the following code would be used:

```
pstatement.executeQuery();
ResultSet executeQuery() throws SQLException
```

executes a prepared statement query and returns a reference to the result set.

**Parameters:** None

```
int executeUpdate() throws SQLException
```

executes a prepared statement query that updates, inserts, or deletes a table and returns the rows affected or 0 if nothing is returned.

**Parameters:** None

# Stored Procedures

Stored procedures are SQL equivalents of functions that provide variables, flow statements, and the ability to call system or other stored procedures. Once created and checked for errors, they are compiled and stored in the database registry for later use. Since they are precompiled, stored procedures are used for repetitive tasks and prevent statements from being recompiled for every query. With flow control and variables, they also provide powerful decision-making abilities and parameter passing. In addition, the database server uses its resources to perform the query, eliminating the need for powerful workstations equipped with large amounts of memory.

## CallableStatement

The CallableStatement object is a derived PreparedStatement class that allows a Java application to communicate with stored procedures contained in any DBMS. The syntax may vary between DBMS implementations when calling stored procedures, so the CallableStatement object creates a common interface. Callable statements are written in escape syntax and can take one of two forms: a statement with a result parameter and a statement without a result parameter.

## How to Use Callable Statements

To create a CallableStatement object, a call to the Connection.prepareCall() method is made. This method requires a string utilizing the escape clause syntax as its only argument. This string may take one of the formats listed next.

For stored procedures that return a value:

```
{ ? = call <stored procedure name> [(<parameter> , <parameter> , ...)]}
```

or for stored procedures that do not return a value:

```
{call <stored procedure name> [(<parameter>,<parameter>,...)]}
```

Keep in mind that the parameters are optional but may be required for some stored procedures. Also, placeholders may be used for dynamic parameter values and optional parameter values. Now, look at the following examples that demonstrate using the prepareCall() method:

```
CallableStatement cstatement = new connection.prepareCall("{? = call sp_get_dob
(?)}");
CallableStatement cstatement = new connection.prepareCall("{call sp_set_dob
(?)}");
```

Part

I

Ch

5

The next step is to assign the placeholders some values by using IN, OUT, or INOUT parameters. The java.sql.Connection method:

**CallableStatement prepareCall(String sql) throws SQLException**

returns a CallableStatement reference to a stored procedure call referenced in the sql parameter.

**Parameters:**

sql                 String that uses the escape clause syntax to denote a call to a stored procedure and may contain one or more placeholders ("?")

# Working with *IN*, *OUT*, and *INOUT* Parameters

To register any parameters that are to be passed in, the setXXX methods, inherited from PreparedStatement, are used. These methods are responsible for binding the Java values to the proper SQL data types and converting the values if necessary. It is important to choose the correct setXXX methods to ensure that the proper conversions and/or representations take place. If a specific data conversion is necessary, it is recommended to use the setObject method, which will convert the value to the specified SQL data type.

Next, the returning value or values must be registered for the application to retrieve the values after the stored procedure has executed. To accomplish this, the registerOutParameter() method is used. This method registers the position number with the specific SQL data type in the java.sql.Types class. Parameters may also be considered INOUT parameters if they need to be registered as IN parameters to send values, and OUT parameters to retrieve values after execution. To accomplish this, use the proper setXXX method and the registerOutParameter method in succession.

Once all parameters are registered, the statement may be executed using the executeUpdate() or executeQuery() methods inherited from PreparedStatement. Any parameters registered as OUT or INOUT parameters may be retrieved using the getXXX methods in CallableStatement. Results may be gathered using the getResultSet method inherited from Statement. The following are the java.sql.CallableStatement methods:

**boolean getBoolean(int parameterIndex) throws SQLException**

gets a BIT value, which is converted and returned as a boolean data type.

**Parameters:**

parameterIndex      int referencing the ordinal number of the parameter's position

**byte getByte(int parameterIndex) throws SQLException**

gets a TINYINT value, which is converted and returned as a byte data type.

**Parameters:**

parameterIndex      int referencing the ordinal number of the parameter's position

**`short getShort(int parameterIndex) throws SQLException`**

gets a SMALLINT value, which is converted and returned as a short data type.

**Parameters:**

    parameterIndex        int referencing the ordinal number of the parameter's position

**`int getInt(int parameterIndex) throws SQLException`**

gets an INTEGER value, which is converted and returned as an integer data type.

**Parameters:**

    parameterIndex        int referencing the ordinal number of the parameter's position

**`long getLong(int parameterIndex) throws SQLException`**

gets a BIGINT value, which is converted and returned as a long data type.

**Parameters:**

    parameterIndex        int referencing the ordinal number of the parameter's position

**`float getFloat(int parameterIndex) throws SQLException`**

gets a FLOAT value, which is converted and returned as a float data type.

**Parameters:**

    parameterIndex        int referencing the ordinal number of the parameter's position

**`double getDouble(int parameterIndex) throws SQLException`**

gets a DOUBLE value, which is converted and returned as a double data type.

**Parameters:**

    parameterIndex        int referencing the ordinal number of the parameter's position

**`Numeric getNumeric(int parameterIndex, int scale) throws SQLException`**

gets a NUMERIC value, which is converted and returned as a java.sql.Numeric data type.

**Parameters:**

    parameterIndex        int referencing the ordinal number of the parameter's position

    scale        int specifying the desired number of digits to the right of the decimal

**`String getString(int parameterIndex) throws SQLException`**

gets a CHAR, VARCHAR, or LONGVARCHAR value, which is converted and returned as a string data type.

Part

I

Ch

5

**Parameters:**

parameterIndex     int referencing the ordinal number of the parameter's position

**byte[] getBytes(int parameterIndex) throws SQLException**

gets a BINARY, VARBINARY, LONGVARBINARY value, which is converted and returned as a byte[] data type.

**Parameters:**

parameterIndex     int referencing the ordinal number of the parameter's position

**Date getDate(int parameterIndex) throws SQLException**

gets a DATE value, which is converted and returned as a java.sql.Date data type.

**Parameters:**

parameterIndex     int referencing the ordinal number of the parameter's position

**Time getTime(int parameterIndex) throws SQLException**

gets a TIME value, which is converted and returned as a java.sql.Time data type.

**Parameters:**

parameterIndex     int referencing the ordinal number of the parameter's position

**Timestamp getTimestamp(int parameterIndex) throws SQLException**

gets a TIMESTAMP value, which is converted and returned as a java.sql.Timestamp data type.

**Parameters:**

parameterIndex     int referencing the ordinal number of the parameter's position

**void registerOutParameter(int parameterIndex, int sqlType) throws SQLException**

registers a parameter as an OUT parameter so that it may be used with getXXX methods for data retrieval.

**Parameters:**

parameterIndex     int referencing the ordinal number of the parameter's position

sqlType            int representing a java.sql.Types SQL data type

```
void registerOutParameter(int parameterIndex, int sqlType, int scale) throws
➥SQLException
```

registers a parameter as an OUT parameter so that it may be used with getXXX methods for data retrieval.

**Parameters:**

| | |
|---|---|
| parameterIndex | int referencing the ordinal number of the parameter's position |
| sqlType | int representing a java.sql.Types SQL data type |
| scale | represents the desired number of digits to the right of the decimal |

**Suggestions When Retrieving Data**  Due to the limitations of DBMSs, it is suggested that all result sets be retrieved before the OUT parameters are retrieved. This is because some DBMSs destroy result sets after queries made to any other data are performed. If multiple result sets are expected, use the getMoreResults() method to retrieve all result sets before retrieving the OUT parameters.

When retrieving OUT parameter data, it is important to know whether the data was a SQL NULL value. When the data is returned as NULL, it will be a null, 0, or false value. The wasNull() method will return true if the last getXXX method was a SQL NULL value.

```
boolean wasNull() throws SQLException
```

returns true if the last getXXX method value was a SQL NULL.

**Parameters:** None

**Handling Large Parameter Values**  When dealing with large IN parameters, the setAsciiStream, setBinaryStream, and setUnicodeStream methods, inherited from PreparedStatement, may be used to load the parameter values in smaller chunks. However, when retrieving OUT parameter values using the getXXX methods, there is no way to retrieve that data using streams. The data must be retrieved in one large chunk, so it is important to use a data type that can store the full value or the data will be truncated. As mentioned in an earlier chapter, it is possible to retrieve ResultSet data in small chunks, so only OUT parameters are affected.

Part
I

Ch
5

# When to Use Statements, Prepared Statements, and Callable Statements

Table 5.2 summarizes the pros and cons of the various Statement classes and may help when deciding which class to use.

**Table 5.2    Determining Statement Class Differences**

| Class | Pros | Cons |
|-------|------|------|
| Statement | Code easy to build; data retrieval simple; good choice for one-time execution | Not optimized until executed; requires SQL statement to be built by code |
| PreparedStatement | Optimized for multiple uses | More code required; not good for one execution |
| CallableStatement | Prevents clients from doing all of the work; clients do not require excess amounts of hardware | Requires the most code for proper usage |

# From Here...

This chapter has presented two new Statement classes: the PreparedStatement and CallableStatement. With the information provided in this chapter, you will be able to understand the proper syntax and usage of these classes. In addition, you now should understand how to use these classes to send and retrieve large result sets, and the advantages and disadvantages of using these classes in place of the generic Statement class. The following chapters present background to this chapter, and additional information related to the JDBC package:

- Chapter 3, "A Simple JDBC Application," covers the basic connections, drivers, and driver management associated with the JDBC and introduces a framework for the rest of Part I.

- Chapter 4, "Executing SQL Statements," discusses how to query a SQL database and use getXXX methods to retrieve results.

- Chapter 10, "Delivering the Application," covers the considerations that need to be understood when delivering a large Java JDBC application, and how to plan for optimizations when building SQL tables and applications.

# CHAPTER 6

# Retrieving Database Information

The JDBC API provides a common interface to relational databases. This abstraction from a single-vendor's implementation facilitates simple porting of applications between back-end databases.

With increasing pressure on Information Technology departments, a trend has been forming that pushes much of the responsibility of extracting information from corporate databases on the end user. This has been made possible through the use of sophisticated tools that simplify the task of presenting enterprise data to end users. Wizards, QBE (Query by Example), and GUI report writers facilitate end users in finding information. Much of this technology is made possible by giving applications the ability to query information about the contents of a database.

In order to implement the "information at your fingertips" motto made popular by Microsoft, the data must be made available to the layman. Hierarchical, relational, and object databases all have some sort of metadata concept. The metadata describes the information in the database. Properly interrogated metadata provides all the necessary information about the database to present to an end-user for querying. It is the metadata that is initially presented to the user, who then will decide what information is

## Querying information about the database

Several different types of applications require that information about the database be discovered at run-time. The `DatabaseMetaData` class offers several methods for performing this task.

## Checking SQL support

The JDBC offers mechanisms to determine the level of support that a DBMS has available.

## Convenience methods

A number of convenience methods are presented in this chapter that help the programmer to query information about a database in a simple fashion.

important, select only that data and send the program off to retrieve a custom request. The following items typically vary among database management systems; for this reason, the JDBC provides facilities for an application to query the DBMS about their support for the item:

**Physical containers for data**—Database devices, binary files, and so on

**Logical containers for data**—Catalogs, tables, and so on

**Vendor-specific information**—Delimiter character, ANSI version, and so on

**The data type**—numbers, strings of characters, graphic images, and so on ■

# Missing Metadata

ANSI SQL guidelines have a well-defined Data Definition Language (DDL) for creating data structures and their accompanying metadata. The DDL explicitly states the syntax for creating tables, views, and the like. It does not state how the DBMS should store the metadata that describes the structure. Vendors' database catalogs will typically contain similar information, but using different syntax and structure. The JDBC will abstract the programmer from the most common metadata issues. In certain cases, applications require additional metadata that is not part of the DBMS catalog.

It is common for the application to implement additional metadata tables that hold extra information about the catalog that the vendor does not implement. Report writers will often store additional information about the data structures in proprietary tables. Information on column names, fonts, font size, and other related information that is important to an application, will reside in application-specific metadata tables. Since these tables are not part of the JDBC, application-specific APIs are required to interrogate the information.

Since most vendors use slightly different features and terms for referring to those features, the JDBC provides several standard methods for retrieving the same *type* of information regardless of the target database. This is one of the true strengths of the JDBC in support of portability.

## The *DatabaseMetaData* Class

At the heart of retrieving database information is the `DatabaseMetaData` interface. Since JavaSoft defines this API as an interface and not a class, JDBC vendors are responsible for coding all of the methods that the specification defines. JDBC vendors often will have several options for retrieving database information. The specification attempts to guarantee the programmer that regardless of the vendors' implementation, the results will be the same. This assumption is largely true, with notable differences in performance.

A `DatabaseMetaData` object must be returned from the `Connection` object in order to use any of the available methods. The `Connection` object has a special method for performing this feat called `getMetaData()`. Listing 6.1 shows an example of returning a `DatabaseMetaData` object. All of the methods in this chapter require that this object first be returned before any of its methods can be called.

```
public abstract DatabaseMetaData getMetaData() throws SQLException
```

returns an instance of the DatabaseMetaData class.

**Arguments:** None

**Listing 6.1    Returning a _DatabaseMetaData_ Object**

```
try {
new jet.bridge.JetDriver(); // instantiate your JDBC driver!

// Connect to the data source
Connection conn = DriverManager.getConnection("jdbc:jet.jettp://www.someURL.com/
someDataSource", "UserId","Password");

    DatabaseMetaData dmd = conn.getMetaData();
} catch (SQLException se) {System.out.println(se);}
```

# Querying Database Limits and Restrictions

The JDBC has over 50 methods for querying the limits and restrictions of either a database management system or the driver that is responsible for communicating with the DBMS. Many of these calls were written to distinguish true DBMS systems from "dumb" files with search engines. Currently, several ODBC drivers are available to read flat files, comma-delimited files, Excel Spreadsheets, and so on. These files were never intended to be treated as full-blown database systems. Since ODBC drivers are available, they will appear as a full-blown system to an application. Thus, it is necessary for applications that are designed to manipulate data on unknown target databases to query the limits and restrictions of either the driver or the DBMS itself.

A complete listing of the method calls that are available in the DatabaseMetaData object are presented in Appendix E, "The JDBC API." Most of the methods return a Boolean result, where true states support for the feature and false states that the feature is not supported.

```
System.out.println("Suports Full Outer Joins ? " +
conn.getMetaData().supportsFullOuterJoins()
```

will return either true or false, stating the support for the feature.

# Checking SQL Support

Relational databases have grown significantly in the last several years. Each vendor has been attempting to meet the prerequisites that Ted Codd presented, while at the same time creating a product that differentiated itself from its competitors. The ANSI group has long been attempting to provide a definition for standard interfaces to relational databases. The SQL-86 document was a first attempt at describing basic relational functionality; that was quickly replaced by the SQL-89 standard. But once again, SQL-89 fell far short of the needs of commercial vendors. Unfortunately, vendors were forced to implement work-arounds for features that were not described, thus leading to a divergence in the SQL languages. The ANSI SQL-92 document was

Part

I

Ch

6

introduced to provide a standard means to perform many of the tasks that most commercial databases had already put in place. Realizing that it would take time for vendors to switch to new naming conventions, and in some instances adding new features, the ANSI committee created three levels of ANSI-92 support to slowly migrate RDBMS to the new standard:

- **Entry Level**—The Entry level roughly equates to full support of the SQL-89 Standard. In some cases, new features replaced older features or corrected errors.

- **Intermediate Level**—Approximately half of the new features added in the Full SQL-92 are defined as part of the Intermediate level. These are the features that the vendors could easily implement or already had implemented.

- **Full Level**—The Full ANSI SQL implementation defines all characteristics and features as defined by the SQL-92 standard. This includes difficult-to-implement features as well as those that are not used often.

Currently, virtually all commercial databases support the Entry level requirements. Several of the larger commercial databases support the Intermediate level, while only a handful support all of the features in SQL-92, the Full implementation. Most commercial vendors are working toward full support and the products should reflect this desire in the next couple of years.

The JDBC provides three methods of the `DatabaseMetaData` object that will query a database to determine its level of ANSI support:

```
supportsANSI92EntryLevelSQL()
```

```
supportsANSI92IntermediateSQL()
```

```
supportsANSI92FullSQL()
```

Test your DBMS level of support:

```
System.out.println("Entry Level ? "
+conn.getMetaData().supportsANSI92EntryLevelSQL());

System.out.println("Intermediate Level ? " +
conn.getMetaData().supportsANSI92IntermediateSQL());

System.out.println("Full Level ? "+ conn.getMetaData().supportsANSI92FullSQL());
```

# Catalog versus Database

The term "catalog" means different things to different vendors. Some vendors will interchange the term "catalog" with "database." The "database" term more accurately describes the physical container of data and its related structures. "Catalog" is more accurately used to describe the list of logical schemas and the data and related structures they contain. The data in a database may or may not be located on the same physical server as the catalog (although typically it is). The catalog presents all of the major containers for holding information accessible by a database server. In distributed DBMSs, this may include databases that are physically located on a different machine. In this case, the local catalog will describe information about the data definitions, but specific information about the DBMS and its implementation constraints will reside on the remote machine.

# Obtaining Catalog Data

A list of the catalogs from a database server can be returned by using the `getCatalogs()` method of the `DatabaseMetaData` class. This command returns a list of the catalogs as a standard JDBC ResultSet. Listing 6.2 shows a method that retrieves all of the catalogs for a given connection. The data is stored in a Vector for easy retrieval. Listing 6.3 is an example of displaying the information in the Vector.

`public abstract ResultSet getCatalogs() throws SQLException`

returns a list of the catalog names. The result set has one column named `TABLE_CAT`.

**Arguments:** None

### Listing 6.2  *getCatalogs* Example

```
//-------------------------- getCatalogs()
    public Vector getCatalogs(Connection conn){

      boolean notdone = true;
      String Catalog_Name;
      Vector Catalog_List = new Vector();
      try{
        DatabaseMetaData dmd = conn.getMetaData();
        ResultSet rs = dmd.getCatalogs();
  while (notdone) {
          notdone = rs.next();
          if (notdone) {
              Catalog_Name = rs.getString(1);
              Catalog_List.addElement(Catalog_Name);
          } // end of if
        } // end of while
      } // end of try
      catch (SQLException se) { System.out.println(se);}
      finally { return Catalog_List;}
    } // end of getCatalogs
```

### Listing 6.3  *getCatalogs* (Display)

```
Vector v1 = getCatalogs(conn);      // Invoke the getCatalogs convenience method.
for (int i=0;i< v1.size(); i++) {      // Dump the contents of the Vector.
      System.out.println((String)v1.elementAt(i));}
```

Part

I

Ch

6

# Review of Schemas

The *schema* is a concept that was invented to relate multiple tables, views, and other database objects together. The purpose of the schema is to avoid naming conflicts. Thus, if two different applications need a table that would have the same name, a schema name can be prefixed to the name to qualify it. As more and more tables were added to corporate systems, SQL-92 added the concept of a "catalog" as presented earlier. The catalog introduces another higher level object that can break schemas into related sections and provides another naming level, so that even the largest corporations can use meaningful naming conventions without the concern of naming conflicts.

The schema notation is often used in larger DBMSs but is often left out completely in smaller, single-user, and departmental database systems. In this case, JDBC returns a `null` value for functions that return a schema name. The schema is also called different names by different database systems. You can find the equivalent to schema in your target system by issuing the following command:

```
System.out.println("Schema Name :" + conn.getMetaData().getSchemaTerm());
```

To return a list of schema names, use the `getSchema()` method of the `DatabaseMetaData` object. This will return a list of the schemas in the current connection. Listing 6.4 presents a convenience method to return all of the schemas in a vector.

**public abstract ResultSet getSchemas() throws SQLException**

returns a list of the schema names in the current database.

**Arguments:** None

**Listing 6.4   Example of *getSchemas()***

```
public Vector getSchemas(Connection conn){

       boolean notdone = true;
       String Schema_Name;
       Vector Schema_List = new Vector();
       try{
         DatabaseMetaData dmd = conn.getMetaData();
         ResultSet rs = dmd.getSchemas();

         while (notdone) {
            notdone = rs.next();
            if (notdone) {
               Schema_Name = rs.getString(1);
               Schema_List.addElement(Schema_Name);
            } // end of if
         } // end of while
       } // end of try
       catch (SQLException se) { System.out.println(se);}
       finally { return Schema_List;}
    } // end of getSchemas
    //-------------------------- getSchemas()
```

The catalog and schema name are often used in conjunction with a database object to fully qualify the target object. In this scenario, the fully qualified name is specified in dot notation:

```
CatalogName.SchemaName.DatabaseObject
```

# Retrieving Database Objects

The JDBC relies on several methods to obtain information on the database objects. Different methods are used for discovering tables, stored procedures, foreign and primary keys, indexes, and so on. Most of the methods will return the information as a result set. Each result set has one or more columns that contain specific information on the database object.

We have created a series of container objects that the result sets can be moved into. Each container object has special accessor and mutator methods for accessing and modifying the data, without violating encapsulation principles. The container classes also have a `toString()` method that allows an instance of the object (which directly relates to one record in the result set) to be displayed as a string.

In addition, several "convenience methods" are introduced that perform the redundant effort of looping through result sets and copying data into its correlating container object. Each record in the result set is put into its own copy of a container object. Each container object is then added to a `Vector`. The `Vector` object can easily be traversed to view the results of the query.

# Table and View Metadata

Table and View information can be retrieved from three different `DatabaseMetaData` method calls:

- **`getTableTypes()`**—A list of the types of tables/views in a database
- **`getTables()`**—A list of the tables/views
- **`getTablePrivileges()`**—A list of access rights to table information

## Table Types

Since each DBMS implements different types of tables that are stored in databases, the `getTableTypes()` method is used to return all of the types of tables used in the active database. An enumerated list of table types is presented in Table 6.1.

**Table 6.1   Valid Table Types**

| Data Type | Description |
| --- | --- |
| TABLE | A user-defined table. |
| VIEW | A view of a table. |
| SYSTEM TABLE | A table that is specific to the vendor's DBMS |
| GLOBAL TEMPORARY | A temporary table that is accessible from all sessions |
| LOCAL TEMPORARY | A temporary table that is accessible only by the session that created it |

*continues*

Part

I

Ch

6

**Table 6.1    Continued**

| Data Type | Description |
|-----------|-------------|
| ALIAS | A secondary name for a table |
| SYNONYM | An ANSI name for a data type |

**Listing 6.5    Example of *getTableTypes***

```
//--------------------------- getTableTypes()
    public Vector getTableTypes(Connection conn){

      boolean notdone = true;
      String Table_Name;
      Vector Table_List = new Vector();
      try{
        DatabaseMetaData dmd = conn.getMetaData();
        ResultSet rs = dmd.getTableTypes();

while (notdone) {
          notdone = rs.next();
          if (notdone) {
            Table_Name = rs.getString(1);
            Table_List.addElement(Table_Name);
          } // end of if
        } // end of while
      } // end of try
      catch (SQLException se) { System.out.println(se);}
      finally { return Table_List;}
    } // end of getTableTypes
```

# Table Listings

After determining the types of tables that are available in the target database, the getTables() method of the DatabaseMetaData object may be called to return a list of the tables. This will return table information only in the active database (as determined by the Connection object). The information that is returned is described in Table 6.3.

**Method:**

```
public abstract ResultSet getTables(String catalog, String schemaPattern,
String tableNamePattern, String types[]) throws SQLException
```

**Arguments:** See Table 6.2.

**Table 6.2    Arguments for *getTables()***

| Argument | Description |
|----------|-------------|
| catalog | The name of the Catalog that has the tables |

| Argument | Description |
|---|---|
| schemaPattern | A pattern (using "%" and "_") for designating the schemas |
| tableNamePattern | A pattern (using "%" and "_") for designating the tables |
| types[] | A string array of table types that will be returned (see getTableTypes) |

**Table 6.3 Return Values for *getTables()***

| Number | Name | Type | Description |
|---|---|---|---|
| 1 | TABLE_CAT | String | The catalog the table is part of; (may be null) |
| 2 | TABLE_SCHEM | String | The schema the table is part of; (may be null) |
| 3 | TABLE_NAME | String | The table name; No Patterns |
| 4 | TABLE_TYPE | String | A table type. Typical types are TABLE, VIEW, SYSTEM TABLE, GLOBAL TEMPORARY, LOCAL TEMPORARY, ALIAS, SYNONYM |
| 5 | REMARKS | String | Explanatory remarks on the table |

The result set from getTables will always return the same set of columns. We have created an object that mimics the structure of the result set. A set of methods are defined for accessing and modifying the data in the object, as well as a toString() method for debugging purposes. The Table_Info class presented in Listing 6.6 has all of the basic features necessary to capture table information.

**Listing 6.6 *Table_Info* Listing**

```
public class Table_Info {

    public String Table_Cat="";
    public String Table_Schem="";
    public String Table_Name="";
    public String Table_Type="";
    public String Remarks="";

    // ------------------------ Accessors
    public String getTable_Cat() {return this.Table_Cat;}
    public String getTable_Schem() {return this.Table_Schem;}
    public String getTable_Name() {return this.Table_Name;}
    public String getTable_Type() {return this.Table_Type; }
    public String getRemarks() {return this.Remarks;}
```

*continues*

Part

I

Ch

6

**Listing 6.6 Continued**

```
    // ------------------------ Mutators
    public void setTable_Cat(String Table_Cat) {this.Table_Cat=Table_Cat; }
    public void setTable_Schem(String Table_Schem)
➡{this.Table_Schem=Table_Schem;}
    public void setTable_Name(String Table_Name) { this.Table_Name=Table_Name;
➡}
    public void setTable_Type(String Table_Type) {this.Table_Type=Table_Type;}
    public void setRemarks(String Remarks) {this.Remarks=Remarks;}

    public String toString() {
        return "Catalog :" + this.Table_Cat +"  Schema :"+ this.Table_Schem +
        "  Table :"+ this.Table_Name + "  Type :"+this.Table_Type +
        "  Remarks :"+this.Remarks;
    }
} // end of class Table_Info
```

Now that we have an object to store our table information, the DatabaseMetaData object can be queried for the actual table information. Two methods with the same name are used to return the information. Note that when getTables is called, the Java Virtual Machine will determine which method to call based on the invoking methods arguments signature (see Listing 6.7).

**Listing 6.7 Example of *getTables()***

```
//-------------------------- getTables()
    pubic Vector getTables(Connection conn,String database){
        // Return all types of tables.
String types[] ={"TABLE", "VIEW", "SYSTEM TABLE", "GLOBAL","TEMPORARY",
"LOCAL TEMPORARY", "ALIAS", "SYNONYM"};
return getTables(conn,database,types);
    }

    //-------------------------- getTables()
    public Vector getTables(Connection conn,String database,String types[]){

    boolean notdone = true;
    Vector Table_List = new Vector();
    try{
        DatabaseMetaData dmd = conn.getMetaData();     // get a DatabaseMetaData
➡object
        ResultSet rs = dmd.getTables(database,"%","%",types);     // Retrieve
➡the table info.

        while (notdone) {
            notdone = rs.next();     // retrieve the next record
            if (notdone) {
                Table_Info ti = new Table_Info();     // Create a container
```

```
➥object.
            ti.setTable_Cat(rs.getString(1));     // Fill the container with
➥the
            ti.setTable_Schem(rs.getString(2));    // actual values.
            ti.setTable_Name(rs.getString(3));
            ti.setTable_Type(rs.getString(4));
            ti.setRemarks(rs.getString(5));
            Table_List.addElement(ti);           // Add this records container
➥to a vector
          } // end of if
        } // end of while
      } // end of try
      catch (SQLException se) { System.out.println(se);}
      finally { return Table_List;}
    } // end of getTables
```

# Table Privileges

Database security mechanisms allow login IDs only with proper access to work with the appropriate database objects. Since most databases support several applications each with its own set of users, it important to maintain table level security. The JDBC uses the method getTablePrivileges() to return each user's access rights for each table. Table 6.4 describes the arguments that are sent to the method. Table 6.5 describes the information that is returned from the method call.

**Method:**

```
public abstract ResultSet getTablePrivileges(String catalog, String
schemaPattern, String tableNamePattern) throws SQLException
```

**Arguments:** See Table 6.4.

**Table 6.4**  *getTablePrivileges* **Arguments**

| Argument | Description |
|---|---|
| catalog | Name of the catalog that the table is in. Note that an explicit catalog must be named and that patterns are not acceptable. "" retrieves the tables without a catalog; null means drop catalog name from the selection criteria. |
| schemaPattern | The name of the schema that the table belongs to, or a pattern of schema names, for example ("Job%"); "" retrieves the tables without a schema |
| tableNamePattern | The name of the table, or a pattern for table names, for example ("employee%") |

Part

I

Ch

6

**Table 6.5    Returned Columns from *getTablePrivileges()***

| Number | Name | Type | Description |
|--------|------|------|-------------|
| 1 | TABLE_CAT | String | The catalog name that the table is part of (may be null) |
| 2 | TABLE_SCHEM | String | The schema name that the table is part of (may be null) |
| 3 | TABLE_NAME | String | The actual table name |
| 4 | GRANTOR | String | The user that granted access to the table (may be null) |
| 5 | GRANTEE | String | The user that was granted access to the table |
| 6 | PRIVILEGE | String | The type of access that was granted, for example (SELECT, INSERT, UPDATE, REFRENCES, and so on) |
| 7 | IS_GRANTABLE | String | "YES" if grantee is permitted to grant access to others; "NO" if not; null if unknown |

The privileges shown in Table 6.6 are defined in ANSI SQL 92. Note that the ANSI SQL 92 also provides for column-level security. This feature is supported in JDBC via the getColumnPrivileges command which is presented later in this chapter.

**Table 6.6    Privilege Types**

| Privilege Name | Description |
|----------------|-------------|
| Select | Permission to view the data |
| Insert | Permission to add new records |
| Update | Permission to modify existing data |
| Delete | Permission to remove records |
| References | Permission on referential integrity constraints |
| Usage | Protects access to domains, character sets, collations, and translations |

Table privileges are returned in a result set. Each row returned corresponds to a table/user security right. The class presented in Listing 6.8 contains a standard data container for holding table privilege information. A Table_Privileges object can be populated using the example code presented in Listing 6.9.

### Listing 6.8  *Table_Privileges* Information Class

```
public class Table_Privileges {

    public String Table_Cat="";
    public String Table_Schem="";
    public String Table_Name="";
    public String Grantor="";
    public String Grantee="";
    public String Privilege="";
    public String Is_Grantable="";

    // ------------------------ Accessors
    public String getTable_Cat() {return this.Table_Cat;}
    public String getTable_Schem() {return this.Table_Schem;}
    public String getTable_Name() {return this.Table_Name; }
    public String getGrantor() {return this.Grantor;}
    public String getGrantee() {return this.Grantee;}
    public String getPrivilege() {return this.Privilege;}
    public String getIs_Grantable() {return this.Is_Grantable;}

    // ------------------------ Mutators
    public void setTable_Cat(String Table_Cat) {this.Table_Cat=Table_Cat;}
    public void setTable_Schem(String Table_Schem)
➥{this.Table_Schem=Table_Schem;}
    public void setTable_Name(String Table_Name) {this.Table_Name=Table_Name;}
    public void setGrantor(String Grantor) {this.Grantor=Grantor;}
    public void setGrantee(String Grantee) {this.Grantee=Grantee;}
    public void setPrivilege(String Privilege) {this.Privilege=Privilege;}
    public void setIs_Grantable(String Is_Grantable)
➥{this.Is_Grantable=Is_Grantable;}

    public String toString() {
        return "Catalog :" + this.Table_Cat +"  Schema :"+ this.Table_Schem +
        "  Table :"+ this.Table_Name + "  Grantor :"+this.Grantor +
        "  Grantee :"+this.Grantee+"  Privilege :"+this.Privilege+
        "  Is_Grantable :"+this.Is_Grantable;
    }
} // end of class Table_Privileges
```

### Listing 6.9  Retrieving Table Privileges

```
public Vector getTablePrivileges(Connection conn,String database){

    boolean notdone = true;
    String Table_Name;
    Vector Table_List = new Vector();
    try{
      DatabaseMetaData dmd = conn.getMetaData();
      ResultSet rs = dmd.getTablePrivileges(database,"%","%");

      while (notdone) {
```

*continues*

Part

I

Ch

6

**Listing 6.9   Continued**

```
            notdone = rs.next();
            if (notdone) {
               Table_Privileges tp = new Table_Privileges();
               tp.setTable_Cat(rs.getString(1));
               tp.setTable_Schem(rs.getString(2));
               tp.setTable_Name(rs.getString(3));
               tp.setGrantor(rs.getString(4));
               tp.setGrantee(rs.getString(5));
               tp.setPrivilege(rs.getString(6));
               tp.setIs_Grantable(rs.getString(7));
               Table_List.addElement(tp);
            } // end of if
         } // end of while
      } // end of try
      catch (SQLException se) { System.out.println(se);}
      finally { return Table_List;}
   } // end of getTablePrivileges
```

The example presented in Listing 6.9 returns all of the table privilege data for all tables in the specified database, regardless of the schema name.

# Retrieving Stored Procedures Metadata

Canned report writers typically allow for some type of Query by Example for simple requests. Often, more complex code is required to return the desired answer set. This may include joining several tables, creating temporary tables, or performing cursor processing. Obviously, information departments cannot expect end users to create this type of complex query. A simple solution to the problem is to create a set of stored procedures that perform the complex querying. The end user should be presented with variables that they may manipulate and customize the query to their needs. Stored procedures are convenient means to package SQL statements together. Most DBMSs support some type of scripting language that can be used inside stored procedures in addition to DDL and DML statements.

Rather than coding in specific information about each stored procedure in an application, it would be nice if the application could discover the metadata of the stored procedure at runtime. The JDBC uses two methods for dynamically discovering information on stored procedures:

- `getProcedures()`—Returns a list of stored procedures
- `getProcedureColumns()`—Returns the input, output, and result set column information

## Listing Stored Procedures

The `getProcedures()` method of the `DatabaseMetaData` object is used to retrieve a list of procedures and related information. Listing 6.10 presents a container class for storing information on procedures, and Listing 6.11 shows a convenience method used to populate the

`Procedure_Info` container class. Table 6.7 describes the arguments that are sent to the method, and Table 6.8 describes the information that is returned. The constants that are passed into the method are described in Table 6.9.

**Method:**

```
public abstract ResultSet getProcedures(String catalog, String schemaPattern,
String procedureNamePattern) throws SQLException
```

**Arguments:** See Table 6.7.

**Table 6.7    Arguments for *getProcedures()***

| Argument | Description |
|---|---|
| catalog | The name of the catalog to interrogate |
| schemaPattern | A schema name or a wildcard pattern to search on |
| procedureNamePattern | A procedure name or a wildcard pattern to search on |

**Table 6.8    Return Values for *getProcedures()***

| Number | Column Name | Type | Description |
|---|---|---|---|
| 1 | PROCEDURE_CAT | String | procedure catalog (may be null) |
| 2 | PROCEDURE_SCHEM | String | procedure schema (may be null) |
| 3 | PROCEDURE_NAME | String | procedure name |
| 4 | reserved for future use | | |
| 5 | reserved for future use | | |
| 6 | reserved for future use | | |
| 7 | REMARKS | String | explanatory comment on the procedure |
| 8 | PROCEDURE_TYPE | short | kind of procedure (Options in Table 6.6) |

**Table 6.9    Procedure Type Constants in *DatabaseMetaData***

| Constant Name | Value | Description |
|---|---|---|
| procedureResultUnknown | 0 | May return a result |
| procedureNoResult | 1 | Does not return a result |
| procedureReturnsResult | 2 | Returns a result |

Part

I

Ch

6

**Listing 6.10   Stored Procedure Information Container Class**

```
public class Procedure_Info {

    public String Procedure_Cat="";
    public String Procedure_Schem="";
    public String Procuedure_Name="";
    public String Procedure_Type="";
    public String Remarks="";


    // ------------------------ Accessors
    public String getProcedure_Cat() {return this.Procedure_Cat;}
    public String getProcedure_Schem() {return this.Procedure_Schem;}
    public String getProcedure_Name() {return this.Procedure_Name;}
    public String getProcedure_Type() {return this.Procedure_Type;}
    public String getRemarks() {return this.Remarks;}


    // ------------------------ Mutators
    public void setProcedure_Cat(String Procedure_Cat)
{this.Procedure_Cat=Procedure_Cat;}
    public void setProcedure_Schem(String Procedure_Schem)
{this.Procedure_Schem=Procedure_Schem;}
    public void setProcedure_Name(String Procedure_Name)
{this.Procedure_Name=Procedure_Name;}
    public void setProcedure_Type(String Procedure_Type)
{this.Procedure_Type=Procedure_Type;}
    public void setRemarks(String Remarks) {this.Remarks=Remarks;}


    public String toString() {
        return "Catalog :" + this.Procedure_Cat +"  Schema :"+
this.Procedure_Schem +
        " Proc. :"+ this.Procedure_Name + "  Type :"+this.Procedure_Type +
        " Remarks :"+this.Remarks;
    }
} // end of class Procuedure_Info
```

**Listing 6.11   Convenience Method for Retrieving Stored
Procedure Information**

```
//-------------------------- getProcedures()
    public Vector getProcedures(Connection conn,String database){

      boolean notdone = true;
      Vector Procedure_List = new Vector();

      try{
       DatabaseMetaData dmd = conn.getMetaData();
       ResultSet rs = dmd.getProcedures(database,"%","%");
```

```
while (notdone) {
        notdone = rs.next();
        if (notdone) {
            Procedure_Info pi = new Procedure_Info();
            pi.setProcedure_Cat(rs.getString(1));
            pi.setProcedure_Schem(rs.getString(2));
            pi.setProcedure_Name(rs.getString(3));
            pi.setProcedure_Type(rs.getString(7));
            pi.setRemarks(rs.getString(8));
            Procedure_List.addElement(pi);
        } // end of if
    } // end of while
} // end of try
catch (SQLException se) { System.out.println(se);}
finally { return Procedure_List;}
} // end of getProcedure
```

# Returning Stored Procedure Columns

In addition to retrieving procedure names and types, input and output parameters are available as well. The JDBC defines six types of procedure columns (Table 6.10). Table 6.11 describes the arguments to invoke the method, and Table 6.12 describes the information that is returned from the method call.

## Table 6.10 Procedure Column Types

| *DatabaseMetaData* Constant | Value | Description |
| --- | --- | --- |
| procedureColumnUnknown | 0 | Information on this column is not known. |
| procedureColumnIn | 1 | The column is only an input parameter. |
| procedureColumnResult | 2 | The column is part of the result set. |
| procedureColumnInOut | 3 | The column is an input parameter whose updated value is sent back to the calling program. |
| procedureColumnOut | 4 | The column is an output parameter whose value is sent back to the calling program. |
| procedureColumnReturn | 5 | The column is a return code/value from the procedure. |

**Part**

**I**

**Ch**

**6**

**Method:**

```
public abstract ResultSet getProcedureColumns(String catalog, String
schemaPattern, String procedureNamePattern, String columnNamePattern) throws
SQLException
```

**Arguments:** See Table 6.11.

**Table 6.11    Arguments for *getProcedureColumns***

| Argument | Type | Description |
|---|---|---|
| catalog | String | The name of the catalog that the Proc. is part of |
| schemaPattern | String | The name of the schema or a wild card pattern that matches 0 or more schema names that the procedure is expected to be part of |
| procedureNamePattern | String | The actual name of the stored procedure or a wild card pattern that matches 0 or more stored procedure names |
| columnNamePattern | String | A column name or a wild card pattern that matches 0 or more column names |

**Table 6.12    Return Values for *getProcedureColumns***

| Number | Name | Type | Description |
|---|---|---|---|
| 1 | PROCEDURE_CAT | String | Procedure catalog (may be null) |
| 2 | PROCEDURE_SCHEM | String | Procedure schema (may be null) |
| 3 | PROCEDURE_NAME | String | Procedure name |
| 4 | COLUMN_NAME | String | Column/parameter name |
| 5 | COLUMN_TYPE | short | Kind of column/parameter; see Table 6.10 |
| 6 | DATA_TYPE | short | SQL type from java.sql.Types |
| 7 | TYPE_NAME | String | SQL type name |
| 8 | PRECISION | int | Precision |
| 9 | LENGTH | int | Length in bytes of data |
| 10 | SCALE | short | Scale |
| 11 | RADIX | short | Radix |
| 12 | NULLABLE | short | Can it contain NULL |
| 13 | REMARKS | String | Comment describing parameter/column |

The code presented in Listing 6.12 is the wrapper class for storing procedure column information. The developer may want to change the scope for the attributes based on the needs of the application.

## Listing 6.12   Storing Procedure Column Metadata

```java
public class Procedure_Columns {

    public String Procedure_Cat="";
    public String Procedure_Schem="";
    public String Procedure_Name="";
    public String Column_Name="";
    public short Column_Type=0;
    public short Data_Type=0;
    public String Type_Name="";
    public int Precision=0;
    public int Length=0;
    public short Scale=0;
    public short Radix=0;
    public short Nullable=0;
    public String Remarks="";

    // ------------------------- Accessors
    public String getProcedure_Cat() {return this.Procedure_Cat;}
    public String getProcedure_Schem() {return this.Procedure_Schem;}
    public String getProcedure_Name() {return this.Procedure_Name; }
    public String getColumn_Name() {return this.Column_Name; }
    public short getColumn_Type() {return this.Column_Type;}
    public short getData_Type() {return this.Data_Type;}
    public String getType_Name() {return this.Type_Name;}
    public int getPrecision() {return this.Precision;}
    public int getLength() {return this.Length;}
    public short getScale() {return this.Scale;}
    public short getRadix() {return this.Radix;}
    public short getNullable() {return this.Nullable;}
    public String getRemarks() {return this.Remarks;}

    // ------------------------- Mutators
    public void setProcedure_Cat(String Procedure_Cat)
{this.Procedure_Cat=Procedure_Cat;}
    public void setProcedure_Schem(String Procedure_Schem)
{this.Procedure_Schem=Procedure_Schem;}
    public void setProcedure_Name(String Procedure_Name)
{this.Procedure_Name=Procedure_Name;}
    public void setColumn_Name(String Column_Name)
➥{this.Column_Name=Column_Name;}
    public void setColumn_Type(short Column_Type)
➥{this.Column_Type=Column_Type; }
    public void setData_Type(short Data_Type) {this.Data_Type=Data_Type;}
    public void setType_Name(String Type_Name) {this.Type_Name=Type_Name;}
    public void setPrecision(int Precision) { this.Precision=Precision;}
    public void setLength(int Length) {this.Length=Length;}
    public void setScale(short Scale) {this.Scale=Scale;}
    public void setRadix(short Radix) {this.Radix=Radix;}
    public void setNullable(short Nullable) {this.Nullable=Nullable;}
    public void setRemarks(String Remarks) {this.Remarks=Remarks;}
```

Part

I

Ch

6

*continues*

**Listing 6.12   Continued**

```
    public String toString() {
        return "Catalog :" + this.Procedure_Cat +        " Schema :"+
this.Procedure_Schem +
        " Proc. :"+ this.Procedure_Name +        " Col. Name
➥:"+this.Column_Name  +
        " Col. Type :"+this.Column_Type  +        " Data Type
➥:"+this.Data_Type  +
        " Type Name :"+this.Type_Name  +        " Precision :"+this.Precision
➥+
        " Length :"+this.Length  +        " Scale :"+this.Scale  +
        " Radix :"+this.Radix  +        " Nullable :"+this.Nullable  +
        " Remarks :"+this.Remarks;
    }
} // end of class Procedure_Columns
```

The source code presented in Listing 6.13 is an example of how information can be retrieved for columnar information. This code, along with the code in Listing 6.12, can be used to capture column information and store it in an object whose life span may be longer than that of the ResultSet object.

**Listing 6.13   Retrieving Procedure Column Information into a Container**

```
//----------------------------- getProcedureColumns()
    public Vector getProcedureColumns(Connection conn,String database){

        boolean notdone = true;
        Vector Procedure_List = new Vector();

        try{
          DatabaseMetaData dmd = conn.getMetaData();
          ResultSet rs = dmd.getProcedureColumns(database,"%","%","%");

          System.out.println("***** Procedure_Columns");
          TopOfLoop:
          while (notdone) {
             notdone = rs.next();
             if (notdone) {
                Procedure_Columns pc = new Procedure_Columns();
                pc.setProcedure_Cat(rs.getString(1));
                pc.setProcedure_Schem(rs.getString(2));
                pc.setProcedure_Name(rs.getString(3));
                pc.setColumn_Name(rs.getString(4));
                pc.setColumn_Type(rs.getShort(5));
                pc.setData_Type(rs.getShort(6));
                pc.setType_Name(rs.getString(7));
                pc.setPrecision(rs.getInt(8));
                pc.setLength(rs.getInt(9));
                pc.setScale(rs.getShort(10));
                pc.setRadix(rs.getShort(11));
                pc.setNullable(rs.getShort(12));
                pc.setRemarks(rs.getString(13));
```

```
                    Procedure_List.addElement(pc);
             } // end of if
          } // end of while
       } // end of try
       catch (SQLException se) { System.out.println(se);}
       finally { return Procedure_List;}
    } // end of getProcedure
```

# Obtaining Column Information

Column information is often used to offer an end user a choice of columns to view in a report, change sort orders, perform aggregation functions, or limit the result set based on certain values. Regardless of the use, the application must have two critical pieces of information: the name of the column and knowledge of the user's security rights to access it. The JDBC provides this functionality via the following functions:

getColumns()

getColumnPrivileges()

## Column Information

The JDBC uses the getColumns() method to retrieve the fields in a table or view. Table 6.13 describes the arguments that are sent to the method, and Table 6.14 describes the information that is returned. The constants that are passed into the method are described in Table 6.15.

**Method:**

public abstract ResultSet getColumns(String catalog, String schemaPattern, String tableNamePattern, String columnNamePattern) throws SQLException

**Arguments:** See Table 6.13.

**Table 6.13   Arguments for *getColumns* Method**

| Argument | Type | Description |
| --- | --- | --- |
| catalog | String | Name of the catalog the index is part of |
| SchemaPattern | String | The name of a schema or a wild card pattern that matches 0 or more schemas |
| TableNamePattern | String | The name of a table or a wild card pattern that matches 0 or more tables |
| ColumnNamePattern | String | The name of a column or a wild card pattern that matches 0 or more column names |

Part

I

Ch

6

**Table 6.14  Return Values from *getColumns()***

| Number | Column Name | Type | Description |
|--------|-------------|------|-------------|
| 1 | TABLE_CAT | String | Name of the table catalog (may be null) |
| 2 | TABLE_SCHEM | String | Name of the table schema (may be null) |
| 3 | TABLE_NAME | String | Name of the table |
| 4 | COLUMN_NAME | String | The column name |
| 5 | DATA_TYPE | short | SQL type from java.sql.Types |
| 6 | TYPE_NAME | String | Data source dependent type name |
| 7 | COLUMN_SIZE | int | The column size; for char or data types this is the maximum number of characters, for numeric or decimal types this is precision. |
| 8 | BUFFER_LENGTH | | Currently not used |
| 9 | DECIMAL_DIGITS | int | The number of fractional digits |
| 10 | NUM_PREC_RADIX | int | Radix (typically either 10 or 2) |
| 11 | NULLABLE | int | Are NULLs allowed? See Table 6.15 |
| 12 | REMARKS | String | Comments describing the column (may be null) |
| 13 | COLUMN_DEF | String | The columns default value (may be null) |
| 14 | SQL_DATA_TYPE | int | Currently not used |
| 15 | SQL_DATETIME_SUB | int | Currently not used |
| 16 | CHAR_OCTET_LENGTH | int | For char types, the maximum number of bytes in the column |
| 17 | ORDINAL_POSITION | int | The position of the column in the table |
| 18 | IS_NULLABLE | String | "NO" means column definitely does not allow null values; "YES" means the column might allow null values. An empty string means nobody knows. |

**Table 6.15  Constants for *Null* options**

| Constant | Value | Description |
|----------|-------|-------------|
| columnNoNulls | 0 | Column might not allow NULL values |
| columnNullable | 1 | Column definitely allows NULL values |
| columnNullableUnknown | 2 | It is unknown if the column accepts nulls |

The source code presented in Listing 6.14 is a `wrapper` class for storing information on columns. This code is utilized in Listing 6.15, where the `Column_Info` object is populated with data from the `ResultSet` object.

---

**Listing 6.14** *Container* **Class for Column Information**

```
public class Column_Info {

    public    String Table_Cat="";
    public    String Table_Schem="";
    public    String Table_Name="";
    public    String Column_Name="";
    public    short Data_Type=0;
    public    String Type_Name="";
    public    int Column_Size=0;
    public    int Decimal_Digits=0;
    public    int Num_Prec_Radix=0;
    public    int Nullable=0;
    public    String Remarks="";
    public    String Column_Def="";
    public    int SQL_Data_Type=0;
    public    int SQL_DateTime_Sub=0;
    public    int Char_Octet_Length=0;
    public    int Ordinal_Position=0;
    public    String Is_Nullable="";


//---------------Accessors
    public String getTable_Cat() {return this.Table_Cat; }
    public String getTable_Schem() {return this.Table_Schem; }
    public String getTable_Name() {return this.Table_Name; }
    public String getColumn_Name() {return this.Column_Name; }
    public short getData_Type() { return this.Data_Type;}
    public String getType_Name() {return this.Type_Name;}
    public int getColumn_Size() {return this.Column_Size;}
    public int getDecimal_Digits() {return this.Decimal_Digits; }
    public int getNum_Prec_Radix() {return this.Num_Prec_Radix; }
    public int getNullable() {return this.Nullable;}
    public String getRemarks() {return this.Remarks; }
    public String getColumn_Def() {return this.Column_Def; }
    public int getSQL_Data_Type() {return this.SQL_Data_Type;}
    public int getSQL_DateTime_Sub() {return this.SQL_DateTime_Sub; }
    public int getChar_Octet_Length() {return this.Char_Octet_Length; }
    public int getOrdinal_Position() {return this.Ordinal_Position;}
    public String getIs_Nullable() {return this.Is_Nullable; }

//--------------- Modifiers
    public void setTable_Cat(String Table_Cat) { this.Table_Cat=Table_Cat; }
    public void setTable_Schem(String Table_Schem) {this.Table_Schem=Table_Schem;}
    public void setTable_Name(String Table_Name) {this.Table_Name=Table_Name;}
    public void setColumn_Name(String Column_Name) {this.Column_Name=Column_Name; }
    public void setData_Type(short Data_Type) {this.Data_Type=Data_Type;}
    public void setType_Name(String Type_Name) {this.Type_Name=Type_Name; }
    public void setColumn_Size(int Column_Size) {this.Column_Size=Column_Size;}
```

*continues*

Part

I

Ch

6

**Listing 6.14 Continued**

```
  public void setDecimal_Digits(int Decimal_Digits)
{this.Decimal_Digits=Decimal_Digits;}
  public void setNum_Prec_Radix(int Num_Prec_Radix) {
this.Num_Prec_Radix=Num_Prec_Radix;}
  public void setNullable(int Nullable) {this.Nullable=Nullable; }
  public void setRemarks(String Remarks) {this.Remarks=Remarks; }
  public void setColumn_Def(String Column_Def) {this.Column_Def=Column_Def;}
  public void setSQL_Data_Type(int SQL_Data_Type)
➡{this.SQL_Data_Type=SQL_Data_Type; }
  public void setSQL_DateTime_Sub(int SQL_DateTime_Sub)
{this.SQL_DateTime_Sub=SQL_DateTime_Sub; }
  public void setChar_Octet_Length(int Char_Octet_Length)
{this.Char_Octet_Length=Char_Octet_Length;  }
  public void setOrdinal_Position(int Ordinal_Position)
{this.Ordinal_Position=Ordinal_Position;}
  public void setIs_Nullable(String Is_Nullable) {
➡this.Is_Nullable=Is_Nullable;}

  // ----
  public String toString() {
  return   "Table_Cat :"+Table_Cat+   "Table_Schem :"+Table_Schem+
  "Table_Name :"+Table_Name+    "Column_Name :"+Column_Name+
  "Data_Type :"+Data_Type+    "Type_Name :"+Type_Name+
  "Column_Size :"+Column_Size+   "Decimal_Digits :"+Decimal_Digits+
  "Num_Prec_Radix :"+Num_Prec_Radix+   "Nullable :"+Nullable+
  "Remarks :"+Remarks+    "Column_Def :"+Column_Def+
  "SQL_Data_Type :"+SQL_Data_Type+   "SQL_DateTime_Sub :"+SQL_DateTime_Sub+
  "Char_Octet_Length :"+Char_Octet_Length+   "Ordinal_Position
➡:"+Ordinal_Position+
  "Is_Nullable :"+Is_Nullable;
  }

}
```

**Listing 6.15 *Convenience* Method for Returning Column Information**

```
//-------------------------- getColumns()
public Vector getColumns(Connection conn,String catalog,String schemaPat,String
tablePat,String columnPat){

     boolean notdone = true;
     Vector CI_List = new Vector();
     try{
        DatabaseMetaData dmd = conn.getMetaData();
        ResultSet rs = dmd.getColumns(catalog,schemaPat,tablePat,columnPat);

        System.out.println("***** Column Info");
        while (notdone) {
           notdone = rs.next();
           if (notdone) {
                Column_Info ci = new Column_Info();
                ci.setTable_Cat(rs.getString(1));
```

```
                    ci.setTable_Schem(rs.getString(2));
                    ci.setTable_Name(rs.getString(3));
                    ci.setColumn_Name(rs.getString(4));
                    ci.setData_Type(rs.getShort(5));
                    ci.setType_Name(rs.getString(6));
                    ci.setColumn_Size(rs.getInt(7));
                    ci.setDecimal_Digits(rs.getInt(9));
                    ci.setNum_Prec_Radix(rs.getInt(10));
                    ci.setNullable(rs.getInt(11));
                    ci.setRemarks(rs.getString(12));
                    ci.setColumn_Def(rs.getString(13));
                    ci.setSQL_Data_Type(rs.getInt(14));
                    ci.setSQL_DateTime_Sub(rs.getInt(15));
                    ci.setChar_Octet_Length(rs.getInt(16));
                    ci.setOrdinal_Position(rs.getInt(17));
                    ci.setIs_Nullable(rs.getString(18));

                    CI_List.addElement(ci);
            } // end of if
        } // end of while
    } // end of try
    catch (SQLException se) { System.out.println(se);}
    finally { return CI_List;}
} // end of getColumns
```

## Column Privilege Information

The ability to grant column-level privilege is a new feature of ANSI SQL-92. Previously, this feat was carried out by creating views with only the fields in the view that a user (or set of users) should have access to. This often leads to hundreds of views being created to support column-level security on tables. Obviously, this situation is a nightmare if table fields change; all views must be reconstructed to support the new table structures.

The flip-side of the security equation is to grant all users access to all fields in a table and control the access through the client application (very popular in client/server). Unfortunately, this method requires that every application reimplement security mechanisms for each application, thus a new nightmare is created by either hard-coding security rules into a compiled application, or by creating additional tables that act as security descriptor tables for the real tables.

The issue of column-level security is growing in importance. Inter-company commerce is leading the way for direct database-to-database communication between business partners. A growing trend is to create a front-end application and deliver the application to your business partner. If a business partner is given access to your data source, you CANNOT rely on the partner to only use the front-end application you provide to access the data. Consider the possibility that the partner uses an application such as Microsoft Access, plus the appropriate ODBC driver to connect directly to your data-source, thus bypassing all application-level security. For this reason, the use of table- and column-level security is of considerable importance.

Part

I

Ch

6

The JDBC implements column level security via the `getColumnPrivileges` method of the `DatabaseMetaData` object. Table 6.16 lists the arguments for the method and, Table 6.17 identifies the return values.

**Method:**

```
public abstract ResultSet getColumnPrivileges(String catalog,
String schema, String table, String columnNamePattern) throws SQLException
```

**Arguments:** See Table 6.16.

**Table 6.16   Arguments for *getColumnPrivileges()***

| Argument | Type | Description |
| --- | --- | --- |
| catalog | String | The name of the catalog that the column belongs to |
| schema | String | The name of the schema that the column belongs to |
| table | String | The name of the table that the column is a field of |
| ColumnNamePattern | String | A column name or a wildcard pattern that matches 0 or more column names |

**Table 6.17   Columns Returned from *getColumnPrivileges()***

| Nbr. | Column Name | Type | Description |
| --- | --- | --- | --- |
| 1 | TABLE_CAT | String | table catalog (may be null) |
| 2 | TABLE_SCHEM | String | table schema (may be null) |
| 3 | TABLE_NAME | String | table name |
| 4 | COLUMN_NAME | String | column name |
| 5 | GRANTOR | String | grantor of access (may be null) |
| 6 | GRANTEE | String | grantee of access |
| 7 | PRIVILEGE | String | name of access Column 7—(SELECT, INSERT, UPDATE, REFERENCES, and so on) |
| 8 | IS_GRANTABLE | String | "YES" if grantee is permitted to grant to others; "NO" if not; null if unknown |

The source code presented in Listing 6.16 is a `container` class for storing information on columns privileges. This code is utilized in Listing 6.17, where the `Column_Privilege_Info` object is populated with data from the `ResultSet` object.

## Listing 6.16 *Container* Class for Column Privileges

```
public class Column_Privilege_Info {
  //--------------------- Declarations

  public String Table_Cat="";
  public String Table_Schem="";
  public String Table_Name="";
  public String Column_Name="";
  public String Grantor="";
  public String Grantee="";
  public String Privilege="";
  public String Is_Grantable="";


    //--------------------- Accessors

  public String getTable_Cat() {return this.Table_Cat;}
  public String getTable_Schem() {return this.Table_Schem; }
  public String getTable_Name() {return this.Table_Name;}
  public String getColumn_Name() {return this.Column_Name;}
  public String getGrantor() {return this.Grantor;}
  public String getGrantee() {return this.Grantee;}
  public String getPrivilege() {return this.Privilege;}
  public String getIs_Grantable() {return this.Is_Grantable;}
  //--------------------- Mutators

  public void setTable_Cat(String Table_Cat) {this.Table_Cat=Table_Cat;}
  public void setTable_Schem(String Table_Schem) {this.Table_Schem=Table_Schem;}
  public void setTable_Name(String Table_Name) { this.Table_Name=Table_Name;}
  public void setColumn_Name(String Column_Name) {this.Column_Name=Column_Name;}
  public void setGrantor(String Grantor) {this.Grantor=Grantor;}
  public void setGrantee(String Grantee) {this.Grantee=Grantee;}
  public void setPrivilege(String Privilege) { this.Privilege=Privilege;}
  public void setIs_Grantable(String Is_Grantable)
{this.Is_Grantable=Is_Grantable;}

//----
  public String toString() {
    return    "Table_Cat :"+Table_Cat+   " Table_Schem :"+Table_Schem+
    " Table_Name :"+Table_Name+   " Column_Name :"+Column_Name+
    " Grantor :"+Grantor+   " Grantee :"+Grantee+
    " Privilege :"+Privilege+   " Is_Grantable :"+Is_Grantable;
  }
}
```

Part

I

Ch

6

## Listing 6.17 *Convenience* Method for Returning Column Privileges

```
//--------------------------- getColumnPrivileges()
    public Vector getColumnPrivileges(Connection conn,String catalog,String
schema,String table,String columnPat){

    boolean notdone = true;
```

*continues*

**Listing 6.17 Continued**

```
          Vector CPI_List = new Vector();
          try{
            DatabaseMetaData dmd = conn.getMetaData();
            ResultSet rs = dmd.getColumnPrivileges(catalog,schema,table,columnPat);

            System.out.println("***** Column Privilege Info");
            while (notdone) {
                notdone = rs.next();
                if (notdone) {
                    Column_Privilege_Info cpi = new Column_Privilege_Info();
                    cpi.setTable_Cat(rs.getString(1));
                    cpi.setTable_Schem(rs.getString(2));
                    cpi.setTable_Name(rs.getString(3));
                    cpi.setColumn_Name(rs.getString(4));
                    cpi.setGrantor(rs.getString(5));
                    cpi.setGrantee(rs.getString(6));
                    cpi.setPrivilege(rs.getString(7));
                    cpi.setIs_Grantable(rs.getString(8));
                    CPI_List.addElement(cpi);
                } // end of if
            } // end of while
          } // end of try
          catch (SQLException se) { System.out.println(se);}
          finally { return CPI_List;}
        } // end of getColumnInfo
```

# Determining Unique Columns

The determination of unique columns is critical in performing Update and Delete operations on tables. Typically, an application will attempt to determine the best fields to be used in the Where clause of a SQL statement for performing DML operations. Different database management systems consider different fields the "best" fields to use. The method getBestRowIdentifier can be used to return information on row identifiers. Table 6.18 lists the arguments for the getBestRowIdentifier method, and Table 6.19 provides the return value information.

The most common options are:

- The primary key for the table
- An automatically generated unique key (surrogate key)
- All of the fields in the table
- The columns whose statistics show the highest cardinality

**Method:**

```
public abstract ResultSet getBestRowIdentifier(String catalog,
String schema, String table, int scope, boolean nullable) throws SQLException
```

**Arguments:** See Table 6.18.

**Table 6.18    Arguments for *getBestRowIdentifier***

| Argument | Type | Description |
|----------|------|-------------|
| catalog | String | The name of the catalog that the table is part of |
| schema | String | The name of the schema that the table is part of |
| table | String | The name of the table for which the field identifiers are desired |
| scope | int | The transitory nature of the table life (see Table 6.19) |
| nullable | boolean | A flag noting if nullable fields can be returned as "best identifier fields" |

**Table 6.19    Return Values for *getBestRowIdentifier***

| Number | Name | Type | Description |
|--------|------|------|-------------|
| 1 | SCOPE | short | The scope of the result; see Table 6.19 |
| 2 | COLUMN_NAME | String | The name of the column that is a "best identifier" |
| 3 | DATA_TYPE | short | A SQL data type from java.sql.Types |
| 4 | TYPE_NAME | String | The DBMS name for the data type |
| 5 | COLUMN_SIZE | int | The precision/length |
| 6 | BUFFER_LENGTH | int | (not used) |
| 7 | DECIMAL_DIGITS | short | The scale/digits to right of decimal |
| 8 | PSEUDO_COLUMN | short | Value noting if the column is "pseudo" (see Table 6.20) |

## Pseudo Columns

A pseudo column is generally considered a column that is defined by the database management system. Typically, they are fields that the DBMS generates a value for such as timestamps and auto-increment fields. Table 6.20 lists the pseudo column indicators.

Part

I

Ch

6

**Table 6.20    Pseudo Column Indicators**

| Value | Description |
|---|---|
| bestRowUnknown | The field may or may not be pseudo column. |
| bestRowNotPseudo | The field is NOT a pseudo column. |
| bestRowPseudo | The field is a pseudo column. |

The source code presented in Listing 6.18 is a container class for storing information on the best row identifiers. This code is utilized in Listing 6.19, where the BestRowIdentifier_Info object is populated with data from the ResultSet object.

**Listing 6.18    *Container* Class for *BestRowIdentifier* Information**

```
public class BestRowIdentifier_Info {

    //--------------------- Declarations
    public    short Scope=0;
    public    String Column_Name="";
    public    short Data_Type=0;
    public    String Type_Name="";
    public    int Column_Size=0;
    public    int Buffer_Length=0;
    public    short Decimal_Digits=0;
    public    short Pseudo_Column=0;

    //--------------------- Accessors
    public short getScope() {return this.Scope;}
    public String getColumn_Name() {return this.Column_Name;}
    public short getData_Type() {return this.Data_Type;}
    public String getType_Name() {return this.Type_Name;}
    public int getColumn_Size() {return this.Column_Size;}
    public int getBuffer_Length() {return this.Buffer_Length;}
    public short getDecimal_Digits() {return this.Decimal_Digits; }
    public short getPseudo_Column() {return this.Pseudo_Column;}

    //--------------------- Mutators
    public void setScope(short Scope) {this.Scope=Scope;}
    public void setColumn_Name(String Column_Name) {
➥this.Column_Name=Column_Name;}
    public void setData_Type(short Data_Type) {this.Data_Type=Data_Type; }
    public void setType_Name(String Type_Name) {this.Type_Name=Type_Name; }
    public void setColumn_Size(int Column_Size) {this.Column_Size=Column_Size;}
    public void setBuffer_Length(int Buffer_Length)
{this.Buffer_Length=Buffer_Length;}
    public void setDecimal_Digits(short Decimal_Digits)
{this.Decimal_Digits=Decimal_Digits;}
    public void setPseudo_Column(short Pseudo_Column)
```

```
➥{this.Pseudo_Column=Pseudo_Column;}

  public String toString() {
    return    "Scope :"+Scope+      "Column_Name :"+Column_Name+
    "Data_Type :"+Data_Type+     "Type_Name :"+Type_Name+
    "Column_Size :"+Column_Size+    "Buffer_Length :"+Buffer_Length+
    "Decimal_Digits :"+Decimal_Digits+    "Pseudo_Column :"+Pseudo_Column;
  }
}
```

The source code presented in Listing 6.19 is the convenience method for easily identifying the best row information. Note: This code relies on the source code presented in Listing 6.18.

**Listing 6.19** *Convenience* **Method for** *BestRowIdentifier*

```
//-------------------------- getBestRowIdentifier()
    public Vector getBestRowIdentifier(Connection conn,String catalog,String
schema,String table,int scope,boolean nullable){

    boolean notdone = true;
    Vector BRI_List = new Vector();
    try{
      DatabaseMetaData dmd = conn.getMetaData();
      ResultSet rs =
➥dmd.getBestRowIdentifier(catalog,schema,table,scope,nullable);

      System.out.println("***** BestRowIdentifier Info");
      while (notdone) {
        notdone = rs.next();
        if (notdone) {
            BestRowIdentifier_Info bri = new BestRowIdentifier_Info();

            bri.setScope(rs.getShort(1));
            bri.setColumn_Name(rs.getString(2));
            bri.setData_Type(rs.getShort(3));
            bri.setType_Name(rs.getString(4));
            bri.setColumn_Size(rs.getInt(5));
            bri.setBuffer_Length(rs.getInt(6));
            bri.setDecimal_Digits(rs.getShort(7));
            bri.setPseudo_Column(rs.getShort(8));
            BRI_List.addElement(bri);
        } // end of if
      } // end of while
    } // end of try
    catch (SQLException se) { System.out.println(se);}
    finally { return BRI_List;}
  } // end of getBestRowIdentifier
```

Part

I

Ch

6

# Retrieving Information on Keys and Indexes

Key and index information is a valuable asset in the creation of ad hoc query tools. Often, column information from multiple tables is presented to end users, who are then expected to join the tables accordingly. End users joining tables? Unfortunately, yes, the majority of tools on the market still expect end users to perform the task of denormalizing the tables that the data modeler was so proud of creating. Obviously, this could be avoided by pre-joining common tables and storing them as either views or stored procedures. But in the cases where the types of joins are not known to the application, the user may be forced to decipher relational algebra.

As information specialists, we can alleviate this issue by first creating the appropriate primary and foreign keys as well as adding indexes to commonly searched fields. Index and Key information could then be presented to the user showing the natural relationships in the data; potentially enforcing that the data be joined only via the keyed or indexed columns. Allowing end users to query on non-key field/non-indexed columns usually results in incorrect answer sets and poorly constructed queries that bring even the largest database servers to their knees.

---

### Knowledge Data Discovery Tools

The movement toward data-warehouses, data-marts, and data-mining (knowledge data discovery tools) emphasizes the need for properly defining the relationships between the tables. These new tools rely heavily on keys to denote data relationships. Data-mining tools cannot be expected to discover the "diamonds" of information in the vast repositories of corporate data without properly defined relationships. If you are not currently specifying key information, you may want to strongly consider doing so; the issue appears to be gaining in importance.

---

## Primary Key Information

Information about the primary key(s) on a table can be queried by using the `getPrimaryKeys` method. The arguments for this method are presented in Table 6.21. The structure of the primary key return values is listed in Table 6.22.

**Method:**

```
public abstract ResultSet getPrimaryKeys(String catalog, String schema, String
table) throws SQLException
```

**Arguments:** See Table 6.21.

**Table 6.21   Arguments for *getPrimaryKeys()***

| Argument | Type | Description |
| --- | --- | --- |
| catalog | String | The name of the catalog that the table is part of |
| schema | String | The name of the schema that the table is part of |
| table | String | The name of the table that has the desired primary keys |

**Table 6.22   Return Values for *getPrimaryKeys()***

| Number | Name | Type | Description |
|--------|------|------|-------------|
| 1 | TABLE_CAT | String | The name of the catalog that the table is part of |
| 2 | TABLE_SCHEM | String | The name of the schema that the table is part of |
| 3 | TABLE_NAME | String | The table name |
| 4 | COLUMN_NAME | String | The name of the column |
| 5 | KEY_SEQ | short | The sequence number within the primary key |
| 6 | PK_NAME | String | The name of the primary key (may be null) |

The source code presented in Listing 6.20 is a container class for storing information on the primary key(s). This code is utilized in Listing 6.21, where the PrimaryKey_Info object is populated with data from the ResultSet object.

**Listing 6.20   A *Container* Class for Storing Primary Key Information**

```
public class PrimaryKey_Info {

    public    String Table_Cat;
    public    String Table_Schem;
    public    String Table_Name;
    public    String Column_Name;
    public    short Key_Seq;
    public    String PK_Name;

    //-------------------- Accessors

    public String getTable_Cat() {return this.Table_Cat; }
    public String getTable_Schem() {return this.Table_Schem;  }
    public String getTable_Name() { return this.Table_Name;  }
    public String getColumn_Name() {return this.Column_Name;  }
    public short getKey_Seq() { return this.Key_Seq;}
    public String getPK_Name() { return this.PK_Name;  }
    //-------------------- Mutators
    public void setTable_Cat(String Table_Cat) {this.Table_Cat=Table_Cat;}
    public void setTable_Schem(String Table_Schem) {
➥this.Table_Schem=Table_Schem;}
    public void setTable_Name(String Table_Name) {this.Table_Name=Table_Name; }
    public void setColumn_Name(String Column_Name) {this.Column_Name=Column_Name;}
    public void setKey_Seq(short Key_Seq) { this.Key_Seq=Key_Seq;}
    public void setPK_Name(String PK_Name) {this.PK_Name=PK_Name;}
```

Part

I

Ch

6

*continues*

---

**Listing 6.20   Continued**

```
public String toString() {
  return      "Table_Cat :"+Table_Cat+    "Table_Schem :"+Table_Schem+
  "Table_Name :"+Table_Name+    "Column_Name :"+Column_Name+
  "Key_Seq :"+Key_Seq+    "PK_Name :"+PK_Name;  }

}
```

---

The source code presented in Listing 6.21 is the convenience method for easily identifying the primary key. Note: This code relies on the source code presented in Listing 6.20.

**Listing 6.21   A *Convenience* Method for Storing Primary Key Information in a *Container* Object**

```
//------------------------- getPrimaryKeys()
    public Vector getPrimaryKeys(Connection conn,String database){
    // Doesn't allow patterns
      boolean notdone = true;
      Vector PK_List = new Vector();
      try{
        DatabaseMetaData dmd = conn.getMetaData();
        ResultSet rs = dmd.getPrimaryKeys(database,"dbo","Authors");

        System.out.println("***** Primary Keys");
        TopOfLoop:
        while (notdone) {
            notdone = rs.next();
            if (notdone) {
                PrimaryKey_Info pi = new PrimaryKey_Info();
                pi.setTable_Cat(rs.getString(1));
                pi.setTable_Schem(rs.getString(2));
                pi.setTable_Name(rs.getString(3));
                pi.setColumn_Name(rs.getString(4));
                pi.setKey_Seq(rs.getShort(5));
                pi.setPK_Name(rs.getString(6));
                PK_List.addElement(pi);
            } // end of if
        } // end of while
    } // end of try
    catch (SQLException se) { System.out.println(se);}
    finally { return PK_List;}
    } // end of getPrimaryKeys
```

# Index Information

The indexes for a table can be queried by using the getIndexInfo. Information regarding the index type as well as statistics on the index is available. Table 6.23 presents the arguments for the getIndexInfo method. Table 6.24 shows the structure for the data that is returned to the program. In Table 6.24 the TYPEs identified have the following meaning: tableIndexStatistic identifies the table statistics that are returned in conjunction with a table's index descriptions, `tableIndexClustered` is a clustered index, `tableIndexHashed` is a hashed index, and `tableIndexOther` is some other style of index.

**Method:**

```
public abstract ResultSet getIndexInfo(String catalog, String schema, String
table, boolean unique, boolean approximate) throws SQLException
```

**Arguments:** See Table 6.23.

**Table 6.23  Arguments for *getIndexInfo***

| Argument | Type | Description |
|---|---|---|
| catalog | String | The catalog that the index belongs to |
| schema | String | The schema the index belongs to |
| table | String | The table the index is on |
| unique | boolean | True indicates to return only indices for unique values; False indicates to return indices regardless of whether unique or not. |
| approximate | boolean | True indicates that the result is allowed to reflect approximate or out-of-data values; False indicates that results are requested to be accurate. |

**Table 6.24  *getIndexInfo* Return Values**

| Number | Column Name | Type | Description |
|---|---|---|---|
| 1 | TABLE_CAT | String | Table catalog (may be null) |
| 2 | TABLE_SCHEM | String | Table schema (may be null) |
| 3 | TABLE_NAME | String | Table name |
| 4 | NON_UNIQUE | boolean | Can index values be non-unique? false when TYPE is tableIndexStatistic |
| 5 | INDEX_QUALIFIER | String | Index catalog (may be null); null when TYPE is tableIndexStatistic |
| 6 | INDEX_NAME | String | Index name; null when TYPE is tableIndexStatistic |
| 7 | TYPE | short | Index type |

*continues*

Part

I

Ch

6

**Table 6.24    Continued**

| Number | Column Name | Type | Description |
|---|---|---|---|
| 8 | ORDINAL_POSITION | short | Column sequence number within index; zero when TYPE is tableIndexStatistic |
| 9 | COLUMN_NAME | String | Column name; null when TYPE is tableIndexStatistic |
| 10 | ASC_OR_DESC | String | Column sort sequence, "A" => ascending, "D" => descending, may be null if sort sequence is not supported; null when TYPE is tableIndexStatistic |
| 11 | CARDINALITY | int | When TYPE is tableIndexStatisic, then this is the number of rows in the table; otherwise, it is the number of unique values in the index |
| 12 | PAGES | int | When TYPE is tableIndexStatisic, then this is the number of pages used for the table; otherwise, it is the number of pages used for the current index |
| 13 | FILTER_CONDITION | String | Filter condition, if any (may be null) |

A container class for the index information is presented in Listing 6.22. This object is populated by the source code presented in Listing 6.23.

**Listing 6.22    A *Container* Class for Index Information**

```
public class Index_Info {

    //-------------------- Declarations

    public    String Table_Cat="";
    public    String Table_Schem="";
    public    String Table_Name="";
    public    boolean Non_Unique=false;
    public    String Index_Qualifier="";
    public    String Index_Name="";
    public    short Type=0;
    public    short Ordinal_Position=0;
    public    String Column_Name="";
    public    String Asc_Or_Desc="";
    public    int Cardinality=0;
    public    int Pages=0;
```

```java
    public   String Filter_Condition="";

    //--------------------- Accessors

    public String getTable_Cat() {return this.Table_Cat;}
    public String getTable_Schem() {return this.Table_Schem;}
    public String getTable_Name() {return this.Table_Name;}
    public boolean getNon_Unique() {return this.Non_Unique;}
    public String getIndex_Qualifier() {return this.Index_Qualifier;}
    public String getIndex_Name() {return this.Index_Name;}
    public short getType() {return this.Type;}
    public short getOrdinal_Position() {return this.Ordinal_Position; }
    public String getColumn_Name() {return this.Column_Name; }
    public String getAsc_Or_Desc() {return this.Asc_Or_Desc;  }
    public int getCardinality() {return this.Cardinality; }
    public int getPages() {return this.Pages;}
    public String getFilter_Condition() { return this.Filter_Condition; }
    //--------------------- Mutators

    public void setTable_Cat(String Table_Cat) {this.Table_Cat=Table_Cat; }
    public void setTable_Schem(String Table_Schem) {this.Table_Schem=Table_Schem;}
    public void setTable_Name(String Table_Name) {this.Table_Name=Table_Name;}
    public void setNon_Unique(boolean Non_Unique) {this.Non_Unique=Non_Unique;}
    public void setIndex_Qualifier(String Index_Qualifier)
{this.Index_Qualifier=Index_Qualifier;}
    public void setIndex_Name(String Index_Name) {this.Index_Name=Index_Name;}
    public void setType(short Type) {this.Type=Type;}
    public void setOrdinal_Position(short Ordinal_Position)
{this.Ordinal_Position=Ordinal_Position;}
    public void setColumn_Name(String Column_Name) {this.Column_Name=Column_Name;}
    public void setAsc_Or_Desc(String Asc_Or_Desc) {this.Asc_Or_Desc=Asc_Or_Desc;}
    public void setCardinality(int Cardinality) {this.Cardinality=Cardinality; }
    public void setPages(int Pages) {this.Pages=Pages;}
    public void setFilter_Condition(String Filter_Condition)
{this.Filter_Condition=Filter_Condition;}

    public String toString() {
     return      "Table_Cat :"+Table_Cat+    "Table_Schem :"+Table_Schem+
     "Table_Name :"+Table_Name+    "Non_Unique :"+Non_Unique+
     "Index_Qualifier :"+Index_Qualifier+    "Index_Name :"+Index_Name+
     "Type :"+Type+    "Ordinal_Position :"+Ordinal_Position+
     "Column_Name :"+Column_Name+    "Asc_Or_Desc :"+Asc_Or_Desc+
     "Cardinality :"+Cardinality+    "Pages :"+Pages+
     "Filter_Condition :"+Filter_Condition ;
    }
   }
}
```

The source code presented in Listing 6.23 utilizes the container class in Listing 6.22. It populates the Index_Info object with detailed information from the ResultSet object.

Part

I

Ch

6

*continues*

**Listing 6.23  A *Convenience* Method for Retrieving Index Information**

```
//------------------------- getIndexInfo()
    //Doesn't support Patterns!
    public Vector getIndexInfo(Connection conn,String database){

      boolean notdone = true;
      Vector Index_List = new Vector();
      try{
        DatabaseMetaData dmd = conn.getMetaData();
        ResultSet rs = dmd.getIndexInfo(database,"dbo","Authors",false,true);

        System.out.println("***** Index_Name");
        TopOfLoop:
        while (notdone) {
          notdone = rs.next();
          if (notdone) {
            Index_Info ii = new Index_Info();
            ii.setTable_Cat(rs.getString(1));
            ii.setTable_Schem(rs.getString(2));
            ii.setTable_Name(rs.getString(3));
            ii.setNon_Unique(rs.getBoolean(4));
            ii.setIndex_Qualifier(rs.getString(5));
            ii.setIndex_Name(rs.getString(6));
            ii.setType(rs.getShort(7));
            ii.setOrdinal_Position(rs.getShort(8));
            ii.setColumn_Name(rs.getString(9));
            ii.setAsc_Or_Desc(rs.getString(10));
            ii.setCardinality(rs.getInt(11));
            ii.setPages(rs.getInt(12));
            ii.setFilter_Condition(rs.getString(13));
            Index_List.addElement(ii);
          } // end of if
        } // end of while
      } // end of try
      catch (SQLException se) { System.out.println(se);}
      finally { return Index_List;}
    } // end of getIndexInfo
```

# From Here...

This chapter has focused on returning information about a specific database. The techniques presented here allow an application to interrogate a relational database management system and capture information regarding its current databases. This information is especially valuable for the writing of ad hoc queries.

- Chapter 7, "Object/Relational Mapping," discusses the issues associated with mapping an object-oriented language like Java to a relational database.

- Chapter 8, "Multithreaded Database Applications," introduces issues associated with the creation of large, multithreaded database applications that interface with database systems.

- Chapter 9, "Using Object Databases," covers the current state of object database management systems and their ability to interface with the Java language.

Part

I

Ch

6

# Object/Relational Mapping

It has been estimated that the majority of data stored in computer format now resides in relational databases. For years, corporate I.T. shops have been moving their flat files and hierarchical data to more modern relational databases. Companies like Oracle, Sybase, and IBM have produced powerful engines that can crunch significant amounts of data in a very short period of time. At the same time, advances in software engineering have emerged, specifically in the object-oriented world. A general acceptance of object-oriented techniques, along with languages like Java that were created with objects in mind, have propagated object-oriented programming into the mainstream. While relational database vendors were tasked with storing, retrieving, and processing large amounts of data, the object-oriented people were tasked with designing software that could be reused and componentized to produce a higher level of quality in the software. Both groups have pursued noble goals, each approaching a problem in the manner that was appropriate for their problem domain. Unfortunately, the application programmer has been left trying to put a square object into a round relational hole. The fit is not as snug as most developers would like. ■

## Mapping Java objects to relational tables

A common problem with writing Enterprise applications is matching a software object to a database table. This issue is addressed throughout this chapter.

## Building object wrappers by hand

One method for having Java interact with legacy systems is to build object wrappers. These wrappers act as an abstraction layer between your application and the database.

## Using tools for object mapping

Several third-party tools are available to help keep application objects and relational tables synchronized. This chapter covers several of the issues that should be addressed in reviewing automated tools.

# Why Use an RDBMS?

For quite some time, object database systems have been available and, recently, several vendors have introduced a hybrid "object/relational" database. Both of the aforementioned solutions are designed to work with object-oriented languages but, in addition, they are designed to work with complex data. If relational databases were not designed to work with object-oriented front ends, then why use them? There are several good reasons.

- All of the company's data already resides in relational databases and your application needs to access it. If you are writing screens to existing databases, it may be overkill to redesign the entire database to meet the needs of a single application.

- The development staff is already incurring a learning curve associated with Java and object-oriented technology. Adding another component of complexity is not feasible to complete the project in the allocated time period or budget. Remember, we are solving problems the best way, not necessarily the most fun way.

- The application is best suited for an RDBMS. Certain applications are better suited for use with an RDBMS. These include large number-crunching systems that work on simple data types. Not every Java front end should use an ODBMS on the back end.

- Data Warehousing, Data Mining, Data Replication, or Relational Report Writers will be used with the data. The software that has been created to ride on top of relational databases is quite impressive. Tremendous gains have been made in giving users access to the data they require through sophisticated report writers that work with data warehousing tools. Many of the relational databases can synchronize their data with other relational databases—a big step forward in global computing. Most data mining tools work only with relational databases to extract the "diamonds" of information from your vast amounts of insignificant data. Vendors are working on porting all of these tools to work with ODBMSs but the versions that work with the RDBMSs are typically a generation ahead.

# The Issues

We have stated that using relational databases to store object attributes can be a painful task. One of the most common issues in performing this feat is doing the initial mapping of objects to database structures. Several challenges are presented in creating a layer of software that maps the objects to the structures; these include: reviewing data normalization, creating the appropriate object inheritance hierarchies, and several other obstacles presented later. The second major issue is keeping the objects and relational structures synchronized. Thus, when a change is made to the database, the change must be propagated to the object container that reflects the data, and vice versa. The last, and perhaps most significant issue, is the tweaking of the system to perform the object/relational mapping in a robust manner while preserving the elegant coding styles enabled by object-oriented languages.

# The Options

Several options exist today that help application developers in molding object and relational technologies. The most popular solutions include:

- Building object wrappers by hand
- Automation tools for forward and reverse engineering
- IDE SQL pre-parsing tools
- ODBMS style APIs for RDBMS servers

This chapter focuses on the first two options listed here.

# Building Object Wrappers by Hand

Hand-built object wrappers are perhaps the most time-consuming of the methods, but offer an application a truly customized solution. The process typically involves a DBA and an object modeler, who will negotiate the pros and cons of various object models and their mappings to relational models. The starting point is based on the needs of the application. Typically, one of the following scenarios holds true:

- Need new front-end (relational tables are built; objects are new)
- Need new back-end (relational tables are not built; objects are already built)
- Need new front- and back-end (brand new application, with new data)

Based on these needs, we can choose a method for bridging our gap via one of two methods: forward engineering or reverse engineering.

## Forward Engineering

Forward engineering is the process of taking an existing object model and creating the appropriate relational table structures to store the objects in a persistent manner. Forward engineering is typically used when an application leans strongly on object-oriented methodologies. The developer may have gathered requirements, using Jacobsen Use Cases, and performed analysis and design using OMT. With all of the hard work already implemented to engineer an application, the persistence of the objects is considered an afterthought. Thus, forward engineering is more commonly used for applications that do not rely on heavy database access.

## Reverse Engineering

The reverse engineering model is used when a relational database already exists, and an object-oriented front-end (or middleware) is to be created. Reverse engineering is very common in large corporations where vast amounts of data have been accumulated over years in relational databases. The feasibility of converting this data to ODBMS is little to none. In these cases, the existing E/R (entity relation) diagrams are studied and reverse engineered into object models.

# Creating Object Relational Mappings

Several techniques exist that aid in mapping objects to relational databases. The designer must determine what the goals are. Generally, either the database or object design must be altered in ways that are not always preferred.

**The Golden Rule**    Perhaps the Golden Rule of object relational mapping is:

### Tables = Classes, Column Field = Attributes, Rows = Instances

That is, a table in a relational database can map to a class in an object system. A column field in a relational table can be stored as an attribute in a class. Each field in the table then becomes an additional attribute in the class definition. Now that we have mapped our table fields to our class attributes, we have to figure out how to process multiple rows. This is accomplished by instantiating a new instance of our class for each row in the table.

If we have a table with three fields, `Name`, `Hits`, and `Misses`, we could have a class with the same three attributes, mapping them on a one-to-one basis. For every row that has our `Name`, `Hits`, and `Misses`, we must instantiate a new instance of our class that holds our attribute containers. Mapping our columns to attributes is a good place to start, but as we get into more complex database designs, the issues grow more complex.

The Golden Rule will work for most of your simple mappings, and is typically used in circumstances where cursor processing is used. Cursor processing assumes that you will be looking at your data a row at a time. Often the application requires that you work with your data by the column. This can present a challenge; the size of the challenge will be determined by answering two questions:

1.  Am I working with a whole column or an aggregation on a column?
2.  Do I know the number of rows that will be returned every time, or will the number vary over time?

**Whole Column versus Aggregation**    Applications that deal with columnar data will often only perform aggregate functions on the data. Our baseball application might perform a query that is concerned with only a single column (batting average) and, within that, only on the highest average. Although we are working with columnar data, we are working with only a single row. Since it is a single row, we can treat it as if we were doing row processing. Hence, we could create a class:

`Highest_Batting_Average`, with one attribute `Highest_Average`.

And create a view that maps to the class:

```
Create view Highest_Batting_Average as
Select distinct max(Batting_Average) from Averages
```

where our attribute `Highest_Average` maps to our aggregate function `max(Batting_Average)`. Since we have chosen an aggregate function, we can assume that only a single row will be returned. This means only one instance of our `Highest_Batting_Average` class will have to be instantiated:

`Columnar Data, Unknown Row Counts`

Certain applications require data to be manipulated on a column-by-column basis. Imagine needing to deploy certain functions on the `Batting_Average` column that are not part of your relational database functions. The coach wants to know what the standard deviation is for all of the averages. In this scenario, we know that we want to work with a single column, yet we cannot use a normal RDBMS function, so we move the contents of the column into a sub-type of a non-fixed length container class such as a `Vector`. Our extended `Vector` class would then contain appropriate methods for manipulating the data that it contained:

```
public class Batting_Average_Col extends Vector {
        public float getStandardDeviation() {
      // perform column manipulation
        }
}
```

**Identification**   Relational tables use primary keys as the mechanism for determining a unique row in a table. In many databases, the primary key consists of fields that are part of the records contents. Our employee record may contain:

```
Employee_Sys_Id     int          not null
Employee_FName    Char(15)        not null
Employee_Lname      Char(25)         not null
Employee_Soc_Sec_No   Char(9)         not null
```

In our employee record, we have two potential unique identifiers: The `Employee_Sys_Id` or the `Employee_Soc_Sec_No`. Knowing that our fictitious company is global, with employees around the world, we decided not to use an American notation (such as Social Security number) as the unique identifier. Instead, we have created an `Employee_Sys_Id` whose number is system-generated for each new employee. Neither the `Employee_Sys_Id` nor any of its digits has any significance, thus the `Employee_Sys_Id` is the perfect candidate for our unique identifier. The `Employee_Sys_Id` can then be embedded in other tables, serving as a foreign key that will relate multiple tables together.

In our Java system, we have not been concerned with unique identifiers for instances of classes. The Java Virtual Machine has taken care of assigning unique names to all of our classes, as well as to all of our objects, and hidden it all from the programmer. Thus, storing the same information in an object might look like this:

```
public class Employee () {
       public String Employee_Fname;
       public String Employee_Lname;
       public String Soc_Sec_No;
}
```

Note that we have removed the field `Employee_Sys_Id`. System-generated keys that are common in relational databases may serve no purpose in an object, or they may serve a very important role to the application. This is one of the decisions that must be made; will the database's system-generated IDs be stored in the object for later retrieval, or will some combination of data fields be used in the object to uniquely qualify a row of data?

The answer depends on the application. Many tables do not have a unique key, even when all the fields combined are used; thus, they depend solely on system-generated IDs for their uniqueness. Obviously, in this case the database wins; the table keeps its identity field and the class gets a new attribute to store the field. In our employee table, we could probably combine the Social Security number plus the first and last name to create a unique identifier. But would searches on several strings in our database return the values in the allotted time? Would extra indexes have to be created on all of these fields to compensate for the slower returned values? Probably. In most cases, you will find it easier to add the relational IDs to the classes.

The other possibility is using the unique object ID that the Java Virtual Machine creates as the primary key in the table.

This is not advised at this point in time for a couple of reasons:

1. The object identifier is usually several bytes in length, and smaller, more efficient keys can be used, such as surrogates.

2. The Java Virtual Machine does not guarantee that an object identifier will be globally unique across multiple JVMs. This introduces the possibility of two JVMs instantiating an object with duplicate values.

The use of an object identifier in a DBMS is different than the use of a primary key. If one of the values in the primary key changes, the identifier to the row has changed. This is not the case in an object identifier. The object ID is never dependent (or even aware) of the data inside of the object that it references. Thus, maintenance of referential integrity is lessened when object IDs are used. Consider a table that holds a person's last name plus Social Security number as the primary key:

Table Name: `Person`

Fields: `Last_Name, Soc_Sec_Nbr, First_Name,Phone_Nbr`

Values : `Hendricks, 999880000, Stacey, 555-555-1212`

If `Stacey` were to marry, and change her last name to `Smith`, all tables that referenced `Hendricks, 999880000` would have to be updated to reference `Smith, 999880000`. If an object identifier were used, it would not be affected by the change in the data. It would still point at the same row in the table and be completely unaware of changes to the data, thus preserving referential integrity.

## Explicitly Stating Primary Keys in a Class

Before reviewing the options for noting a primary key in a class, a quick review of terminology on keys is needed. Most texts on relational databases distinguish three types of keys for row identification: candidate key, primary key, and alternative key. A candidate key is the set of attributes (fields) that uniquely describe a row (tuple) in a table (relation). Since a table can have multiple fields (or combinations of fields) that uniquely describe a row, the term "primary key" is used to denote which key will be the primary or default that is used when referencing a table. Any candidate keys that were not the primary key are considered alternative keys.

Earlier we noted the similarities in object IDs and primary keys. One important concept to remember is that the object ID is a mechanism that is used internally to the Java system. Thus, the object ID becomes the mechanism for one object to refer to another object. From an external standpoint, the users of an application will still refer to the data by its name. That is, a user will enter a record describing a Person (object/table) that they want to delete. The user has no knowledge about the object ID nor any concern for it. This means that at some point, the data that the user has identified must be matched to the object. Thus, even within the class, we must identify the primary key of the table that holds the data.

# Data Normalization

Ted Codd once claimed that he borrowed the term "normalization" from Richard Nixon, who at the time was attempting to "normalize" relations with China. At times, the task of normalizing foreign relationships may seem easier than normalizing our data. Luckily, there are fleets of dedicated DBAs rattling off the rules for the fourth normal form or Boyce-Codd normal form, making sure that all of the application developers store their data in accordance with the rules. Yet object-oriented developers tend to see the world in a slightly different way...

A rule of thumb in potentially modifying your table normalizations is: DON'T! A wise man once said, "Don't screw with the relational model." We must remember the reasons for performing data normalization:

- Preserve data integrity
- Reduce storage space
- Facilitate flexible queries
- Reduce access time via small unique keys

Thoroughly reconsider making changes to the database model if you can see that it may have a derogatory effect on any of the items in the preceding list.

# Alternatives

Developers will often find scenarios where the Golden Rule will not work for their application. Rather than modifying the physical data structures, the use of views or stored procedures should be evaluated. Both views and stored procedures provide a mechanism to abstract a table.

**One Object Uses Some of the Fields from a Single Table**   The View can be used to reduce the number of columns that are visible to an application by selecting only the desired rows:

We desire an object that contains Name, and/or Hits and Misses, yet our table contains much more data: Name, Hits, Misses, Walks, Strikeouts, Runs, and so on.

To match our class to only the appropriate fields in our table, we create a view that selects only the desired information:

Part

I

Ch

7

```
Create View Baseball_Info as
        Select Name, Hits, Misses from Averages
```

We now have an object that has a one-to-one match with our desired class structure.

**One Object Uses Fields from Multiple Tables**    Cases where a single object references fields from multiple tables should be questioned. Good object models will usually look just like third normal form. Remember that third normal form states that if, and only if, for all times, each row consists of a unique identifier together with a number of mutually independent values, where each attribute directly describes the information identified by the primary key, then the table is in third normal form. This is the same design goal that we should have for our objects. Consider a class definition that holds the following information:

Class Name: `Player_Info`

Attributes : `Fname, Lname, Date_of_Birth, Team_City, Team_Name`

Views can make multiple tables appear as a single table (or object) by joining the tables together. This means that we can normalize our tables as far as we want, but we can bring them back to third normal form by using a view. This technique simplifies the movement of information between objects and relational databases.

# Mapping Object Relations

Database designers take great care in modeling the relations between the tables. After the relations are determined, an entity/relation diagram (E/R) is created that explains the relationships in the data. A similar feat must be performed on the objects that will hold our data at runtime. Several types of class relations are known; the most common, which we will explore, are:

- Binary, Ternary, and N-ary Associations
- Finite Aggregation
- Generalization (Inheritance)

**Binary, Ternary, and N-ary Associations**    Binary and ternary associations describe conceptual connections between classes. An example of a binary association is that of a client and consultant relationship. One might say, "A client has a consultant," or "A consultant has a client." This relationship shows a one-to-one relationship between clients and consultants. In addition, we could add, "A client may have multiple consultants," or "A consultant may work for many clients," thus denoting a many-to-many relationship. This type of relationship is generally modeled in one of two ways:

1. Association Objects
2. Attribute Pointers

We can look at our many-to-many relationship between client and consultant by using each of these techniques.

***Association Objects***    In addition to the Consultant and Client classes, an additional class is used to relate the two classes (Client_Consultant_Assoc). In addition to relating the Client and

Consultant objects, this class holds any information that is significant in their relationship. In this example, the Billing_Rate can vary between a Client and a Consultant:

```
public class Client {
     String          Client_Name;
}

public class Consultant {
     String          Consultant_Name;
}

public class Client_Consultant_Assoc {
     Client              Client_Object;
     Consultant     Consultant_Object;
     float          Billing_Rate;
}
```

Use of association objects is preferred when additional information needs to be stored that is significant to the relationship such as the `Billing_Rate`. This type of object model can efficiently be ported to the relational model using our Golden Rule. The `Client` class becomes a table, the `Consultant` class becomes a table, and the `Client_Consultant_Assoc` class also becomes a table. If possible, system keys would be added to both the `Client` and `Consultant` table, resulting in the following definitions:

```
Create Table Client as
        ( Client_Sys_Id          int,
          Client_Name           char(40))

Create Table Consultant as
        (Consultant_Sys_Id      int,
         Consultant_Name      char(40))

Create Table Client_Consultant as
        (Client_Sys_Id          int,
         Consultant_Sys_Id      int,
         Billing_Rate           float)
```

**Attribute Pointers**   The Attribute Pointer identifies an instance of a class that directly relates to another class. Since Java does not support the traditional notion of a Pointer (as found in C, C++, and so on), the Attribute Pointer is declared as a member object. Each class contains an attribute that points at the other class:

```
public class Client {
        String Client_Name;
        Consultant Current_Consultant;
}

public class Consultant {
        String Consultant_Name;
        Client Current_Client;
}
```

The Golden Rule can be applied to Attribute Pointer relationships. Our `Client` and `Consultant` classes would be represented as:

Part

I

Ch

7

```
Create Table Client as
        ( Client_Sys_Id          int,            //Primary Key
        Consultant_Sys_Id        int,            // Foreign Key to Consultant Table
Client_Name              char(40))

Create Table Consultant as
        (Consultant_Sys_Id       int,            // Primary Key
        Client_Sys_Id            int,            // Foreign Key to Client Table
        Consultant_Name char(40))
```

Attribute Pointers are very common when a one-to-one relationship exists. In our model presented previously, we have limited our `Client` class to only have one `Consultant`, while our `Consultant` can work only with one `Client`. This model would not lend itself to our example; thus, we may use some sort of container object that points to the other class:

```
public class Client {
        String Client_Name;
        Vector Current_Consultant;         // A Vector of Consultant objects
}

public class Consultant {
        String Consultant_Name;
        Vector Current_Client;             // A Vector of Client Objects
}
```

Although we chose a `Vector` to hold multiple instances of an object, we could have used arrays, linked lists, `Bags`, `Collections`, `Enumerations`, or any other container object that Java can support. Implementing a one-to-many or many-to-many relationship will usually be done using the techniques presented in Association Objects, where a new table is created that holds the relationships between the `Clients` and the `Consultants`.

**Finite Aggregation**    The aggregate relation (sometimes called a containment hierarchy) describes relations between objects where one object is part of another object. Associations describe a relationship where one object uses, or communicates with another object, where the aggregation states that one class is composed of other classes. The container class could be composed of multiple classes, each of these could in turn also be composed of multiple classes, and the containment could continue on until all leaf classes are uncovered. Finite Aggregation varies from Association in Java only by the context in which the objects are used. In both cases, the objects will appear as attributes to the class. Thus, implementing persistence on the classes does not vary from that of Association.

**Inheritance and Relational Tables**    The generalization/specialization concepts associated with inheritance can be easily converted to the relational model. In essence, inheritance moves the common attributes found in multiple classes to a new abstract class. The classes that "lost" their attributes can then inherit from the abstract class, which "gives" the properties back to the class. This same metaphor of moving common attributes to a different container can easily be applied to the relational model. Only in this case, we are moving the attributes (or fields) to a new common table. This model extends our Golden

Rule with a clause stating that abstract classes can have a one-to-one relationship with tables.

Consider the following mapping found in many corporate environments.

A company needs to capture information on its business partners. These partners consist of several types of companies: suppliers, distributors, customers, and so on. Noticing that each of these entities has some common characteristics, such as company name, address, phone, and so on, we opt to create an abstract class of type Business that contains all of the common characteristics:

```
public class abstract Business {
String Company_Name;
        String Phone_Nbr;
}
```

We then extend our abstract Business class to create containers for our Suppliers, Distributors, and so on:

```
public class Supplier extends Business{
        int On_Time_Pct; // percentage of deliveries that were on time
        int In_Full_Pct;   // percentage of deliveries that were in full
}

public class Customer extends Business{
        Credit_Standing;  // Current credit rating with our company
        boolean Favored_Status; // Is this a favored customer?
}
```

There are two primary options we have in mapping these classes to a relational database:

1. **Option One**—Map each concrete class to a table and each abstract class to a table.

2. **Option Two**—Combine the attributes of the concrete class with the attributes of its super classes and map each concrete + abstract combination to a table.

***Option One***  This scenario would produce the following tables for the classes described previously:

```
Create Table Business as
        (Business_Id       int not null,
Company_Name Char(40),            Phone_Nbr      Char(10))

Create Table Supplier as
        (Business_Id       int not null,
On_Time_Pct       int,
        In_Full_Pct       int)

Create Table Customer as
        (Business_Id       int not null,
Credit_Standing       Char(1),
        Favored_Status  bit)
```

In this case, each concrete class maps to a table and each abstract class maps to a table. Notice that we added a system-generated key called Business_Id. This key is essential for joining our Business table to either our Supplier or Customer table. We can now create a view that ties our general Business information to the more concrete business type:

```
Create View Business_Supplier as
        Select Company_Name, Phone_Nbr, On_Time_Pct, In_Full_Pct
        From Business, Supplier
        Where Business.Business_Id = Supplier.Business_Id

Create View Business_Customer as
        Select Company_Name, Phone_Nbr, Credit_Standing, Favored_Status
        From Business, Customer
        Where Business.Business_Id = Customer.Business_Id
```

Most advanced RDBMSs can generate a system key for a table. These keys are usually implemented as incremental counters. Any time a record is inserted into a table that has an identity field (the counter), the identity field for the row is assigned a value one larger than the highest number already assigned. Unfortunately, a given table is not aware of the identity values being assigned to other tables. Thus, in our example, if three rows were inserted into our Business_Supplier table, and three rows were inserted into our Business_Customer table, they would each be assigned identity values of (1,2,3). These values are fine for distinguishing unique rows in their respective tables, but they would conflict with one another when used as a foreign key in the Business table. To avoid this issue, the developer may be forced to use a homemade routine for assigning values to the identity field. Doing this bypasses the conflict of key issue, but restricts us from using a very nice feature that is built into the database, system-generated keys.

Another obstacle in mapping abstract classes to tables is the issue of inserting, updating, and deleting. It is a simple task to retrieve our data, as we saw with our views (Business_Customer and Business_Partner), but changing data in joined tables is a more complex issue. Some relational databases allow DML commands to be used with tables that are joined, but the majority do not. This means that the developer must make an extra effort to preserve referential integrity on all Inserts, Updates, and Deletes.

The Identity field obstacle along with the DML challenge is usually enough to steer most developers away from this style of mapping. Yet several of the respected object-oriented methodologies recommend this approach (Jacobson, Rumbaugh). This method may appear to be a good solution, but in practice it presents several challenges that usually outweigh its merits.

**Option Two**   An alternative approach is to combine the attributes of the concrete class and all of its super-classes into a single table. Thus, our Business example would produce the following two tables:

```
Create Table Supplier as
        (Supplier_Id     int not null,
Company_Name Char(40),
        Phone_Nbr     Char(10),
On_Time_Pct     int,
        In_Full_Pct     int)

Create Table Customer as
```

```
        (Customer_Id      int not null,
Company_Name Char(40),
        Phone_Nbr       Char(10),
Credit_Standing       Char(1),
        Favored_Status  bit)
```

In this scenario, we have moved the `Company_Name` and `Phone_Nbr` field to both tables. This option allows the application to easily perform Inserts, Updates, and Deletes, as well as implement system-generated keys without concern for conflict. Notice that we did not try to share a common key, giving each table its own system-generated key instead.

# Synchronization Tools

Bridging the gap between relational databases and object-oriented applications can become quite an effort. Vendors have realized that the need to automate the synchronization of the two sides is a necessity for very large applications. Two different types of synchronization tools have come to market. The database companies and the database modeling companies are pushing tools to reverse engineer relational databases into object models, while ODBMS companies and object modeling groups have created forward engineering tools that will create table structures that mimic the classes in an application. Both sets of tools fulfill a distinct requirement. One is geared for writing applications where an RDBMS is already populated, while the other takes a clean-slate approach. Perhaps more important than forward or reverse engineering is answering some even more basic questions about the automation software:

- Does it support the Golden Rule?
- How are Association and Aggregation handled?
- How is Inheritance handled?
- Does it "remember" from one session to the next?
- Are DML statements generated?

## Does the Tool Support the Golden Rule?

Be wary of tools that do not map a class to a table, or any of the extensions to the Golden Rule that were mentioned. Proprietary mapping techniques may bind a project to a particular vendor's tool. Most tools currently require that a container class is present at compile time. As extensions to the Java language continue to unfold, developers should keep their eyes on the concept of the meta-class. This concept allows a new class to be created and used at runtime. Thus, the attributes of the class could be determined at runtime. This would facilitate using a system that could reach into a relational database and dynamically create the appropriate container class. Currently, the `ResultSet` object attempts to mimic the concept of a meta-class, in that the fields inside of the object change in accordance with the `Select` statement that was issued, but the `ResultSet` object has several limitations when used in this context.

**Limitations in ResultSet Class**    The ResultSet class appears to work much like a meta-class, but it has several limitations. In a meta-class, not only can the value of its contents change at runtime, but the number of attributes, their names, and types can also change. The ResultSet object attempts to mimic this by providing methods that allow a program to enumerate the attributes, their types, values, and so on. The ResultSet object was designed for a one-way movement of data from a relational database into an object-oriented world (for example, Retrieve only). The container classes that we have created in this chapter represent buffers that can act as a bi-directional utility for movement of data (for example, Insert, Update, Delete and Retrieve). Although the ResultSet object can perform cursor processing, it was not designed to be a robust mechanism for modifying data. The designers of the JDBC crippled the ResultSet object by not providing for backward scrolling, or bookmarks. For this reason, we have added our container classes that, in many cases, will initially be populated with data from a ResultSet object, but later will be used for performing updates, deletes, and inserts.

**Are DDL Scripts Created and Executed?**   The basis of forward engineering tools is the creation of relational data structures from an object model or from Java source code. Typically, the tools will create table structures and save the structure in a file. Others will connect to the data source and create the structures automatically.

# Portability to an ODBMS?

Many of the packages that are available from Object Database vendors have created a single interface that will help in transitioning a move from a relational database to an object database. This is accomplished by providing the application with an interface that is consistent between the two back-ends.

When considering the procurement of tools to aid in development, you may want to answer the following question:

*Can multiple back-end databases be supported within a single application?*

Several of the newer tools support the need for storing objects in multiple databases, regardless of the relational engine. The tool does not assume that only a single engine is used, and offers the luxury of picking the database the object will be stored in.

# Issues in Reverse-Engineering Tools

■ **Are object models created?**   Reverse-engineering tools will usually take the data structures in a relational database and create an object model. Most of the tools apply the Golden Rule and match a table to a class. Some have the ability to recognize the relationships in the data (foreign key relationships become object associations, and so on).

■ **Is Java code created (shell classes)?**   In addition to the object model, the tool should generate tight Java source code for each class that is created. This code is used as a shell container to hold the data. It may be a subclass of a class that has some persistence logic built into it. The shell container class is usually extended by the application to add business or logic rules. It is usually not modified, because subsequent regenerations of the database would re-create the class and any changes would be lost.

■ **Is any intelligence built into the objects?** Some tools add basic logic to the generated classes. If a class is acting as an object container for a table (where certain fields didn't allow nulls), and the application attempted to insert a new record, the class would be smart enough to notify the application of the problem rather than attempt a costly call to the database.

# SQL3 & ODMG-93

The ODMG-93 is a specification that has come out of the Object Database Management Group and is well-supported among the ODBMS vendors. It specifies an (ODL) Object Definition Language much like the Data Definition Language in SQL. It also supports an OQL (Object Query Language), much like the Data Manipulation Language in SQL. One of the goals of the group was to create the OQL as a superset to standard queries in the relational model. Thus, any Select statement that runs on relational tables works with the same semantics and syntax on collections of ODMG objects. The ODMG provides for a set of features that goes beyond the boundaries of traditional relational databases providing for complex objects, object identity, and so on. This means that, from a query perspective, an ODBMS that supports the ODMG-93 standard can accept SQL queries that were designed to work with relational databases. Obviously, design issues arise in the direct porting of data from a relational database to an ODBMS.

While the ODMG has approached the issue from an object database vendor's perspective, the SQL3 group has approached the same problem from a relational database vendor's view. The SQL3 standard supports all of the notions that were created in prior SQL specifications, but adds new functionality to extend the relational model into an object-oriented world.

# Object/Relational Databases

A new breed of databases has come out in the last few years that attempts to bridge the object database and relational database technologies. These are generally known as Object/Relational Databases. Perhaps the best known of these is from a company called UniSQL. The UniSQL product takes the relational model and extends it to work in an object-oriented environment. UniSQL supports the concept of encapsulation, whereby a method can be stored with the data in the database. Method calls can then be made to operate on the data. In addition, the UniSQL product has direct support for inheritance. This allows a "table" to inherit the properties of another table, thus preserving inheritance hierarchies. Perhaps the single strongest feature is direct preservation of attributes. While most normal relational systems can store only a system-defined type (int, char, and so on), UniSQL can store an instance of a class as a field.

In addition to the efforts made in object/relational circles, the ODBMS vendors have made strides in creating products that work with SQL syntax and then can easily bind to object-oriented languages. Chapter 9, "Using Object Databases," covers the advantages of using an ODBMS with the Java language.

Part
I

Ch
7

# From Here...

This chapter introduced many of the factors that should be weighed in writing object-oriented applications in Java that interface with relational databases. Many solutions exist for overcoming this issue, and no one solution is correct in all situations. Each project must determine what the appropriate answer is for its own needs.

- Chapter 8, "Multithreaded Database Applications," introduces issues associated with the creation of large, multithreaded database applications that interface with database systems.

- Chapter 9, "Using Object Databases," covers the current state of object database management systems and their ability to interface with the Java language.

- Chapter 10, "Delivering the Application," covers many of the options that are available to the corporation for delivering a production-ready system to the user community.

# CHAPTER 8

# Multithreaded Database Applications

**Why use threads?**

Understand the benefits of using threads and when you use them.

**Review threads**

Review the concepts of threads.

**Advanced thread topics**

Understand the advanced thread topics, such as monitors, synchronization, and thread groups.

**Demonstrate a threaded JDBC application**

Assemble an example of a threaded JDBC class.

**Threaded JDBC issues**

Evaluate several issues when using threads with JDBC applications.

**E**ach application can be thought of as a process, using its own memory areas for data and code. Within each application is the possibility of one or more threads. These threads allow tasks related to the application to be performed in parallel, allowing independent processing to be made when other tasks are idle. Designing multiple threads in an application can sometimes be time-consuming since third-party libraries and a strong knowledge of thread theory may be required. However, Java has included a library of thread classes and interfaces to allow the developer access to the power of the underlying operating system, with a smaller degree of a learning curve. Powerful, multithreaded applications may be designed in a fraction of the time necessary in other languages, and they will function on multiple platforms. This prevents the developer from being forced into understanding the specifics of thread programming for the particular platform target. ■

# Why Use Multiple Threads with JDBC?

So far, all of the applications presented in this book have been designed within one thread—the primary thread. The primary thread is the single thread assigned to a Java application when the virtual machine is invoked. All application instructions from start to finish are executed within the context of the primary thread. This means that no two methods may be executing in parallel. When designing simple applications, this is satisfactory; however, developing large applications using only one thread can lead to poor application performance.

To increase the performance of larger applications, multithreading should be used. Determining what processes should merit a thread can be determined by evaluating the application's processes. Processes that slow down the application, at least to the end user, should be designed in a separate thread. This can allow a user to continue working while data is being computed for future use. In addition, an application may continue to flow in the correct direction without interruption. Also, JDBC calls executed from threads can allow other applications running on the user's PC to continue executing smoothly by cooperating with the operating system.

In addition, using a separate thread for background loading can ensure that the user gets a response from the application as it is retrieving large result sets. Using this technique prevents users from assuming the application isn't working should it not start quickly. It also allows for quicker user interaction during login procedures, since the retrieval of the data will not occupy the system resources.

Finally, moving queries such as large unions into a separate thread will allow users to interact with the application. Most long database queries will cause the application to block, preventing further execution of the application until the results return. Users may then have the option of interrupting the long process instead of being forced to wait for the full duration of the query.

> **CAUTION**
>
> Using multiple threads with the JDBC package may allow the user to interrupt important data manipulation. Be sure to include data-safe routines should a user attempt to close a frame or other user interface that could end the query.

# Reviewing Thread Concepts

The Java Thread class allows programmers to design an object as a thread. Whenever an applet or application is started, the Java VM starts the primary class (specified by the applet tag or the class given on the command line) as a thread. It then becomes a member of the virtual machine's primary threadgroup, and is started.

The Thread class is an abstract class that defines how a thread should be implemented. In addition, it defines several methods for controlling the state and properties of the thread. The heart of the Thread class is in the run() method. Any statements inside of the run() method are executed until one of the following occurs: there are no more statements in the run method to execute, the thread's `stop()` method is called, or a terminal exception is thrown that has not been caught.

To create a thread, simply subclass the `Thread` class and provide a `run()` method containing any code that the thread will process. Here is a simple framework for a `thread` object:

**Listing 8.1  An Example of Using the *Thread* Class**

```
public class SimpleThread extends Thread {
public void run () {
    while (true) {
      // do any processing
}
}
```

The class in Listing 8.1 demonstrates a simple thread that will operate continuously until it is halted. Threads do not have to continue forever; they may operate only once, several times, or continuously. The code in Listing 8.2 will instantiate a thread and begin its execution. Notice that the code after the `start()` method will execute after the thread is started. This indicates that the two threads are operating concurrently.

**Listing 8.2  Implementing the New *Thread* Class**

```
public static void main (String args[]) {
    SimpleThread thread=new SimpleThread();
    thread.start();
    System.out.println ("After the thread is started");
 }
```

## Runnable

Using the technique just covered, it's easy to create a thread that extends the `Thread` class. But how do you handle the task of creating a thread that already has an inheritance requirement? This is where the `Runnable` interface would be appropriate. For instance, if an object must extend the `Frame` class, the option of extending `Thread` isn't available. By using the `Runnable` interface, this class could be implemented as a thread. An example is shown in Listing 8.3.

**Listing 8.3  A Frame that Implements *Runnable***

```
public class ThreadFrame extends Frame implements Runnable {

 public void run () {
    while (true) {
      try { Thread.sleep (500);} catch (InterruptedException e) {
      System.out.println ("Got exception : "+e);
 }
   }
 }
```

To start the class as a thread, Listing 8.4 would be used:

### Listing 8.4 Implementing the *ThreadFrame* Class

```
public static void main (String args[]) {
ThreadFrame frame;
Thread Runner=new Thread (frame);
Runner.start();
}
```

This is a simple example of using the Runnable interface. The important things to remember when using the Runnable interface include:

- The run() method must be specified and is executed when a new thread is called.

- Instantiate a thread with the Runnable class as an argument. This will alter the target of the thread object to the Runnable implementation and invoke its run() method once the start() method of the Thread is called.

- Any references to sleep() inside of a Runnable implementation must be called statically. This is because the Runnable interface doesn't define the standard thread methods, such as sleep(), yield(), and so on.

Another option when designing Runnable implementations is to include a Thread as a member object and create methods to handle the starting and stopping of the Thread. For instance, Listing 8.5 is a new class, ThreadFrame2, which will encapsulate the need to start and stop a thread into the object itself:

### Listing 8.5 A Second Implementation of the *ThreadFrame* Class

```
public class ThreadFrame2 extends Frame implements Runnable {
    Thread Runner;
  public void start () {
    if (Runner == null) {
        Runner = new Thread (this);
        Runner.start();
    }
}

  public void run () {
    while (true) {
      try { Thread.sleep (500);} catch (InterruptedException e) {
      System.out.println ("Got exception : "+e);
}
    }
  }

  public void stop () {
```

```
        if (Runner != null && Runner.isAlive())
            Runner.stop();
        Runner=null;
    }
}
```

## Suspend, Resume, and Stop

Once a thread has been started using the start() method, the thread begins running until there are no more instructions in the run() method, or a serious error occurs. To force a thread to stop running, the stop() method is used. This will cause the thread to cease execution, it is removed from its thread group owner, and the thread is assigned a null value (this procedure is detailed later in the chapter).

Whenever a thread needs to be paused for an indefinite amount of time, the suspend() method is called. The thread will then stop executing at the line where it is currently, and not start again until the resume() method is invoked. The thread then begins processing at the next statement from where it left off. Listing 8.6 is an example of the suspend(), resume(), and stop() methods.

**N O T E**   When using suspend(), keep in mind that the resume() method executes the statement where it left off. If the thread is designed to act upon time-dependent data, the thread data may need to be refreshed before its execution resumes. ▪

**Listing 8.6    A Demonstration of Pausing, Resuming, and Stopping a Thread**

```
public boolean handleEvent (Event evt) {
  if (evt.id == Event.ACTION_EVENT && evt.target == startButton) {
    startButton.disable();
    stopButton.enable();
    t.resume();
    return true;
  } else
  if (evt.id == Event.ACTION_EVENT && evt.target == stopButton) {
    stopButton.disable();
    startButton.enable();
    t.suspend();
    return true;
  }
  if (evt.id == Event.ACTION_EVENT && evt.target == exitButton) {
    t.stop();
    System.exit (0);
    return true;
  }
  return super.handleEvent (evt);
}
```

# Prioritizing

Every Java thread has a priority number. Most `thread` objects inherit the priority number of their parent thread. To change the default priority, use the `setPriority()` method. The priority number may be in the range of 1 (`Thread.MIN_PRIORITY`) to 10 (`Thread.MAX_PRIORITY`). Whenever the thread scheduler has to pick a thread to operate with, it will pick the highest thread priority. The thread chosen will keep running until the thread:

■ yields by calling the `yield` method.

■ ceases to be runnable, by entering the `blocked` state or dying.

■ is replaced by a higher priority thread that has become runnable, usually by the thread having slept long enough or a `resume()` was invoked.

The default priority setting for threads is 5 (`Thread.NORM_PRIORITY`). Note that higher priority threads always have precedence over lower priority threads. Listing 8.7 is an example of how to change thread priority.

■ `final void setPriority(int newPriority)`

sets the priority of a thread

**Parameters:**

`newPriority`: integer ranging from 1 (lowest) to 10 (highest) for priority

■ `public final static int MAX_PRIORITY = 10`

constant that represents the highest priority state (10)

■ `public final static int MIN_PRIORITY = 1`

constant that represents the lowest priority state (1)

■ `public final static int NORM_PRIORITY = 5`

constant that represents the normal priority state (5)

---

**Listing 8.7   Changing the Thread Priority**

```
Thread thread=new SimpleThread ();
thread.setPriority (Thread.MIN_PRIORITY);
thread.start();
```

---

# Thread States

Understanding the various thread states that a thread object can cycle through is important to understanding advanced threading techniques. The states a thread may be labeled as include `new`, `runnable`, `blocked`, and `dead`. This section discusses each of these states and the criteria in which they enter and exit these states.

***new***   When a thread is instantiated with the `new` operator, a thread is said to be in the `new` state. The `start()` method is called, which allocates the memory and establishes itself with the operating system. No lines of code are executed during the `new` state.

***runnable***   Once the `start()` method has finished, the thread moves from the `new` state to the `runnable` state. The thread is then capable of running, although it may not begin running until the Virtual Machine allows the thread to run. Once the thread begins running, the instructions in the `run()` method begin execution. Note that a thread is still in the `runnable` state, whether it is executing or not, as long as it is not in the `blocked` or `dead` states.

***blocked***   A thread may enter the `blocked` state due to one of five reasons.

1. The `sleep()` method is called.
2. The `suspend()` method is called.
3. The thread calls the `wait()` method.
4. The thread calls an I/O method that blocks, meaning that the thread cannot continue execution until the operation returns control.
5. A thread has attempted to enter the same *synchronized* method as another and must wait until the first is finished.

To move out of the `blocked` state, four things must happen.

1. If sleeping, the thread must expire the `sleep` time.
2. If suspended, the thread's `resume()` method must be called.
3. If `wait()` was called, the owner of the monitor must call `notify()` or `notifyAll()`.
4. A blocking I/O operation must complete and return control to the thread.

Please note that calls made to attempt to remove the thread out of a state that is uncontrollable, such as a blocking I/O call, will be unsuccessful and will remain blocked. If a method is invoked that is incompatible with its current state, an `IllegalThreadStateException` is thrown. For example, calling a `suspend()` method on a thread that is not currently `runnable` will cause this exception to be thrown.

***dead***   A thread moves into the `dead` state when one of two things happen.

1. The thread has finished executing the `run()` method.
2. The thread's `stop()` method has been invoked.

A thread's state may be determined by using the `isAlive()` method. This method will return `true` if the thread is `runnable/blocked` and `false` if it is in the `new` or `dead` states.

```
final boolean isAlive()
```

> determines if the thread is `runnable/blocked`

> **Returns:** `True` if the thread is `runnable/blocked`, `false` if it is `new` or `dead`

# Thread Groups

Dealing with multiple threads at once can be commonplace for some applications. However, if a user interrupts a function, or the application needs to stop all of the threads at once, a more useful method of thread manipulation may be used—thread groups. A thread group identifies a group of threads by a name, and allows the application to stop, suspend, and resume all of the threads in a group (see Listing 8.8). Thread groups may also be nested, allowing groups inside of groups if applications necessitate this need.

### Listing 8.8 A Demonstration of Using the *ThreadGroup* Class

```
public static void main (String args[]) {

    // create a new thread group
    ThreadGroup g = new ThreadGroup ("Timers");

    // First, create a new constructor for the SimpleThread class to allow a
    ➡ThreadGroup
    // Now, instantiate three objects, all part of the group
    Thread thread1=new SimpleThread (g);
    Thread thread2=new SimpleThread (g);
    Thread thread3=new SimpleThread (g);

    // now, start all of the threads at once
    g.start();
}
```

**public ThreadGroup(String name)**

creates a new ThreadGroup with the given name.

**Parameters**:

name: String containing the desired ThreadGroup name.

**public ThreadGroup(ThreadGroup parent, String name)**

creates a new ThreadGroup with the given name and is a child of the given ThreadGroup.

**Parameters**:

parent: ThreadGroup that will be the parent of the new ThreadGroup

name: String containing the desired ThreadGroup name.

**public int activeCount()**

returns the number of active threads in the ThreadGroup and any child ThreadGroups.

**Parameters**: none

returns an integer containing the number of active threads.

**public void list()**

displays information about the ThreadGroup to the default console device. Useful for debugging.

**Parameters**: none

```
public final void suspend()
```

suspends all threads in the ThreadGroup.

**Parameters**: none

```
public final void resume()
```

resumes all threads in the ThreadGroup.

**Parameters**: none

```
public final void stop()
```

stops all threads in the ThreadGroup.

**Parameters**: none

# Synchronization

When working with multiple threads within an application, it is imperative to understand how the application is actually functioning. Whenever two or more threads are attempting to call the same method that alters data, problems may arise that can cause errors to creep into your application, which may disrupt information.

In an attempt to understand synchronization fully, let's examine how the Java Virtual Machine handles threads. When threads operate on values that are shared between objects, the value will be copied into the current thread's memory area. This requires the value to be read from the actual storage area and copied into the temporary storage. The thread may then operate on the value as it needs to. When finished, the value will be read from the temporary storage area and written back to main memory. Should several threads attempt to access the same value and attempt to alter its state, the value could become corrupt. This corruption is likely to occur since several CPU cycles may expire before the value is read, copied, and written to the temporary area.

The synchronization modifier requires a thread to complete the execution of a body of statements and move the temporary value to its permanent location before another thread may continue. This is called monitoring, and is a very standard concept when handling threading issues. A monitor is the mechanism by which the virtual machine tracks the current thread and all waiting threads for a given synchronized body.

**N O T E**  Although this example states that values are moved from "main memory" to "temporary memory," the virtual machine does not partition memory in this fashion. The terminology has been used only for simplicity. ■

When an object begins execution of a synchronized body, the object is said to be in ownership of the synchronized object. This means that it is the only object that is allowed execution of the synchronized statements.

What happens if an object, such as an array, needs to be synchronized? Since there are no methods within an array, the `synchronized()` statement allows an object to gain ownership of the object's monitor. Using the `synchronized()` statement gives the developer the ability to invoke a method in a `synchronized` state, even when the method isn't declared `synchronized`. It also allows public members to be altered in a synchronized manner, preventing corruption from other running threads. Listing 8.9 demonstrates the correct usage of the `synchronized()` statement.

**Listing 8.9  Example of Using the *Synchronized* Statement**

```
public synchronized void doSomething() {
  // insert some data manipulation here
}
```

# wait/notify

Now, consider what will happen to a `synchronized` method that requires a specific condition for proper execution. If the condition cannot be met immediately, the thread must wait for the condition to exist. However, in a `synchronized` method, the thread cannot allow any other thread to execute the code until the original thread is finished. To alleviate this problem, Java has two methods, `wait()` and `notify()`, that allow the next thread in the queue to execute the method. The `wait()` method:

- allows the current thread to be suspended, allowing the next thread in the queue to execute the method.
- will remain suspended until a `notify()` method is invoked.
- will cause the thread to resume and make another attempt when the `notify()` method is called.

The use of `wait()` and `notify()` is especially useful in a producer/consumer relationship, where all threads are attempting to achieve a common goal. Note that the `wait()` and `notify()` methods can be invoked only by an object that has monitor ownership. As you may recall, the ownership of a monitor is gained by the use of the `synchronized()` statement or by calling the `wait()` or `notify()` methods from a synchronized body.

When dealing with the `notify()` method, keep in mind that there is a level of uncertainty when multiple threads may be chosen for the notify target. This is due to the thread implementation being dependent upon the actual native implementation of thread handling. Should circumstances arise that would allow multiple threads to enter a `wait()` state, the `notifyAll()` method should be used.

The `notifyAll()` method broadcasts a `notify()` call to each waiting thread in the wait queue. Use of this method ensures that threads are not forgotten and left in the `wait()` state. Listing 8.10 is an example of the `wait()`, `notify()`, and `notifyAll()` methods.

### Listing 8.10   A Demonstration of the *wait()* and *notify()* Methods

```
public class Account {
float Total=0;

public synchronized void Withdraw (float value) {
    while ((Total-value) < 0 ) {
        // Insufficient funds. Wait until their are funds to withdraw (Nice
        ➥bank!)
        System.out.println ("Thread Asleep");
        try { wait();} catch (InterruptedException e) {}
    }
      System.out.println ("Old Value: "+Total);
      Total -= value;
      System.out.println ("New Value: "+Total);
}

public synchronized void deposit (float value) {
    Total+=value;
    notifyAll(); // let all waiting threads know that more money has been
entered
}
}
```

`public final void notify()`

wakes up the next Thread waiting on the object's monitor.

**Parameters**: none

`public final void notifyAll()`

wakes up all threads waiting on the object's monitor.

**Parameters**: none

`public final void wait() throws InterruptedException`

waits to be notified by another thread of a change to this object.

**Parameters**: none

`public final void wait(long timeout) throws InterruptedException`

waits to be notified by another thread of a change to this object, or until a time limit expires.

**Parameters**:

   timeout: number of milliseconds to wait for a notification

`public final void wait(long timeout, int nanos) throws InterruptedException`

waits to be notified by another thread of a change to this object, or until a time limit expires.

**Parameters**:

> `timeout`: number of milliseconds to wait for a notification

> `nanos`: number of milliseconds to wait for a notification

# Developing a Multithreaded JDBC Example

Putting all of the thread concepts together, the next step is to create an example of using threads with the JDBC. This example will demonstrate two concurrent threads. The first will be the primary thread, and display a "tick" message once a second. The second will establish a connection to the database and insert 200 rows of data into a sample table. In addition, the second thread will print the start and stop times, so that a feel of concurrent events is shown.

First, let's examine the requirements that must be met to properly design a JDBC-enabled thread. Although certain JDBC drivers allow more than one statement to be executed simultaneously using the same connection object, it is recommended to use individual connection instances for each concurrent process. This provides the greatest flexibility when drivers may change, and ensures the application will function should a driver's properties be altered in a future revision.

The thread's `run()` method should contain a `sleep()` invocation. This ensures that the thread allows other threads to process and doesn't use 100% of the CPU processing time. Additionally, several well-placed `sleep()` calls throughout the complex methods will also alleviate any large processing times.

Finally, be sure to call the cleanup methods, such as `close()`, to ensure that unnecessary JDBC objects are closed in case the thread is halted. This also reduces the amount of connections to the database and the amount of memory used.

Listing 8.11 shows the complete listing for the demonstration. The output is shown in Figure 8.11.

---

**Listing 8.11   Implementing a Multithreaded JDBC Class**

```
import java.sql.*;
import java.io.*;
import java.util.Date;

public class DBThread extends Thread {
   Connection connection;
   Statement statement;
   ResultSet results;

   String name;

   public DBThread(String s){
       //init the DB objects
       name=s;
```

```
        try {
         Class.forName("jet.bridge.JetDriver").newInstance();
          connection = DriverManager.getConnection("jdbc:jet:enterprise","sa","");
        } catch (Exception e) {
          System.out.println ("INIT exception :"+e);
        }
         }

public void simpleInsert () {
    try {
          statement=connection.createStatement ();
          for (int i=0;i<200;i++) {
              try {
                 sleep (50);
              } catch (InterruptedException e) { System.out.println ("Thread
interrupted! "+e);}
            statement.executeUpdate ("INSERT into test values ("+i+")");


          }
    } catch (SQLException e) { System.out.println ("Got Exception while
      ➥inserting: "+e);}
      statement.close();
}

public void run () {
    while (true) {
      try {
         System.out.println (name+" start time: "+new Date());
          simpleInsert();
         System.out.println (name+" has finished inserting 200 rows at : "+new
         ➥Date());
         sleep (10000);
      } catch (InterruptedException e) { System.out.println ("Thread interrupted!
        ➥"+e);}
      }
}

public static void main (String args[]) {
  // instantiate and start the thread
  DBThread db=new DBThread ("Thread");
  db.start();

  // loop for about 30 seconds, allowing the thread a chance to operate three
times
  int time=0;
  while (time<30000) {
    try {
      Thread.sleep (1000);
    } catch (InterruptedException e) {System.out.println ("Thread interrupted
      ➥:"+e);}
    time+=1000;
    System.out.println ("Tick");
  }
  db.stop();
}
}
```

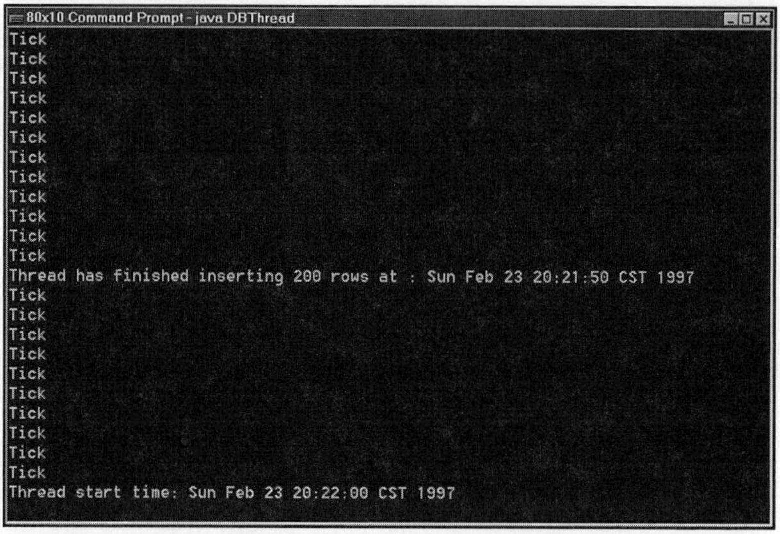

**FIG. 8.1**
Output window from
DBThread.java.

```
80x10 Command Prompt - java DBThread
Tick
Tick
Tick
Tick
Tick
Tick
Tick
Tick
Tick
Tick
Tick
Thread has finished inserting 200 rows at : Sun Feb 23 20:21:50 CST 1997
Tick
Tick
Tick
Tick
Tick
Tick
Tick
Tick
Tick
Thread start time: Sun Feb 23 20:22:00 CST 1997
```

# Using *PipedStreams* for Thread Notification

The java.io package includes two stream classes, PipedInputStream and PipedOutputStream, which allow threads within the same virtual machine to send and receive data. This gives threads a stream from which notification messages may be sent, or data may be traded.

Using the PipedStream class is straightforward and offers simple byte reading and writing. The PipedInputStream provides two read() methods, which allow reading one byte at a time, or an array of bytes. In addition, it defines an available() method, which returns the number of bytes currently in the stream. The PipedOutputStream provides two write() methods for sending a single byte or array of bytes. Both stream classes include a connect() method, which links a PipedInputStream to a PipedOutputStream. Listing 8.12 demonstrates the use of PipedStream classes for sending data from one thread to another.

**Listing 8.12  A Demonstration Using the *PipedStreams***

```java
import java.util.Date;
import java.io.*;

public class PipedCounter extends Thread {
  PipedOutputStream pout;
  int counter;
  public PipedCounter (PipedInputStream pin) {
    counter=0;
    try {
      pout=new PipedOutputStream (pin);
    } catch (IOException e) {
      System.out.println ("Got IO Exception: "+e);
```

```
      }
    }
    public void run () {
      while (true) {
        // increment counter and send result to PipedOutput

        counter++;
        try {
          pout.write (counter);
    } catch (IOException e) {
      System.out.println ("Got IO Exception writing: "+e);
    }

        try {
          sleep (1000);
        } catch (InterruptedException e) {System.out.println ("Interrupted");
        }
      }
    }
  }

}
```

The guidelines for using PipedStreams include:

- PipedStreams must be connected in at least one direction for proper communication.
- A receiving thread should poll the stream occasionally to determine if any new data has been sent (−1 indicates no data).
- A message in the form of an integer or byte array may be sent to another thread by using the write() method.
- For a thread to receive the data, it must periodically check its stream by calling the read() method.

# Avoiding Potential Obstacles

When writing multithreaded JDBC applications, keep in mind several pitfalls that may be encountered. These pitfalls can include thread deadlocking and JDBC driver thread support. Each of these problems can cause potential hazards and may even lead to long debugging sessions should they be encountered. Following are discussions of each problem, and suggestions for avoiding them.

# Deadlocks

Deadlocks are potentially the most hazardous situations a multithreaded environment can encounter. Deadlocks occur when two or more threads encounter a situation in which they freeze, or hang, and cannot proceed. This can be explained using the simplest deadlocking case, involving two threads. Thread A owns a monitor on Object A, and is waiting for ownership of Object B's monitor. Thread B owns a monitor on Object B, and is waiting for ownership of Object A's monitor. Figure 8.2 demonstrates this scenario.

The Java Virtual Machine cannot protect applications from entering a deadlock state, so it is up to the Java developer to ensure that an application can never enter this situation. Several algorithms are documented throughout the Internet and published in many books which can reduce or eliminate this situation, but are beyond the scope of this book. Please take caution when designing multithreaded applications to prevent deadlocks from occuring.

**FIG. 8.2**
Understanding the potential hazards of deadlocking and their origins.

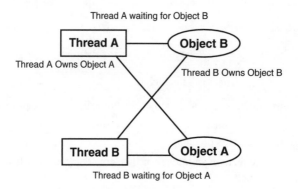

Thread A waiting for Object B

**Thread A**   **Object B**

Thread A Owns Object A   Thread B Owns Object B

**Thread B**   **Object A**

Thread B waiting for Object A

**Thread Deadlock**

# Database and Driver Support

Although Java is a multithreaded language, support for multiple simultaneous database operations may be restricted on several different levels, including database level and driver level. Databases, including mSQL, do not support simultaneous operations and therefore cannot benefit from multithreaded JDBC applications. In addition, some third-party JDBC drivers do not support simultaneous operations, such as the JDBC-ODBC Bridge from Intersolv and JavaSoft. Please refer to the proper documentation before attempting to develop multithreaded JDBC applications using certain JDBC drivers and DBMSs.

# From Here...

In this chapter, multithreaded JDBC applications were introduced. We discovered when and why to use them, as well as potential pitfalls when creating multithreaded database applications in Java. However, when providing all but the simplest application with multiple threads, applications will run smoother and the users will see a cleaner application. This not only creates confidence for the end user, but also with the company for which the application was written. Applying these techniques, as well as techniques from other chapters, can create a scalable, efficient application.

- Chapter 3, "A Simple JDBC Application," covers the basic connections, drivers, and driver management associated with the JDBC, and introduces a framework for the rest of Part I.

- Chapter 4, "Executing SQL Statements," discusses how to query a SQL database using getXXX methods to retrieve results.

- Chapter 10, "Delivering the Application," covers the considerations that need to be understood when delivering a large Java JDBC application, and how to plan for optimizations when building SQL tables and applications.

# Using Object Databases

Object database systems have been growing in features and popularity since their original inception. Much of this popularity is due to the means of storing and retrieving objects in their natural state. Only after writing applications that require persistence and using a relational or flat-file system do they get very interested in the Object Database Management System (ODBMS). Large, object-oriented applications require extensive analysis and design. During this period, a great deal of time is spent identifying the objects, their attributes, operations, and collaborations. This information is usually modeled in detail to aid in the organization and long-term maintenance of the system. Use of a database management system that does not facilitate objects in their natural state will force the developer to create abstraction layers between the desired object model and the model that is required by the persistence engine. The ODBMS does not hamper the object model of a large system, but instead it enables the system to easily perform persistently. For this reason, it is expected that the use of object databases will be propelled forward with the popularity of the Java language.

Object database systems have undergone a critical eye from the development community since their inception. Early versions of object database systems were lightweight in features and not always as robust as their relational counterparts. Over the years, the ODBMS has matured to a stable and reliable option for developing mission-critical applications. That is not to say that relational database management systems do not have a lead on the ODBMS; systems from vendors such as IBM, Oracle, Sybase, and Microsoft generally have had several years to tweak their engines and user interfaces. These companies offer strong products that have been time-tested. A key criterion in determining whether you should use the ODBMS instead of the Relational Database Management System (RDBMS) is identifying the importance of keeping your objects in their natural state when they are stored to a persistent device. ■

# ODBMS Standards

The lack of standardization between early object databases was a huge hurdle in achieving commercial success. For this reason, the major vendors agreed that it would be better to work together to create a common application interface to store, manipulate, and retrieve data. From this realization grew the Object Database Management Group (ODMG). This is an organization that consists of several of the major vendors for the purpose of creating and maintaining the standards for object databases. The ODMG has four levels of membership that influence the standard:

1. **Voting Members:**

     GemStone Systems

     IBEX Computing

     O2 Technology

     Object Design

     Objectivity

     POET Software

     UniSQL

     Versant Object Technology

2. **Reviewer Members:**

     Andersen Consulting

     CERN

     Electronic Data Systems (EDS)

     Fujitsu Software Corporation

     Hitachi

     Lockheed Martin

     Microsoft

     MITRE Corporation

NEC Corporation

ONTOS

Persistence Software

Sybase

Unidata

VMARK Software

3. **ODMG Academic Reviewers:**

Klaus R. Dittrich

Roger King

Barbara Liskov

David Maier

J. Elliot Moss

Marvin Solomon

Stan Zdonik

4. **ODMG Staff Members (1997):**

Rick Cattell
ODMG Chair
Java Work Group Chair

Jeff Eastman
ODMG Vice Chair
Object Model Chair
Smalltalk Binding Editor

Douglas K. Bary
ODMG Executive Director

Mark Berler
Object Model and ODL Editor

Sophie Gamerman
OQL Editor

David Jordan
C++ Binding Editor

Henry Strickland
Java Binding Editor

# Review ODMG-93—Release 1.2 versus 2.0

At the time of this writing, the official ODMG standard is the 1.2 release. Several items are undergoing change and a release of 2.0 is expected sometime in 1997. Part of this release should be the Java Binding Specification. This will be the formalized method for using Java to communicate with an ODBMS that complies with the ODMG standard.

## State of the Java Binding Specification

The Java Binding Specification is a work in progress at the time of this writing. This chapter is provided to give developers a sneak preview of the type of functionality that is expected in the final release of the specification. Several vendors have adopted the early release of the specification and have the appropriate ODMG specifications. Examples used in this chapter have been tested using the Poet 4.0 ODBMS with their ODMG class library.

# Relational versus Object Database Concepts

The majority of development done with Java continues to use relational databases for storage. For those individuals who come from a relational background, Table 9.1 will help define new ODMBS concepts based on your previous relational background.

**Table 9.1   ODBMS Concepts**

| RDBMS Concept | Definition | ODBMS Concept |
| --- | --- | --- |
| Database | A mechanism for storing information in a logically associated fashion. | Database |
| Table (Relation) | A matrix of rows and columns used to store records of the same type. | The ODBMS does not have a true equivalent. The `Extent` object can be viewed as a mechanism to refer to all objects of the same type. |
| Row (Tuple) | A row is a group of logically related information. The row is synonymous with a record of information. | An instance of a class |
| Column (Attributes) | A column is the set of all occurrences of a specific field across all rows. | All instances of an attribute or member object for a class |
| Field | A cell in a relational table, that is, an attribute for a specific row. | An attribute in a class |
| Surrogate Key | A mechanism to uniquely identify a record of data. The characters used in the identifier have no meaningful significance. | Object ID |

| RDBMS Concept | Definition | ODBMS Concept |
|---|---|---|
| Foreign Key | A set of attributes or an identifier in one table that identifies a record in a foreign key. The member object points to another object that is related to the original object. | A member object performs a similar function as the second table |
| Candidate Key | The attributes of a record that uniquely identify it from all other records. The ODMG ODL does define the notion of KEY. | Not yet supported by Java |
| SQL-92 | A standard for defining and manipulating data in a database. | SQL3 or ODMG-93 |
| DML -Data Manipulation Language | A set of commands used to manipulate the data in the database. | The OQL (Object Query Language) performs the Select functionality of an RDBMS. The Insert, Update, and Delete mechanisms are done through separate API calls. |
| DDL - Data Definition Language | A set of commands used to describe the containers that will hold the data. | ODL (Object Definition Language) |
| Index | The index is a means to quickly locate a record in a database. The index is usually maintained by the ODBMS. | Index |

# ODMG Class Libraries

There are two primary means for writing Java/ODBMS applications. One is to use a Java class library that was written by the ODBMS vendor that has an API specific to the vendor's package. This option will usually include all of the commands that the vendor offers, but it may lock the application into using vendor proprietary operations. The second method is to use a class library that conforms to the ODMG standard. Again, the library will probably be written by the ODBMS vendor or by a third party. This option allows an application to swap out ODMG class libraries. Hence, an application can easily be modified to use a variety of different object database systems.

In our applications, we are importing a class library from the POET corporation. The classes that are used implement an interface that is specified by the ODMG and by JavaSoft:

```
import COM.POET.odmg.*;
```

It is expected that JavaSoft will release a package that will be imported into your application that facilitates callbacks into the vendor's package. In this scenario, you import the JavaSoft package and later specify which vendor's ODMG driver should be used, as JavaSoft has done for the JDBC package.

# ODBMS Concepts

Object databases have several new concepts that developers must embrace. We will look at several of the key concepts that are necessary to work with an ODBMS:

- Storage
- Transient and Persistent
- Object Identity
- Retrieving Data
- Collections (Bag, List, Set, and Varray)
- Extents
- Reachability

## Storage

A basic notion of object databases is when an object is stored, all of the member objects are stored with it (see Figure 9.1). In relational databases, you would typically "insert" all of the data into their respective tables one at a time. In the ODBMS world, if an object has references to other objects (member objects), then all of the member objects are automatically stored with the original object. In addition, all of the relationships that were intact while the instances were in memory remain intact while they are stored in the persistent medium.

**FIG. 9.1**
Storage of objects versus tables.

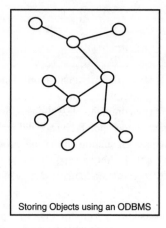

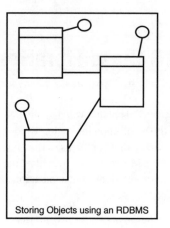

Storing Objects using an ODBMS

Storing Objects using an RDBMS

## Transient versus Persistent

Objects are usually described by their properties and operations. Another important aspect of an object is defining its lifetime. In most cases, an object is instantiated, some computations are done, and the object is destroyed. Thus, the "life" of the object is only for the period of time that the object remains in memory. Generally, the term persistent in object terms implies that the object (or a portion of it) was saved to some medium.

Java defines the keyword "transient" to define variables that will not be persistent. In the JDK 1.0 and 1.1, the use of the term transient is ignored. This allows programmers to develop applications with the future in mind. If you have identified which fields should be transient versus persistent, they can be noted without any detrimental effect to the system. When full ODBMS persistence is supported, the application will require minimal maintenance. In addition, defining items as transient helps to document the life of the field. Listing 9.1 shows how certain fields can be designated as transient.

### Listing 9.1   Defining Transient Fields

```
class Point {
    // Not stating "transient" implies that the field is persistent
        int x, y;
    // Fields described as "transient" will not be persistent
transient Color PointColor;
}
```

**N O T E**   Several vendors have released libraries that allow for local or lightweight storage of objects to a device. "Persistent Storage Engines (PSE)" are a simple means to dump the contents of an object to a file so that it can be read back in at a later point in time. Usually the PSE does not have sophisticated facilities for performing intensive searches on sets of objects that a full-fledged ODBMS will have. They are generally used when an application needs to temporarily save the state of an application (or a portion of the application). ▪

## Object Identity

A core concept of object database systems is Object Identifiers. In essence, an Object ID is a unique value that is system assigned. It is very similar in concept to the surrogate key in relational database systems. A new Object ID is assigned for every instance of the object. Many object database systems also support the Class ID concept, where a unique ID is assigned to each class.

Currently, object database management systems are not given a range of acceptable Object ID values. Hence, the ID of an object stored in one ODBMS may be the same as an ID stored in a different database. The Object ID is unique within its own storage domain. Listing 9.2 shows the Object ID.

---

**Listing 9.2    Object Identity**

```
try
    {
        // Instantiate a new object & bind it to a database object.
            MyClass myObject = new MyClass();
db.bind(myObject, name);
            // Get the Object ID & print it out.
ObjectId id=ObjectServices.getObjectId (myObject);
System.out.println ("Object ID: "+id);
        }
 catch (ODMGException e1)
        {
      System.out.println(e1);
}
catch (ODMGRuntimeException e2)
        {
      System.out.println(e2);
        }
```

---

# Retrieving Data

An object database that adheres to the ODMG standard can retrieve information from the database through a variety of ways:

- An arbitrary name can be "bound" to an object. This name becomes a handle to the object and can be used to retrieve the object. (Keywords: `bind`, `lookup`)

- When an object is put into the ODBMS, it may be added to a `collection` object. This `collection` object then acts as a starting point for locating the desired object. (Keywords: `Collection`, `Set`, `Bag`, `List`, `Varray`)

- Regardless of how an item was added to the database, all instances of the same class can be returned to a client. The object that facilitates returning all persistent instances of a class is the `Extent`. (Keyword: `Extent`)

- Relational databases support the Structured Query Language (SQL) for retrieving items from a database. The ODMG standard has a similar facility called the Object Query Language (OQL), which performs many of the same feats. (Keyword: `OQL`)

# Collections

Collections allow an object to contain lists of references to other objects, or to contain other objects directly (see Listing 9.3). If the `Person` class contains a list called "children," the following code looks up the president and lists his children.

---

**Listing 9.3    Collections**

```
Person p = (Person)database.lookup("President");
Enumeration e = p.children.createIterator();
while (e.hasMoreElements())
```

```
{
Person c = (Person)e.nextElement();
System.out.println(c.name); // prints the person's name
}
```

The Java object binding specification identifies four types of collections (see Table 9.2). An additional type of dictionary is expected with the ODMG-93 Release 2.0.

### Table 9.2    Collection Types

| Ordering | Uniqueness | Allowances |
|----------|-----------|------------|
| List | Programmer specifies order | Duplicates are allowed |
| Bag | System maintains order | Duplicates are allowed |
| Set | System maintains order | Duplicates are not allowed |
| Varray | Programmer specifies order, array metaphor | Duplicates are allowed |

*List*    The List object is a collection of ordered elements. Objects can be referenced by using an index. The List collection is similar in nature to a linked list, where items can be added to the middle of a list as easily as they can be appended to the end. It is common to use the List collection when items should be stored in a predetermined order, yet the items will be added in a random order.

Operations supported for Lists:

```
public void replaceElementAt(long index, Object obj) throws
CollectionIndexOutOfRangeException

public void removeElementAt(long index) throws CollectionIndexOutOfRangeException

public Object retrieveElementAt(long index) throws
➥CollectionIndexOutOfRangeException

public long findElement(Object obj)

public void insertElementAfter(Object obj, long index) throws
CollectionIndexOutOfRangeException

public void insertElementBefore(Object obj, long index) throws
CollectionIndexOutOfRangeException

public void insertElementFirst(Object obj)

public void insertElementLast(Object obj)

public Object removeFirstElement() throws CollectionIndexOutOfRangeException

public Object removeLastElement() throws CollectionIndexOutOfRangeException

public Object retrieveFirstElement() throws CollectionIndexOutOfRangeException
```

```
public Object retrieveLastElement() throws CollectionIndexOutOfRangeException

public List concat(List other)

public void append(List other)
```

**Bag**    The Bag collection facilitates holding items that do not need to be stored in a predetermined order and regardless of duplicate values. Typically the Bag is the collection that requires the least amount of processing overhead, thus for simple operations it will usually be the quickest.

Operations supported for Bags:

```
public Bag unionWith(Bag otherBag)

public Bag intersectionWith(Bag otherBag)

public Bag differenceWith(Bag otherBag)
```

**Set**    A Set defines a collection of items. Sets are often used in conjunction with other Sets. Several methods are available to compare the contents of Sets, or create new Sets based on the contents of other Sets. Duplicate items are not allowed within a single Set.

Operations supported by Sets:

```
public Set unionWith(Set otherSet);

public Set intersectionWith(Set otherSet);

public Set differenceWith(Set otherSet);

public boolean isSubsetOf(Set otherSet);

public boolean isProperSubsetOf(Set otherSet);

public boolean isSupersetOf(Set otherSet);

public boolean isProperSupersetOf(Set otherSet);
```

**Varray**    The Varray collection defines a set of ordered items where an index is used to retrieve a specific object. Unlike arrays that have a fixed amount of storage locations, the Varray facilitates growable arrays.

Operations for variable length arrays (Varray):

```
public void replaceElementAt(long index, Object obj) throws
CollectionIndexOutOfRangeException

public void removeElementAt(long index) throws CollectionIndexOutOfRangeException

public Object retrieveElementAt(long index) throws
➥CollectionIndexOutOfRangeException

public long findElement(Object obj) // returns -1 if not found

public void resize(long newSize)
```

# Extent

In addition to adding objects to collections for easy access, the ODMG Java binding allows an application to reference all objects of a given type. It is extremely important to be able to access all persistent objects in the database, not just the named roots. The Extent class is used to access all the objects of a given class which have been stored in the database (see Listing 9.4). Whenever an object is stored, a reference is added to the extent associated with the object's class. The object database management systems will automatically take care of creating and maintaining the extent for a class.

### Listing 9.4   Using *Extent*

```
// Create an extent of all stored instances of the person class in the specified
database
Extent allPersons = new Extent(database, "Person");
Enumeration e = allPersons.createIterator();

// Loop through all of the instances & print out the persons name
while (e.hasMoreElements()) {
    Person c = (Person)e.nextElement(); // Don't forget to cast!
    System.out.println(c.name);
}
```

Typically, developers will name the extent the same as the class name, but in its plural form. An extent can be used to step through all the objects in a given class, to position directly to specific offsets, or to perform a query on the objects of a class. Its constructor specifies a database and a class name (see Table 9.3).

### Table 9.3   Operations Supported for *Extent*

| Method | Operation |
| --- | --- |
| public void advance() | Positions to the next element of the extent. |
| public long cardinality() throws ODMGException | Returns the number of elements in the extent. |
| public Object currentElement() | Returns the next element of the extent without advancing the cursor. |
| public boolean findKey(Object obj) throws ODMGException | Searches first occurrence of a member. |
| public void finish() | Updates the extent to not point to any element. |
| public String getClassName() | Returns the name of the class this extent enumerates. |
| public String getIndex() | Returns the name of the index that specifies the sort order. |

*continues*

**Table 9.3   Continued**

| Method | Operation |
|--------|-----------|
| public boolean hasMoreElements() | Returns true if the extent contains more elements. |
| public boolean isEmpty()throws ODMGException | Returns true if the cardinality of the extent is zero. |
| public Object nextElement() | Returns the next element of the extent. |
| public void previous() | Positions to the previous element of the extent. |
| public void reset() | Positions to the first element of the extent. |
| public void setIndex(String indexName) throws ODMGException | Sets the name of the index that specifies the sort order. |

**N O T E**   The support for extents varies by vendor. At the time of this writing, the ODMG group is debating the required level of support for extents. ▪

Listing 9.5 shows the steps necessary to create a connection to a database, work with a transaction, bind/store instances, and retrieve the information again. It accomplishes this by issuing two separate queries, demonstrating some of the changes between relational SQL and the ODBMS format.

**Listing 9.5   Using *Extent* to Enumerate**

```
// establish a db connection
     Database db = Database.open("poet://LOCAL/my_base",
➥Database.openReadWrite);

    // instatiate some objects and push them to the DB
    Transaction txn = new Transaction(db);
    txn.begin();

    try
    {
        Employee emp1=new Employee ("Joe Smith","555-55-5555");
        db.bind (emp1,null);

        Employee emp2=new Employee ("Lucky Schmoe","777-77-7777");
        db.bind (emp2,null);

        // commit changes to the database

        txn.checkpoint();
        System.out.println ("Employees created and commited");
        // print all stored instances of MyClass

        System.out.println ("\nRetrieving a list for enumeration");
```

```
        Extent employees = new Extent(db, "Employee");
        System.out.println ("\nList retrieved. The objects are: ");
        while (employees.hasMoreElements())  {
            System.out.println(employees.nextElement());
        }
    }
    catch (ODMGException exc)
    {
        txn.abort();
        throw exc;
    }
    catch (ODMGRuntimeException exc)
    {
        txn.abort();
        throw exc;
    }
    txn.commit();
}
```

The following is the output from Listing 9.5:

```
Employees created and committed
Retrieving a list for enumeration
List retrieved. The objects are:
Employee Name: Joe Smith   SSN: 555-55-5555
Employee Name: Lucky Schmoe  SSN: 777-77-7777
```

## Transaction

The ODMG persistence model specifies that all persistent objects be created within a transaction. To do this, the programmer creates a transaction object and uses the begin(), commit(), and abort() methods to manage the transaction:

```
Transaction txn = new Transaction();
txn.begin();
... // Persistent objects are always created
... //  within a transaction.
txn.commit();
```

Creating a persistent object and assigning members is no different than performing the same operations with a non-persistent object, except that this must be done within a transaction.

## Storing Named Objects

At this point, the object still does not reside in the database. To store an object, a database object must be created, and the bind() method is called to assign the object to the database. The bind() method also gives a name to the object if one is specified.

The bind() method does not actually store the object; this is done automatically when the transaction commits. If the transaction is aborted, the object is never stored. Here is the code which is needed to create an object, bind it to the database, and store it by committing the transaction (see Listing 9.6).

---

**Listing 9.6   Committing *Transaction*s**

```
Transaction txn = new Transaction();
txn.begin();
Person p = new Person();
p.name = "George Washington";
database.bind(p, "President");
txn.commit();
```

---

Once a named object is in the database, it can be retrieved using the `lookup()` method: Note that when the object is returned it is of type `Object`. It must be cast back to its original class.

To store an object without creating a name for it, the `bind()` method is called using `Null` for the name parameter. Persistent objects without names can be retrieved from the database using `extents`, which will be described later.

# Persistence Through Reachability

In Java, the relationships among objects are expressed by references—if a `Person` object has a reference to the person's spouse, the spouse can always be accessed via this reference. In order to ensure that a Java object read from the database looks and acts exactly like the original Java object, all referenced objects are stored when an object is stored. Therefore, if a person has a spouse, that spouse will be stored if the person is stored (see Listing 9.7).

---

**Listing 9.7   Using *Transaction***

```
Transaction txn = new Transaction();
txn.begin();
Person p = new Person();
p.name = "George Washington";
     Person q = new Person("Martha Washington");
     p.spouse = q;
     database.bind(p, "President");
txn.commit();
```

---

In general, storing an object stores the entire network of objects referenced by that object. Once the person and his or her spouse have been stored, we can read the person from the database using the `lookup()` method and use the spouse reference to access the spouse. In the following code, we read the `president` object and print out the name of the `president`'s spouse (see Listing 9.8).

---

**Listing 9.8   Performing a *Lookup***

```
Person p = (Person)database.lookup("President");
System.out.println(p.spouse.name); // Prints "Martha Washington"
```

---

# OQL—Object Query Language

The Java bindings allow queries to be formulated by using Object Query Language (OQL), the query language specified by the ODMG standard for object databases. OQL is similar to SQL. Here is a sample query, which specifies conditions as a string and returns a set of objects that meet the conditions (see Listing 9.9).

Part

I

Ch

9

**Listing 9.9   OQL Query**

```
String qs = "define extent allPersons for Person;" +
"select p from p in allPersons  " +
"where p.name = \"Sculley\";";
OQLQuery query = new OQLQuery(qs);
Object result = query.execute();
```

If the query returns a collection of objects, an Enumeration may be used to step through the objects in the set (see Listing 9.10). This code prints out each element in the set (assuming that the element is a type that can be printed this way).

**Listing 9.10   Display Elements**

```
Enumeration e = ((CollectionOfObject)result).createIterator();
while (e.hasMoreElements()) {
System.out.println(e.nextElement());
}
```

The references among objects can be used in query conditions. It can also be used to formulate quite complex queries. Consider the following query (see Listing 9.11).

**Listing 9.11   Query with an *Extent***

```
// create an extent that references all instances of the Invoice object.
define extent allInvoices for Invoice;

// Define the query
select    i
from      i in allInvoices,
        e in i.entries
where       e.product.list_price < 10
and         e.product.list_price > 4
and         i.customer =  F*;
```

This query finds all invoices for customers whose names begin with "F" that have entries for products whose price is between 4 and 10. Despite the complexity of the query, the query itself is quite readable because it uses the semantics of the Java classes directly to formulate conditions.

After a query is created, the execute() method can be called to return the results. The type of the object returned can vary depending on the specifics of the query. Listing 9.12 shows an example of how the query can be executed and results dealt with.

**Listing 9.12   Performing an OQL Query and Printing the Results**

```
{
            System.out.println("\nSelecting all Employee Objects");
            String qs = "define extent allEmployees for Employee;" +
            "select p from p in allEmployees   ";

            OQLQuery query = new OQLQuery(qs);
            Object result = query.execute();
            if (result instanceof CollectionOfObject) {
                Enumeration e = ((CollectionOfObject)result).createIterator();
                while (e.hasMoreElements())
➥System.out.println(e.nextElement());
            } else
                System.out.println(result);
        }


        {
            System.out.println("\nSelecting any Employee Objects that are in
➥Dept 2");

            String qs = "define extent allEmployees for Employee;" +
            "select p from p in allEmployees " +
            "where p.dept.Dept_Nbr = 6789";

            OQLQuery query = new OQLQuery(qs);
            Object result = query.execute();
            if (result instanceof CollectionOfObject) {
                Enumeration e = ((CollectionOfObject)result).createIterator();
                while (e.hasMoreElements())
➥System.out.println(e.nextElement());
            } else
                System.out.println(result);
        }
```

The following is the output of Listing 9.12:

```
Selecting all Employee Objects
Employee Name: Joe Smith   SSN: 555-55-5555
Employee Name: Lucky Schmoe  SSN: 777-77-7777
Employee Name: Paul Order   SSN: 1234-56-7890
Employee Name: Number Nine   SSN: 999-99-9999

Selecting any Employee Objects that are in Dept 2
Employee Name: Lucky Schmoe  SSN: 777-77-7777
Employee Name: Paul Order   SSN: 1234-56-7890
```

# ODL—Object Definition Language

The ODMG defines a set of syntax for defining the objects that will be saved in the object database. Each object has a set of attributes that will be saved. Relationships, including cardinality between objects, are identified, and keys for the object are noted.

Several vendors have created alternative methods for creating empty data structures inside the ODBMS. The following diagram (Figure 9.2) depicts some of the most common methods.

**FIG. 9.2**

Methods for creating Object Schemas.

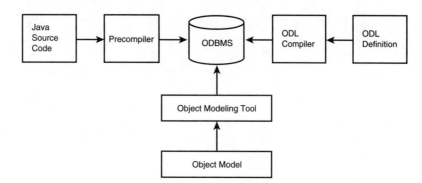

# From Here...

This chapter has presented an overview of the ODMG specification for object database management systems. Just as relational databases revolutionized the storage of data during the last decade, ODBMS will alter the way companies organize and store their data. Understanding and using ODBMS will provide companies with powerful tools for gathering, storing, retrieving, and exchanging information.

- Chapter 3, "A Simple JDBC Application," will cover the basic connections, drivers, and driver management associated with the JDBC, and introduce a framework for the rest of Part I.

- Chapter 4, "Executing SQL Statements," discusses how to query a SQL database and use getXXX methods to retrieve results.

- Chapter 7, "Object/Relational Mapping," discusses the mapping of relational tables to Java objects.

# CHAPTER 10

# Delivering the Application

**S**everal software industry reports have stated that the single reason to use the Java language is for its ability to be quickly rolled out. Through the use of Java-enabled network computers or through Java-enabled browsers, applications can easily be deployed. This model suggests that the application be reloaded each time the user runs the application. Anyone who has done a massive rollout of a client/server system knows that it can be a very costly effort. Resources are needed to fix bugs, control revisions, and, perhaps most costly, to redistribute the software to potentially thousands of users. After a system goes out, developers generally say their prayers and hope that all the bugs were caught. The Java model that has been praised by the press appears to alleviate many of the roll-out concerns. It also creates new issues, such as the amount of time that it takes to send a large Java application to a client, especially when the bandwidth is minimal. This chapter reviews the options for delivering Java applications and suggests methods to overcome some of the common obstacles. ■

**Storing the application**

Review the options for storing the application code.

**Options for executing Java on the client**

Java facilitates several models for running Java applications on the client. This section reviews the options.

**Code replication mechanisms**

Code replication schemes have been popularized by the Java environment.

**Addressing slow load times**

Several methods can be used to address the slow load times associated with large Java applications.

**Delivery via the Internet**

Using the Internet to deliver applications can be a very effective means to reach your business partners.

# Which Delivery Model to Use?

Perhaps the first question you need to answer is this: "What type of delivery model will the application use?" The most common options are illustrated in Table 10.1.

### Table 10.1   Delivery Model Options

| Location Where Java Code Is Stored | Vehicle for Executing the Java Application/Applet |
|---|---|
| Web Server | Web Browser |
| Network File Server | Web Browser |
| Local Hard Drive | Web Browser |
| Network File Server | AppletViewer |
| Local Hard Drive | AppletViewer |
| Network File Server | Java Virtual Machine (local) |
| Local Hard Drive | Java Virtual Machine (local) |
| Network File Server | Java Virtual Machine (Network) |
| Local Hard Drive | Java Virtual Machine (Network) |
| Castanet Transmitter | Castanet Tuner |
| Web Server | Network Computer |

## Storage Options for the Runnable Code

In most client/server applications, there are two choices for delivering the application. You either put the code on the network or you put it on the local PC. These options still exist with Java applications; in addition, there are some new options.

**Web Servers**   Much of Java's popularity is based on the applets that people have loaded from Web servers. The applet's dynamic loading architecture demonstrates a simple way to move some runnable piece of Java code from a server to a client. Like all delivery mechanisms, Web servers have their pros and cons.

**Web Server Pros**   The Web server is a very viable option for delivering small applications to a large number of people. This is the category that most of the Java applets on the Internet fall into and obviously it is the choice for Internet applets. Using Web servers for intranet applications is also an option. If the application needs to cross several sub-nets, rather than having a client machine map to several file servers, it may be easier to have an HTML page point to the IP address or host name of the Web server.

**Web Server Cons**   Unfortunately, most Web servers are not tuned to deliver large applications. Most servers are unable to determine which files make up an application and only send those files as the client asks for them. This inability tends to slow down the delivery process. This problem is partially overcome by compressing the Java `.class` files. An additional problem with Web servers is in granting security rights. Most large corporations have several network administrators that spend quite a bit of their time verifying that only the proper people have access to their own applications. Many Web servers do not offer the ability to keep certain people out of applications. Makers of the Web servers recommend that either hidden pages be used to house the Java applets or to use a CGI-secured page.

---

### What Is a Hidden Page?

A *hidden page* is an HTML document whose URL address is not published or linked in from any other HTML pages. Only users who know the proper URL can access the page. This type of security keeps many individuals from accessing documents that they shouldn't. In no way consider this a good security practice. It will not keep the address from traveling by way of word-of-mouth or through hackers' newsgroups.

---

Part
I

Ch
10

Although not directly a problem with Web server technology, a problem does exist in the manner in which servers are operated. Currently, many Web servers are not kept in traditional glass houses where operations staff can manage the hardware and the status of the software. If Web servers are to be used to deploy production applications, they should have the same attention paid to them that a file server has. This includes UPS power backup, mirrored hard drives, and housing in a safe and secure environment.

Both Web server and Web browser technology rely on the TCP/IP protocol. Many organizations either do not have support for this networking protocol or only have a mixed network environment that only has partial support. The Java language does not directly rely on the TCP/IP protocol, and thus this protocol should not be considered a disabler in deploying Java applications.

**File Servers**   File servers, such as those from Novell and Microsoft, are perhaps the most common means for delivering applications. Although Web servers may displace the use of file servers to deploy Java applications, you should still strongly consider file servers.

**File Server Pros**   Virtually every company has a file server of some kind. This technology is both stable and mature. Administrative tools are usually advanced and the feature sets that the file servers have are generally robust. Typically, individuals are available on-site who have extensive experience in dealing with file server issues. It has been my experience that when a file server goes down, it gets immediate attention, whereas when a Web server goes down people do tend to it, but in a less immediate fashion.

**File Server Cons**   Without a doubt, the largest problem in delivering applications via a file server is getting all of the clients to map a drive letter to the file server. This process usually requires having an individual go from machine to machine setting up network mappings. This burden can be alleviated by using network boot routines. These routines are used to automatically map a client machine to as many file servers as needed.

As with Web servers, some period of time is required to load the software across the network. Most networks still move data at 10 megabits per second. Newer hardware and networking protocols will move the traffic at 100 megabits per second. This will tremendously decrease the amount of time that an application takes to load off of a network. It may be worthwhile to review your networking architecture as well as your future plans to determine how crucial an issue this will be.

**Local Hard Drives**    Stand-alone applications are quite common in the PC environment. It is not unusual for an application to be stored on a network file server and then loaded onto the local hard drive of a computer. Expect for less software to be loaded locally in the Java arena. History tells us that if there is a quicker way to load an application, people will probably use it, regardless of the operational cost.

*Local Hard Drive Pros*    The most obvious benefit of running software from a local hard drive is the reduction in load time. This benefit may be dwindling in importance as faster networking technology is making its way into enterprises. Fast Ethernet and ATM solutions are moving data at a much faster rate. As companies move to these technologies, the need for local copies of software will reduce. Another benefit of having the code local is for security reasons. If the application itself is considered confidential, it may be intercepted by third parties if the application is transferred over the network.

*Local Hard Drive Cons*    Because of the revision control and configuration management issues associated with running corporate applications from a local hard drive, it is not generally recommended that you do this. Reloading Java files to hundreds of PCs can be a very time-consuming and costly operation. In addition, the costs associated with hard drive usage must be considered.

If load time is an issue, consider using a mix of storage mediums. One potential option is to load all of the common classes such as the Java packages and third-party class libraries to the local hard drive and only deliver the application software through the network. This hybrid will make most of the software easily accessible by the virtual machine, while putting the more volatile software in a network environment where it can be updated quickly.

# Options for Executing Java on the Client

You have seen that there are several options for storing Java code on servers for multiple clients to easily access. The decision of which method to use will go in hand with the solution for executing the Java code on the client machine.

**Web Browsers**   Web browsers, such as Netscape Navigator and Microsoft Internet Explorer, are the most popular means of executing Java applets due to their ability to conveniently download software at runtime. The Web browser has the ability to load a complete application to the local hard drive and then send the code to a Java virtual machine that is packaged with the Web browser. It should be noted that not all Web browsers have the ability to execute Java applets. All of the popular browsers including those from Microsoft and Netscape do have this functionality. The Web browser vendors have faced a number of hurdles in the integration of the Java Virtual Machine into their HTML browsers. Issues of security, fast downloads, and a consistent look and feel have been raised. Each new version of the browser software fixes many of the problems that the user community has raised.

*Web Browser Pros*   Much of the popularity of Java is based on its ability to run inside of most Web browsers. A user can be surfing through HTML documents, encounter one that has a Java applet built into it, and, without the user explicitly performing any function, the Java applet will load and begin execution. This model of integrating, loading, and executing takes users to a whole new level of simplicity. Because the code is loaded from scratch each time, the user is guaranteed to get the latest copy of the software (if they are using either a Web server or a file server). By embedding applications directly into HTML, an application can easily be delivered with the associated documentation. Developers will save time by not having to package special online help routines in various formats.

Perhaps the best reasons to use a Web browser for executing Java applications are still in the future. Netscape has stated that its browser will support the IIOP standard for distributed communications (Internet Inter-Operability Protocol). This could launch a new wave of distributed, event-based computing that supports peer-to-peer and multi-tiered environments. In addition, Netscape is also working with vendors to support object persistence at the client. This is essential to performing offline computing activities. The network model that most browsers use may eventually be augmented with data and code replication schemas, such as those available from Marimba (see "A Closer Look at Castanet"). It is clear that Netscape is making a commitment to turning a simple tool like a browser into a powerful enterprise computing environment. This effort will only raise the bar of competition for companies like Microsoft and IBM/Lotus.

*Web Browser Cons*   Perhaps the big question is why should any application embed a Java Virtual Machine inside of itself? Should all Java applications be deployed with a JVM? Drawing the line in determining which applications should have a JVM is a tricky issue. Technologies such as PointCast, LotusNotes, and others are looking at embedding this technology inside their products. Many people believe that the Java Virtual Machine belongs in the operating system and that it does not belong in every shrink-wrapped piece of Java software that hits the market. Web browsers have a certain set of features that make them attractive. Java Virtual Machines also have a set of features that distinguish them from their competition. Relying on

Part

I

Ch

10

a combination browser/JVM technology may force users to pick a technology. Abstracting the browser from the underlying JVM will allow a company to pick the proper technology for the job. Relying on your Web browser to be your Java platform may not be a good strategic move. If your operating system embeds a JVM into it, it may be wiser to launch your Java applications from the JVM owned by the operating system.

**Additional Notes on Web Browser Usage**    Industry analysts such as the Gartner Group and Forrester Research believe that the use of Web browsers is the area where the greatest cost savings will be. Early estimates state that the cost of maintaining a PC that uses the Web browser will be significantly less than the current model of loading software at each client. The early numbers suggest that the cost of ownership could be reduced by 30 to 40 percent. This estimate makes the following assumptions:

- Companies that have diverse client computing platforms (Windows, Macintosh, UNIX, and so on) will be able to use a single browser across the various platforms to execute a Java application. Perhaps more importantly, the application will behave uniformly across the platforms.

- Individuals in companies will not spend an unusually large amount of time loading browser software. Early indications have shown that users will download new versions of the browser software from the Internet and spend significant amounts of time installing and testing the latest browser.

Making these assumptions may be a leap-of-faith for the seasoned information specialist. Before hopping on the browser bandwagon, developers and managers should strongly consider all of the options.

**Java Virtual Machines**    The Java Virtual Machine is the runtime interpreter for Java byte-code. Java Virtual Machines (JVM) are typically packaged with other software such as groupware products or browsers. In addition, the JVM can be used as a stand-alone application. Java applications can be launched from command lines or icons by specifying the name of the JVM followed by the application name and classpath.

**AppletViewer**    The AppletViewer utility that is packaged with the JDK from JavaSoft was intended to be a vehicle for testing Java applets. It was not intended to be a means to roll out production applications. Unless JavaSoft invests in the product, beefing up its functionality, it should be avoided in the production arena.

**Compiling Java Code to Binary**    One item of contention in the Java society is the compiling of Java code to native machine code. Java purists believe that the primary perks of Java are its machine-independent nature and its dynamic loading model. To Java purists, the very notion of compiling a Java application disgusts them. But in the corporate world, you are writing software in response to a business problem. The technical means to achieving the solution must be of a secondary nature. If an application does not work fast enough using a JVM or a Just-in-Time Compiler, then a very acceptable solution is to compile the application.

Compiling a Java application will present some new challenges:

- Delivery via a Web browser is no longer an option.
- Versions must be recompiled for each platform that will be used.
- Dynamic loading of classes will not be possible.

Compiling an application has its benefits as well:

- Compiled applications typically will run several times faster than those interpreted by standard JVMs or by just-in-time compilers.
- When delivering an application via a removable medium (CD-ROM, diskette, and so on) it may be much easier to deliver a single executable file than delivering a Java Virtual Machine plus the application.
- The signing of JVM license agreements can be avoided by building executables, usually royalty-free.
- Decompilers for the executable are not currently available, whereas bytecode files can easily be reverse engineered into the original source. (See "The Mocha Controversy" in Chapter 11.)

**Network Computers**   The Network Computer (NC) is a topic of much interest today. Unfortunately, the industry has not quite agreed to exactly what an NC is. Generally, people agree that an NC has the following characteristics:

- It is a piece of hardware that has a CPU and local memory.
- The machine can easily be connected to a network.
- The machine connects to standard peripherals like video, keyboard, and mouse.

Although not consistent across all vendor offerings, several other common characteristics can be noted:

- The machines are usually less expensive than a personal computer.
- The machine depends fully on the network to load software.
- The machine does not have a local hard drive for persistence.
- The machine has a built-in Java Virtual Machine.

Several characteristics that vary widely by vendor include:

- CPU: Intel, Motorola, Sun, and so on
- Boot-up software
- Number of peripherals: Flash cards, multiple serial ports, parallel ports, expansion cards, and so on

Most of the excitement that has been generated by the Network Computer is the lower cost of delivery. If the NC uses a truly dynamic load model, there would be no need to ever install or upgrade software. In addition, the NC is typically a much less complex environment than the

Part

I

Ch

10

PC. Administration costs and procurement costs are typically much lower than found in a comparable PC environment. Unlike the PC, the NC is a new architecture that has not been proven. With the emphasis that hardware vendors are putting behind the architecture, one can assume that eventually this platform will be a very viable option.

# Code Replication Mechanisms

The Web browsers demonstrated that there were easier ways to roll out applications to large numbers of people. A new genre of applications are employing techniques to automatically replicate software between server and client locations. This delivery model offers some of the best features of Web browsers without some of the negatives. By using a replication schema, the user can be assured that they are running the latest version of the software. Typically, a tool (such as Marimba's Castanet or Lotus Notes) will be responsible for updating local client code with any changes that may have been made on the server. Since the code is run locally, rather than downloading the entire piece of software each time, the amount of time to load the application can be significantly reduced.

Most of the replication tools are still in their infancy, but their future looks very promising. Users should eventually expect the replication tools' "desktop" to mix the delivery of canned software with the delivery of internally developed systems. As these products mature, features such as integrated security, usage monitors, persistence repositories, and pay-per-use functionality will be included.

**A Closer Look at Castanet**   In early 1996, several of the original members of the Java development team left the newly formed JavaSoft business division to start a new Java company named Marimba. Within a few months, the group presented their first product, Castanet. The Castanet software performs code synchronization to client machines using several different components.

1. **Castanet Transmitters**—The transmitter is the server where one puts a production application after it is completed. The transmitter sends normal Java applets/applications across the network on what Marimba has dubbed "Channels."

2. **Channels**—Using the television metaphor, the channel implies that it is a service that is always available, waiting for a client to "tune in" to the program. In this case, the program isn't a TV show but a Java application. The channel also can be used to deliver multiple types of content such as music or pictures. The current state of the channel architecture does not support real-time streaming, so delivery of multimedia content on demand is currently out of its scope.

3. **Castanet Tuners**—The tuner software is the portion that runs on each client's computer. Each tuner can subscribe to as many channels (or Java applications) as the user is interested in. A tuner downloads the Java code from a transmitter. If the code on the transmitter has changed since the last download, only the changed code is sent to the client. By keeping the code cached at the client, the tuner is able to launch a Java application much more quickly than browsers can.

4. **Castanet Repeaters**—In order to scale the delivery of code to thousands of users, the Castanet technology uses a series of repeaters. Each repeater accepts the latest version of the software from the transmitter, and then takes the responsibility to deliver the code to the tuners. As many repeaters can be added as necessary to create a scalable architecture.

**The Future of Replication**    The Castanet suite presents a simple model for delivering applications to large numbers of people without the downside of reinstalling or long download times. This model will surely be used by other vendors. Companies like PointCast have already developed software that uses the Internet to "broadcast to subscribers." A natural evolution of their software is to not only move content, but to also get in the business of moving software. The Lotus company has extensive experience in code replication techniques from their Lotus Notes product. The Lotus (IBM) group is a strong supporter of the Java initiative; it would be very surprising if they failed to enter this market with a top-notch product. Last, Microsoft could enter this arena. Why? If there is money in a particular market, Microsoft tends to find its way to that corner of the world.

The players in code and data replication facilities are still coming out. Regardless of which vendor is used, large information shops should take a strong look at using this technology. The ability to redeploy a large application is in line with the iterative or spiral methodologies supported in most client/server shops today, and it has a place in the client/networking shops of tomorrow.

**Part**

**I**

**Ch**

**10**

# Application Load Time

Several of the issues associated with choosing a model to deliver a Java application were based on the amount of time it would take for the application to load. This problem is partially due to network speeds, but other factors play a role as well.

## Virtual Machine Byte Code Checks

Much of the blame in slow loading Java applications is improperly placed on network speeds or slow browsers. Actually, the Java security model is one of the culprits. Remember that the Java Virtual Machine will run a byte code verifier on each class as it is loaded in. This process will verify that the Java compiler did not improperly create the `.class` file, and no hacker modified the byte code in its native format. Load times will eventually decrease as new, faster algorithms for checking the byte code are released. Until then, verify that the problem is not a network issue by loading the software from a local source.

## Modular Design

The term "Modular Design" has a different meaning in Java than it would have had in most languages. Typically, a system is modular if it has been broken into distinct pieces. This process facilitates writing very large applications by taking a large problem and breaking it down into many smaller problems. Java takes this concept one step farther. In addition to breaking the development into modules, Java applications can dynamically load the modules at runtime. This means that if a piece of an application is not used during a session, then it is never read from the source (hard drive, network, and so on) nor is time spent verifying its byte code or loading it into memory. This type of modular design, also known as delayed construction, will be essential in writing applications that are based on the pure networking model where the applet or application is loaded across the network from scratch each time. The BootStrap application that is presented in Listing 10.1 will also work for loading modules.

The dynamic loading model obviously will work only for applications that maintain a persistent connection to the file source. Many Web applications are designed where the user can download an applet, and then disconnect from the Internet while continuing to use the applet. This scenario will not work for the dynamic loading model since the user will not be aware of when the files would be loaded from the Web server.

# Perceived Load Time

By performing dynamic loading of modules you can actually reduce the amount of time that is required for an applet or application to load. In addition to the actual load time is the perceived load time, that is, the amount of time that a user believes it takes for an application to load. For some reason, Java programmers have forgotten about two of the oldest tricks in the book: the splash screen and the progress bar. Neither of these items actually speeds up the load process, but they often reduce the user's annoyance of not knowing whether the application is loading or not.

**The Splash Screen**    The splash screen is perhaps the simplest means to distract the user while an application is loading. A splash screen often doubles as the "About" window under the "Help" menu. Typical splash screens will display:

- Product or system name
- Company name and logo
- Product version number
- Copyrights and license information

Splash screens will usually extend the Window class. (A Window is a top-level window with no borders and no menubar.) There are two tricks to implementing a splash screen; one is the loading of the image into the window, whereas the other is the implementation of a delayed construction routine (see the section, "Delayed Construction"). Listing 10.1 is the source code for a splash screen.

## Listing 10.1  *SplashScreen* Source Code

```java
import java.awt.*;

public class SplashScreen extends Window {

    Image img;
```

```
    public SplashScreen(String FileName) {
      super(new Frame());
      // All image functionality in applications comes from the default
      ➥toolkit.
      this.img = Toolkit.getDefaultToolkit().getImage(FileName);
      this.show();
    }

    // imageUpdate is called when the specified image is done loading.
    public boolean imageUpdate(Image img, int flags, int x, int y, int w, int h){
      if ((flags & this.ALLBITS) !=0) {
        // resize the window to be the same size as the image.
        this.resize(img.getWidth(this),img.getHeight(this));
        this.show();
      }
      return true;

    }

    public void paint(Graphics g) {
      // Actually draw the image.
      g.drawImage(img,1,1,new Color(191,191,191),this);
    }
  }
```

**The Progress Bar**    The progress bar, like the splash screen, will slow down the actual load time for an application. It will reassure the user that the system is actually doing something, which tends to be their greatest concern.

In order to implement either the splash screen or the progress bar, delayed construction techniques must be used. Remember that in a normal application, the application will not start until the entire application is loaded in. By this time, it is too late for either the splash screen or the progress bar to serve its purpose.

Since the JDK didn't package a progress bar as a standard widget, and most progress bars behave differently, I have opted not to show the implementation details of growing a progress bar. Rather, I have created a delayed construction routine that can load class files one at a time. All your application needs is a list of files that the BootStrap routine can read in and loop through!

# Delayed Construction

The delayed construction routine is a small application that loads quickly into memory. After loading, the routine can be used to load the application that the user wants to execute. Since your Java application is responsible for loading the application (rather than the browser or the default class loader), techniques such as progress bars and splash screens can be kicked off prior to the completion of the application load routine.

Listing 10.2 shows an example of a delayed construction routine called BootStrap. Without rewriting a ClassLoader routine, it would be difficult to obtain the granular level of loading that takes place. When an application specifies a class to load, by default all dependent classes are loaded automatically. Thus, if you were to load the mainframe class of your application, one call to the class loader would load the entire application by default. On the other hand, if you were to look at your application as a tree hierarchy, where the top root node is the `public static void main` class and all nodes below it are classes that the are used in the application, one would realize that the application could be loaded from the leaf nodes up, rather than the root node down. By doing this, you can call for each class by name, which gives you the granularity to control a progress bar.

---

**Listing 10.2  *BootStrap* Source Code**

```java
import java.io.*;

public class BootStrap {

    public static void main (String args[]) {

        byte[] input = new byte[25];

        try {
            //Load the splash screen first.
    //Remember to double up your backslashes in Strings!
            SplashScreen ss = new SplashScreen("d:\\t10.gif");

            //Begin loop, read file names from some source....
                System.in.read(input);
                String s = new String(input,0x00);
                System.out.println(s.trim().length());
                Class tf = Class.forName(s.trim());
                tf.newInstance();
            // end loop
            System.in.read(input);
        }
        catch (IOException ioe) {System.out.println(ioe);}
        catch (InstantiationException ie) {System.out.println(ie);}
        catch (ClassNotFoundException cnfe) {System.out.println(cnfe);}
        catch (IllegalAccessException iae) {System.out.println(iae);}
    } // end of the main method

} // end of class BootStrap
```

---

The `BootStrap` routine gives the application more control over the loading of the `.class` files. Control over the loading of the `java.*` packages will be limited; thus, the first call to load a GUI class will probably result in the loading of several of the AWT classes. By using the `Class.forName()` and the `newInstance()` methods, entire modules can be loaded dynamically by merely instantiating the main class for the module.

# Avoiding the "Auto-Launch" Syndrome

Java Applets have been praised for their ability to automatically launch, but this feature also can be a nuisance on low-bandwidth networks (like modem access to the Internet). One option is to use a "Delayed Construction" technique along with a Launch Button. In this scenario, a small applet is loaded and presents the user with a button. The button will usually say something like, "Launch Application." If the user clicks the button, the application will be loaded and started. Often an applet will contain several launch buttons, offering the user a menu of applications to choose from. Listing 10.3 shows the applet Launch Button routine.

### Listing 10.3   Applet Launch Button Routine

```
import java.applet.*;
import java.awt.*;

public class LaunchApplet extends Applet
{
    Button LaunchButton = new Button("Launch");
    public void init()
    {
        setLayout(new FlowLayout());
        add(LaunchButton);
    }

    public boolean handleEvent(Event e)
    {
       if(e.target == LaunchButton)
       {
            theFrame tf = new theFrame();
            tf.resize(200,200);
            tf.show();
       }
        return false;
    }


}

class theFrame extends Frame
{
    public boolean handleEvent(Event e)
    {
       if(e.id == Event.WINDOW_DESTROY)
       {
        System.exit(0);
       }
        return false;
    }
}
```

Part
I

Ch
10

## Compression Techniques

Due to the slow downloading times of Java code from Web servers, several companies have implemented techniques for compressing .class files into a single file. Currently, there are three popular methods to compress multiple files into a single file. They are shown in Table 10.2.

### Table 10.2   Multiple File Compression

| Compression Name | File Extension | Supported By |
| --- | --- | --- |
| Java Archive | .jar | JavaSoft |
| ZIPped File | .zip | Netscape (old JavaSoft method) |
| Cabinets | .cab | Microsoft |

**Java Archive Files**   The .jar file is new to the JDK 1.1. It solves the largest problem of delivering large applications via a Web server, which is the sending of each file in a separate transaction. By moving all of the .class files, graphic files, data files, and audio files into a single file, a tremendous amount of time can be saved in the transfer. In addition, the Java Archive format relies heavily on the compression techniques that are used in the traditional zipped format. Additionally, individual entries in a JAR file may be digitally signed by the author to authenticate their origin.

**Creating Java Archive Files**   The JDK 1.1 introduces a new utility appropriately called "Jar.exe". This tool is used from the command line to create a new .jar container and add the .class files to the container. In addition, certain information about the files is stored in a new file called the manifest file.

As with most of the JDK command line tools, the Jar utility accepts several flags to change options. The Jar utility does not require using a hyphen character in front of the parameter, and the parameters can be strung together.

> **c**         Creates a Java archive file.
>
> **t**         Lists the contents of an existing .jar file.
>
> **m**        Specifies a manifest file to add to the .jar.
>
> **x** *file*    Extracts all files, or just the named files. If the file name is omitted, then all files are extracted; otherwise, only the specified file or files are extracted.
>
> **f**         If the preceding flag was "c," then "f" specifies the name of the new .jar file. If the preceding flag was "t" or "x," then "f" identifies the .jar file to be listed or extracted.
>
> **v**         Switches to verbose output.

To add all .class files in the current directory, use:

```
jar cvf brandNewJar.jar *
```

When adding files to .jar, the directory path will be added if the Jar utility is not run from the same directory as the .class files or if the directory path is specified when adding the files. This is acceptable if you are importing a class library and the directory structure needs to be maintained; otherwise, it may put your classes in a location where the browser or AppletViewer cannot find them. To verify that the files are placed in the correct location, list the contents of the .jar file.

To list the contents of an existing Java archive, use:

```
jar tf someExistingJar.jar
```

Using directory structures in .jar files is common for storage of data files. Typically, a directory would be created for each type of data:

```
\images\t1.gif
\images\t1.gif
\images\t1.gif
\audio\muzac.au
\audio\country.au
```

Jar files have the ability to be digitally signed. More information on digitally signing a .jar can be found in the security section.

***Launching Java Archive Files***    To launch an applet from a .jar, use the Applet tag in your HTML document, as shown in Listing 10.4.

---

**Listing 10.4**   ***Applet* Tag**

```
<applet code=BootStrap.class
  archives="BootStrap.jar"
  width=200 height=200>
  <param name=MainFile value="TheMainClass">
</applet>
```

---

Files can be shared between Java archives by specifying multiple .jar files for a given resource:

```
    archives = "classes.jar +  System1.jar +   FrameWork.jar"
```

**Zipped Files**    The JDK 1.0x has built-in support for using .zip files that are in accordance with the PKWARE standard. The JDK is packaged with all of the files in the classes.zip file for easy reference. Currently, files that are stored in .zip format cannot be compressed. Most of the major zipping utilities allow files to be added using no compression techniques. Utilities such as WinZip support this feature, as well as the ability to store long file names. Many of the older zip routines will truncate the file names to the DOS 8.3 notation. Since the Java class files must mimic the name of the object, truncating file names will cause severe trouble!

Listing 10.4 shows the HTML tag used to launch an applet that is stored in a .zip format. The archive keyword will point the browser to the location of the .zip file. If no path is specified, the browser assumes that the file is in the same directory as the HTML document that is launching it. If .class files are used that are in packages, the directory structure that describes the package name must be moved in its entirety to the .zip file. If a package of COM.MyCompany.Project1 was used, the files in the package should be stored in the .zip file using a directory structure like: \COM\MyCompany\Project1\MainFile.class. Make sure that directory and file names remain in the correct case as they are transferred to .zip containers.

Listing 10.5 shows the syntax that is used to launch an applet when the Java byte code is stored in a .zip file.

**Listing 10.5  *Applet* Tag for Zipped Files**

```
<applet archive="AllFiles.zip"

  code="MainFile.class"

  width=100 height=100>

    </applet>
```

**Cabinet Files**  Microsoft supports a file format called Cabinets for the storage of Java .class files. Currently, Microsoft is the only company that is supporting this technique. The life expectancy of this format may be limited with the announcement of the .jar file from JavaSoft. Most large-scale development projects are expected to use the Java Archive over the Cabinet. To obtain more information on using Cabinets, please reference the Microsoft Web site at **http:\\www.microsoft.com\java**.

# Delivery via the Internet

The Internet has received significant attention in the computing arena since the advent of the World Wide Web and the browser. The Internet was designed to be a mission-critical network that could "survive" a nuclear war. As the twenty-first century nears, users are less concerned about a nuclear war taking the Net down, and more concerned about the traffic of millions of users bringing it to a halt. This has not kept ambitious companies from leveraging the Internet as a vehicle for communication.

Enterprises are looking at using the Internet in three ways:

1. To deliver public information to the masses.
2. To deliver semi-private information to business partners.
3. To deliver private information to remote sites and offices.

# Delivery to the Masses

The exact number of users on the Internet seems to be an area of controversy; some agencies have put the number of users at 30 million, while others have stated numbers closer to 80 million. Regardless, the Internet is a popular tool that more and more people are joining daily.

Most companies have created a "Web presence," meaning they have put information about their company out on the Web. This will usually include: Company history, product information, support documents, marketing material, and so on. This type of information is fairly static in nature; that is, they are documents whose content do not change very often.

A handful of companies have created "dynamic" Web pages. The dynamic Web page is one whose content is changed based on input from the user. Typically, a user will request some piece of information from an HTML interface and send their input to a CGI routine located on a Web Server. The CGI routine will perform a database lookup and format the returned data as an HTML document. This document is then sent back to the client's Web browser where they can view the data. Since the data is presented in HTML format, the advanced user interface techniques are not available to the user. For instance, HTML does not have the ability to perform client-side integrity checks. This lack of functionality is often diminished by using JavaScript to enhance functionality. Although Javascript can perform many features that HTML cannot, it is still a scripting language, not a full-fledged programming language like Java.

Only a few companies have deployed Java applications to the public. This is mostly due to the long amount of time that it takes for an application to be downloaded. With the use of Java Archive files, browser caching techniques, and faster communication lines, the delivery time for Java applets will become much more acceptable. Companies should be planning for the scenario where applications are delivered to the end-user or consumer of their products or services.

**Part**

**I**

**Ch**

**10**

---

### Notes on CGI

CGI is an acronym for Common Gateway Interface. CGI is a specification for receiving and sending data. A CGI routine is usually a compiled piece of code written in C or C++ that is placed on a Web Server. The CGI routine is designed to accept input from HTML documents, process the information, and then send formatted data back to the client. Java-based CGI template files are available at the Gamelan site, **www.gamelan.com**.

---

# Delivery to Business Partners

One of the most popular uses of the Internet in the enterprise is using the Internet as a communication vehicle to trading partners, suppliers, vendors, resellers and customers. Previously, corporations conducted business by phone, fax, mail, or in person. The Internet adds another means to conduct business, and an efficient one at that. Intercompany commerce on the Internet is expected to continue to grow at a rapid pace. New security mechanisms are allowing private transactions to take place on public lines. JavaSoft has recognized that the Java language can play an important part in intercompany commerce and has created a new API that facilitates transactions. This API is called the Java Electronic Commerce Framework, or JECF.

The JECF is designed to be a standard way for Java applications to perform basic commerce. JECF is in a design phase at the time of this writing, but its intent is to facilitate digital cash and provide a mechanism for securely purchasing items over the Internet.

The JECF does not discuss many of the standard transactions that occur in everyday business. For years, companies have been using ANSI X.12 (E.D.I., or Electronic Data Interchange) records for moving data between trading partners in a standard way. The X.12 transactions are typically used in a batch environment. Java, with its event-driven model, offers an excellent alternative to performing batch transactions. This would allow a company to update its suppliers or distributors of information in a near-real-time manner. Rather than waiting for a batch of records to be accumulated, each transaction or record would be sent to the trading partner. The trading partner would either accept or deny the transaction, but would always send a reply back to the originator in a timely fashion. Unfortunately, many of the standard transactions that are defined in X.12 have not been ported to an event-driven model. This is forcing businesses that want to use the Internet/Java/Transaction model to develop proprietary transaction sets. One can assume that a more open and robust architecture is not far away.

## Delivery to Remote Offices

Most large companies have branch offices located in remote environments. Traditionally, these companies have created their own internal network to communicate between offices. With the advent of the Internet, many companies are looking at using this infrastructure to provide a low-cost alternative to proprietary networks. A new breed of networks have emerged that are often referred to as Virtual Private Networks. The VPN can be defined as a secure intranet on the Internet that uses software or hardware to ensure data integrity and enforce privacy. Advantages of the VPN include:

- Allows you to use the Internet as a low-cost wide area backbone
- Reduces leased-line telecommunications costs
- Supports low-cost telecommuting and organization-to-organization communications
- Uses authentication and encryption features to ensure secure business-critical communication over the Internet
- Frees IS managers from the burden of building and managing private networks

Virtual Private Networks are usually implemented in both hardware and software. The hardware may double as a router or as a secured firewall station. Software is used to verify authentication between remote sites and implement encryption of data. Many of the VPN packages are now built directly into firewall solutions, while others are used as add-ons, complementing the overall security package.

The introduction of the VPN has enabled a new means of delivering enterprise applications to remote sites. Java and its network delivery model are able to take full advantage of this architecture. Installations of fat clients typical of the client/server era can be avoided. This model offers the ease of delivering a mainframe application (green screen sessions) with the robust GUI features found in client/server applications in one mechanism.

## Delivery to an International Audience

Java has a strong appeal to global companies. With the release of the JDK 1.1, Java has taken on an even stronger flair. A tremendous amount of support for multi-byte characters is now available. The common English character sets ASCII and EBCDIC both require a single byte to uniquely identify a character. Multi-byte storage containers enable complex character sets like Kanji to be represented in Java applications. The `InputStream` and `OutputStream` classes were augmented with a new set of classes for manipulating UNICODE characters (a two-byte character set). Other changes will be included in the new package `java.text` which supports text formatting, sorting, and so on. Additional support for localization resources is expected soon. Throughout the JDK, it is apparent that JavaSoft is attempting to make the language a viable environment for writing multilingual applications.

Part

I

Ch

10

# Online Help

The close relationship between Java and HTML browsers should be used to its fullest. Because a Java applet can be embedded directly into an HTML browser, it makes sense to create user documentation in HTML. Java applications have the ability to launch a browser if one is not open, and then pull up the desired HTML page.

In addition, many companies are using the internal Web pages as a holding ground for all of their Java applets. Web pages that hold applets will have links to other Web pages that also contain applets. This creates a simple method for navigating internal documentation and full-blown Java applets in the same medium (see Listings 10.6 and 10.7).

### Listing 10.6    HTML/Applet Navigation

```
<HTML>
<title>Java Applet Demo</title>
<h1> Page 1 </h1>
<applet code="OnlineHelp.class" width=400 height=650>
</applet>
</HTML>


import java.applet.*;
import java.awt.*;
import java.net.*;
```

*continues*

## Listing 10.6   Continued

```java
public class OnlineHelp extends Applet
{
    Canvas c;
    Button b;
    AppletContext ac;

    public void init()
    {
        ac = this.getAppletContext();
        Panel p = new Panel();
        setLayout(new FlowLayout());
        b = new Button("Goto Page 2");
        p.add(b);
        add(p);
    }

    public void paint(Graphics g)
    {
        g.drawString("Applet # 1",50,50);
    }

    public boolean handleEvent(Event e)
    {
        if ((e.target == b) && (e.id == Event.MOUSE_DOWN))
        {
            try
            {
                ac.showDocument(new URL("file:///D¦/Cafe/Projects/
                ➥Page2.html"),"_self");
            }
            catch(MalformedURLException mue) { System.out.println(mue);}
            return true;
        }
        return false;
    }
}
```

## Listing 10.7   The Target HTML File and Applet

```html
<HTML>
<title>Java Applet Demo</title>
<h1> Page 2 </h1>
<applet code="Page2.class" width=400 height=650>
</applet>
</HTML>
```

```java
import java.applet.*;
import java.awt.*;
import java.net.*;

public class Page2 extends Applet
```

```
{
    Canvas c;
    Button b;
    AppletContext ac;

    public void init()

    {
        ac = this.getAppletContext();
        Panel p = new Panel();
        setLayout(new FlowLayout());
        b = new Button("Goto Page 1");
        p.add(b);
        add(p);
    }


    public void paint(Graphics g)
    {
        g.drawString("Applet # 2",25,25);
    }

    public boolean handleEvent(Event e)
    {
        if ((e.target == b) && (e.id == Event.MOUSE_DOWN))
        {
            try
            {
             ac.showDocument(new
            URL("file:///D¦/Cafe/Projects/Throw_Away/OnlineHelp.html"),"_self");
            }
            catch(MalformedURLException mue) { System.out.println(mue);}
            return true;
        }
        return false;
    }
}
```

# From Here...

We have discussed many of the options for delivering a full-scale Java application. In addition to deployment options, there are several other issues related to the secured delivery of the application. The JDK 1.1 introduced several new features for ensuring a secured delivery.

- Chapter 11, "Securing Enterprise Information," discovers the dangers of moving sensitive information over the Internet and intranets.

- Chapter 12, "Introduction to Distributed Computing," will cover the basic concepts of distributed computing including DCE, RPC, and CORBA.

- Chapter 14, "Remote Objects," covers the basic RMI model, presents the RMI package, and demonstrates how it brings distributed computing to Java.

- Chapter 15, "Advanced RMI Concepts," discusses using RMI to tackle larger applications and expands on the topics in Chapter 14.

# CHAPTER 11

# Securing Enterprise Information

**S**ecurity is a top concern for large and small corporations. The Internet poses many threats from intruders. JavaSoft introduced the applet security model to remedy many of the issues associated with real-time, mass publication of software over a public medium. ■

### Understanding the Java security model

Discover the "sandbox" security model, as well as other advanced techniques that Java uses to ensure secured applications.

### Applet signing

Applet signing is a means of verifying the ownership of an applet. This section shows you how to sign your own applets.

### Decompiling Java byte-code

A new security risk has been uncovered with decompiler technology. Understand the risks that are associated with the decompilation of your code.

# Applet Security Model

Since applets can be loaded from any Web server on the Internet, the designers realized that it would be essential to modify their security model. Several limitations were introduced for applets in the JDK 1.0:

- Applets cannot read or write from the local hard drive. This means that a "bad" applet cannot modify or delete files on your local system, nor can it read sensitive documents and transmit them to a third party.

- All applets that are not signed are tagged with a disclaimer at the bottom of each window. The disclaimer reads that the application is not to be trusted. This prevents people from writing applications that would attempt to look like another application (like your e-mail client) and ask you for your password. After entering the password in the malicious applet, it could be sent back to the author of the applet.

- Applets can open a socket network connection only to the machine from which they were serviced (usually the Web server that housed it). This prevents an applet from passing through a firewall, then opening a socket connection to a database server (or other secure device) and guessing user IDs and passwords. If the applet were able to successfully find a secure device and break the security, it could read information and pass it back to a third party, without the user of the applet ever knowing. Perhaps more devastating, the applet could destroy information on the device.

- Applets cannot make calls to the operating system nor make any "native" code outside of the Java Virtual Machine. This includes calling any dynamic link libraries or executables on the client machine. If applets could make native calls, virtually all of the security would go out the window.

The applet security model is often referred to as the sandbox. The model suggests that an applet is allowed to happily play in its own sandbox. It should be able to do anything that it wants (in accordance with applet guidelines) without the user ever worrying about viruses or other malicious attacks. Overall, the sandbox model is an ideal means for delivering a simple piece of code to a mass audience. This model does not work for all types of applications. More sophisticated software requires writing files to hard drives or making socket connections. For this reason, Javasoft introduced applet signing.

## Applet Signing

The applet security model is a very limiting model to work within, especially for large robust applications. The security restrictions were put in place primarily because of the anonymity of the Internet. If individuals could write applets that damaged a user's hard drive, or stole information on a mass scale, people would eventually just stay away from the Web altogether. Obviously, this wasn't a viable choice; hence, the designers decided to loosen the security model on applets, but only if users explicitly state that they trust the applet will do no harm to their system or network.

How does the user know that the applet won't damage his or her system? Well, it all comes back to trust; either you trust the individuals or company that wrote and deployed the application or you don't. In order to establish trust, it must be determined whether the applet came from the source that we believe it came from. That is, did the individual or company that claims to have published this applet really publish it, or is someone acting as an impostor? Like a police officer who has pulled over a speeding motorist, the officer will note the license plate of the vehicle and ask the driver for his or her identification. The Web browser takes a similar precaution. To determine whether a group is really who they say they are, the Web browser will ask to see their ID. That means that people who publish software on the Internet must get a driver's license for the information superhighway.

**Trusted Applets**   Just as automobile drivers go to the local Department of Motor Vehicles and show their credentials like birth certificates and Social Security cards, software publishers on the Internet must go to a certificate authority (CA). The CA will perform background checks on the individual or group. If everything turns out OK, they will give you a certificate that states that you are who you say you are. They will keep this information on-hand and online so that others can verify that you are who you say you are. The certificate that you are issued is a unique identifier and is merely a series of bytes. The file that the software publisher is given is known as the "certificate."

**Certificates**   The certificate is your identification on the Internet. You may now publish software and present your ID to potential users. The users of the application now have the ability to look at your ID, determine whether they trust you, and run the software if they desire. The purpose of the certificate is to generate confidence in the legitimacy of a public key.

The next problem is verifying that the certificate that you were issued really belongs to you. Going back to our earlier example, it is much like verifying that you didn't steal someone else's driver's license. The driver's license, although not a perfect mechanism, uses two pieces of information to reduce this possibility. The combination of a picture of the individual and a description (hair color, weight, gender, etc.) diminishes the possibility of impostors using a fake ID. The certificate authority also uses two pieces of information, a public and a private key.

**Public and Private Keys**   The public and private keys are merely a series of bytes. By themselves they mean nothing; together they provide the necessary information to unlock the security mechanisms on Web browsers or other secured devices. The public and private keys are generated by either the CA or by a user who has an appropriate tool for generating keys (Java has a tool for generating keys called JavaKey). After generating the two keys, the user hides the private key from everyone. The public key is sent to the certificate authority and a copy is kept by the group publishing the software.

The group that wants to publish a Java applet on the Web should have the following items:

- Their Java application (all of the `.class` files)
- A digital certificate that identifies you or your organization
- A public key that you and some trusted group have (like a certificate authority)
- A private key that only you have

Typically, a software publishing company will create separate sets of keys for each application. Thus, if one key is stolen (or broken), the other applications are not compromised.

The certificate helps to verify that a public key is associated with an individual or company. It does not suggest that the software was not modified or potentially dangerous. It merely ties a public key to a responsible party. Certificates are generally used as a supplement to digitally signed software.

**Digital Signatures**    At this point, a "digital fingerprint" of the Java application can be taken. This fingerprint is used to verify that the application was not changed between the time that the developer fingerprinted the application up until the time the application arrived at a remote machine. In order to accomplish this, a utility is used to read the Java files and generate a new file that acts as a "signature" to the original file. When the application gets to the client machine, the signature is regenerated. The two signatures are compared to each other to verify that no changes took place. The slightest change in a signed application will cause the digital signature verification process to fail.

To verify that a third party did not intercept the application and provide a new signature, the application is signed with the private key. Only the public key of the publisher can decrypt the hash code for the application. Thus, the intended user of the application must either have the public key or have access to a certificate authority that has a copy of the key and is willing to send it to the user.

JavaSoft currently supports the Digital Signature Algorithm (DSA) for signing applets. DSA specifies an algorithm for generating public and private keys and for signing files. DSA is part of a larger initiative known as the Digital Signature Standard. This standard is currently supported by the U.S. government and was selected by NIST and NSA as the standard for digitally signing material. The DSA standard is often criticized for slow verification of signatures and for a lack of key exchange capabilities. RSA support is currently not available, but this situation could easily change.

**Clients and Digital Signatures**    Some client software is used to launch your Java applet/application. Typically, the launching software is a Web browser but could be any software that has a Java Virtual Machine (JVM). The client software will receive a Java applet/application, a digital signature, and potentially a certificate. It will then look for a local copy of the public key that is associated with the digital signature. If one is not stored locally, a CA may be used. In this scenario, the client software will use either an intranet or the Internet to find the preferred CA. A communication link will be established between the client and the CA. The CA will then use information on the certificate to locate the public key of the publisher. It will then send back information regarding itself and the public key. The user is then shown the information about the software publishing group, as well as information about the CA. The public key is then used to decipher the digital signature accompanying the application. If the application has been modified, the user will be notified and the JVM will refuse to launch the application. If the application was not modified, the user is prompted to accept or deny the execution of the software. If the user accepts, the application is launched. Although this sounds like a lot is going on, the aforementioned steps all take place within a few seconds.

**Digitally Signing Java Files**    A new utility was introduced in the JDK 1.1 called Javakey. This utility is used to create a digital signature for an applet based on public/private key technology. Javakey can only be used with the new Java Archive containers (.jar files). The following lists the steps necessary to create a digital signature for your applet:

1. Create an ID for a "Signer," the individual whose credentials are used in the signing of the applet.

   ```
   javakey -cs Scott true
   ```

   -cs = create a signer

   Scott = An arbitrary name for a signer account

   true = Is the signer trusted?

2. If the signer does not have a public/private key set, we will need to either obtain one from a certificate authority or generate our own. To generate our own, we can use javakey again.

   ```
   javakey -gk Scott DSA 512 Scott_Pub Scott_Priv
   ```

   –gk = generate keys

   Scott = The account the keys will be generated for.

   DSA = The digital signing algorithm that should be used.

   512 = The length of the key in bytes.

   Scott_Pub = The name of an output file that will hold the public key.

   Scott_Priv = The name of an output file that will hold the private key.

3. Create a certificate that identifies the signer. Eventually, we may use a certificate that was generated by a CA, but this is not currently supported. The javakey tool can use a "directive" file that contains information about the signer to create a certificate. But first, the certificate directive file must be created. Listing 11.1 is an example of one.

Part
I

Ch
11

### Listing 11.1   Certificate Directive File

```
#
# Information about the issuer (required).
#
issuer.name=Scott

#
# The certificate to use for the signing (required).
#
issuer.cert=1

#
# Information about the subject (required).
#
subject.name=Scott
subject.real.name=Scott Campbell
subject.org.unit=Marketing
```

*continues*

---

**Listing 11.1 Continued**

```
        subject.org=ACME
        subject.country=USA

        #
        # Information about the certificate (required).
        #
        start.date=1 Jan 1997
        end.date=1 Dec 1997
        serial.number=1001

        #
        # Name of the file to which to save a copy of the certificate
        ➥(optional).
        #
  out.file=Scott.cer
```

---

4. Compile the directive file for the certificate using javakey.

   ```
   javakey -gc Scott_cert_dir
   ```

   `-gc` = generate certificate

   `Scott_cert_dir` = the input file

5. Add the Java bytecode files to a Java Archive file (`.jar`) using the "jar" utility.

   ```
   jar -cf NewJarFile.jar *.class
   ```

   `-cf` = create file

   `NewJarFile.jar` = arbitrary name for the new output `.jar` file

   `*.class` = the input files that should be added to the `.jar` file

6. Create a digital signature directive file (see Listing 11.2). This file will contain information specific to the applet that is being signed.

---

**Listing 11.2 Digital Signature Directive File**

```
#
        # This is the directive file used by javakey to
        # sign a JAR file.
        #

        # The name of the signer that we added to the database.
        signer=Scott

        # A signer may have multiple certificates; what certificate number is
        ➥this one?
        cert=1

        # If certificate chaining were supported, we would note the number of
        ➥levels.
        chain=0
```

```
# The name to give to the generated signature file and associated
➥signature
# block. This must be 8 characters or less.
signature.file=ScottSig
```

7. After a directive file for the digital signature is created, we can apply the digital signature to the `.jar` file.

   `javakey -gs App1.sf  NewJarFile.jar`

   `-gs` = generate signature

   `App1.sf` = The signature directive file.

   `NewJarFile.jar` = A jar file that the signature will be applied to.

   The output of this operation will be a new archived file named `NewJarFile.jar.sig`. This file will contain the original contents of the `.jar` file and will also contain a digital signature. This file, as well as the original `.jar` file, can be viewed by using "zip" utilities. It may be a good idea to unzip your final signature file to verify that the contents are as expected.

8. The output file, `NewJarFile.jar.sig`, is usually renamed, and the `.sig` is removed from the name.

9. The applet may now be launched from a Java Virtual Machine that supports applets. This includes the appletviewer utility as well as browsers like Netscape Navigator and Microsoft Explorer. See "Java Archive File" in Chapter 10 for more information.

Part
I

Ch
11

# What Does It Mean to Be a CA?

The credentials for becoming a CA have not yet been ironed out. At this point, anyone who wants to act as a CA can do so. This situation will change as the importance of having credible authorities on the Internet increases. Several government bodies have been looking at this issue. Without credible agencies, the certificate that is issued has very little significance. If anyone can issue drivers' licenses, what good is the license? People will be forced to look closely at each certificate that is presented. If the certificate was created by a CA that has little or no merit, the user must then be responsible to use caution in accepting the software. The design of the certificate allows for multiple certificates to accompany a piece of software. This concept is known as *certificate chaining*. In essence, it allows a user to be presented with the information on a CA. If the user is not familiar with this CA, the user has the option of looking at a higher level certifying authority. Thus, a chain of certificates can be presented to the user until he or she finds a CA agency that they are comfortable with. If none are found, the user has the option of denying the software.

# The Mocha Controversy

In mid-1996, a developer released a new application that shook the Java community, Mocha. This software could reverse engineer the bytecode that was produced from a standard Java compiler. It turned the `.class` files into `.java` files, or source files. This meant that anyone could download an applet off the Web using Netscape Navigator, or their favorite browser. They could then look in the directory where the Java `.class` files were cached, and point the Mocha software at the cached files. Minutes later, a set of Java source code files would be produced. Suddenly, anyone who wanted the source code to any Java applet could easily obtain it. Obviously, this horrified developers and software companies that had invested huge amounts of time and money in developing these applications. The possibility for pirating or hacking was enormous.

Many applications were designed to hold user ID and password information directly in the client. A hacker could easily decompile the applet, view the source code, and immediately find the user ID and passwords necessary to infiltrate the software.

Software companies were concerned that dishonest developers would reverse engineer their multimillion-dollar packages, modify them, and make them their own. Obviously, this threat was a very real concern. Many people were outraged that this software was released on the Internet, while others were relieved. What Mocha did was wake up developers to the possibility that their code could easily be snatched. The author of Mocha had two choices: one was to release the software and give the Java community a wakeup call, the other was to keep the code a secret. If the code had never been released, the world may have never known about the insecurity. The truly diabolical developers would have written the same tool and decompiled canned software for their personal gain. Mocha may have been a blessing in disguise.

# Avoiding Decompilation

The author of the tool did perform a marketing trick that even Microsoft would have been proud of. After releasing the tool that could break into anyone's software, he released a tool that would "obfuscate" or scramble some of the contents to make the decompilation process much more difficult. This tool was called Crema. JavaSoft also recognized the problem that Mocha created and was also looking at a tool that could obfuscate the bytecode. At the time of this writing, JavaSoft is still considering this possibility. Note that obfuscation tools do not deny reverse engineering, they only make it harder to work with the reverse-engineered code by changing `.class`, attribute, and method names to painfully ugly syntax. The tool can modify the code only in places where it references other obfuscated code. In other words, if the code references the standard Java classes, like `Frame`, or `Window`, this code would be presented clearly. This means that a "de-obfuscation" tool could be created to help in the unscrambling of the source code.

When compiling a Java application, most compilers offer two modes of output. One is for debug mode, and the other is for release mode. Developers who do not use the obfuscation tools should always release their code using the "release" setting on their compiler. This will produce the bytecode without much of the symbolic references.

# The Future of Secured Code

Obfuscation utilities will help secure an application only to a certain point. Many have suggested that encryption routines be used on the bytecode files. But at some point in time, the files must be decrypted and stored in memory. Any time that a version of the software is decrypted in memory, a routine could be built to move the contents of memory to the hard drive and re-create the original `.class` files. Building locks that cannot be broken has been an endless goal. Since most languages now have reverse-engineering tools like Mocha, developers must assume that corrupt individuals may perform illegal activities, but this should not stop the advancement of software engineering.

The following listings show the different levels of obfuscation that are available. We have taken the "Splash Screen" example from Chapter 10 to demonstrate code decompilation.

Listing 11.3 shows the original source code for the class.

Listing 11.4 shows the source code that was generated from a decompiled class when the compiler was set to the "Release Mode."

Listing 11.5 shows the source code that was generated from a decompiled class when the compiler was set to the "Debug Mode."

Part

I

Ch

11

### Listing 11.3  Original *SplashScreen* Source

```
// This example is taken from Chapter 10, "The Splash Screen." The code is
// designed to be run from a JVM, but could be altered to work for a browser.
import java.awt.*;
public class SplashScreen extends Window {
    Image img;
    public SplashScreen(String FileName) {
        super(new Frame());
      // Swap out the toolkit for browser execution.
        this.img = Toolkit.getDefaultToolkit().getImage(FileName);
        this.show();
    }
    // Update the image after it has been loaded from disk.
    public boolean imageUpdate(Image img, int flags, int x, int y, int
w, int h) {
        if ((flags & this.ALLBITS) !=0) {
            this.resize(img.getWidth(this),img.getHeight(this));
            this.show();
        }
        return true;
    }
    public void paint(Graphics g) {
        g.drawImage(img,1,1,new Color(191,191,191),this);
    }
}
```

### Listing 11.4 Reverse-Engineered *SplashScreen* Source Code When Compiled in "Release" Mode

```java
import java.awt.*;
import java.awt.image.ImageObserver;

public class SplashScreen extends Window
{
    Image img;
    public SplashScreen(String string)
    {
        super(new Frame());
        img = Toolkit.getDefaultToolkit().getImage(string);
        show();
    }
    public boolean imageUpdate(Image image, int i1, int j1, int k, int
i2, int j2)
    {
        if ((i1 & 32) != 0)
        {
            resize(image.getWidth(this), image.getHeight(this));
            show();
        }
        return true;
    }
    public void paint(Graphics g)
    {
        g.drawImage(img, 1, 1, new Color(191, 191, 191), this);
    }
}
```

Notice that the variable names were changed, comments were removed, but everything else is intact.

### Listing 11.5 Reverse-Engineered *SplashScreen* When Compiled in "Debug" Mode

```java
import java.awt.*;
import java.awt.image.ImageObserver;

public class SplashScreen extends Window
{
    Image img;

    public SplashScreen(String FileName)
    {
        super(new Frame());
        img = Toolkit.getDefaultToolkit().getImage(FileName);
        show();
    }
```

```
    public boolean imageUpdate(Image img, int flags, int x, int y, int
w, int h)
    {
        if ((flags & 32) != 0)
        {
            resize(img.getWidth(this), img.getHeight(this));
            show();
        }
        return true;
    }

    public void paint(Graphics g)
    {
        g.drawImage(img, 1, 1, new Color(191, 191, 191), this);
    }
}
```

Notice that all variable and method names are intact.

# From Here...

The applet security model, along with digital signatures, certificates, and obfuscating tools, will protect against many types of malicious intruders. These are tactics in a much larger battle. It is necessary to create a strategic security plan that covers all aspects of securing enterprise information. Only when all pieces of the plan are implemented can one be reasonably confident that their information is secure. Hacking and cracking techniques are constantly improving. The security plan should be reviewed on a regular basis to adapt to the changing techniques used by unwanted intruders and information thieves.

■ Chapter 12, "Introduction to Distributed Computing," will cover the basic concepts of distributed computing including DCE, RPC, and CORBA.

■ Chapter 13, "Object Serialization," discusses how Java can move objects using streams for storage and persistence.

# Remote Method Invocation (RMI)

# Introduction to Distributed Computing

Java Enterprise computing falls in the broad area of Distributed Computing. In this section, we see what constitutes Distributed Computing, how and when it started, where and why it is happening, and we also look at its advantages and complexities. Finally, the main Distributed Computing architectures—sockets, remote procedure calls, distributed objects, and distributed object frameworks—are introduced. ■

## Distributed Computing

What is it and is it something new? Who are the potential users of Distributed Computing?

## Making a business case

Given that Distributed Computing can be harder and costlier, why must business consider it?

## Making a technical case

Where does Distributed Computing fit technically in the Enterprise?

## Advantages

What are the potential advantages of Distributed Computing and what needs to be done to achieve them?

## Complexities

You will get a conceptual overview of the complexities of Distributed Computing and how they should be approached.

## Distributed Computing architectures

You will briefly learn about the architectures used to build distributed applications. These are covered in more detail later in the book.

# Introducing Distributed Computing

Computing is an exciting industry. Ever since its beginnings about five decades ago, it has been continuously evolving. Like a fascinating novel, it builds on its previous chapters. Individuals and organizations, of all sizes and inclinations, make their rich contributions in the forms of innovation, technology, alliances, promises, and visions. They sometimes reap enormous fortunes by being with the right idea and product at the right time, while at other times the most calculated gigantic efforts by the biggest players fail absolutely. A dynamic industry like computing is fascinating enough to watch, and exhilarating to participate in.

Every so often in this dynamic industry, the plot evolves to a level where it acquires a new character. A new era of computing begins, providing new levels of enablement to humanity. A whole new domain of knowledge and products reshape the future of business, leisure, home, and community lifestyle. Inventions of the first computer, transistors, multiuser operating systems, microprocessor, personal computer, database systems, and local area networks (ethernet) are some of the historical milestones.

The new chapter of the story, the new era of computing that we are witnessing now, promises to be far more unique than anything we have witnessed so far. Its impact on the human race is comparable to that of the invention of the telephone and air travel, both of which suddenly made the planet Earth a much smaller place. It is delivering new experiences for an individual—for business, fun, learning, social, and political interaction—without so much as leaving the comfort of his or her favorite seat at home or office. Its impact on business is no less significant. A small corner store, with the right product, now has nearly the same chances of being discovered, in any part of the world, as those of a large corporation.

This new era is that of Distributed Computing!

## What Is Distributed Computing?

A distributed system is a collection of autonomous computers linked by a network, with software designed to produce an integrated computing facility. In lower-level technical terms, distributed computing is inter-process communication between two processes running in different address spaces, located on the same computer or on different computers connected using a network (see Figure 12.1).

**FIG. 12.1**

Inter-process communication between different processes constitutes Distributed Computing.

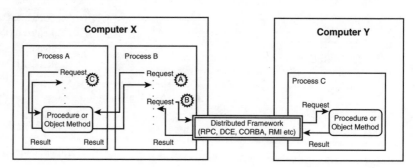

Distributed systems are implemented on platforms ranging in size from a few workstations on a local area network to the Internet—a worldwide interconnected collection of local and wide area networks comprising thousands or even millions of computers. Other examples of large distributed systems are automatic teller machine networks providing worldwide withdrawal facilities and international airline reservation systems. The Internet is, of course, the largest and most well-known example of a distributed system.

## When and How Did Distributed Computing Begin?

The beginnings of distributed computing can be traced to two to three decades ago, when communication infrastructure had yet to evolve into being a critical part of computing. Distributed Computing first emerged in military, academic, and research organizations. ARPAnet and UseNet, the early forms of the Internet, originated with such purposes. Due to low communication speeds and reliability, distributed computing took the form of only slow file transfers between computers at that time.

With the arrival of local area networks (LANs) in the 1980s, suddenly data transfer speeds on the local area network were comparable to data transfer speeds between hard disk and memory of a computer. It resulted in the growth of network operating systems such as Novell, Banyan, Appletalk, and Microsoft Windows Network, and standard networking protocols such as NetBIOS. Wide area networks (WANs) based on packet-based protocols such as TCP/IP and X.25 matured in the late 1970s and continued to evolve during the 1980s.

Most of the evolution of client/server computing can also be attributed to the 1980s. Starting gradually with large- and mid-range computers using UNIX and other proprietary operating systems, it was only with the arrival of the personal computers that the client/server captured a big mindset in the market. With the arrival of Microsoft Windows 3.x and Windows NT-based BackOffice products, client/server products started to become available to a much wider user base.

During most of the 1980s, the Internet, though gradually making its way from academic and military beginnings to commercial organizations, was still largely found in big organizations. E-mail, news, and ftp were still its main uses—all of them centered around file transfer. In 1992, Mark Andreeson and Tim Berners-Lee, along with others, brought hypertext-based document browsing to the Internet...and the rest is history. HTTP-based Web browsers have brought a very friendly and highly intuitive graphical user interface to the Internet or the World Wide Web, commonly known as just the Net or the Web. NCSA's Mosaic and Netscape's Navigator were the earliest browsers. Today, Netscape Navigator and Microsoft's Internet Explorer share most of the browser market. Use of the Internet technology within an organization, nothing new to a number of universities and organizations around the world, has become known as the intranet. Information retrieval and distribution—be it within an organization, in a community or suburb or city, or around the world—has acquired a new level of proficiency. It has created virtual communities around the world, who share common goals and interests.

From its roots in earlier research by Sun, 1994 saw the introduction of Java, and it has made every Web browser in the world a first-class (as good as a locally connected client of that computer) client of any computer connected to the Internet. This enablement has redefined the Internet (and intranets) as a Distributed Computing and application delivery platform, whose reach is as wide as all parts of the world reachable by phone.

# Where Is Distributed Computing Happening?

The push to integrate various computing facilities is coming from many directions and can be witnessed in many circumstances.

**Business Integration**    In large corporations, departmental computers of the late 1970s and early 1980s have been replaced by the departmental LANs or two-tier client/server application systems. But increasingly, customers are demanding that corporations deal with them as a single entity, rather than the customer having to deal with multiple departments of large corporations; or if already dealing with a single interaction, they should be serviced instantly across the whole corporation without delays along department boundaries. Increased globalization of a large number of businesses has also necessitated a much greater agility in the marketplace for all the corporations involved. This requires the ability to bring to market new products and alter current product offerings in the minimum time possible. Speeding a product to market and demand for integrated customer service have required that corporations integrate their disparate systems spread in various departments and divisions.

**Popularity of the Internet**    But the single largest distributed system, now with nearly global awareness, is the Internet. Its growth has reached a level where there is a case for all other wide area distributed systems to become a part of the Internet, thus making the Internet a part of the consumer telecommunications infrastructure. Whereas many of the existing large distributed systems (automated banking facilities of various types, and airline reservations systems to name a few) have used proprietary and "closed" technology and approaches, the Internet, with all its openness, has nearly become secure and dependable enough to become a generic platform for delivery of all distributed applications. The target audience of these distributed systems may be as small as a local organization or as widespread as the whole connected world. The number of people connected to the Internet has reached a level where the Internet has become a publishing medium in its own right. It is on its way to becoming as ubiquitous as the telephone. It has made it possible for any corporation to treat any person in the world, connected to the Net, as a potential customer.

Typical users of distributed systems, other than the large corporations, now include schools; students; professions and professionals of all kinds; businesses of all sizes; politicians; local, county, state, and federal governments; ethnic communities; and other "virtual" communities who may share one of the huge range of common interests.

# Why Distributed Computing?

One of the key questions we need to answer is why we need Distributed Computing. Distributed systems are generally more complex than their single node counterparts and therefore more expensive to implement and maintain. Before committing additional time and resources to a distributed environment, it is important to examine the need first. Let us look at both business and the technical reasons.

Businesses are increasingly discovering marketing, customer service, and product management requirements that can be fulfilled only by using distributed technology. These businesses have to invest in the Internet or other Distributed Computing technology based on the nature of their specific markets, products, and customers.

On the other hand, the computing environment in many organizations has already evolved to a distributed environment. In such organizations, existing investment in technology has to be managed with more focus on building a distributed environment.

We will now look at both business and technical reasons for choosing distributed technology.

**Business Reasons**    First, look at a number of reasons the business and the marketplace are starting to require solutions which cannot be delivered without distributed technology.

*Agility in the Marketplace*    Increased competition is leading all businesses to respond to market forces quickly. This response can come in the form of new or altered product lines, establishing distribution channels in previously unexplored markets and, in general, customizing business offerings in other ways dictated by the market.

This requires integrating various information systems and subsystems within the organization. Many of these information systems are built on heterogeneous technology. Java-based intranets, with Internet access to customers, suppliers, and partners, can be combined with middleware platforms like DCE and CORBA and can be used to build a highly responsive business.

*New Levels of Customer Service*    A business providing highly cost-effective service to its customers has a very strong edge over the competition. Customers of banking, insurance, utility, and other service-based industries have come to expect a single point of contact to be able to service all their needs.

This level of service requires a customer's request to flow smoothly through various parts of the servicing organization. In its lifetime, the request may pass through information systems that are on different technical platforms, operate in distant parts of the organization, or require close coordination between multiple accountable persons. Distributed technology provides the solutions to meet these requirements.

*Adoption of Intranets*    Dissemination of information and process management are key components of today's industries. The early 1990s have seen business concentrate on re-engineering its business processes in order to minimize costs and maximize the value of its products and services.

By implementing information retrieval and distribution systems using open Internet-based solutions, such as e-mail and newsgroups, businesses have successfully reaped returns on investments in hundreds of percents, if not more.

***Geographically Distributed Customer Base***   A large number of organizations and businesses have a customer base spread very widely over large geographical areas. Examples are utilities, banks, insurance companies, various levels of government, and the tourism industry—just to name a few.

Traditionally, these industries were serviced by the branch networks of these businesses. Human operator-staffed or automated phone-based servicing followed next. Phone-based service, although substantially cheaper than a branch network, does not provide a user-friendly interface.

Use of interactive, Internet-based, client/server, front-end applications for customer service provides a relatively inexpensive and user-friendly solution. Internet-delivered client/server applications are Distributed Computing applications requiring careful planning and design. During 1995 and 1996, electronic commerce standards for the Internet also have matured, elevating the Internet's status to a shopping mall or complex.

***Employee Enablement***   As discussed earlier, a single point of customer service has become a key objective of modern business. Front desk employees responsible for actioning customer requests have to be fully enabled and authorized to implement it. Distributed technology may be used to integrate multiple systems within an organization for information retrieval and to action the customer request.

***Workflow Management***   Focus on analysis and re-engineering of the business processes has enabled the existence and survival of lean and mean businesses in the 1990s. Organizations are now looking to implement systems which implement flexible business processes. Such systems allow business processes to be altered without requiring large system changes. These systems typically integrate information systems with groupware such as Lotus Notes.

Most workflow management systems evaluate the work that needs to be done and automatically route it through the organization in a way that meets or exceeds performance objectives while minimizing costs. Internet-based workflow management, still in its early days, when available will enable virtual teams spread over different parts of the world to work together very closely.

Workflow management systems manage the organization's workload in a distributed environment. Distributed technology is the core of their implementation mechanism.

***Mobile and Virtual Workforce and Partnerships***   Flexible working hours and venues, allowing working parents (and all employees in general) balanced lifestyles, are nothing new. Sales and Field Service staffs, whose role by nature involves travel, also must be able to work at remote locations at all kinds of possible hours. In some industries, contract workers may never have face-to-face contact with the employer or customer and carry out the required work at a distant location. Due to globalization of the business, partners and suppliers may be located anywhere in the world.

All these situations require facilities by which the remotely located person is able to participate in the organization. Communication facilities and applications necessary to achieve that objective are based on Distributed Computing.

**Technical Reasons**    In the previous section, business forces driving the need for distributed technology were looked at. In this section, you look at technical opportunities that, by using distributed technology, can provide an enrichment of the overall technical environment in an organization.

*Integrate the Desktop into Overall Architecture*    We are currently outgrowing widespread use of two-tier client/server architectures. The Internet and intranets are making significant contributions to the design of infrastructure required for a true network of distributed services. Domain Name Service (DNS), Internet Time Service, various Kerberos-based or other Certificate Servers (e.g., VeriSign and so on), and Electronic Commerce Servers are examples of general services that are likely to proliferate in a distributed computing world.

By virtue of Java and ActiveX being first-class clients in this distributed world, even a personal computer or workstation is as equal a citizen of the distributed world as any of the biggest Internet servers.

This is a long journey for mass-scale desktop computers which started out as stand-alone personal computers and workstations. Having progressed through large-scale use of local area networks and two-tier client/server architectures, we are now on the threshold of a new era of distributed client/server computing.

*Integrate Heterogeneous Proprietary Environments*    The Internet is an excellent example of a huge network of hundreds of thousands or even millions of computers, running multiple hardware and software platforms, interoperating successfully. With the arrival of Java and ActiveX, it has progressed from being an information retrieval and distribution platform to an application delivery platform, which was previously the realm of operating systems.

For organizations struggling with getting multiple hardware and operating systems platforms to interoperate, it (the Internet) is providing an excellent model for information and application delivery. Being an open platform, it promises to be much less costly to acquire and maintain, due to large economies of scale being available.

*Improving WAN Bandwidth*    One of the most crucial enabling factors for popularity of two-tier client/server architecture on local area networks was data transfer speeds comparable to those between local memory and hard disk of a personal computer. Latest communication technologies, such as ATM, are capable of data transfer speeds of a minimum of several hundred megabits per second—compared to about 10–100 megabits per second for the ethernet. Specialized ATM networks will be capable of several gigabits per second.

Part

II

Ch

12

This will help wide area network data transfer speeds to approach the levels of speed between a computer and its peripherals. A lot of investment in national and international communication backbones needs to happen before this will be a reality. With the current high growth of Internet use, this investment is already happening.

# Advantages of Distributed Computing

The difference between stand-alone or non-distributed and distributed computing can be compared to that between a one-person "team" versus a real team of many members. When properly structured, a Distributed Computing environment provides more resources, possibility to grow easily, flexibility of usage, and higher availability, to name a few.

You will now look at some of the benefits of Distributed Computing in detail.

## Resource Sharing

A stand-alone system must have dedicated access to all the resources it ever needs to use. A resource, in general, can be data, a software or hardware device like a color printer, a fax modem, or a server like an Internet search engine. There are obvious drawbacks to having dedicated resources for a stand-alone system, cost being the most obvious one. By opting for a resource shared amongst a large number of users, a quality resource (hard disk, search engine, printer, and so on) with a much better price-to-performance ratio can be used.

When extended to software services-based resources, a lot of common functionality can be built as services available on the Internet. Certificate servers, such as VeriSign, are examples of such servers. Large organizations can choose to have their own servers; but for applications where transaction volume does not justify their own dedicated servers, pay-for-use services available in the public domain over the Internet will provide ideal value.

## Scalability

Distributed systems operate effectively and efficiently at many different scales. The smallest possible distributed system probably consists of two workstations networked together, optionally with a file server. A distributed system centered around a local area network may consist of hundreds of workstations and many file, print, and other special-purpose servers. Local area networks may be further networked together, resulting in internetworks. Internetworks can contain thousands of workstations, forming a single distributed system, enabling resources to be shared among all of them.

The objective of scalability in the design of distributed systems has led to a design philosophy in which no single resource—hardware or software—is assumed to be in restricted supply. As the demand for a resource grows, it should be possible to extend the system to meet it.

**N O T E**  Designing a scalable distributed system, although a very valuable objective, can be hard.
Key to designing a scalable system is to choose a design option where the work involved in
processing any single request to access a shared resource should be nearly independent of the size of
the network. Replication of data, and servers and caching at various levels, are some of the techniques
to achieve scalability. ■

## Access Flexibility

Access flexibility is one of the most fundamental advantages of distributed systems. Access to
data and services is delivered to the point where it is actually needed. Whether it is the shop
floor in a factory, or a remote Internet user in a remote corner of a far-away country, data and
service can be made available regardless of the distance from the provider of the service. It is
very common to find hundreds and even thousands of users from scores of countries using the
largest of the Internet servers at the same time. On some of these servers, it is possible to view
the demographic spread of the users in real-time.

## Fault-Tolerance

Computer systems, like all "nearly" perfect things in the world, sometimes fail. Distributed
systems have provided one of the main techniques for building fault-tolerant computer systems. At the hardware level, identical *hot standby* machines have been used in parallel in Automatic Teller Machine networks. In a distributed system, redundancy can be planned at a finer
level—individual servers, both at hardware and software level, can be replicated. The servers
can be designed to detect faults in their peers. When a fault is detected in one server, clients
are redirected to the remaining servers. By such techniques, tolerance to some of the hardware faults can be provided in a distributed system at a lower cost, compared to hardware level
redundancy. Built-in fault-tolerance in any system, of course, results in better availability.

Part
II

Ch
12

## Uniform User Interface

By integrating heterogeneous hardware and software platforms in a single distributed system,
a generic view of the Distributed Computing environment is created. This also results in a
consistent, and even identical, user interface across various operating platforms. Differing
feature sets, syntax, or user interfaces and semantics for the same facility on various operating
platforms have been a great source of productivity loss and costly training of users. Various
Internet clients—for example, World Wide Web browsers, ftp, and telnet clients—are examples
of a high level of uniformity in the user interfaces.

## Exploit the Desktop Price/Performance Revolution

As we have already seen, scalability of distributed systems is achieved by adding additional
resources as and when required. When compared to a stand-alone system, a distributed system
of the same capacity may be implemented using multiple smaller machines. To achieve fault-
tolerance, servers may be developed such that they can run on any of the machines in the
distributed system—some of these machines can now be the high-end workstations. Thus,
some of the processing may be moved from very expensive mainframes and other legacy
boxes to much less expensive operating platforms.

The recently available distributed platforms, like CORBA, combined with dynamically downloadable applications written using Java, make such flexible environments a reality. Using such platforms, a high degree of flexibility of server platforms can be achieved.

## Transparency

Transparency is one of the most elegant features of well-designed distributed systems. The International Standards Organization's Reference Model for Open Distributed Processing (RM-ODP) identifies many types of transparency. Distributed Computing platforms such as DCE and CORBA implement a large number of these transparencies. Some of the key transparencies are:

- **Access Transparency** enables local and remote information objects to be accessed by using identical operations.

- **Location Transparency** allows you to access objects whose physical location may not be known to you.

- **Concurrency Transparency** enables several processes to run concurrently, using shared information objects, without interference between them.

- **Replication Transparency** allows the client applications to use the best possible information object, for the given purpose, from a set of multiple instances of information objects—created to increase reliability and performance.

- **Failure Transparency** enables concealment of faults to the extent possible, allowing users and application programs to complete their tasks despite some hardware and software failures.

## Openness

Openness of a given system defines whether it can be extended in various ways. To be open, a system must specify its interfaces and their semantics. Openness has two aspects: technical and commercial. On a technical level, an open system's design must provide interfaces that can be used to extend the original system. On a commercial level, such interfaces must be published openly.

Success of distributed systems depends largely on open systems. UNIX was an early example of highly open and extendible systems. The computing industry's annoyance with vendors with closed systems is very well known.

Looking at all the benefits of Distributed Computing, it is not hard to see the relevance of the adage "the whole being greater than the sum of the parts." In the next section, we look at the complexities of distributed systems. These have to be managed adequately to achieve fine-tuned-cost-effective distributed systems.

# Complexities of Distributed Computing

Distributed systems are built by networking and integrating multiple stand-alone machines. Interconnection of various machines adds a new set of complexities. In this section, you will see some of these complexities in more detail. They may look daunting to begin with, but most of these already have solutions, products, and methods to manage them.

The leading middleware solutions, DCE and CORBA (discussed later in the chapter), provide elegant ways of managing some of these complexities. Other complexities have to be managed by a suitable design process and approach. Most of the popular database products (Oracle, DB2, Microsoft Access, Microsoft SQL Server, to name a few) have already started supporting distributed database functionality. CORBA specifies distributed query and transaction services which provide a unified way of accessing and updating various databases across a distributed system. Let us look at some of the key complexities in detail.

# Multiple Failure Modes

Where on one hand, a system with multiple components can offer the benefits of scalability and fault-tolerance; on the other hand, a larger number of components implies more ways in which the components can fail. With each node added to a network, the number of possible failures rises exponentially. Many of these failure modes constitute partial failure. In such circumstances, the non-failed part of the distributed system may be able to continue to work, though at a reduced level of functionality.

Distributed system design has to be able to detect partial failures and reconfigure itself to switch to an alternative mode of operation in a systematic fashion.

# Concurrency Control

In multiuser database management systems, the DBMS processes transactions from various users in a manner such that:

- Either the transactions are processed completely or not at all (atomicity of transactions).
- Any committed updates to the database are permanent (durability of transactions).
- Each user has a consistent view of the database, even during the transient states experienced during life cycles of various parallel transactions (consistency of the database).
- Users are isolated from updates done by other users until the other users' updates are committed (isolation of transactions).

These properties of database updating apply to all types of resources available in a distributed system. Distributed database management is a complex area which has been steadily developing in the last decade. Most of the major database products now support distributed transaction processing of some form.

Before opting to use distributed database systems, one must be sure it is absolutely necessary. Distributed database systems—if not properly designed, planned, and configured—can be the source of heavy data communication loads on the network and can be hard to maintain over the life cycle.

Part
II

Ch
**12**

In situations requiring distributed databases, it is currently common to use the simplest form (read-only). Most of the time, it is possible to design around this requirement.

## Possible States of the Distributed System

Software design, by nature, involves processing a given system's states that are of interest to the application, while handling all possible states adequately. The possible number of states of a given application determines its complexity. With higher complexity, design and testing become more expensive and less reliable.

In a distributed environment, the total number of states for a distributed application is very high, simply due to the fact that multiple states exist in parallel on various nodes of the distributed system. Therefore, additional effort is required in designing and testing distributed applications.

The complexity of distributed systems is easier to manage with an object-oriented approach. Encapsulation and elegant exception handling found in object-oriented design address the challenges of Distributed Computing head on. Distributed object frameworks like CORBA, DCOM, RMI, and many others in the research field have proven this beyond a doubt. In a procedural model, managing the complexity of a distributed system is much harder.

## Processing Flow Design

Processing flow is easy to control in a single-threaded process, even on a multiuser (not necessarily multi-processor-based) operating system. It acquires extra complexity in a multithreaded application. In a distributed environment, multiple processes with multiple threads on multiple nodes may exist simultaneously. Achieving proper synchronization across multiple nodes requires new mechanisms.

Both DCE and CORBA models of the distributed environment, discussed later in this chapter, provide event services which are used by applications to coordinate their activities across a distributed network. In an Internet or intranet application, the event services enable the setting of data-push applications from the server (for example, a stock price ticker application where data is refreshed from the server at fixed intervals), eliminating the need for regular polling by the client.

## Security

Enforcement of security, even in a stand-alone server, is very important. In a distributed system, all the features that make it convenient for legitimate users also make it convenient for an illegitimate user. Data, as it travels on the wire, and in the case of the Internet through unknown machines, is exposed to eavesdropping and tampering. Not only the potential users, but also the computers requesting information, need to be authenticated.

Distributed security technology, increasingly becoming common knowledge, has progressed to a level where dependable distributed security infrastructure can be put in place. RSA-based public key encryption and Kerberos-based certificate servers form the foundations of distributed security.

## Performance Estimation

A Distributed Computing system, although presenting a unified view to the end user, is, in many ways, an assembly of individual computer systems. Loads on the overall system may arrive in a variety of combinations from the individual systems and the outside world. Performance management of a distributed system will require performance management of each individual system as well as for the system as a whole.

For these reasons, modeling, analyzing, and forecasting the performance of a distributed system are much more complex than they are for a stand-alone system. Usually the users or sponsors paying for the system require advance guarantees of the quality of service and performance required from the overall system.

Distributed Systems Management Technology has come a long way during the last decade. The growing size of LANs and WANs in large companies has already made that a necessity. The leading, distributed, object-based, application frameworks (CORBA) come with server load management tools that operate on the distributed system as a whole. Easy management of performance and reliability of distributed systems is key to their widespread acceptance in the commercial environment.

# Discovering Distributed Computing Architectures

Distributed Computing Architectures specify the infrastructure that delivers the benefits of distributed processing and also helps manage its complexities.

We will first examine the basic mechanisms available to communicate between two processes running on different address spaces, which can be on the same machine or on two different computers. Sun remote procedure calls (Sun RPC), DCE remote procedure calls (DCE RPC), CORBA IDL method invocation, and Java Remote Method Invocation are the most popular or important standards in use. You will look at their unique features in this section.

Distributed Computing frameworks, like DCE and CORBA, provide a unified view of the Distributed Computing environment. They provide a simple, manageable interface to the application developer and environment manager for development and administration of the distributed system. Distributed Computing frameworks play an instrumental role in helping manage the enormous complexity of a large distributed application environment.

# Remote Process Communication

No, the title of this section is not a wrong expansion of RPC, which is commonly understood to stand for Remote Procedure Call. In this section, we look at how the basic remote procedure call has evolved from socket-level communication to hardware-independent and object-oriented forms.

There are many variations of the remote procedure call, which vary mainly in the data format used on the wire. CORBA and Java introduce their own object-oriented representations to communicate parameters and results between processes on different nodes.

**The Basics of Sockets**　At the hardware level, two computers are connected using the hardware ports designated for the purpose. At the lowest application level, a program can write data to these ports and read data from these ports. Use of sockets for communication programming is nothing new to developers on UNIX-like systems. Java makes socket-based network programming much easier by providing a rich set of classes in the `java.net` package.

**Participating Components**　The basic process of using sockets is very similar to using files, also known as streams. Figure 12.2 shows the process of using sockets for inter-process communication.

**FIG. 12.2**

Sockets are one of the basic mechanisms for inter-process communication.

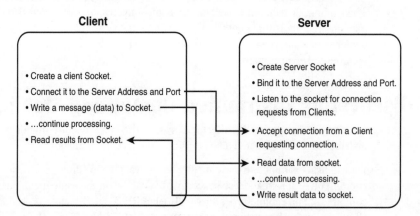

**Client**

- Create a client Socket.
- Connect it to the Server Address and Port
- Write a message (data) to Socket.
- ...continue processing.
- Read results from Socket.

**Server**

- Create Server Socket
- Bind it to the Server Address and Port.
- Listen to the socket for connection requests from Clients.
- Accept connection from a Client requesting connection.
- Read data from socket.
- ...continue processing.
- Write result data to socket.

**Flow of Control**　In order to communicate, two processes must first establish a connection. The server process is listening for a connection and the client will be asking for a connection. Figure 12.2 illustrates the server creating a socket, binding it to an address (IP address and port), and listening for a connection. The client creates a socket and then requests a connection to the server port. The server accepts the connection and creates a socket for the current connection. From this point on, the client can write to this socket and the server can read from it. When the server wants to send some results back to the client, operations are reversed.

**Using Sockets for Transferring Data**    Data transferred on socket connections is plain character data, which means it does not have any application-specific type or structure. Both processes participating in the communication should agree on a protocol and format of messages to be exchanged.

**Types of Remote Process Communication**    For client/server communication to be as close to a normal sub-routine call in a non-distributed environment, it should be possible to pass the call parameters, with their data types, to the server. The server in turn should return results as a type sub-routine or function would. We will now look at techniques which provide a higher level mechanism compared to socket-based inter-process communication. Sun remote procedure calls and Distributed Computing Environment (DCE) remote procedure calls are examples of procedural models. CORBA IDL method invocations using IIOP and Java Remote Method Invocation (Java RMI) are examples of inter-process communication in the object-oriented model.

# Remote Procedure Calls (Sun RPC and DCE RPC)

In a non-distributed or local procedure call, a sub-routine, procedure, or function is invoked with a number of parameters, each of which is of a given type. The objective of remote procedure calls is to provide the same ease of programming for invoking a remote procedure.

**Participating Components**    Figure 12.3 shows the main components of a general remote procedure call setup.

**FIG. 12.3**

Remote Procedure Calls convert parameters and results to a standard external format.

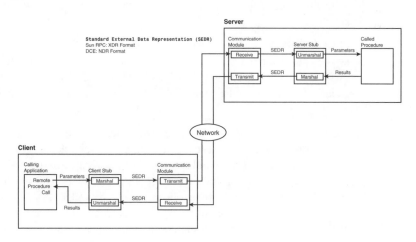

The client makes a local call to the client stub procedure. The client stub procedure is responsible for converting procedure parameters to a format suitable for transmission on a communication line. This representation generally indicates the number of parameters in the request, and the types and values of each—each value being of a predefined length or format. This process of converting parameters to a format suitable for transmission is known as *marshaling*.

The Sun RPC standard uses a format known as XDR (External Data Representation). It provides a format which is independent of programming language, operating system, and hardware word sizes of the client and server environments. Whenever it is possible to ascertain that the client and server platforms are identical, conversion to and from a standard external representation is avoided to gain some performance improvement. DCE remote procedure call uses a format known as NDR (Network Data Representation).

The target procedure name or suitable identifier is also transmitted as part of the request to the server. Sun RPC uses Program IDs (numeric) to identify programs. DCE RPC assigns UUIDs (Universally Unique Identifiers)—which, once generated, are unique in time and space; i.e., they are never repeated—for identifying all its resources, including programs.

The communication layer on the client end transmits the program identification along with marshaled parameters. On the server end, a process reverse of that on the client end takes place. An RPC daemon on the server extracts a Procedure ID or name. The server stub receives the request parameters and converts them from XDR or NDR to suit the operating system and the programming language used in the server program. This step is known as *unmarshaling*.

The server program completes the required processing and returns the results to the client program. Returning of the result value(s) follows the same steps of marshaling, transmission, and unmarshalling, as followed for the request parameters during invocation call from the client.

**Interface Definition**   As is the obvious explanation, the client need not be aware of the operating system, programming language, or location of the server machine. It knows only an interface, with its signature, it can use. This interface is specified by using the *Interface Definition Language (IDL)*. Both Sun RPC and DCE RPC have their own variants of interface definition language.

Any new interface is first described using IDL syntax. It is compiled to produce client- and server-side stubs. These stubs also handle communication-related error conditions that can arise during transmit and receive stages. DCE RPC assigns a unique UUID to each interface, whereas Sun RPC uses Program Name and Version Numbers. This information (UUIDs or Program Name and Version Numbers) is stored in a central database, along with server program information and signature of the calls. Client and server stubs are then used to build the respective client and server application programs.

**Binding**   In a flexible distributed system, multiple copies of a server process may be initiated to improve performance and availability. Binding is the process of associating a given request to the most suited server process for that request.

**Product Maturity**   Sun RPC is a very popular remote procedure call implementation. Having started with various UNIX variants, it is now supported on nearly all platforms. DCE, on the other hand, goes much beyond a remote procedure call mechanism. The DCE is a fully distributed environment framework providing distributed directory, time, security, file, event, and network management services. Many mature commercial DCE products on all major operating platforms are available. Due to being the first Distributed Computing framework, DCE is already in extensive use in many large corporations around the world.

# CORBA IDL Method Invocation

The latter half of the 1980s and 1990s have seen a strong adoption of object-oriented technology. Object-oriented technology offers excellent advantages for modeling of complex systems and is therefore very well-suited for distributed applications.

Common Object Request Broker Architecture (CORBA) is the basic mechanism by which objects can invoke methods on a remote object transparently. To the client object, it appears as a normal local method invocation, thus resulting in transparent invocation of the remote method. The distributed communication layer which delivers this functionality is called an Object Request Broker (ORB). CORBA is the centerpiece of the Object Management Architecture (OMA), the overall distributed objects standard published by Object Management Group. OMA and CORBA are discussed in more detail in Chapter 16, "CORBA and Object Management Architecture (OMA)."

Sunsoft has announced full support for CORBA IDL, starting with Java 1.1. For example, Java applets will be able to invoke methods on CORBA objects located anywhere on the Internet. Netscape will also be including Internet Inter-ORB Protocol (IIOP) support in Navigator clients and all its server products. IIOP is an object-oriented equivalent to XDR or NDR data representation, discussed in the section on Remote Procedure Calls. IIOP is the standard, on-the-wire, object representation protocol used by CORBA-compliant ORBs to interoperate successfully. A large number of object-oriented and object-relational database vendors are also in the process of providing IIOP compatibility.

Figure 12.4 shows the client/server communication in a CORBA-distributed objects environment. Client object, Client stub, Server skeleton, and Server object are very similar to the remote procedure call paradigm, except that they support object-oriented paradigm. The Client object invokes server object methods on a local proxy contained in the Client stub, which, using the ORB, passes the method invocation to the actual remote object.

Like remote procedure calls, CORBA method invocations are language- and operating system-independent. This requires externalization of an object's state, followed by its marshaling to achieve a suitable format for transmission. On the receiving end, the process is reversed. To pass references to objects, CORBA provides interoperable object references (IORs) which we will describe in detail in Chapters 16 and 17.

**FIG. 12.4**

CORBA Method Invocation facilitates method invocation on remote objects.

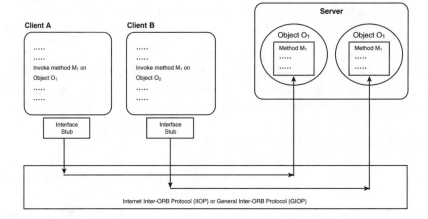

## Java Remote Method Invocation

Distributed systems based on procedural model, as well as the CORBA IIOP model for distributed objects programming, are language- and operating system-neutral. For both of them, data is converted to a standard interoperable format (XDR for Sun RPC, NDR for DCE, and IIOP for CORBA).

But, Java itself is operating platform-neutral. Distributed systems developed using Java should not have to incur the overhead of converting data to an external format on the sending end and back again on the receiving end. Java Remote Method Invocation (Java RMI) provides just such a mechanism. Java RMI is a part of the Java Enterprise API released by Sun, which consists of JDBC for relational database connectivity, Java IDL for interfacing to CORBA applications, and Java RMI for allowing developers to seamlessly distribute Java objects across an enterprise.

Please refer to Figure 12.5 for an overview of the Java RMI Application Architecture. A more detailed discussion appears in Chapters 11 and 14.

RMI transport mechanism uses object serialization to read and write object streams across the network. The RMI API allows a flexible interface between remote objects, allowing them to invoke methods remotely as if they were in the same virtual machine address space.

**FIG. 12.5**
Java Remote Method
Invocation (RMI) allows
you to invoke methods
of remote Java objects.

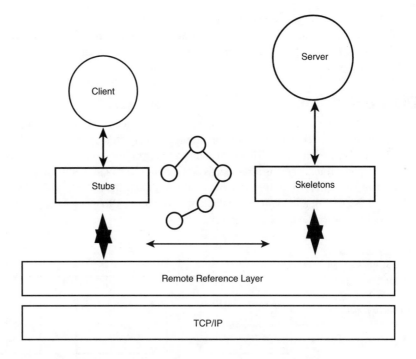

# A Unified View of the Distributed Environment

Let us go back about three or four decades in computing history and examine the birth of operating systems as we know them today. Before the invention of operating systems, each programmer had to manage devices, load and unload programs (i.e., manage memory), and carry out a number of similar repetitive utility tasks that today we take for granted. Files, directories, variable name spaces (through virtual machines and runtime environments), and software interrupts for inter-process communication are some of the operating system facilities that we use regularly.

A great deal of research into the architecture of distributed systems has already been carried out. Distributed operating systems and shared memory management architectures, which can control the whole distributed environment as a single entity, are still at the research and development stage. On the other hand, industrial strength distributed application frameworks such as DCE and CORBA are already available. These frameworks provide a "unified view" of the local environments to the application developer, using distributed files, directories, software interrupt (event) services, and much more—thus making the task of developing distributed applications much easier.

Part
II

Ch
12

We shall briefly describe an overview of the two main distributed application frameworks, namely Distributed Computing Environment (DCE) from the X/Open Group (previously Open Systems Foundation) and Object Management Architecture (OMA) from Object Management Group.

# Distributed Computing Environment (DCE)

Distributed Computing Environment provides a set of C programming language interfaces that support the construction and integration of client/server applications in heterogeneous distributed environments. DCE specification and reference model is currently controlled by the X/Open Group, which is a standards-setting body with about 300 member companies and other organizations from the I.T. industry and academic institutions. DCE was originated by Open Systems Foundation (OSF), which merged with the X/Open Group in February 1996. Figure 12.6 shows the DCE architecture.

**FIG. 12.6**
DCE was the first standardized architecture for building distributed applications.

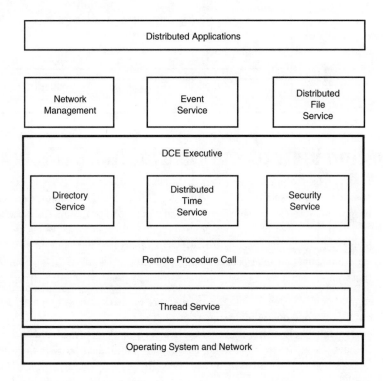

DCE consists of the following components:

- Directory services which support local DCE administration domains, or cells, and inter-cell name resolution.

- A Distributed Time Service (DTS) that synchronizes clocks on all hosts in a DCE cell, as well as among cells.

■ Security services which provide authentication of clients and servers, authorization of clients to access servers, and privacy and integrity of data transmitted between clients and servers.

■ A Remote Procedure Call mechanism where clients invoke server procedures without a knowledge of location of servers within the network, types of hardware and operating system on which they run, and what data representation they use.

■ A Posix-based threads package, supporting creation and management of multiple threads of control within a client or a server.

■ An event service to provide a common way for system and user applications to generate, forward, filter, process, and log events.

■ Distributed File Service (DFS) implements a single logical file system that is available throughout an entire cell and across cell boundaries.

■ Network Management Option (NMO) provides a mechanism for system management applications to access system information throughout the distributed system using standard protocols such as SNMP.

The X/Open Group has established a World Wide Web task force to enable Java client applets to communicate to DCE-based servers. More information about the DCE-Web Project can be found at **http://www.osf.org/www/dceweb/index.html**.

# Object Management Architecture and Common Object Request Broker Architecture (OMA and CORBA)

Object Management Architecture (OMA) provides an object-oriented view of the distributed computing environment. Rich semantics of the object-oriented model are used to specify multiple levels of abstractions, starting with operating systems and network services to business level distributed objects. Common Object Request Broker Architecture is the core of OMA, delivering object level connectivity across the network.

OMA is published by the Object Management Group (OMG), a consortium currently consisting of about 700 information technology vendors and other interested institutions. OMG was founded in 1989, with the first CORBA 1.2 specification being published in 1991-92. The current CORBA 2.0 specification, published in 1994, was finally adopted in the second half of 1995.

Figure 12.7 shows the components of the CORBA architecture. The Object Request Broker (ORB) is the "core object bus," connecting various objects on the distributed system. It lets objects transparently make requests to—and receive responses from—other objects located locally or remotely.

CORBA Services are essential services required for implementing objects. Specifications for a majority of services have been specified. Industry implementations of core services like naming, life cycle, persistence, and event services are already available. Query and transaction services, related to database transactions, have been announced and are likely to become available soon from the database vendors. Specifications for some of the services are still being finalized. OMG invites submissions for standardization of various parts of OMA, with the submissions discussed, fine-tuned, voted upon, and finally adopted by OMG.

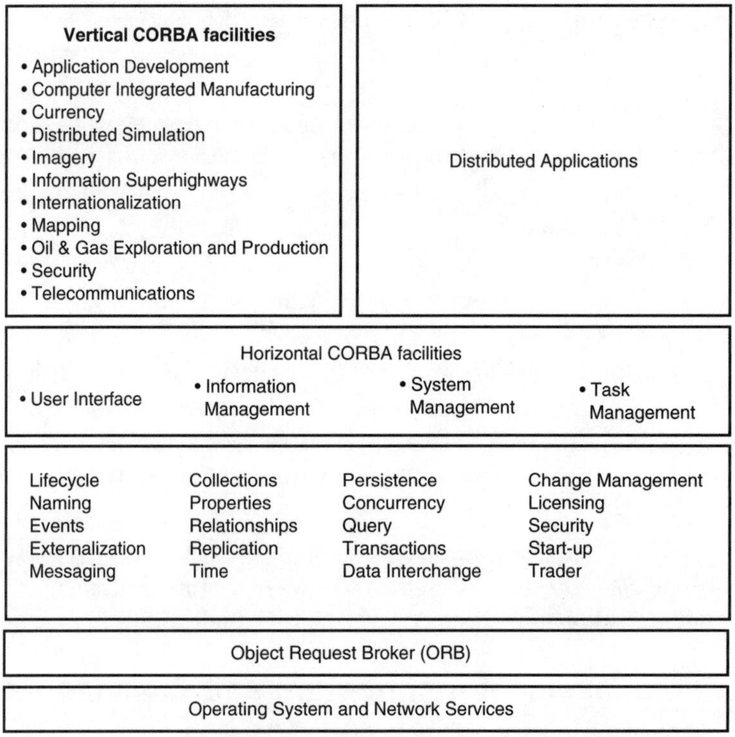

**FIG. 12.7**

Object Management Architecture (OMA) provides an object-oriented architecture for distributed applications.

**Vertical CORBA facilities**

- Application Development
- Computer Integrated Manufacturing
- Currency
- Distributed Simulation
- Imagery
- Information Superhighways
- Internationalization
- Mapping
- Oil & Gas Exploration and Production
- Security
- Telecommunications

Distributed Applications

Horizontal CORBA facilities

- User Interface
- Information Management
- System Management
- Task Management

| | | | |
|---|---|---|---|
| Lifecycle | Collections | Persistence | Change Management |
| Naming | Properties | Concurrency | Licensing |
| Events | Relationships | Query | Security |
| Externalization | Replication | Transactions | Start-up |
| Messaging | Time | Data Interchange | Trader |

Object Request Broker (ORB)

Operating System and Network Services

CORBA facilities are higher level services for building applications. They are split between horizontal and vertical facilities. Horizontal facilities are application domain-independent and fall into the categories of user interface, information management, system management, and task management. Vertical facilities support specific application domains like business objects for finance, health care, and manufacturing industries.

Java and OMA are both object-oriented and thrive in a distributed environment. Java provides an excellent programming language and a virtual machine platform for runtime portability. OMA, in addition to providing connectivity for distributed objects, has a rich set of services which can augment Java's distributed application development strengths. OMA and CORBA have attracted wide acceptance from the development and database vendor community. Sun Microsystems, Java's originator has, on the other hand, announced IIOP support through the Java-IDL component of JDK Version 1.1.

At the time of writing, Sun looks inclined to move Java IDL to a future release of JDK. The current version of Java-IDL is in alpha stage. However, just like the normal JDK, it is not compulsory to use Sun's Java-IDL distribution for all Java-CORBA connectivity. Java-CORBA development tools are available from a number of leading ORB vendors, such as Visibroker and Orbix. In fact, the Java-IDL or Java-CORBA example applications are based on Visibroker for Java and OrbixWeb products. Evaluation versions of these products can be downloaded from the respective vendors' Web sites.

# Index of Common Problems

| Planning for Distributed Applications | |
|---|---|
| **If You Have This Problem...** | **You'll Find Help Here...** |
| Presenting a case to business | p. 227 |
| Proving technical benefits of Distributed Computing | p. 229 |

| Building Distributed Applications | |
|---|---|
| **If You Have This Problem...** | **You'll Find Help Here...** |
| Choosing appropriate remote communication mechanism | p. 237 |
| Understanding a unified view of Distributed Environment | p. 241 |

# From Here...

Java RMI and CORBA are object-oriented programming methods for distributed applications, rather than being just object-based. You also saw the complexity issues of distributed applications. Java RMI and CORBA are covered in more detail later in the book.

- See Chapter 2, "JDBC Data Types," and Chapter 3, "A Simple JDBC Application," to understand in detail and use JDBC.
- See Chapter 11, "Securing Enterprise Information," to understand Java RMI in more detail.
- Proceed to Chapter 13, "Object Serialization," to build a Java RMI client and server application.
- See Chapter 16, "CORBA and Object Management Architecture (OMA)," and Chapter 17, "WWW Applications Development Using CORBA," to understand IIOP, IDL, and CORBA in more detail.
- Proceed to Chapter 18, "Incorporating Java, JDBC, and CORBA: A Sample Application," to build a simple server and client application using Java, CORBA, and JDBC.

**Part**

**II**

**Ch**

**12**

# CHAPTER 13

# Object Serialization

When developing all but the simplest applications, the need will arise to store an object's contents. To fulfill this need, objects are usually designed with a method of loading and saving current settings to a text file. Not only does this require excessive time to develop the routines, but the data may become subject to tampering. To reduce the development time for object storage, the `java.io` package has been extended to include object serialization. Object serialization adds another tool in the developer's kit by allowing objects to be stored with their current state intact.

The concept of storing the current object state is not new, and is sometimes referred to as object persistence. The goal is to store an object's contents in a manner that allows proper restoration at another time, possibly in another application. In addition, any members of the object should be stored also, providing a clean representation of the object as a whole. To properly illustrate, imagine a class that contains fields such as a name and an employee number. An instance of the class contains data such as Joe Smith and 555-55-5555. For the object to be labeled persistent, it should store all of the fields and their current states. The object's data is sent to a storage device, such as the local hard drive, when the object is written. When an application wants to restore the object, a new object instance of the class is created containing the values `Joe Smith` and `555-55-5555` which were retrieved from the storage device.

Object serialization is designed to follow the concepts of persistence. When an object is serialized, the object and its members are converted into a graph. The graph provides information about the primary class and any member classes and primitive fields. This allows the deserialization process to have enough information to correctly restore the object. Next, the current state of each member object and field is written to the device. In addition, all fields and members of the superclasses in the hierarchy are stored also. The graph and accompanying data are then available for future deserialization.

The `java.io` package provides seven primary classes for supporting object serialization. These classes include:

- `ObjectOutput`
- `ObjectInput`
- `Serializable`
- `Externalizable`
- `ObjectOutputStream`
- `ObjectInputStream`
- `ObjectInputValidation`

These classes form the core of object serialization and were designed to achieve several goals. These goals include:

- A simple but expandable implementation
- Maintaining the proper Java object representation when serialized
- Provide expandability for remote object implementations
- Expandable to support object persistence
- Require class implementation only for customization requirements
- Allow custom external format implementations

This chapter will discuss the rules of using object serialization, the proper use of serialization, and custom implementations. ■

# Rules of Serialization

Object serialization is responsible for producing a stream that contains information about an object or series of objects. For a class to become eligible for stream transmission, it must implement either the `Serializable` interface or `Externalizable` interface. Each interface offers a different method of storing and retrieving the objects. They also determine if the object may be stored using the Object Stream class format or if the class must define its own method of storage.

## Serializable

The Serializable protocol is used to define the representation of an object that may be transferred through a stream. The representation used for the stored object provides enough information for the object to be restored at a later time with its current state intact. It also allows different versions of the same object to be declared compatible. This provides the newer object with the capability of restoring itself to a previous state.

The Serializable interface is used to define an object that wants to use the Serializable protocol for its storage format. The object must implement the java.io.Serializable interface and may:

- Mark fields that do not want to be persistent using the transient keyword
- May implement the writeObject() method to define additional information to be saved
- May implement the readObject() method to read the format given in the custom writeObject() method, modify any member objects or attributes after retrieval, or implement custom code for initialization

Once the object implements java.io.Serializable, the object is then subject to storage and retrieval with little or no custom implementation code.

## Externalizable

Externalizable objects require a custom method to properly store and load their states. When Externalizable objects are being stored, the identity of the class is saved but the rest is left to the class implementation. Externalizable classes must implement the java.io.Externalizable interface, and are also:

- required to implement the writeExternal() method for object storage. This method defines the storage format and its state.
- required to implement the readExternal() method for object retrieval and is the complement to the writeExternal() method. It must reverse the process implemented in the writeExternal() method but may also include initialization code for member objects and attributes.

**N O T E** Defining a class as externalizable allows custom implementations of object storage and retrieval but can introduce security compromises. The writeExternal() and readExternal() methods are public and may be used to alter the state of private information such as attributes and methods. Keep this in mind when developing externalizable objects. ▓

Part

II

Ch

13

# Reviewing Standard Streams

Before examining object serialization in greater detail, a review of Java's standard streams is necessary. Java provides the concept of streams for transporting data from an application to a sequential file, a random-access file, or even another thread. The classes that provide each of these stream types are numerous. To understand object serialization, the core stream classes will be reviewed.

## InputStream and OutputStream

InputStream and OutputStream are abstract classes that define the most primitive input and output methods. They include the ability to: read/write a byte, read/write series of bytes, determine if any bytes are in the current stream, skip bytes during a read, flush a buffer when writing, and close the stream. These classes provide a base class from which new streams may be defined with additional functionality.

## DataInput and DataOutput

DataInput and DataOutput are interfaces that define a stream with methods that may read or write basic Java types. They define readXXX() and writeXXX() methods, such as readInt() and writeInt(), for each of the fundamental Java data types. The DataInputStream and DataOutputStream classes implement the DataInput and DataOutput interfaces and provide a complete stream implementation for reading and writing Java data types. Used in conjunction with the FileOutputStream and FileInputStream classes, a Java application can store computational results, data entries, and other information to a local file.

# Writing Objects

The primary motivation for most Java developers to use object serialization is for storing an object to a device. To accomplish this using the java.io package, the ObjectOutput and ObjectOutputStream classes were added. This section demonstrates using the new java.io classes to store objects to common output streams, such as a local file.

## ObjectOutput

ObjectOutput extends the DataOutput interface and defines additional methods for storing a byte, an array of bytes, and objects. It extends DataOutput to include the ability to write basic Java data types. Classes that implement the ObjectOutput interface are defined as a class capable of storing object information, attributes, and additional member objects. The ObjectOutputStream class implements the ObjectOutput interface.

Methods defined in ObjectOutput are similar to OutputStream and include: write(), flush(), and close(). The interface also defines a writeObject() method, which is used to write an object.

## ObjectOutputStream

The ObjectOutputStream is responsible for writing primitive data types and objects to an OutputStream. It writes all primitive types of an object by using the writeXXX() methods defined in the DataOutput interface. The constructor requires an OutputStream implementation to which the serialized data is stored. Object graphs are used to store the object structure and are written to the OutputStream. The object graph allows the object to be re-created from an ObjectInputStream by another method or application. The class is also responsible for tracking the list of objects that have been serialized, preventing circular references from being traversed multiple times. All objects written to the ObjectOutputStream will be contained in the same stream, such as a local file.

Objects that are sent to an ObjectOutputStream must implement java.io.Serializable or java.io.Externalizable. The class name, signature, attribute values, and member object values are gathered and transported to the OutputStream for storage. References to other objects, such as member objects, are also written in the same fashion. In the case of multiple references to a stored object, a mechanism known as reference sharing is used to maintain the object's structure when retrieved and reconstructed. Reference sharing also prevents the same object from being written to the output stream multiple times, increasing the size of the serialized data.

## transient

To prevent an object's field from being serialized, the transient keyword may be used. Any field defined as transient will not be serialized, preventing storage and persistence. This modifier is often used to protect valuable object data from being stored externally or to prevent unnecessary fields such as counters and flags from being stored. Reasons for protecting an object's data may include: preventing fields from being restored before a specific state exists, protecting system resources, and protecting sensitive settings. Transient fields are usually assigned a private modifier for further protection.

## Writing an Object Using *ObjectOutputStream*

Listing 13.1 demonstrates how to write an object to a local file using the ObjectOutputStream. The constructor provides a FileOutputStream for the object to be written. A call to writeObject() with the object to save starts the serialization process and sends the result to the local file. These results include the name and id fields of the SimpleObject object. Finally, the ObjectOutputStream is flushed and closed.

**Listing 13.1    Code Portion Demonstrating the Use of *ObjectOutputStream***

```
public void saveObject () {
  SimpleObject so=new SimpleObject ("Object Number 1",1);
  try {
          FileOutputStream fout=new FileOutputStream ("test.object");
          ObjectOutputStream sout=new ObjectOutputStream (fout);
          sout.writeObject (so);
          sout.flush();
          sout.close();
      fout.close();
```

*continues*

Part

II

Ch

13

### Listing 13.1 Continued

```
        } catch (IOException e) {
          e.printStackTrace();
          System.out.println (e);
        }
    }

class SimpleObject implements java.io.Serializable{
    String name;
    int id;

    public SimpleObject (String n, int i) {
      name=n;
      id=i;
    }

    public String toString () {
        return "NAME: "+name+" ID: "+id;
    }
}
```

# *writeObject*

ObjectOutputStream provides the writeObject() method for writing objects to the OutputStream. This method is responsible for gathering the required object information and writing it to the OutputStream. Multiple objects may be written to the OutputStream using multiple writeObject() calls. It is the responsibility of the retrieving application to read the objects in the same order for proper restoration.

The defaultWriteObject() method in the ObjectOutputStream class is responsible for writing all of the non-static and non-transient fields of the class. When an object is serialized, the defaultWriteObject() method is called. This method provides the basic serialization protocol and handles storing the object states. A class that implements the java.io.Serializable is given an option to provide a custom writeObject() method. This option allows a class to include additional information about its state or its environment. If the class includes a writeObject() method, it is called in place of the defaultWriteObject() method. When implementing a custom writeObject() method, a call to the defaultWriteObject() method is issued first, followed by additional writeXXX() methods containing custom data. defaultWriteMethod() may be called only from an object's custom writeObject() method or a NotActiveException will be thrown. Listing 13.2 shows a short example of implementing a custom writeObject() method.

### Listing 13.2  An Example of Implementing a Custom *writeObject()* Method

```
class SimpleObject2 implements java.io.Serializable {
    private void writeObject(java.io.ObjectOutputStream stream)throws
IOException {
```

```
        stream.defaultWriteObject ();
        stream.writeUTF ("Example 2 using a custom writeObject method");
    }
// rest of code here
}
```

It is recommend to declare the custom `writeObject()` method private to prevent external objects from prematurely invoking the method. In addition, calling the `defaultWriteObject()` method ensures that the object is fully represented and all fields are stored. Note that the `ObjectOutputStream.writeObject()` method determines which method to call: the `defaultWriteObject`, a custom `writeObject()` implementation, or the `writeExternal()` method.

## *writeExternal*

When an object implements the `Externalizable` interface, the object must define its own format or representation. The definition must be contained in the `writeExternal()` method of the class. It is the responsibility of the `writeExternal()` to capture the states of all fields, as well as coordinate with its superclasses. Coordination with the superclasses is important so that previously defined external formats are maintained and the object design remains intact.

Designing the `writeExternal()` method presents a large amount of freedom. The `ObjectOutputStream` that is calling the `writeExternal()` method is passed as the only argument. This gives the method complete access to the `writeXXX()` methods of the `ObjectOutputStream` for saving primitive fields and member objects. Listing 13.3 shows a simple externalizable object and its `writeExternal()` method.

### Listing 13.3   A Demonstration of Defining an *Externalizable* Class

```
class ComplexObject implements java.io.Externalizable{
    SimpleObject so1,so2;

    public void writeExternal(java.io.ObjectOutput out){
        try {
        out.writeObject (so1);
      // write a simple string in the UTF 16-bit string format
        out.writeUTF ("Custom String inside of two objects!");
        out.writeObject (so2);
        } catch (IOException e) {
          System.out.println (e);
        }
        System.out.println ("WriteExternal!!");

    }
}
```

Part

II

Ch

13

# Reading Objects

Once an object has been serialized and transported using an OutputStream, the object may then be restored, or deserialized. This is accomplished by using several classes that complement the ObjectOutputXXX classes. These classes include ObjectInput, ObjectInputValidation, and ObjectInputStream.

## *ObjectInput*

The ObjectInput interface provides methods for retrieving byte, byte arrays, and Java objects from a stream. The interface extends DataInput which defines additional methods for retrieving primitive Java data types. Classes that implement the ObjectInput interface, such as ObjectInputStream, are able to retrieve stored Java objects and member fields.

ObjectInput defines several methods similar to InputStream, including: read(), skip(), and close(). In addition, the interface defines a method called readObject(), which is used to retrieve an object from storage.

## *ObjectInputValidation*

ObjectInputValidation is an interface that is used for callbacks when an object has finished deserializing of all objects and fields contained in its graph. This interface is used for object validation once an object has been loaded. The only method defined in the interface is validateObject(). It will throw an ObjectInvalidException should any errors occur during the validation process.

## *ObjectInputStream*

ObjectInputStream is responsible for the reconstruction of an object or objects that were stored using the ObjectOutputStream class. It processes the object deserialization and ensures that an object may be reconstructed from the given information. The class is responsible for keeping a list of the objects that have already been deserialized and also maintains the state of the stream.

The constructor requires an InputStream implementation for the source of the data. The constructor then calls the readStreamHeader() method to determine if the InputStream data contains information that has been generated from an ObjectOutputStream writeheaderMethod(). If the header is valid, the process to move through the stream contents begins. It starts reconstructing the saved data for the object from the InputStream implementation. Data is read by using the readXXX() methods implemented from the ObjectInput interface. Should any data be encountered that doesn't belong in the reconstructed object, it is thrown out. If data is not available for a specific object field, the field is set to its default value. The latter condition is common when a newer version of the saved object has added extra fields to its definition.

## Reading an Object Using the *ObjectInputStream*

Listing 13.4 shows the code for loading the SimpleObject stored by the code in Listing 13.1. It first creates a new FileInputStream pointing to the file the object was previously written. It then passes the file stream to the constructor of the new ObjectInputStream object. Next, it invokes the readObject() method which retrieves the object, casts it to the proper object type, and prints it to the console. When restoring serialized objects, the code must declare the proper class for casting during compile-time. This excludes dynamic casting and forces the developer to know what kind of class to cast the data. Finally, it closes the streams to finish the method.

### Listing 13.4   Code Portion Demonstrating the Use of *ObjectInputStream*

```
public void loadObject () {
   try {
           FileInputStream fin=new FileInputStream ("test.object");
           ObjectInputStream sin=new ObjectInputStream (fin);

             SimpleObject so2=(SimpleObject) sin.readObject();
           System.out.println (so2);

 sin.close();
     fin.close();
     } catch (IOException e) {
       e.printStackTrace();
       System.out.println (e);
     } catch (ClassNotFoundException e){
       e.printStackTrace();
       System.out.println (e);
     }
   }
```

Output:

*NAME: Object Number 1 ID: 1*

## *readObject*

As shown in the previous Listing 13.4, ObjectInputStream contains a method called readObject() which is responsible for traversing the stream and reconstructing the next object available. It is the responsibility of the application to ensure the objects are read in the proper order for the restoration process to proceed correctly, should multiple objects be stored in the stream.

Should a class implement a custom writeObject() routine, the class is required to implement a custom readObject() routine for properly restoring the additional data. It is also important to ensure that data is read in the proper order when implementing the custom code. If this precaution is not taken, the deserialization could fail for any object not read at the correct time.

The deserialization process will call the `defaultReadObject()` method if a custom `readObject()` method has not been implemented. This method is responsible for implementing the standard deserialization process. Should an error occur during the process, one of the following Exceptions will be thrown: `IOException`, `ClassNotFoundException`, or `NotActiveException`. The `NotActiveException` will be thrown only if a call to the `defaultReadObject()` method is made outside of a custom `readObject()` method.

Listing 13.5 shows the complementary code to the example in Listing 13.2. The `readUTF()` method is used to retrieve the custom string sent to the local file in the custom `writeObject()` routine shown earlier.

**Listing 13.5    Implementing a Custom *readObject()* Method**

```
private void readObject(java.io.ObjectInputStream stream) throws IOException,
ClassNotFoundException {
    stream.defaultReadObject();
    System.out.println (stream.readUTF ());
  }
```

It is recommended to declare the custom `readObject()` method private to prevent external objects from prematurely invoking the method. In addition, calling the `defaultReadObject()` method ensures that the object is fully represented and all fields are stored.

# readExternal

If an object implements the `Externalizable` interface, the `readObject()` method will invoke the object's `readExternal()` method when the object is to be retrieved. The `readExternal()` method should complement the `writeExternal()` method to ensure that all data is properly retrieved and restored. As with the `writeExternal()` method, it is the responsibility of the class to coordinate with its superclasses and ensure proper restoration of all object fields. Also, the `ObjectInputStream` that invoked the custom method is passed to `readExternal()` to provide the `readXXX()` methods associated with reading Java primitives and objects. Listing 13.6 shows the code for `readExternal()` that complements the code in Listing 13.3.

**Listing 13.6    A Demonstration of Defining an *Externalizable* Class**

```
class ComplexObject implements java.io.Externalizable{
    SimpleObject so1,so2;

public void readExternal(java.io.ObjectInput in){
try {
        so1=(SimpleObject)in.readObject ();
        System.out.println (in.readUTF ());
        so2=(SimpleObject)in.readObject ();
      } catch (IOException e) {
        System.out.println (e);
```

```
        } catch (ClassNotFoundException e) {
            System.out.println (e);
        }
    }
}
```

# Versioning Objects

During the development of a Java application, a serialized object will often require new fields or modifications to its overall structure. This can cause problems when attempting to restore a serialized object that was saved from an older version. To overcome this obstacle, the concept of versioning has been introduced into object serialization.

Versioning provides a list of compatible and incompatible changes that the object serialization protocol can handle if a class changes over time. It also attempts to handle the changes automatically, preventing special conversion methods for the new object version. It will handle only classes that are Serializable since it has control of the stored object format for these classes. This requires Externalizable classes to implement a custom version control system.

## Versioning Responsibilities

It is the responsibility of the new, or evolved, class to meet the requirements necessary to remain compatible with previous versions of itself. To retain this compatibility, two steps are necessary. First, it must follow the guidelines set by the serialization protocol for compatible and incompatible changes. Second, it must specify which class it is compatible with by specifying the SerialVersionUID of the class with which it wants to remain compatible. This prevents two classes with the same name from attempting to restore incompatible object data.

## Compatible and Incompatible Changes

For versioning to occur properly, the new class must follow several guidelines. Table 13.1 lists the compatible changes that can be made to a new object version for proper deserialization to occur. Table 13.2 lists the changes that prevent versioning from proceeding properly.

**Part**

**II**

**Ch**

**13**

**Table 13.1   Compatible Object Versioning Changes**

| Action | Comment |
|---|---|
| Adding Fields | Fields may be added to a new version and will be assigned the default value for the type, such as null. |
| Adding Classes | New classes may be added and will be assigned the default value, such as null. |

*continues*

**Table 13.1    Continued**

| Action | Comment |
|--------|---------|
| Removing Classes | Member classes may be deleted and will be detected when deserialized. Primitive types will be discarded, but members of the deleted class will be created in case of references later in the stream. Garbage collection will occur when the stream is reset or destroyed. |
| Adding `read/writeObject` | New versions may implement a customized `readObject()` method, but should call `defaultReadObject()` before reading custom data. The new `writeObject()` should call `defaultWriteObject()` to ensure the required data is written before optional data. |
| Removing `read/writeObject` | Old `read/writeObject` methods may be removed; the default `read/writeObject` methods will be used and custom data discarded. |
| Adding `java.io.Serializable` | Similar to adding fields, there will be no available data, so the class will be initialized to its default values. Caution: Subclassing non-serializable classes requires the class's superclass to contain a no-argument constructor so the class may be initialized. |
| Removing `java.io.Serializable` | Similar to removing the class, the data for the class is read and discarded. |
| Changing field state | Changing a field from static to non-static or transient to non-transient is similar to adding a field. Data for the field will not be available when read causing the field to be initialized to its static field or initialized to its default value. |

**Table 13.2    Incompatible Object Versioning Changes**

| Action | Comment |
|--------|---------|
| Deleting Fields | The new class will not write the deleted field, which allows the new class to evolve forward. Problems may occur if the old version attempts to read the new file, since the field will be initialized to its default value and may not be in its proper state. |
| Moving classes in the hierarchy | Class data will appear in the wrong order should a class change its parent or location. |

| Action | Comment |
|---|---|
| Changing `static`/`transient` states | This is similar to deleting a field and will have the same repercussions should a field move from non-static to static or non-transient to transient. |
| Changing a field type | Data is written in a form specific to its type and cannot be read as another data type. This will cause a `read` to fail because of the mismatch. |
| Changing `read`/`writeObject` method | Changing the order in which the `readObject` or `writeObject` methods `write` data will cause the restoration to fail. It will also fail if the default data is not written when it was or written when it wasn't before. |
| Changing to `Externalizable`/ `Serializable` | `Externalizable` classes are not compatible with `Serializable` classes since the reading and writing implementations are incompatible. |

# Using *serialver*

Distributed with version 1.1 of the Java Development Kit is a command-line utility called `serialver`. It displays the Stream Unique IDentifier number, or SUID, for a specific class. This number is a unique hashcode value for the class and is defined by the class name, fields, and methods it contains. The proper syntax for using `serialver` is:

```
serialver [-show] [classname][classname...]
```

The optional -show switch displays a graphical frame for a friendlier user interface. Sample output from the `serialver` command is in the form:

[classname] [serialVersionUID = number]

Example:

```
serialver SimpleObject
```

returns:

```
SimpleObject:    static final long serialVersionUID = 1177034771972299918L;
```

The string returned from `serialver` is used to specify a new class as compatible with an older version of the same class. This is accomplished by including the static field declaration in the new class declaration. This value represents the unique SUID assigned to the object and allows the serialization protocol to attempt versioning when restoring a new class from older data.

For example, to determine the SUID for a class name `myClass`, execute the `serialver` command:

```
serialver myClass
```

Next, add the following line to a new version of `myClass`:

```
static final long serialVersionUID= thenumber;
```

Part

II

Ch

13

The new `myClass` is now prepared to read object data stored by the previous version. In addition, any new versions of the class that require reading an older version may attempt to do so by simply adding the `serialVersionUID` to the class declaration.

# Implementing Versioning

To demonstrate the complete steps necessary when implementing a class that can handle versioning, let's expand on the class `SimpleObject` that was used in the previous examples for this chapter.

**Step 1: Determine the New Class Needs** The first step is to determine what changes need to be made. For this example, we want to add a new `String` field, named "another." Does this fit within the bounds of versioning compatibility? According to Table 13.1, it does. Add the new field to the definition and go to Step 2. If it didn't, we would need to determine if the change is required and if it was worth losing the capabilities of versioning. We could also determine if the change could be made in a different way to eliminate any problems with versioning.

**Step 2: Determine the SUID of the Older Class** The next step is to use the new `serialver` command to determine the SUID of the older class. For this example, the following command line is needed:

```
serialver SimpleObject
```

The output is:

```
SimpleObject: static final long serialVersionUID= -1177034771972299918L;
```

**Step 3: Insert the SUID as a Class Constant** Using the result from Step 2, insert a `serialVersionUID` field in the new class declaration:

```
static final long serialVersionUID= -1177034771972299918L;
```

**Step 4: Put It Together and Execute the New Code** Gathering the information from previous steps, the new class code is presented in Listing 13.7. Compare the code with the `SimpleObject` class in Listing 13.1. Finally, use the `loadObjects()` code in Listing 13.4 to create a simple application that loads the same file from Listing 13.4 but uses the new class (Listing 13.8).

---

**Listing 13.7   A New Version of *SimpleObject***

```
class SimpleObject implements java.io.Serializable{
    String name;
    int id;
    String another;
    static final long serialVersionUID= -1177034771972299918L;

    public SimpleObject (String n, int i,String a) {
      name=n;
      id=i;
      another=a;
    }
```

```java
    public String toString () {
        return "NAME: "+name+" ID: "+id+" another:"+another;
    }
}
```

## Listing 13.8   A Simple Application to Demonstrate Versioning

```java
import java.io.*;

public class Example4{
    public Example4() {
        loadObject();
    }

    public void loadObject () {
      try {
          FileInputStream fin=new FileInputStream ("test4.object");
          ObjectInputStream oin=new ObjectInputStream (fin);

          SimpleObject nso=(SimpleObject) oin.readObject();
          System.out.println (nso);
      oin.close();
      fin.close();
      } catch (IOException e) {
        e.printStackTrace();
        System.out.println (e);
      } catch (ClassNotFoundException e){
        e.printStackTrace();
        System.out.println (e);
      }
    }

    static public void main(String args[]) {
        Example4 f=new Example4 ();
    }

}
```

# Object Serialization Security Issues

Security issues associated with Java applications typically cover issues that exist within the Java Virtual Machine. However, object serialization presents additional issues, including security from external sources. Though not all of the problems that occur outside of the virtual machine are preventable, steps may be taken to reduce the amount of outside tampering. This section presents several security issues associated with object serialization, as well as several solutions and preventative measures.

Part
II

Ch
13

# Serialization Security by Design

Object serialization was designed to provide a simple, yet robust mechanism for transforming Java objects into byte representations. This design was kept simple to prevent large holes in security. The following is a summary of the security designs for object serialization:

- Serialization is restricted to objects implementing java.io.Serializable, and java.io.Externalizable. Fields and objects that shouldn't be serialized may be marked by the transient keyword.

- Serialization stores only object values; deserialization always creates new objects with these values and will not overwrite an existing object.

- Code loading during the deserialization process is restricted by the same security model enforced on the rest of the application.

- Externalizable objects provide opportunity for custom serialization, but the implementation is required to provide security mechanisms and protections.

# Using *transient* as Partial Security

Designing a serialized class that uses system resources may open security for an application if they are not managed properly. Improper design would involve allowing public access to member objects that use resources such as file systems. The member object, if public or publicly accessible by accessor methods, may be altered to point to a local file before serialized. This may give an application access to the resource at a later time, when it normally wouldn't be allowed. This loophole may be closed by tagging resource members with the transient keyword, protecting the resource from being stored when the object is serialized. Careful planning and use of the transient declaration may help protect an application from being used for something other than that for which it was designed.

# External Serialization

Some classes contain code that require particular states to exist before actions may occur. Should a class be stored in a state that does not reflect the currently correct state, application errors may occur. In addition, incorrect data may be loaded from a corrupted file that could cause an application to go awry. To prevent this, extra validation code should be included after serialization occurs. This may be included in a custom readObject() method, or within the method(s) responsible for starting the loading process.

# Encrypted Streams

Finally, the object serialization mechanism was designed for the greatest flexibility for transmission. Since the abstract InputStream and OutputStream classes are used for the readObject() and writeObject() method arguments, special stream classes may be used. These stream classes may be a special stream filter, or a custom stream such as encryption streams, for data transmission.

# Serialization Exceptions

All exceptions that are thrown during object serialization are subclasses of ObjectStreamException. ObjectStreamException is a subclass of java.io.IOException and therefore allows applications to catch IOException and determine the proper course of action by using the instanceOf operator. Table 13.3 lists all subclasses of ObjectStreamException and the common reason(s) for being thrown.

**Table 13.3   Object Serialization Exceptions**

| Exception | Reason |
|---|---|
| InvalidClassException | The class cannot be used to restore an object due to: non-matching version numbers, class contains inconsistent data types with stored data, class is not public, class does not have a no-argument constructor |
| NotSerializableException | Class is not a Serializable class—thrown during readObject() and writeObject() only |
| StreamCorruptedException | Invalid stream header or control information invalid/not found |
| NotActiveException | Thrown if registerValidation() is not called during a readObject() method |
| InvalidObjectException | Thrown when a deserialized object can't be made valid |
| OptionalDataException | Thrown when primitive data is found when object data is expected during a readObject() |
| WriteAbortedException | Thrown when an exception is encountered while data is being written to a stream |

# Serializing Objects Using Relational Databases

Part
II

Ch
13

So far, the serialization techniques presented were used to store objects to a local file for later retrieval. Using this technique is tolerable for most small to mid-size applications, but not for large-scale applications. The local file system is too slow and cumbersome to store large amounts of data, especially when attempting to read or write a file multiple times in a session. In addition, file persistence doesn't allow multiple users to access data efficiently and may cause poor application performance. To satisfy large-scale applications that must handle large amounts of users and data, a relational database may be used.

Relational Database Management Systems (RDMSs) currently exist in many corporate networks and provide many advantages when using serialization. These advantages, along with the side effects, will be outlined in this section. Finally, a technique for storing object data to an RDMS will be presented and example code provided.

# Advantages of Using an RDMS

Using an RDMS can provide several advantages when combined with object serialization, including: large user support, fault-tolerant design including crash recovery, abundance of tools and software, and performance gain when handling data.

Handling a large number of users is very important when developing scalable applications. Using local file systems requires an application to read the entire file each time data is requested, producing unsatisfactory results such as low performance, redundant reads, and large room for error. In addition, the input/output performance is low, preventing an application from quickly distributing information to each client efficiently.

In addition, using a local file system leaves the data susceptible to crashes and data loss. Should the storage of data be interrupted by a power shortage, for example, the local data file may be damaged and unrecoverable. However, most RDMSs are designed with fault-tolerance, allowing data recovery and automatic data backup. These features can protect valuable data from being ruined by uncontrollable situations.

In addition, RDMS software can be found easily and is available from many different development companies. This increases the chance of finding a particular software package that fits the development and hardware needs of the application and corporation.

Finally, an RDMS is designed to handle data in an efficient method and may be designed to monitor data requests for added performance. This monitoring, coupled with memory-caching of popular data, can be used to increase data manipulation and response time by several factors over local files. Implementing efficient data manipulation techniques may increase the time-to-market goal for an application and increase development time when using local files.

# Disadvantages of Using an RDMS

An RDMS is not without its faults, however. These include: higher cost for software, incompatible data representations, and additional code for mapping.

The biggest factor of using an RDMS for object storage is the inability to search for data contained in stored fields. The data is stored in byte format and cannot be searched by standard methods. Additionally, the fields cannot be changed easily, but require the object to be deserialized, modified, and serialized again.

Although many low-cost RDMS packages are available, they do not offer the performance advantages and fault-tolerance that many other packages offer. In addition, some cost is associated with third-party tools and drivers necessary for proper implementation and testing.

Another disadvantage of using an RDMS for serialization solutions is the incompatibility of Java objects with relational data types. Relational databases were popularized before object-oriented technologies became mainstream. This requires a Java developer to spend time developing database tables that represent the Java object. Should an object change, the table must also be changed, forcing the data to be exported and imported into the new table. This can cost additional time and money when attempting to maintain Java objects in a relational database.

Finally, additional code must be added to the Java application to map Java objects to the custom database tables. This can increase the size of the application and decrease performance when working with large object structures. Should the object definition change, the code must be updated to accept these changes.

As a general rule of thumb, RDMS storage is a good decision if large amounts of bulk data are needed by multiple clients. It is not a good idea for storing data that requires only minor field modifications.

## Serialization Using BLOBs

This section will present a technique of storing Java objects into a database that accepts data types with sizes larger than 255 bytes. Some databases support data types such as LONGVARBINARY, IMAGE, and BLOBs (Binary Large Objects). These data types may be used to support storage of serialized objects, often called object BLOBs. The technique will build a sample application that stores multiple objects into a database and retrieves them for later use. The database table for this example will contain only one column of type IMAGE and is designed to work with SQL Server. Please refer to a reference manual for the proper data type support in other DBMSs.

**Establishing the Database Connection**   The first step is to establish a connection to the database. Listing 13.9 shows the connection to the database using the JDBC-ODBC Driver from JavaSoft. The code attempts to connect to an ODBC driver named Enterprise.

### Listing 13.9   Application Declaration and Database Connection

```
public class Example6{
    byte[] bytes;

    Connection connection;
    Statement statement;
    ResultSet results;

    public Example6(){
     //init the DB objects
     try {
       Class.forName("sun.jdbc.odbc.JdbcOdbcDriver").newInstance();
       connection = DriverManager.getConnection("jdbc:odbc:enterprise;uid=sa");
     } catch (Exception e) {
       System.out.println ("INIT exception :"+e);
     }
     saveObjects();
     loadObjects();
     }
```

**Using *ByteArrayOutputStream* to Capture the Serialized Data**   The next step is to serialize the objects into a byte array. To accomplish this, the serialization will be directed into a ByteArrayOutputStream. Since ObjectOutputStream accepts any output stream that extends the OutputStream abstract class, this can be accomplished with little effort. Listing 13.10 presents the saveObjects() method that instantiates six objects, serializes them, and stores the data into a byte array. After the data is gathered, the byte array is passed to another method, DBInsert(), which is outlined in the next section.

**Listing 13.10   Using *ByteArrayOutputStream* to Capture the Serialization in Memory**

```
public void saveObjects () {
      SimpleObject sf=new SimpleObject("Testing Object 1",10);
      SimpleObject sf2=new SimpleObject("Testing Object 2",20);
      SimpleObject sf3=new SimpleObject("Testing Object 3",30);
      SimpleObject sf4=new SimpleObject("Testing Object 4",40);
      SimpleObject sf5=new SimpleObject("Testing Object 5",50);
      SimpleObject sf6=new SimpleObject("Testing Object 6",60);
       try {
           // Write an object to a byte array
           ByteArrayOutputStream bout = new ByteArrayOutputStream();
           ObjectOutputStream sout = new ObjectOutputStream(bout);
           sout.writeObject(sf);
           sout.writeObject(sf2);
           sout.writeObject(sf3);
           sout.writeObject(sf4);
           sout.writeObject(sf5);
           sout.writeObject(sf6);

   // capture data into a byte array and insert into the database
           bytes = bout.toByteArray();
           DBInsert (bytes);
       } catch (IOException e) {
         e.printStackTrace();
         System.out.println (e);
       }
       System.out.println ("saveObjects Done!");
    }
```

**Inserting the Objects into the Database**   With the byte array created, it now needs to be inserted into the database as a new row. To accomplish this task, several steps need to be taken. The first step is to create and execute a SQL statement that sets the length of returned IMAGE data types to the maximum size, 2,147,483,647 bytes. This command is SQL Server-specific, and may need to be modified to other DBMS equivalents. Next, a DELETE statement, specific for this example, will be sent to remove any previous objects stored in the database. Finally, a PreparedStatement is created with one in parameter. This parameter is set as a binary stream and assigned to a new ByteArrayInputStream created from the byte array. The statement is then executed to insert the data into the database (see Listing 13.11).

### Listing 13.11 Inserting the Object BLOB into the Database

```
public void DBInsert (byte[] array) {
    try {
      statement=connection.createStatement();
      statement.executeUpdate ("SET TEXTSIZE 2147483647");

      Statement cleanup=connection.createStatement();
      cleanup.executeUpdate ("DELETE storage3");

      PreparedStatement ps=connection.prepareStatement("INSERT into storage
➥values (?)");
      ps.clearParameters();

      ByteArrayInputStream bin=new ByteArrayInputStream(array);
      ps.setBinaryStream (1,bin,array.length);
      ps.executeUpdate ();
    } catch (SQLException e) {
      System.out.println ("DBInsert exception: "+e);
    }
  }
```

**Retrieving the Objects from the Database**   Now that the data has been inserted into the database, it may now be retrieved and restored. To retrieve the data, a SELECT statement is executed and the results gathered into a byte array. The results are gathered into a byte array by using the getBinaryStream() method from the ResultSet class. The data is read from the returned InputStream and stored in a byte array passed to the read() method. The byte array is then returned at the end of the method, shown in Listing 13.12.

### Listing 13.12 Retrieving the Objects from the Database

```
public byte[] DBRetrieve () {
      ByteArrayInputStream bin=null;

    try {
      statement=connection.createStatement();
      results=statement.executeQuery ("SELECT * from storage");

      // get the results, create a new DBEmployee object,  and add it to the
      ➥vector
      results.next();
      InputStream in =results.getBinaryStream (1);
      System.out.println (" — ");
      int next;
      byte[] data=new byte[32767];
      while ( (next=in.read (data)) != -1) {
      }
      return data;
      } catch (java.sql.SQLException e) {
```

*continues*

Part

II

Ch

13

**Listing 13.12   Continued**

```
        System.out.println ("Error retrieving results from the db! "+e);
    }
    catch (IOException e) {
      System.out.println ("Error retrieving results from the db! "+e);
    }
    return null;
}
```

**Rebuilding the Objects**   The final step is to restore the objects in the byte array created from the method in Listing 13.12 to their original states. To accomplish this, the steps used to create the byte array will be reversed. A ByteArrayInputStream will be created from the byte array and passed into a new ObjectInputStream. The objects in the stream may now be read and restored. This loadObjects() method in Listing 13.13 demonstrates the necessary steps, and prints them to demonstrate the success of the restoration.

**Listing 13.13   Restoring the Objects from the Retrieved Data**

```
public void loadObjects () {
  System.out.println ("loadObjects()");
  try {
      // Read the object from the db
      byte[] bytes2=DBRetrieve();

      ObjectInputStream in = new ObjectInputStream(new
      ➡ByteArrayInputStream (bytes2));
      SimpleObject sf10=(SimpleObject)in.readObject ();
      SimpleObject sf20=(SimpleObject)in.readObject ();
      SimpleObject sf30=(SimpleObject)in.readObject ();
      SimpleObject sf40=(SimpleObject)in.readObject ();
      SimpleObject sf50=(SimpleObject)in.readObject ();
      SimpleObject sf60=(SimpleObject)in.readObject ();
      System.out.println
      ➡(sf10+"\n"+sf20+"\n"+sf30+"\n"+sf40+"\n"+sf50+"\n"+sf60);

  } catch (IOException e) {
    e.printStackTrace();
    System.out.println (e);
  } catch (ClassNotFoundException e){
    e.printStackTrace();
    System.out.println (e);
  }
}
```

# From Here...

This chapter has presented an in-depth demonstration of various persistent techniques using Java's Object Serialization API. The API was designed to provide simple, easy-to-use methodology for storing and retrieving objects to storage devices. In addition, it provides extreme flexibility for the developer, allowing custom external protocols to be defined for specialized applications. Using object serialization will help developers reduce the development curve usually associated with converting object states to persistent data and provide a standard method for storing and retrieving Java objects.

- Chapter 12, "Introduction to Distributed Computing," will cover the basic concepts of distributed computing including DCE, RPC, and CORBA.
- Chapter 14, "Remote Objects," covers the basic RMI model, presents the RMI package, and demonstrates how it brings distributed computing to Java.
- Chapter 15, "Advanced RMI Concepts," discusses using RMI to tackle larger applications and expands upon the topics in Chapter 14.

# Remote Objects

So far, developing a Java application has involved writing one or more objects that work together within the same virtual machine. If applications want to communicate with one another, a set of communication routines would have to be developed. This would include routines for encoding and decoding information transmitted between each application.

With the introduction of Remote Method Invocation (RMI), applications may now be distributed between virtual machines. This means that applications may now span computers, or even networks; these distributed applications can now leverage the power of multiple computers to accomplish a common task. ■

**Understanding RMI**

Find out what RMI is and weigh its benefits.

**The RMI model**

Review the Java RMI model and how all of the pieces of RMI fit together.

**RMI architecture**

Understand the RMI Architecture, including the layers of RMI and their responsibilities.

**RMI security**

Fully understand RMI security issues and how they affect RMI applications.

**Building a simple RMI application**

Apply the knowledge to build a basic RMI application.

**Applying RMI**

Expand upon the basic RMI framework, adding advanced techniques.

# What Is RMI?

*RMI* is an acronym for Remote Method Invocation, a new package that was included in the release of the JDK 1.1. RMI provides Java with the ability to execute, or invoke, methods that exist in other virtual machines. These remote objects may exist in another application on the same machine, on another machine on the local LAN or on a remote LAN on the Internet. RMI is based on the Remote Procedure Call (RPC) technology that evolved in the 1980s, which allowed procedures on remote machines to be executed as easily as procedures on the local machine. RMI expands on this principle, adding the object-oriented technologies that have evolved in recent years.

Chapter 15, "Advanced RMI Concepts," will discuss RMI from an abstract, conceptual, and in-depth point of view. As a Java developer, it is important to understand the implications of using RMI, and how RMI can reduce design time and offer a new tool in the developer's belt.

Understanding how RMI works and when it is needed is essential in project assessment. To fully understand RMI, an abstract view of RMI will be presented. This presentation will provide the necessary information for understanding RMI and determining when RMI can be leveraged for better application development.

## Why Was RMI Developed?

In a standard two-tier application model, the application contains the business logic, the user interface, and the interface to the database. As businesses start to change the way they function, the application must be altered to reflect these changes. To prevent large applications from being rewritten, the three-tier application model was developed. In this model, the user interface becomes its own module, and the business logic becomes the middle piece for the application. In addition, multiple applications will use the same business logic module. The business logic becomes responsible for retrieving the information from the database and organizing it for all of the end-user applications. When a business must change its strategy or functions, only the business logic module requires updating. All applications that depend on the same module escape the need for rewriting, thus saving time and expense in code revisions.

The three-tier application must have a communications layer between the business module and the user interface for the design to function properly. This usually means that an application-level protocol must be defined; this perpetuates cumbersome design that leads to errors. With the addition of RMI, the application-level protocol goes away and an easier implementation may be used. Until recently, the three-tier model couldn't be combined easily with object-oriented design. However, with the addition of RMI to the Java package, a truly object-oriented distributed architecture design is available.

The RMI package allows Java developers to design three-tier applications without the worries of building a custom communications layer. In addition, the computing power that becomes necessary for large-scale applications may be moved to a server that is capable of handling the requirements. The user interface may be moved to a workstation that is equipped with less hardware, thus creating a thinner client. This is very important with the addition of network computers in the marketplace. These computers, though powerful, initially will not be equipped with vast amounts of resources. Large-scale applications may now be developed for powerful servers and alleviate the standard, cumbersome client that some current designs require.

## How Does RMI Work?

RMI requires several components to function properly, including a remote interface, remote server, client, and naming registry. Each of these components defines a specific function and communicates using object serialization. Object serialization is a method of converting object hierarchies into byte streams for transportation. This allows Java applications that exist outside of the same virtual machine to communicate with one another.

**The Remote Interface**  The remote interface is responsible for defining the methods that may be invoked by an object in another virtual machine. This interface specifies the method names, parameters, and return values that are required. It is the building block for the application, since the server must implement this interface to be considered a remote object.

**The Remote Server**  The server component provides the implementation of the remote methods, as defined in the remote interface. It also may contain local methods that may be used for additional calculations and processes for the object. The server is required to be exported, which initializes the object as a remote object and allows the object to "listen" for remote method invocations. The server usually extends a remote object class, provided in the java.rmi package, which properly exports the server. However, other alternatives are provided for exporting the object, enabling custom objects to provide remote methods, as well.

**The Client**  Client components are the most flexible components of an RMI application. These components are responsible for obtaining a reference to the remote server and invoking remote methods. They may extend any class and can be member objects of a larger class. Clients also may be defined as remote objects by implementing a different remote interface.

**N O T E**  When clients implement a remote interface, the concept of client and server tend to get confusing. To eliminate this confusion, the object invoking a remote method will be named the client, and the object containing the remote method will be the server. ▪

**The Naming Registry**  Finally, the naming registry component is a bootstrapping mechanism that holds references to remote servers. It must exist on the same machine as the remote server(s) that are registered. Once a server is bound to the registry with a name, a client may obtain a reference to the server by issuing a locate request from the registry. Should the client not find a reference for the name provided in the request, the client will receive an error.

The RMI model brings the three-tier architecture to a more powerful state, and allows the computational requirements of an application to be placed on the server instead of the client. The client then becomes free to operate on more important tasks rather than take up the user's time by making computations that it may not be readily equipped to handle. In addition, since

Part
II

Ch
14

Java is platform-independent, applications may now be distributed across different operating systems. This truly makes Java stand out in the world of distributed computing!

# RMI Benefits

The Java RMI package can benefit application design in several ways:

■ RMI allows passing and returning complex objects, preventing application-level protocol design. This prevents hard-to-find errors from creeping into applications.

■ RMI can provide transaction confirmations after remote methods are completed. This prevents complex handling of transactions that require the client to track lists of transactions and wait for custom confirmation messages that must be decoded and processed.

■ Processing power may be distributed to powerful servers and no longer must depend on slowing down clients for hard computations. This also allows clients to be equipped with less hardware than normal and starts a decline in the endless requirements of stronger clients.

■ True object-oriented designs remain intact due to the object passing abilities of RMI. Applications don't have to be designed with 75 percent object-oriented technology and 25 percent procedural technologies, which alleviates conflicts in design.

■ RMI preserves event-driven programming, allows seamless remote invocations, and doesn't interfere with standard application flow.

■ RMI uses an independent transport layer. It is currently built to use TCP/IP sockets, but may be replaced with future protocol handling without disturbing the application or package as a whole.

■ RMI provides less open communications. Unlike standard socket communications, RMI uses object serialization to communicate with remote applications. This prevents pure text transfers, reducing security compromises. In addition, as Secure Socket Layer or other security protocols become commonplace, it may be used as the transport protocol for an RMI application.

# RMI Penalties

Although powerful, RMI does have some disadvantages:

■ Invoking remote methods has a high overhead. As larger, more complex objects are passed, a time penalty is incurred to convert the objects into the proper format required by the serialization methods.

■ An RMI application is Java-specific. Unlike CORBA, there are no standards for using RMI with other platform-specific software. Currently, the remote methods must be called by a Java application.

■ Development is more difficult. Using RMI to its fullest is sometimes difficult and requires lots of practice and forethought. A poorly designed RMI application can reduce performance to unacceptable levels.

■ When designing peer-to-peer (bi-directional) remote objects, the client cannot extend the applet class, but must extend a remote object class. This forces applets to use a more complex method of performing remote object communications.

## Determining When RMI Is Needed

RMI provides a powerful distributed architecture to Java. When designing an application that will be a three-or-more-tiered application, a decision should be made: *Is RMI right for this project?*

To determine if RMI is right for your project, try to answer the following questions:

1. Can multiple applications leverage common objects on a remote server?
2. Am I going to spend a lot of time creating an application protocol for a standard three-tier application design?
3. Do I need easy expandability into a secure transportation protocol?
4. Would I benefit from complex object passing instead of simple string passing?
5. Will all communication be Java-to-Java?

If the answer to most of these questions is yes, then RMI may be the design choice for your project. If the answer to most of these questions is no, consider if the design of the application may necessitate RMI in future implementations. RMI is not for every project, but can help make a large project easier to manage as it matures.

# The Structure of an RMI Application

To understand how RMI functions, and how remote objects interact, the structure of RMI must be examined. This section shows how all of the pieces of an RMI application interact. It takes some time to fully understand how an RMI application must behave, but it is important when you are designing an application using RMI.

## Client/Server RMI Applications

The client/server RMI application is the most common implementation of distributed architecture. To visualize how a client/server configuration may be designed, imagine a simple banking scenario. A client, which could be a bank representative or an automated teller machine, would get an account number, a transaction type, and an amount. The client would then connect to the server and perform the transaction on the account by invoking the remote method with the proper information. The method would then return the current balance after any adjustments. Figure 14.1 shows how Java classes communicate and the steps necessary to perform remote invocation.

Part
II

Ch

14

**FIG. 14.1**
Client/Server RMI
Application structure.

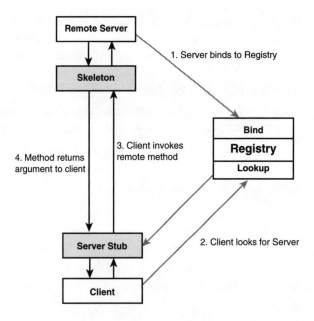

**Structure of a Client/Server RMI Application**

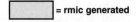 = rmic generated

The first step in designing a client/server RMI application is to design a remote server. It must implement a remote interface, which describes what methods are allowed to be called remotely. The server will contain the remote methods and any additional methods necessary for the server to perform locally. A remote server is required to extend the remote server class included in the *java.rmi.* package. This class provides the necessary functionality to facilitate remote computing.

The next step is to bind the remote server to the registry. The registry is an application that acts as a simple naming device and must reside on the same host as the server. It keeps a list of names and the associated references to the remote server. Once the server is bound to the registry with a name, it may be located by the client.

The client then attempts to locate the name of the server in the registry. If it is found, the registry will return a reference to the remote server, called a *stub*. This stub will be used by the client to invoke remote methods on the server. A stub is actually a special class created by the *rmic* compiler (discussed in the "Command-Line Utilities" section of this chapter) that implements the same remote interface as the server. In addition, the stub provides the necessary methods for communicating to the remote server.

Finally, the client now may invoke remote methods. These methods, defined in the remote interface, are the key to the communications between the client and the remote server. In addition, the remote server may be referenced by more than one client, giving it a one-to-many relationship.

## Peer-to-Peer RMI Applications

Peer-to-peer RMI applications expand on the client/server design by allowing servers to perform callbacks on the client. This design leads to two remote interfaces, and may be used when the server must send information to the client that is event driven. The structure of a peer-to-peer design is shown in Figure 14.2. A simple example of using peer-to-peer would be a chat server and chat client. A chat server would remain idle, waiting for a client to register itself. Once registered, the client would be able to send messages to any other registered clients. When a message is received, the server would invoke a remote method on each client that is registered, informing them of the user who sent the message and the message body. The server would have a reference for each registered client, which it would use when messages arrived. When the client wants to disconnect, it invokes the disconnect method on the server and the server removes the client from its known list.

**FIG. 14.2**

Peer-to-Peer RMI Application structure.

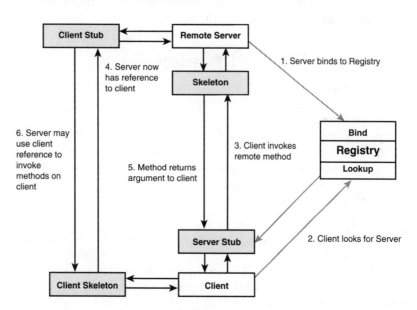

**Structure of a Peer-to-Peer RMI Application**

☐ = rmic generated

Part

II

Ch

14

The steps for building a peer-to-peer application would resemble a client/server design, except for a few minor differences. First, the client invokes a server method that requires a reference of itself as a parameter. The server then has a client stub, and may use this stub to remotely invoke methods on the client. Notice that, although the client still has to perform a registry lookup for the server, the client doesn't have to bind itself with the registry. In addition, the server doesn't have to make a lookup call to the registry for the client, it simply waits for the client to invoke a predefined remote method that accepts a reference to the client.

Another difference is that the client also must define a remote interface. This interface will inform the server of the methods available for remote invocation on the client. The rmic compiler must be used to generate stub/skeleton classes representing the client. These classes will be used by the server when performing remote invocation on client methods.

Finally, the client must meet one of the following criteria:

- It must extend a remote object class such as `UnicastRemoteObject`.
- In case of an Applet, it must contain a member object that extends `UnicastRemoteObject`.
- Implement a remote interface and use the static `UnicastRemoteObject.exportObject()` method to properly allow remote invocations.

# Reviewing the RMI Model

Now that I have presented an overview of using RMI, you are now going to look into applying this knowledge. The Remote Method Invocation package developed by Sun provides a flexible, yet powerful, set of classes and interfaces for developing distributed Java applications. RMI defines a remote object as an object that may have its methods invoked by an object that exists in another Java Virtual Machine. Remote object methods may be invoked across different hosts or on the same host running separate Virtual Machines. Objects using remote method invocation may invoke a method defined by a remote interface on an object that exists in a remote environment.

It is important to understand the similarities between Java objects in a standard object model and objects in the RMI model. Remote methods are defined in the same fashion, and may be passed arguments and return values when finished. Remote objects may be cast to any of the remote interfaces, provided that the implementation allows such a cast to be made. Finally, remote interfaces are allowed to be tested for a particular membership by using the `instanceof` operator.

Java objects do differ from remote objects in several ways, and these differences must be remembered when you are designing RMI applications. First, objects used as arguments or return values are passed by copy. Remote objects, however, are passed by reference. This is because remote objects are actually handled by the remote interface definition, which will be covered later in the chapter. Also, certain methods defined by the `Object` class are handled differently and are modified for remote objects. These methods are defined in the

RemoteObject class. Finally, because of the increased failure rate that may occur when remote objects communicate, your code must deal with a larger number of exceptions, which leads to slower performance.

Now, review the RMI hierarchy so that the relationship between remote objects and the remote interfaces may be understood. RemoteObject is the basic remote class and defines new implementations for basic objects methods such as toString(), hashCode(), and equals(). As shown in Figure 14.3, this class implements the Remote and Serializable interfaces, which ensures that extended classes of RemoteObject may be passed between virtual machines. RemoteServer extends the basic remote object definition by including methods for setting and retrieving log streams. It also provides a method for determining the originating host that invoked a remote method. Finally, UnicastRemoteObject defines a remote object that is capable of exporting itself for remote invocation. It accomplishes this when a copy is instantiated and the constructor exports itself, or by calling its static method with an object that implements a Remote interface.

**FIG. 14.3**

The RMI Class Hierarchy is built from many areas of the JDK.

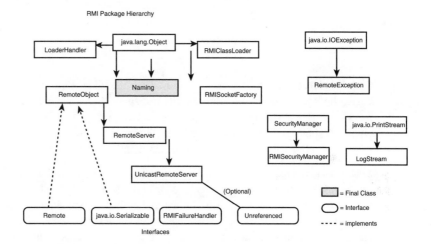

## RMI Architecture

RMI is divided into three layers that provide independent interface and protocol standards. These layers are the stub/skeleton layer, the remote reference layer, and the transport layer. Each of these layers was designed independently, which allows a layer's protocol to be changed to support new transfer protocols. This design will ensure the robustness and longevity of the architecture without requiring the whole implementation to be rewritten, should a new standard evolve in the future.

Part

II

Ch

14

**FIG. 14.4**

Overview of the RMI
Architecture.

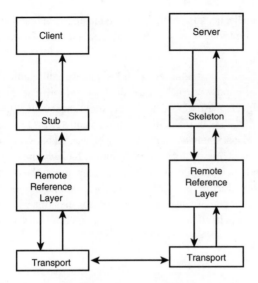

**RMI System Architecture**

**Stub/Skeleton Layer**   The stub/skeleton layer of RMI is responsible for the interface between the RMI and application layers. The transportation of the data is sent via the abstract marshal streams, which use object serialization to transmit Java objects to other virtual machines. All objects transmitted as arguments or return values are passed by copy. The only exception to this rule is when the objects are remote objects, which are passed by reference.

*Stubs* can be thought of as client-side proxies. They implement all of the supported interfaces of the remote object. Stubs are responsible for initiating the call to the remote object through the remote reference layer. They also use marshal streams, obtained from the remote reference layer, facilitating the transportation of data to the upper RMI layers. In addition, they are responsible for informing the remote reference layer that a call should be invoked, and obtain return values from the marshal stream when a method call is finished. Finally, stubs inform the remote reference layer that the call is complete.

The *skeleton* layer is the server-side reflection of a stub. Its duties include gathering arguments from the marshal stream that may be required for a remote object call, invoking a remote object method, and marshaling any results or exceptions from the remote object method to the marshal stream.

Stubs and skeletons are generated using the rmic compiler, and are determined at runtime, meaning that they are dynamically loaded when needed.

**Remote Reference Layer**   The remote reference layer handles the transport interface and protocol. The low-level responsibilities are handled independently of the stub and skeleton layers. Remote reference layers come in many different subclasses and operate in different ways. Each remote object chooses the correct representation of the protocol desired to properly define its uses. Remote reference layers are grouped into two components: the client-side component and server-side component. These two components cooperate and define how each side must handle calls invoked from another remote object.

The client-side component is designed to contain information specific to the remote server or servers. It communicates to the server-side component via the transport layer, and performs the semantics specific to the remote reference. Similarly, the server-side component implements the semantics that correspond to the remote reference just before informing a skeleton of a remote method invocation. Both components utilize a stream-oriented connection to transmit data to the transport layer. This connection stream is handled by the transport layer and operates independently of the remote reference layer.

**Transport Layer**   The transport layer is responsible for setting up, managing, monitoring, listening, and maintaining connections. It also can locate the dispatcher of a target remote object and pass a connection to the dispatcher. A *live reference* is the name given to a representation of an endpoint and an object identifier. It can be used to set up a connection to the virtual machine in which a remote object exists.

The RMI transport system layer consists of four basic components: *endpoint, channel, connection*, and *transport*. An *endpoint* represents an address space, or virtual machine, and can be mapped directly to its transport. With this in mind, a transport instance may be obtained, if the endpoint is known. A *channel* is a conduit between virtual machines and manages connections between local and remote address spaces. A *connection* is the component for transferring data and is synonymous with the input/output processes of a remote object. Finally, a *transport* manages channels and is responsible for setting up channels when it is given an endpoint.

## How RMI Handles Dynamic Class Loading

The three common class loaders used by Java are: the `AppletClassLoader`, the default `ClassLoader`, and the `RMIClassLoader`. Each of these class loaders operates slightly differently, and requires different methods of indicating where to locate the classes. The `AppletClassLoader` is used to retrieve classes used in a Java applet from the codebase attribute inside the `applet` tag. Any other classes that are directly required are also loaded using the `AppletClassLoader`. The default `ClassLoader` is used to load a class which requires the `main()` method to be executed. This class and any other classes required by the application are loaded from the local `CLASSPATH`. Finally, the `RMIClassLoader` is used to load any remote classes, such

Part

II

Ch

14

as stubs, skeletons, and extended classes that are parameters and return values for all remote methods. Classes loaded by the `RMIClassLoader` are located in the following order: the local CLASSPATH, the URL encoded in the marshal stream, and the URL specified by the `java.rmi.server.codebase` property.

Due to the requirements of RMI to have all of the associated classes and interfaces available that are related to invoking remote methods, the RMI design includes a custom class loading system. This system allows the dynamic creation of necessary classes related to remote invocation to be performed at runtime. It may use a variety of class loading techniques specific to Java, depending on the implementation of the remote objects. These techniques, mixed with Object Serialization and a Security Manager, create the complete dynamic class loader. Classes that need to be dynamically loaded by the RMI loader include: remote object classes and their interfaces, stub and skeleton classes, and any other classes that are used as parameter arguments or return values.

The class loader used when a Java class is invoked will depend upon the circumstances of the implementation. Whenever RMI implementations exist, the `RMIClassLoader` class is used to load all classes and interfaces that are used indirectly by the client and server and is invoked after the initial classes are loaded.

## RMI and Garbage Collection

Since object references are handled differently when using RMI, a special garbage collection algorithm was developed for RMI. While still cooperating with the standard Java runtime garbage collection system, the RMI runtime uses a special algorithm, called reference counting garbage collection, to handle the special needs of RMI objects. The RMI runtime keeps track of all live references within each virtual machine. As each reference enters the virtual machine, the reference count is incremented. When the first reference is established, a "referenced" message is sent to the server of the object. As live references are found to be no longer used, the reference count is decremented. Should the last reference get discarded, an "unreferenced" message is sent to the server. Special precautions are taken to eliminate premature removal of the references. This may occur if a network problem exists, confusing the server into thinking the client has crashed or no longer exists.

When a remote object no longer has an active reference, the RMI runtime will assign it as a weak reference, and allow the standard Java virtual machine to dispose of the object properly. This interaction with the standard garbage collection system ensures that the RMI application objects are able to perform normal life cycles, including the finalize cycle.

 **T I P** The RMI package includes an *Unreferenced* interface that may be implemented by remote objects. This interface defines a method called `unreferenced()`, and is invoked when the object no longer has live references. Using this interface can create smarter remote objects; more detail is discussed later in this chapter.

# RMI Configurations

The Remote Method Invocation was designed to be highly configurable. The configurations can be used to leverage different computing requirements based on the needs of the application. With each configuration, the developer must be aware of the advantages along with the disadvantages. The configurations that affect servers, applications, and applets are described in this section.

**Servers**   RMI servers can be divided into three basic categories that describe their behavior: closed, open, and cautious. Each category will have its own special options and configuration, and each also will have its restrictions. The design of the RMI system to handle multiple designs and configurations is one of its strongest advantages.

The closed server can be described as the "selfish" server. These servers will load only classes that are necessary for the server to function properly. All remote interfaces are defined locally and may be used by clients, but will not exist outside of the client's "protective shell," even if the client provides an URL for the class. If a client sends a remote object as a parameter, the server will fail when attempting to use it, unless a stub exists locally. A closed server keeps to itself and does what it is defined to do in the remote interface.

An open server is exactly the opposite; think of it as a "sharing" server. It will set the `java.rmi.server.codebase` property to allow clients to load classes across the network, and allow the server to load classes that are needed for remote objects that the client may want to exchange. The open server will define a security manager and RMI class loader which help to protect the server, but allow more activity to occur.

Finally, a cautious server will establish a security manager just as an open server will, but the definition will be more strict, further limiting its trust with the client. It may even set the `java.rmi.server.useCodebaseOnly` property to true, thus not allowing the client to supply URLs to classes that it wants the server to load.

**Applets**   Applet configurations are typically very secure, since all classes and interfaces will be loaded from the same server. Because applets are restricted to communicate with the host from which they were served, the RMI server and its interfaces will be available only from this server. All remote interfaces used by the client will originate from this server, thus providing a secure application. It is important to note that, along with the stubs/skeletons and applet code, the registry also must be running on the host that serves the applet. This is an important item to note when you are deciding to use applets, because the server must be properly configured to handle such a situation.

**Applications**   Unlike applets, Java applications have a greater number of options, allowing connections to other hosts. This creates a larger number of configuration options for the server and the clients, enabling more robust RMI applications. Java applications typically fall into two categories: local and remote.

Part

II

Ch

14

A local RMI application must load all of its classes from the local source. The only classes that may be retrieved from a network include the stub/skeleton classes and any classes that may be required for the correct functioning of remote methods. This may include classes used as arguments and as return values.

Remote applications, however, may retrieve all classes from a central source. The application must set the `java.rmi.server.codebase` property to the URL that the application and stub/skeleton classes are to be retrieved from. The URL is then embedded inside the class as it is serialized for network loading.

**N O T E**   Note that if a class is found locally, the class will use the local version and not the network version. ▪

# Command-Line Utilities

The RMI package requires the use of two command-line utilities for building RMI applications. These utilities are the rmic compiler and the rmiregistry and are described in this section.

**rmic**   The rmic compiler is used to generate stub and skeleton class files. The compiler requires the targeted class to be compiled already. For example:

```
rmic  HelloImpl
```

will generate stub/skeleton classes for the HelloImpl class file in the current directory. Optionally, use the -d switch to specify the root directory for the generated class files. The command:

```
rmic -d /users/java/rmidemo HelloImpl
```

will generate stub/skeleton classes for the HelloImpl class in the /users/java/rmidemo directory. The following class names generated would be: `HelloImpl_stub.class` and `HelloImpl_skel.class`.

**rmiregistry**   The RMI registry is a simple name server for server-side bootstrapping. It allows remote clients to verify that a remote object exists on the server and retrieve a reference to the object.

General syntax for Win95/NT systems is:

```
start rmiregistry
```

or

```
javaw rmiregistry
```

For Solaris:

```
rmiregistry &
```

To specify a port other than the default 1099, include a port number argument such as:

```
rmiregistry 7777
```

Be sure to specify where the client should look for the port when using the Naming class.

For example:

```
Naming.rebind ("//host:port/class",obj);
```

# Building an RMI Application

Since the fundamentals of RMI have been presented, it's time to build the first RMI application. It will use a client/server approach, allowing a client application to send a string to a remote server. The client will send the string from the command line, and when the remote server receives it, will print it to the standard console.

## Step 1: Verify the JDK Version

RMI requires the Java Development Kit version 1.1 to function properly. Early versions of RMI that work with the JDK 1.02 may still be available, but are not supported by JavaSoft. Also, betas 1 and 2 of the JDK 1.1 suffer a slight performance issue when making method calls to the registry. Try to obtain the most recent version of the JDK for proper functionality.

## Step 2: Plan the Remote Objects

The second step in designing an RMI application requires putting some thought into the remote methods. Selecting methods that will be invoked often will degrade performance. Try to design methods that accomplish multiple tasks with one invocation.

**NOTE** Remember, remote invocations, when used properly, can create very powerful and robust applications. However, keep in mind when designing RMI applications that performance will degrade if a large number of remote methods are defined. Keep remote methods to a minimum so that the overall design doesn't get out of hand. ▪

With this in mind, define what this remote server should do:

- ▪ The server should be responsible for accepting a string argument through a remote method.
- ▪ It should print the string received to the console.

## Step 3: Write the Remote Interface

A remote interface defines the methods that are permitted to be remotely called. This interface also tends to shape the creation of the client/server model, defining what actions the server allows to be performed on the server. Typically, the remote interface will define the method names, parameters, and return values that should be expected when a client invokes a remote method. The interface then will be implemented by the server object.

Remote interfaces must have the following characteristics:

- ▪ It must be public. Otherwise, the client will generate an error when attempting to load the remote object implementing the interface.

Part
II

Ch
14

■ The interface must extend `java.rmi.Remote`.

■ Each method defined in the interface must throw `java.rmi.RemoteException`.

■ A remote object that is used as an argument or as a return value must be referenced by its remote interface, not its implementation class.

Listing 14.1 shows the source to the remote interface:

---

**Listing 14.1   The Remote Interface**

```
public interface RemoteDisplay extends java.rmi.Remote{
  public void display (String s) throws java.rmi.RemoteException;
}
```

---

The `RemoteDisplay` interface is public and extends `java.rmi.Remote`. It defines a remote method named `display()` that accepts a string as an argument and will throw the `java.rmi.RemoteException` should an error occur during the remote invocation of the method.

Now, apply this interface to the development of the remote server.

# Step 4: Write the Server Implementation

The remote server class will implement the `RemoteDisplay` interface created in Step 1. A remote server has the following requirements:

■ It must define a constructor and call the `super()` parent constructor. The constructor must be defined as public and throw `java.rmi.RemoteException`. This exception will be thrown if the object doesn't get exported correctly.

■ It must set a security manager. If no security manager is set, the loading of RMI classes will be denied. This is true even when using locally stored RMI classes.

■ Define a `main()` method that instantiates a copy of the remote object. This will start the "listening" process of the server, provided errors are not encountered during the export process.

■ It must register itself with the naming registry so that it may be found by a client.

■ It must implement an interface that extends `java.rmi.Remote`, which will define the remote methods available to the clients.

Listing 14.2 shows the code for the `DisplayServer` class:

---

**Listing 14.2   The Remote Server Implementation**

```
public class DisplayServer extends java.rmi.server.UnicastRemoteObject imple-
ments RemoteDisplay {
public DisplayServer () throws java.rmi.RemoteException {
    super();
  }
public void display (String s) throws java.rmi.RemoteException {
    System.out.println ("Received:"+s);
```

```
    }
    public static void main (String args[]) {
        // set the security manager
        System.setSecurityManager (new java.rmi.RMISecurityManager());
        .try {
            DisplayServer ds=new DisplayServer();
            // register with the naming server
            java.rmi.Naming.rebind ("DisplayServer",ds);
            System.out.println ("Server bound to registry: DisplayServer");
        } catch (java.rmi.RemoteException e) {
            System.out.println ("Server got Exception: "+e);
        }
        catch (java.net.MalformedURLException e) {
            System.out.println ("Server got Exception: "+e);
        }
    }
}
```

DisplayServer is defined as extending the java.rmi.server.UnicastRemoteObject class. The constructor for display server invokes the superclass constructor. It is important to understand what happens when the superclass constructor is called. The constructor creates and exports a new remote object that will listen to an anonymous port for method invocation requests. Should the object fail to initialize, the constructor will throw java.rmi.RemoteException.

In addition, the server implements RemoteDisplay, which defines a remote method. The display() method will print out the string argument to the console when invoked. The display will be in the format:

Received: string passed

The rest of the requirements for the remote server are met in the main() method. The security manager for the application is set to java.rmi.RMISecurityManager. For specialized applications, a custom security manager may be needed and can be substituted for the default RMI manager. Next, the server is instantiated and bound to the registry. Notice that the new and rebind() calls must be inside of a try/catch block. This is important, since the call to the object's constructor may throw java.rmi.RemoteException should the object fail to export or bind to the registry.

Two methods are available when binding to the registry: bind() and rebind(). If bind() is used and the name is already listed in the registry, a java.rmi.AlreadyBoundException will be thrown. If the rebind() method is used, any name already registered will be discarded and the new object will be linked into the registry.

The registry must be on the same host that will run the server. If the registry is running on a port other than the default, the following format may be used:

```
Naming.rebind ("//myhost:7777/name",obj);
```

Note that a remote server also can contain local methods. Those methods, however, cannot be called remotely and may be used only in the standard Java context.

Part
II

Ch
14

# Step 5: Creating the Remote Client

Remote clients may be of any class type and may function in any normal fashion. For a client to communicate with a remote server, it must follow the following requirements:

- It must use a security manager such as the RMISecurityManager. In the case of an applet, the Applet security manager will work fine. Either of these security managers will satisfy the security manager requirement.

- To communicate with the remote server, it will need to invoke the lookup() method to the registry on the server and retrieve a reference to the server. This will allow the client to know what methods are legal to call and how to handle them.

In this application, the client will:

- Take a command line argument for the string to display

- Locate the server name "DisplayServer" in the registry and obtain a reference to it.

- Display the string argument by sending it to the remote server through a remote method invocation.

Listing 14.3 shows the code for the client application:

### Listing 14.3   Remote Client Application

```
public class DisplayClient {
  public static void main (String args[]) {
    if (args.length != 1) {
      System.out.println ("Proper usage: java DisplayClient [string]");
      System.exit (1);
    }
    System.setSecurityManager (new java.rmi.RMISecurityManager());
    try {
      RemoteDisplay rd = (RemoteDisplay)java.rmi.Naming.lookup ("DisplayServer");
      rd.display (args[0]);
    } catch (Exception e) {
      System.out.println ("Not Bound exception : "+e);}
  }
}
```

In this example, the client uses the java.rmi.RMISecurityManager class as its security manager. Inside the try/catch block is the core of the client. An attempt is made to retrieve a reference to the remote server by requesting a registry lookup for the name DisplayServer. If the client, server, and the registry are all going to be on the same machine, the explicit call to the host running the registry is not needed. If the registry and the remote server will be running on another machine, follow this format:

```
RemoteDisplay rd= (RemoteDisplay) java.rmi.Naming.lookup ("//host/
DisplayServer");
```

Once the registry and entry can be located, the registry will return a remote reference to the server. Notice that we are casting the reference as RemoteDisplay, which is the remote interface that was originally defined. It is important to remember to cast the reference as the interface and not the implementation, or the RMI runtime will throw an exception.

Once the reference is returned, the method is called normally. In this application, the first argument passed in the command line is sent to the server to be displayed. After the reference is obtained from the registry, methods may be invoked normally. However, remember that remote methods have a slightly slower performance and may degrade application speed.

## Step 6: Compiling and Running the Application

Since the RMI package requires extra steps to generate specialized classes and start the RMI Registry, this section will step you through the proper methods to prepare and execute an RMI application.

**Using *rmic* to Generate the Stub and Skeleton Classes**    RMI requires generating a stub and skeleton class using the rmic compiler. To use the compiler, launch rmic with the following options:

```
rmic [-d destination directory] class name [class name] [class name]...
```

The rmic compiler accepts the –d switch followed by the destination directory to store the two files. Multiple class names may be included on the command line, and need only be separated by a space. Be sure to compile the classes before running rmic, since the stub and skeleton classes will be generated from the bytecode of the remote object(s). Also, be sure to specify the implementation class, not the remote interface, as the class name(s) to generate stubs and skeleton classes. For this application, the following command line will work (make sure the current working directory is the directory with the .class files for this project):

```
rmic DisplayServer
```

After the compiler is finished, look at the directory listing for the project directory. Notice that two new files, DisplayServer_Stub.class and DisplayServer_Skel.class, are in the directory. These are the stub and skeleton classes that will be required by the server and the client for the RMI runtime to function correctly.

Remember, the stub and skeleton classes implement that same interface that the remote server implements. These classes are what the client and server use to reference a remote object, such as the server. When a client requests a reference to the remote server from the registry, the stub class is returned as the reference.

When distributing an RMI application, be sure that these new files are located in the same directory that is specified in the codebase property of the server. These files are required for the client to work properly.

Part

II

Ch

14

**Running the Application**   The first step to getting the application running is to launch the registry on the machine that will host the remote server. To accomplish this, use the following command line:

```
(Win95/NT) start rmiregistry
```

```
(Solaris) rmiregistry &
```

This will launch the naming registry and establish itself on port 1099. To change the port number, specify the desired port number after the command, such as:

```
(Win95/NT) start rmiregistry 7777
```

```
(Solaris) rmiregistry 7777 &
```

When modifying the port that the registry will listen to, be sure to change the host URL for the binding call in the server and the lookup call in the client. Without changing the host URL, the server will not be able to bind to the registry and the client will not be able to retrieve a reference from the registry.

Finally, launch the server with the command line:

```
java DisplayServer -Djava.rmi.server.codebase=//<hostname> DisplayServer
```

For example, my system is named lightning, so my command line looks like:

```
java DisplayServer -Djava.rmi.server.codebase=//lightning DisplayServer
```

Now, launch the client:

```
java DisplayClient "example text"
```

The server should receive the message and display it to the console. The client then should resume user control at a shell prompt. Try launching the client from different machines on a network, or launching several instances of the client simultaneously. This will demonstrate the capabilities of RMI and distributed architecture in Java.

Figures 14.5 and 14.6 show what the client and server should look like:

**FIG. 14.5**

Results of the client application.

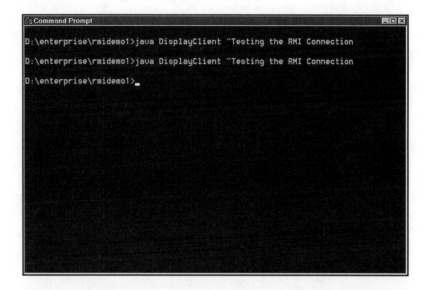

**FIG. 14.6**

Results of the server application execution.

# RMI Security

When designing all but the simplest RMI applications, it is important to understand the extended security techniques associated with the RMI package. Extensions to the standard Java security include enhanced class loading for retrieving classes from an URL and using RMI with network firewalls. This section details these changes and presents explanations on understanding and using these changes.

## Class Loading Security

When a Java application is started, all necessary classes are loaded from the CLASSPATH and are considered to be trustworthy. When an applet loads, all of its necessary classes are loaded through the network connection. A security manager is put in place to protect the user from harmful applets. The same design concept exists in RMI applications that exist in applets—the need for a security manager. The RMI runtime requires that security be in place to protect the RMI server and clients. Without a security manager in place, the RMI runtime will throw an exception and refuse to load classes from the network. This design is used to protect an application and force at least a minimum security level to be in place. Without any type of security, the application may be compromised from an external source.

Part

II

Ch

14

When RMI applications are loaded locally, the security manager usually will not restrict the application. If the application is loaded from a network source by using the RMIClassLoader, the security manager will be used and restrict the client program.

**N O T E** Once a class is loaded using the RMIClassLoader, all classes used by that class suffer the same security restrictions. Plan your dynamic loading carefully!

To relieve some of the restrictions placed on RMI applications by the RMISecurityManager, simply subclass the RMISecurityManager and override the methods necessary to provide the correct implementation needed by the application. Please note that removing some of the protection provided by the RMISecurityManager may have strong implications on an application and must be taken seriously. Java security is beyond the scope of this book, but it is crucial that a programmer understand the Java security model before modifying the security manager.

To force restrictions on an RMI application, no matter how it was loaded, whether locally or through a network, set the property java.rmi.useCodebaseOnly to true. This will prevent the loading of classes from any URL except the one specified in the java.rmi.server.codebase property. The useCodebaseOnly property may be used on either the client or the server, but has no effect on applets.

## RMI Through Firewalls

As the transport layer of the RMI model matured, the ability to use RMI with firewalls was included. This was accomplished by implementing a scheme in which a failed direct connection attempt to a remote object will result in the attempt to connect to the remote object using HTTP (Hypertext Transport Protocol). HTTP is usually trusted by most firewalls, although various levels of security can exist. With this in mind, the transport layer will attempt to send an RMI call inside of the body of an HTTP POST request. Any return information will be sent in the HTTP response. The transport layer will attempt one of the following methods when using HTTP:

1. Some firewall proxies will allow an HTTP request to be redirected to a specific port. If this is allowed, the POST request will be redirected to the proper remote object port. Remote objects, no matter what port they are listening to, are capable of understanding POST formats and sending properly formatted responses.

2. If the firewall will forward requests only to well-known ports, then the call will forward to the HTTP server on port 80 to a CGI routine that will forward the call to the remote server on the same machine.

All of this magic is performed by the RMISocketFactory, which is responsible for creating sockets that transparently provide firewall tunneling, HTTP POST decoding, and POST response encoding. The createSocket() and createServerSocket() methods are responsible for creating these sockets and are described in detail later in this chapter.

Configuring the client to use HTTP is not necessary. It is possible, however, to disable the usage of the HTTP redirection by setting the java.rmi.server.disableHttp property to true.

To configure the server so that it may be found by any remote object outside of the server's domain, the `java.rmi.server.hostname` property should be set. For example, to start the server:

```
java -Djava.rmi.server.hostname=machine.hostname.com Server
```

 **TIP** It is recommended to avoid using the IP address of the server since some proxies will not forward to destinations that are represented only by the IP address and not the host name.

If the firewall proxy doesn't support forwarding requests to any port, the following steps must be taken:

1. An HTTP server on port 80 must be present on the host machine of the remote object(s).
2. A CGI script must be located in the aliased path of `/cgi-bin/java-rmi`.
3. The CGI script must invoke the local Java interpreter to execute a class internal to the transport layer and which forwards the request to the appropriate RMI server port.
4. The CGI script must define properties in the Java VM which have the same names as the CGI 1.0 environment variables.

 **TIP** An example CGI script is available with the Win32 and Solaris distributions of the 1.1 JDK. When setting up the script, be sure to specify the complete path to the Java interpreter for the script to work.

It should be noted that when the RMI transport layer is forced to use the HTTP POST format, the RMI performance will suffer greatly. You also must consider the amount of time that forwarding takes.

**N O T E** Since most HTTP requests may be allowed to occur only in one direction, bi-directional RMI is sometimes not possible. Keep this in mind when designing applications that may be required to operate within a firewall-protected network. ▪

# Building an RMI Chat Framework

The next example RMI application will build a Java chat client and server. It will look similar to Java chat clients that currently exist, but will not require special application protocols. This will produce a more object-oriented application. The client and server will be implemented in a peer-to-peer design, which means that the client and the server will be remote objects.

To understand what the application will require, the features of the application must be outlined. First, the client will:

- Provide a GUI interface with a text field for entering a public message, a user list containing all of the current users registered with the server, and a text area containing all messages sent and received from the server.

**Part**

**II**

**Ch**

**14**

- Register itself with the server to receive messages from all of the other clients.

- Invoke a method on the server with a message entered in the text field of the client.

- Provide a remote method for the server to inform the client of a new message.

- Provide remote methods to add and remove users from its list.

- Remove its registration from the server when exiting.

The server will be responsible for:

- Providing a simple GUI display for showing the current users connected and several statistics related to the clients connected

- Providing remote methods to connect, disconnect, and broadcast a message

- Having added protection against clients that do not disconnect properly and cause an exception to occur

- Invoking remote client methods that inform the client when new users join, and old users leave

- Informing all clients when a message is received from a client

Using this outline of the necessary responsibilities and functions, now start designing the application.

# The Remote Server Interface

Following the same guidelines as outlined in the previous example, the remote interface for the server will contain several core functions. The server will be responsible for connecting clients to the server for discussions, disconnecting the clients when they want to shut down, and broadcasting messages. To accomplish this, the remote server interface will define three methods: connect(), disconnect(), and broadcastMessage(). Listing 14.4 shows the final code for the remote server interface:

**Listing 14.4   The Remote Server Interface**

```
public interface RemoteChat extends java.rmi.Remote
{
    public void connect (ClientInfo client) throws java.rmi.RemoteException;
    public void disconnect (String username) throws java.rmi.RemoteException;
    public void broadcastMessage (String username,String message) throws
java.rmi.RemoteException;
}
```

The connect() method will register the client with the server. The ClientInfo class will be discussed a little later. For now, understand that the ClientInfo class will contain a reference to the client and a string containing the user's name. The disconnect() method will remove the client from registration, while the broadcastMessage() will send a message to all registered clients.

# The Remote Client Interface

The remote client interface will describe the methods that the server will invoke on a registered client. Once a client has registered with the server, the server will be able to perform remote functions on the client. This interface will be responsible for adding users to the client's user list, removing users from the list, and accepting a broadcasted message from the server. The interface is described in Listing 14.5.

**Listing 14.5   The Remote Client Interface**

```
public interface RemoteClient extends java.rmi.Remote
{
    public void message(String username, String message) throws
java.rmi.RemoteException;
    public void addUser (String username) throws java.rmi.RemoteException;
    public void removeUser (String username) throws java.rmi.RemoteException;

}
```

The addUser() method will add a newly registered client to the list of users on the client. removeUser() will be responsible for removing a disconnected user from the client list. Finally, the message() method will display a message to the output area of the client, including the name of the user who sent the message.

# Creating a Custom Security Manager

Since this application will be using the AWT for displaying important server statistics and providing a user interface, the RMISecurityManager class will not be adequate. Since the class prevents the AWT event queue processing from having security permissions, a new class will extend the RMISecurityManager, and will be called ChatRMISecurityManager. Listing 14.6 shows the new class overriding the checkAwtEventQueueAccess() method and removing the call to the method in the RMISecurityManager. The new security manager now will allow the AWT event queue to function as normal.

**Listing 14.6   Extending the Default RMI Security Manager to Release the AWT Restraints**

```
public class ChatRMISecurityManager extends java.rmi.RMISecurityManager
{
    public void checkAwtEventQueueAccess ( ) {
      //super.checkAwtEventQueueAccess ();
      //prevents the security check from being called
    }
}
```

Part
II

Ch
14

**N O T E**  Care must be taken when creating a custom security manager. Releasing too much of an application's security restraints will cause it to become vulnerable to malicious attacks. ▪

## Implementing the Remote Server

The remote server can be divided into four major areas: the remote interface, the custom security manager, the GUI interface, and the remote server implementation. The remote server implementation will be responsible for using the custom security manager, and implementing the remote interface.

The GUI interface will extend the Frame class, and needs only to update its statistics. The information it will be responsible for tracking includes: the current number of client connections, the current user names, the total connections accepted, and the total messages broadcast. Due to space limitations, the code for the ServerFrame class has been left out.

The remote server implementation will be designed to track client connections, the broadcasting of messages, updating the GUI interface, and handling errors. Listing 14.7 illustrates the remote server.

---

**Listing 14.7  The Declaration of the Remote Server Implementation**

```
import java.util.*;
public class ChatServer extends java.rmi.server.UnicastRemoteObject implements
RemoteChat{
    Vector Clients=null;
    ServerFrame frame;

    public ChatServer() throws java.rmi.RemoteException {
        frame=new ServerFrame ();
        frame.show ();
    }

     public static void main (String args[]) {
        System.setSecurityManager (new ChatRMISecurityManager());
        try {
           ChatServer server=new ChatServer();
           java.rmi.Naming.rebind ("//hostname/ChatServer",server);
           server.setStatus ("Accepting Connections");
           System.out.println ("Server bound to the registry");
        } catch (Exception e) {
           System.out.println ("Exception caught: "+e+"\nServer not bound to the
registry");
        }
     }
```

---

The ChatServer class will contain a member object called Clients. Clients will be a *Vector* of registered classes and may be enumerated for broadcasting messages. The logic for handling the registration status of a client is contained within the connect() and disconnect() methods, shown in Listing 14.8.

**Listing 14.8  The Remote Methods *connect()* and *disconnect()***

```
public void connect (ClientInfo client) throws java.rmi.RemoteException {

    // initialize the Client vector if it is null
    if (Clients== null) {
      Clients=new Vector (10,3);
    }

    // add the client to the list if it is not null
    if (client != null) {
      // update all old users with the new user name
      updateClients (client.Username);


      // Now, add the new user to the linked list of Client references and user
➥names
      // Note: we add the new user to the linked list after the updateClients()
      //        to prevent an echo in the user list
      Clients.addElement (client);
    }

    // update the new user with the current user list
    updateUserList (client.Client);

    // add user to the list box
    frame.addUser (client.Username);

    // increment the user count and the total user count
    frame.incCurrent();
    frame.incTotal();
    }

    public void disconnect (String username) throws java.rmi.RemoteException {
        ClientInfo found=null;
        //System.out.println ("Disconnecting User");

        if (Clients != null) { // make sure client didn't call this method
before registering
            Enumeration e=Clients.elements ();
            while (e.hasMoreElements() ) {
              ClientInfo cinfo=(ClientInfo)e.nextElement();
              if (cinfo.Username.equals (username))
                found=cinfo;
            }
        }
        if (found != null) {
          Clients.removeElement (found);
```

*continues*

Part

II

Ch

14

**Listing 14.8    Continued**

```
                // remove the entry from the user list
                frame.removeUser (found.Username);

                // decrement the current user count
                frame.decCurrent ();

                // update current users that user has logged off
                if (Clients != null) { // make sure client didn't call this
➥method before registering
                        Enumeration e=Clients.elements ();
                        while (e.hasMoreElements() ) {
                          ClientInfo cinfo=(ClientInfo)e.nextElement();
                          try {
                            cinfo.Client.removeUser (found.Username);
                          } catch (Exception ex) {
                            System.out.println ("Exception trying to inform client
➥of removed user! :"+ex);
                          }
                        }
                }
        }
        }
```

The broadcastMessage() method (see Listing 14.9) will be responsible for enumerating through the Clients and invoking the remote client method called message(). This method will accept the user name and the message body for transmission entered in the client window.

Considerations need to be made when handling remote callback implementations. When a client invokes broadcastMessage() on the server, problems could arise if a client left the server without calling the disconnect() method. This causes the server to encounter exceptions when remote methods are invoked on a client that doesn't exist. To handle this problem, a local vector named badclients is used to keep track of any client references that caused an exception to occur. If any problems occurred when trying to invoke the remote method, the client's username will be added to the vector. If any entries are in the vector at the end of the method, those entries are removed from the Clients vector.

Keep stability in mind when designing remote callback methods for peer-to-peer RMI applications. Exceptions are capable of happening in RMI due to more circumstances than in standard Java applications. These applications tend to become unstable if designed incorrectly, and can lead to troublesome bugs.

**Listing 14.9    Broadcasting a Message to the Clients**

```
public void broadcastMessage (String username,String message) throws
java.rmi.RemoteException {
        Vector badclients=null;
```

```
        // enumerate through registered clients and invoke the remote method for
➥a new message on each one
        frame.incMessages ();
        if (Clients != null) { // make sure client didn't call this method
➥before registering -- eliminates server crashing
            Enumeration e=Clients.elements ();
            while (e.hasMoreElements() ) {
               ClientInfo cinfo=(ClientInfo)e.nextElement();
               try {
                 cinfo.Client.message (username,message);
               } catch (java.rmi.RemoteException ex) {
                 System.out.println ("Error sending message to a client!
Remov➥ing! :"+ ex);
                   if (badclients == null)
                       badclients=new Vector (10,3);
                   badclients.addElement (cinfo.Username);
               }
               }
            }
        if (badclients != null) {
           // enumerate through problem clients and remove them
           Enumeration en=badclients.elements();
           while (en.hasMoreElements()) {
              String next=(String)en.nextElement();
              try {
                disconnect (next);
              } catch (java.rmi.RemoteException ex2) {
                System.out.println ("Exception trying to remove a bad client!
➥"+ex2);

              }
              badclients.removeElement (next);
           }
        }
    }
```

Since the client application will have a list of users that are currently on the server, the client must be updated when users enter and leave the server's view. To accomplish this, the local methods updateClients() and updateUserList() are used to invoke remote methods to add and remove users in the list.

The updateClients() method (see Listing14.10) is responsible for adding a new user to the lists of the current subscribed users. This method is called from the connect() method on the server, and must be invoked before the user is actually added to the Clients vector. This prevents an echo of the user's name in the new client's list. This method simply enumerates through the Clients and invokes the addUser() remote method on the client.

In contrast, the updateUserList() enumerates through the list of clients and sends each currently registered user name to the new client. This method is called after the client is added to the vector, which echos the new user's name on the list as well. This helps the user know that they are currently joined to the server and may join in the conversation.

Part
II

Ch
14

> **Listing 14.10   Updating Client User Lists**

```
public void updateClients (String username) {
        // iterate through clients and add new user that just joined to their
➥list
        if (Clients != null) { // make sure client didn't call this method
➥before registering
            Enumeration e=Clients.elements ();
            while (e.hasMoreElements() ) {
              ClientInfo client=(ClientInfo)e.nextElement();
              try {
                client.Client.addUser (username);
              } catch (java.rmi.RemoteException ex) {
                System.out.println ("Exception updating user names: "+ex);
              }
            }
        }
    }

    public void updateUserList (RemoteClient client) {
        // iterate through clients and add new user that just joined to their
➥list
        if (Clients != null) { // make sure client didn't call this method
➥before registering
            Enumeration e=Clients.elements ();
            while (e.hasMoreElements() ) {
              ClientInfo user=(ClientInfo)e.nextElement();
              try {
                client.addUser (user.Username);
              } catch (java.rmi.RemoteException ex) {
                System.out.println ("Exception updating user list: "+ex);
              }
            }
        }
    }

}
```

# Implementing the Remote Client

With the server now in place, the client needs to be implemented. The client implementation will be straightforward and will leave most of the hard work to the GUI interface. Notice that, unlike the first RMI application, this client extends UnicastRemoteServer. This is necessary for the client to define remote methods and allow them to be invoked from the server (see Listing 14.11). Following the requirements of an RMI client, the application sets a security manager, instantiates a copy of itself, and shows the login frame for gathering the user's information. It also initializes key member objects for later use, including the chat client's primary frame for conversation (see Listing 14.12).

 **T I P**  Note that the client also implements an interface called RemoteClientListener. This is used for callbacks from the ChatFrame member object when a user has entered a message or exited the application.

## Listing 14.11 Declaration of the Remote Chat *Client* Class

```
public class ChatClient extends java.rmi.server.UnicastRemoteObject
                                         implements RemoteClient,
RemoteClientListener{
    RemoteChat server;
    ChatFrame frame;
    ClientLoginFrame login;
    String Username;
    ClientInfo info;

    public ChatClient () throws java.rmi.RemoteExceptio  {
        super ();
        frame=new ChatFrame (this);
        login=new ClientLoginFrame (this);
        login.show();
    }
    public static void main (String args[]) {
        System.setSecurityManager (new ChatRMISecurityManager() );
        try {
          ChatClient client= new ChatClient ();
        } catch (Exception e) {
          System.out.println ("Error in main! Got: "+e);
        }

    }
```

## Listing 14.12 A Callback Interface for the *ChatFrame* Class

```
public interface RemoteClientListener {
    public void login(String username);
    public void logoff();
    public void sendMessage (String message);
}
```

Three remote methods are defined for the remote client. Since the remote methods actually modify the current state of the user interface and not the remote object itself, methods in the ChatFrame class are called with the arguments sent from the server. The ChatFrame class will add a new message to the text area component, add a new user to the user list, or remove a disconnected user (see Listing 14.13).

## Listing 14.13 Remote Method Implementations

```
public void message(String username, String message) throws
java.rmi.RemoteException {
        frame.addText (username,message);
    }
```

*continues*

**Listing 14.13 Continued**

```
public void addUser (String username) throws java.rmi.RemoteException {
    frame.addUser (username);
}

public void removeUser (String username) throws java.rmi.RemoteException {
    System.out.println ("Removing User "+username);
    frame.removeUser (username);
}
```

Two local methods, login() and logoff(), are responsible for establishing a connection to the remote server, registering as a client, and disconnecting from the server when the user closes the application.

The login() method first creates a new ClientInfo object with the user name entered in the login frame and a reference to the client. It then looks up the remote server, calls the server's connect() method with the ClientInfo object, and shows the chat frame for the user. The logoff() method has the opposite responsiblities. It calls the server's disconnect() method with the user name as an argument. It then closes the application and exits. Finally, the sendMessage() method calls the broadcastMessage() method on the server with the user's name and the message entered in the chat frame (see Listing 14.14).

Listing 14.15 shows the ClientInfo object. Note that the custom object that needs to be passed between remote objects must implement the java.io.Serializable interface. This interface allows the object to be converted to a byte representation, which allows the transfer between different virtual machines.

**Listing 14.14 Methods for Connecting and Disconnecting from the Remote Server**

```
public void login (String username) {
      Username=username;
      info=new ClientInfo (username,this);
  login.hide();
        try {
            server=(RemoteChat)java.rmi.Naming.lookup("//hostname/
➥ChatServer");
            server.connect (info);
            frame.setTitle ("Chat Client -- "+username);
            frame.show();
        } catch (Exception e) {
          System.out.println ("Exception caught: "+e);
        }
    }
    public void logoff () {
        try {
        server.disconnect (Username);
        System.out.println ("Logging off");
        System.exit (0);
```

```
        } catch (java.rmi.RemoteException e) {
          System.out.println ("Exception caught trying to logoff: "+e);
        }
  }

  public void sendMessage (String message) {
        try {
        server.broadcastMessage (Username,message);
         } catch (java.rmi.RemoteException e) {
          System.out.println ("Exception caught trying to broadcast: "+e);
        }
  }
```

**Listing 14.15   A Simple Class to Keep the Client's Information**

```
public class ClientInfo implements java.io.Serializable{
  public RemoteClient Client;
  public String Username;

  public ClientInfo (String username, RemoteClient client) {
    Client=client;
    Username=username;
  }
}
```

# Running the Application

To test the application, follow these steps:

1. Start the RMI registry.
2. Use the rmic compiler to generate the server and client stub and skeleton classes.
3. Start the Chat Server.
4. Start one or more Chat Clients (see Figure 14.8).
5. Log in with a unique user name (see Figure 14.7).
6. Enter a message and see it echo back to all of the connected clients (see Figure 14.9).

Part
II

Ch
14

**FIG. 14.7**
The primary client interface provides a simple user interface.

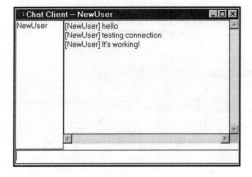

**FIG. 14.8**
The client login screen once execution begins.

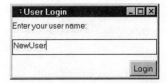

**FIG. 14.9**
Server statistics and current user lists help the developer track the current usage.

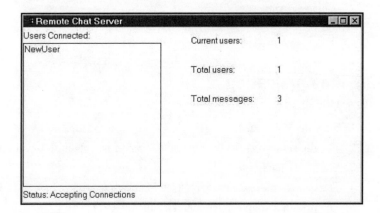

# From Here...

In this chapter, you've been presented with several views of RMI. The first view provided insight into the basics of RMI, including why RMI was developed. The second view demonstrated how RMI functions and the various components of RMI work together. Another view presented a step-by-step procedure to create an RMI application. The final view presented a look at RMI security and its components.

- Chapter 12, "Introduction to Distributed Computing," will cover the basic concepts of distributed computing including DCE, RPC, and CORBA.

- Chapter 13, "Object Serialization," discusses how Java can store objects using streams for storage and persistence.

- Chapter 15, "Advanced RMI Concepts," covers the application of advanced topics in RMI, including integrating RMI with JDBC.

# Advanced RMI Concepts

**C**hapter 14 introduced the basic concepts of Remote Method Invocation (RMI), and provided a simple RMI framework. The distributed computing architecture provided by RMI allows applications to remotely invoke methods on objects that may exist outside the local Virtual Machine.

This chapter will provide a deeper insight into RMI, including proper exception handling, advanced RMI usage, and an RMI class and interface reference. ■

# RMI Exception Handling

Properly handling exceptions is an essential component when designing Java applications. Handling exceptions when using RMI is also important since exceptions may occur because of I/O problems, server-side runtime errors, and loss of connections. Handling exceptions in RMI applications can be accomplished in two ways: server-side handling and client-side handling.

Server-side exception handling involves catching and logging exceptions inside the server's remote methods. For example, suppose a remote server method was responsible for moving data to a distant server. If the distant server isn't currently available, the server must determine the best course of action. This could be making another connection attempt, or logging the error to a file or database with the appropriate debugging information. In either case, the server must be the one to deal with the situation, since the client won't have enough information to make an accurate decision.

Client-side exception handling provides a different method of handling a runtime error. Suppose a banking application invokes a remote method on the bank server to execute a transaction. If the particular account specified in the transaction doesn't have enough funds, the server must inform the client of what just occurred. The client will then allow the user to select another option, including transferring funds from another account. Similar situations allow the client to receive the exception and properly handle the error.

# Building a JDBC RMI Application

To demonstrate the integration of JDBC with RMI, a simple application will be presented. It will show how a client/server JDBC application can be built using RMI without requiring large amounts of custom application protocol. Additionally, it will demonstrate how to design the client for use as an applet or application and includes necessary changes to the client's design to accomplish this design.

Following the same steps used in previous examples, the application's duties need to be defined.

- The server will be responsible for connecting to the database and performing data retrieval and insertion.
- The server will provide two remote methods: one to retrieve the data, the second to insert a new row of data.
- The client will provide a user interface for displaying the current database rows and inserting a new row of data.
- The client will be designed as an application and an applet, and demonstrate the differences between RMI client implementations.

# The Database Configuration

With the definition of the application in place, the database information needs to be defined.

The table will contain some simple but useful information regarding a current employee. The information stored should contain: the first and last name, the office phone and extension, home phone number, primary skill, and secondary skill. It will be called `emp_overview` to separate it from the table names used in previous chapters. Listing 15.1 shows the SQL code to create the table structure.

**Listing 15.1   The SQL Script to Generate the *emp_overview* Table**

```
if exists (select * from sysobjects where id = object_id('dbo.emp_overview') and
sysstat & 0xf = 3)
        drop table dbo.emp_overview
GO

/****** Object:  Table dbo.emp_overview
CREATE TABLE dbo.emp_overview (
        id_num int IDENTITY (1, 1) NOT NULL ,
        last_name varchar (30) NOT NULL ,
        first_name varchar (20) NOT NULL ,
        office_phone varchar (20) NOT NULL ,
        office_ext varchar (5) NOT NULL ,
        home_phone varchar (20) NOT NULL ,
        primary_skill varchar (40) NOT NULL ,
        second_skill varchar (40) NOT NULL
)
GO
```

Note that the code was originally used for SQL Server and may need to be altered to fit other DBMS servers.

In addition to the table, an ODBC driver needs to be established. This example assumes a driver named "enterprise" and will communicate to a SQL-compliant database server. The example database queries are simple, and should not require much custom configuration.

# The Remote Server Interface

Defining the remote server interface, shown in Listing 15.2, should now look familiar. The interface `RemoteDBServer` extends `java.rmi.Remote` and declares two methods: `retrieveData()` and `insertData()`. The `insertData()` method requires an argument of type `DBEmployee`, defined in Listing 15.3. This class represents each column name in the table `emp_overview` with public String members. The constructor initializes the values of the object. Any member may be accessed directly from the application to reduce the code required for this example.

---

**Listing 15.2   The Remote Server Interface**

```
public interface RemoteDBServer extends java.rmi.Remote{
public Vector retrieveData () throws java.rmi.RemoteException;
public void insertData (DBEmployee emp) throws java.rmi.RemoteException;
}
```

---

**Listing 15.3   A Simple Object for Storing DB Results**

```
public class DBEmployee implements java.io.Serializable {
    public String LastName,FirstName,
      OfficePhone,OfficeExt,HomePhone,
      PrimarySkill,SecondarySkill;

public DBEmployee (String ln,String fn,String op,
                   String oe,String hp,String ps,String ss) {
      LastName=ln;
      FirstName=fn;
      OfficePhone=op;
      OfficeExt=oe;
      HomePhone=hp;
      PrimarySkill=ps;
      SecondarySkill=ss;
    }
  }
```

# The Remote Server Implementation

The remote server implementation for this example contains subtle differences from the previous examples. These differences include: extra member objects to reference the database, additional initialization code, and an additional exception-handling framework. The declaration, constructor, and main() method are shown in Listing 15.4. The main() method sets the security manager, attempts to initialize the database connection, and finally binds itself to the server. The binding is attempted last to ensure that the database connection is present before any clients may locate and invoke remote methods on the server.

---

**Listing 15.4   Declaration of the Remote DB Server**

```
import java.sql.*;
import java.util.Vector;

public class DBServer extends java.rmi.server.UnicastRemoteObject
                   implements RemoteDBServer {
    Connection connection;
    Statement statement;
    ResultSet results;
    PreparedStatement psInsert;
```

```
public DBServer () throws java.rmi.RemoteException {
    super();
}
public static void main (String args[]) {
    // set the security manager
    System.setSecurityManager (new java.rmi.RMISecurityManager());
    try {
        // instantiate the remote server
        DBServer db=new DBServer();

        // attempt to initialize the database objects
        db.initDBObjects();

        // Everything must be ok, so let's register with the naming server
        java.rmi.Naming.rebind ("DBServer",db);
        System.out.println ("Server bound to registry: DBServer");
    } catch (java.rmi.RemoteException e) {
        System.out.println ("Server got Exception: "+e);
    }
    catch (java.net.MalformedURLException e) {
        System.out.println ("Server got Exception: "+e);
    }
    catch (Exception e) {
        System.out.println ("Server got Exception: "+e);
    }
}
```

The initObjects() method in Listing 15.5 attempts to instantiate the JDBC-ODBC driver and make a connection to the ODBC driver. It then creates a preparedStatement object that simplifies the insertion of a new set of data into the table. The use of the prepared statement is shown in a later code listing. The method throws Exception which ensures that the server will not bind to the registry if the connection to the database is not established.

The closeConnection() method is responsible for providing the clean-up code. It ensures that a connection exists, and attempts to close the connection. Additional code for final clean-up can be inserted into this method.

## Listing 15.5   Initializing and Closing the Database Connection Objects

```
public void initDBObjects () throws Exception{
    //instantiate a new driver that matches the given Driver
    Class.forName("sun.jdbc.odbc.JdbcOdbcDriver").newInstance();
    connection = DriverManager.getConnection
                ("jdbc:odbc:enterprise;uid=sa");

    // Instantiate the Insert preparedStatement
    psInsert= connection.prepareStatement
                ("INSERT into emp_overview values (?,?,?,?,?,?,?)");
```

*continues*

**Listing 15.5   Continued**

```
    }

public void closeConnection () {

      try {
        // try to close the connection
        if (connection == null)
          System.out.println ("Connection NULL");
        else
          // verify connection has been initialized
          if (connection != null && !connection.isClosed() )
              connection.close();
      }
      catch (java.sql.SQLException e) {
       System.out.println ("Exception trying to close DB connection:"+e);
      }
    }
```

The `retrieveData()` implementation executes the following query:

```
SELECT * from emp_overview
```

Once the statement is executed, it gathers the results from the database, instantiates new `DBEmployee` objects and populates them with the results. The new `DBEmployee` objects are then inserted into a vector that will be returned at the end of the method.

Since all remote methods are required to throw `RemoteException`, this method uses the exception to its advantage. If a `SQLException` is caught while trying to execute a query or gather results, the server prints the exception to the client. In addition, it instantiates a new `RemoteException` with a simple string explaining the problem and attaches the `SQLException` to the new `RemoteException`. The new exception is then thrown, enabling the client to receive the error. Providing this kind of information to the client allows the user to document any error that may occur so the department manager may process the error efficiently.

**TIP**  Using exceptions wisely is an important part of effective Java programming. Without the proper use of exceptions, robust applications tend to become troublesome and can cause large amounts of downtime while trying to debug errors.

The `insertData()` method in Listing 15.6 is similar to the `retrieveData()` method. This method first clears the currently bound parameters of the prepared statement member object. It then binds each member of the new `DBEmployee` object containing new data to each `IN` parameter. Finally, it executes the statement and catches any exceptions that occur. The same design for handling database errors in `retrieveData()` is used. The `SQLException` is passed to the client through a `RemoteException`, should an error occur.

**Listing 15.6    Remote Method Implementations**

```
public Vector retrieveData () throws java.rmi.RemoteException {
        Vector v=new Vector (10,3);

      try {
        // create a statement
        statement=connection.createStatement();
        //execute query and capture results
        results=statement.executeQuery ("SELECT * from emp_overview");

        // get the results, create a new DBEmployee object,
        // and add it to the vector
        while (results.next()) {
          String lname=results.getString (2);
          String fname=results.getString (3);
          String ophone=results.getString (4);
          String oext=results.getString (5);
          String hphone=results.getString (6);
          String pskill=results.getString (7);
          String sskill=results.getString (8);

          DBEmployee emp=new DBEmployee (lname,fname,
                        ophone,oext,hphone,pskill,sskill);
          v.addElement (emp);
        }
      } catch (java.sql.SQLException e) {
        System.out.println ("Error retrieving results from the db! "+e);

        // throw a RemoteException with the exception
        // embedded for the client to receive
        throw new java.rmi.RemoteException
                ("Error retrieving results for the DB",e);
      }

      return v;
  }

/**
 * Inserts a row of data into a database
 */
  public void insertData (DBEmployee emp) throws java.rmi.RemoteException {
      try {
      // clear parameters
      psInsert.clearParameters ();

      // set parameters to new values
      psInsert.setString (1,emp.LastName);
      psInsert.setString (2,emp.FirstName);
      psInsert.setString (3,emp.OfficePhone);
      psInsert.setString (4,emp.OfficeExt);
      psInsert.setString (5,emp.HomePhone);
      psInsert.setString (6,emp.PrimarySkill);
      psInsert.setString (7,emp.SecondarySkill);
```

*continues*

**Listing 15.6   Continued**

```
            // now execute
            psInsert.executeUpdate ();
            } catch (java.sql.SQLException e) {
                System.out.println
                   ("Exception attempting to clear/set parameters for insert: "+e);

             // throw a RemoteException with the exception
             //  embedded for the client to receive
             throw new java.rmi.RemoteException ("Error inserting new row into
             ➥DB",e);
            }
       }
```

# The Client Implementation as an Application

The client will first be designed as an application (Listing 15.7). The main() method instantiates the client and calls the initObjects() method. This method handles setting the security
manager and attempting to locate a reference to the remote server.

**Listing 15.7   Declaration of the Client**

```
import java.awt.*;
import java.util.*;

public class DBClient extends Frame {
    RemoteDBServer db;

public void initObjects () {
        // set-up the security manager
        System.setSecurityManager (new java.rmi.RMISecurityManager());

        try {
           // try to get a stub referencing the remote object by calling lookup
           // with the naming registry. Modify the lookup URL if the server/
➥registry
           // will be located on another machine
           db = (RemoteDBServer)java.rmi.Naming.lookup ("DBServer");

        } catch (Exception e) {
          e.printStackTrace();
          System.out.println ("Not Bound exception : "+e);
        }

    }
```

```
public static void main (String args[]) {
  DBClient client=new DBClient();
  client.initObjects();
  client.show();
}
```

The insertData() method is called from the InsertFrame class, which provides the user interface for gathering information from the user for insertion into the database. It is passed a
DBEmployee object, created in the InsertFrame class, which is then passed on to the remote
method for database insertion.

The retrieveData() method in Listing 15.8 disables the three buttons for the primary menu,
and calls the remote retrieveData() method on the server. The remote method returns a
vector containing all of the data from the database, which has been stored in DBEmployee objects. A copy of the DataFrame class is instantiated for displaying the data.

### Listing 15.8    Invoking the Remote Methods

```
public void insertData (DBEmployee dbe) {
        try {
            db.insertData (dbe);
        } catch (java.rmi.RemoteException e) {
          System.out.println ("Exception while inserting Data to server"+e);
        }
     }

public void retrieveData () {              //disable the buttons until the data is
retrieved
        Insert.disable();
        Exit.disable();
        Retrieve.disable();

            // retrieve the data by invoking the remote method
            try {
        Vector v=db.retrieveData ();

                // hide this frame, move the retrieved data to the new
frame, and show new frame
        hide();
                DataFrame df=new DataFrame(this);
df.show(v);
      } catch (java.rmi.RemoteException e) {
        System.out.println ("Remote Exception occurred during Data retrieval!
"+e);
      } finally {
        Insert.enable();
        Exit.enable();
        Retrieve.enable();
      }

    }
```

# Running the Application

After starting the `rmiregistry`, execute the server and one or more clients. Try inserting some (see Figure 15.1) data into the database by selecting the Insert button on the main menu. After inserting some data into the database (see Figure 15.2), select the Display option and view the data. Notice how fast the data is retrieved and returned to the client (see Figure 15.3). If a new database is needed, simply change the ODBC driver to point to the new database. As long as the table remains the same name, the change is simple.

**FIG. 15.1**

A screenshot of the client's main menu.

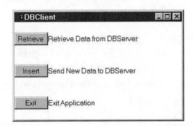

This is an example of the power of RMI when combined with the JDBC package. Powerful clients may be built for showing and entering data into a database, while moving the database interaction to the server. This frees the client for processing other data, making it faster and more efficient. Containing the JDBC code to the remote server allows the server to be placed on a network closer to the database and frees the client from database interaction.

Using this technique can help create powerful clients for the Internet without forcing the client to connect to a database server over slower connections, such as a modem. The data may be obtained by the remote server at a faster connection rate on the local LAN, collecting the data for the client. The benefits of RMI are even more apparent when larger table joins are required, or when data must be filtered from a large database.

# Implementing the Client as an Applet

Converting the client to an applet takes little effort when designing a client/server RMI application. To create an applet that functions the same as `DBClient`, follow these steps:

1. Copy the `DBClient.java` file to the same directory, using the name DBApplet.java.
2. Change the superclass of `DBClient` to Applet and change the name of the class to `DBApplet`.
3. Add a line to import the `java.applet.*` package.
4. Rename the previous constructor to `init()`, adding a call to the `initObjects()` method.
5. Remove the `setSecurityManager()` call in the `initObjects()` method.
6. Remove the `main()` method from the source code.
7. Create an HTML file to launch the applet.
8. Recompile the applet.

**FIG. 15.2**

A screenshot of the client's `InsertFrame` user interface.

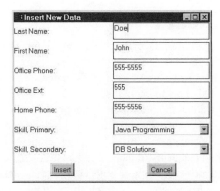

**FIG. 15.3**

A screenshot of the client's `DataFrame` user interface.

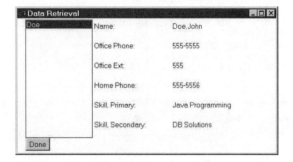

# Running the Applet

The structure of the application remains the same. After making the modifications, launch the applet using the following method:

1. Start the `rmiregistry`.
2. Start the server.
3. Launch the applet using AppletViewer `html filename`.

After using the applet, review the changes made. Notice how they mirror the application, and only fundamental changes need to be made.

**N O T E**    Remember the restrictions associated with applets when designing RMI-enabled applets. These restrictions may cause implementation problems when using applets as clients. The Web server, the Registry, and the RMI server must all reside on the same host machine due to the security constraints enforced by the `AppletSecurityManager`. Plan your client and server configurations accordingly! ▨

# Bootstrapping the Client

The power of RMI becomes apparent as developers begin to understand the full concepts of distributed architecture and the RMI structure. Applications can now be moved to the server, where a central location may hold just a few objects, or even hundreds. As these objects evolve and need to grow, they may need to be updated. Instead of propagating these classes to every machine that may need the update, a simpler method may be used. *Bootstrapping* is a technique that allows Java applications to specify an URL to load a client and all of its associated classes. This opens a whole new perspective into a Java programmer's toolbox and shows the true power of the RMI model. In fact, without using the bootstrapping technique, a client is limited to loading all of its classes, except remote objects, from the local CLASSPATH. The only classes that may be loaded from a network are the stub/skeleton classes and any indirect classes needed for parameters and return values.

The requirements for creating a bootstrapping loader are:

1. Set the security manager to the RMISecurityManager or a user-defined manager.
2. Use the RMIClassLoader.loadClass() method to load the primary class file for the client.
3. Use the newInstance method to create an instance and cast it to Runnable. This requires that the primary class implement runnable.
4. Start the client by invoking the run() method on the primary class.

When using the loadClass() method, the class is loaded from the java.rmi.server.codebase specified URL. If another URL is needed, use the alternate loadClass() method which allows the specification of an URL and class name.

# Using the *LogStream* Class

Included in the RMI package is the LogStream class, which provides a logging function to Java applications. The LogStream class extends java.io.PrintStream, and provides several static and non-static methods.

The non-static methods are responsible for logging text sent to the stream in a detailed format. The format looks similar to the following:

```
<date>:<logname>:<current method>:<text>
```

Each time a string of text is sent to the stream without a carriage return (/n), the text is stored in the stream's buffer. Once a carriage return is sent to the stream, the buffer is entered into the log in the style above. Once the text is sent to the log, the buffer is empty.

The static methods provide a simple naming service for the LogStream objects. The static method setDefaultStream() accepts a PrintStream argument that will be assigned to all newly created logs. A LogStream object is created by the static method log(), which requires a name to be passed as an argument. This name is used in the log entry and enables sharing the same stream for multiple logs. To create a new `LogStream` object, use the static method `log()` in the following format:

```
LogStream newlog=LogStream.log ("MyFirstLog");
```

This example will create a new log named `MyFirstLog` and assign `newlog` a reference to a new `LogStream` object. The reference may now be used for any logging mechanism that accepts an argument of `OutputStream`.

To demonstrate a typical use for the `LogStream` class, examine Listing 15.9 :

### Listing 15.9   Example of Using the *LogStream* Class

```
// retrieve a reference to the default print stream
PrintStream ps=LogStream.getDefaultStream();

// print a sample string to the stream (should go to console)
ps.println ("Testing default");

// create a new log to the file : testing.log
try {
    FileOutputStream fs=new FileOutputStream ("testing.log");
    PrintStream pslog=new PrintStream (fs);
    LogStream.setDefaultStream (pslog);

    // create a new log with the name testinglog1
    ls=LogStream.log ("testinglog1");
    ls.println ("This is a terrific tool for debugging RMI!");
    ls.print ("That's");
    ls.println ("That's all for now!");

    // create a second log name
    LogStream ls2=LogStream.log ("testinglog2");
    ls2.println ("Testing the second log name");
    ls2.println ("That's all for now! (Again)");


} catch (java.io.IOException e) {
  System.out.println ("Exception :"+e);
}
```

Sample Output:

```
Sun Feb 02 21:44:39 CST 1997:testinglog1:main:This is a terrific tool for
debugging RMI!
Sun Feb 02 21:44:39 CST 1997:testinglog1:main:That'sThat's all for now!
Sun Feb 02 21:44:39 CST 1997:testinglog2:main:Testing the second log name
Sun Feb 02 21:44:39 CST 1997:testinglog2:main:That's all for now! (Again)
```

This portion of code demonstrates several things. First, it retrieves a reference to the default stream using the `getDefaultStream()` method. It then uses the reference to print a short phrase to the stream, demonstrating the console is the default stream. Next, the code creates a `FileOutputStream` object using the filename testing.log and passes it to a new `PrintStream` object. By calling the `setDefaultStream()` method with the new `PrintStream` object (pointing to a local file) as an argument, the `LogStream` will now use the stream as the default. It then uses the `log()` method to obtain a reference to a new `LogStream` object using the name "testinglog1." Using the new reference, a few lines of text are sent to the stream. Notice the second and third lines that were sent are concatenated. This is because the second line actually used `print()` instead of `println()`, which doesn't send the carriage-return. The text from line two remains in the buffer until line three is sent, which contains a carriage-return. Finally, a second `LogStream` object reference is obtained. Text is sent to the new object, demonstrating that the two logs use the same stream but are noted as different entry names in the output.

# Logging RMI Applications

Logging remote method invocation occurrences is particularly useful when using RMI. Detailed information such as the date, the client's URL, and the method invoked are captured. By using the `RemoteServer.setLog()` method with a `PrintStream` object, a detailed report of remote method invocations may be kept. To send the output to a local file, use the code sample in Listing 15.10.

---

**Listing 15.10    A Code Segment Demonstrating the Use of RMI Logging**

```
try {
        FileOutputStream fs=new FileOutputStream ("testing2.log");
        PrintStream ps=new PrintStream (fs);
        ds.setLog (ps);
    } catch (java.io.IOException e) {
      System.out.println (e);
    }
```

---

By adding a call to the `setLog()` method of a remote server and invoking a few remote methods, the following output is created:

```
Sun Feb 02 22:20:34 CST 1997:RMI:TCP Accept-2:[james.delphis.com:
sun.rmi.transport.DGCImpl[0:0:0, 2]: java.rmi.dgc.Lease
dirty(java.rmi.server.ObjID[], long, java.rmi.dgc.Lease)]
Sun Feb 02 22:20:35 CST 1997:RMI:TCP Accept-2:[james.delphis.com:
DisplayServer[0]: void display(java.lang.String)]
Sun Feb 02 22:20:35 CST 1997:RMI:TCP Accept-2:[james.delphis.com:
DisplayServer[0]: SimpleRemoteObject exportit()]
Sun Feb 02 22:20:36 CST 1997:RMI:TCP Accept-3:[james.delphis.com:
sun.rmi.transport.DGCImpl[0:0:0, 2]: java.rmi.dgc.Lease
dirty(java.rmi.server.ObjID[], long, java.rmi.dgc.Lease)]
```

Notice how the logging feature of the `RemoteServer` class records information related to remote method invocation calls. This technique can help reduce debug and troubleshooting requirements and increase development time.

# Exporting Objects

The examples in Chapters 13 and 14 demonstrate creating remote objects by extending UnicastRemoteObject. The UnicastRemoteObject class provides a static method for exporting objects that implement a remote interface; in addition, it removes the restrictions of extending UnicastRemoteObject, allowing the object to extend any class. The static method provides the same export functionality as the constructor in UnicastRemoteObject.

A short example of using this method is included in this section. The class SimpleObject, shown in Listing 15.12 extends the class Thread and implements SimpleRemoteObject, shown in Listing 15.11. The next step in this demonstration is to create a function on the server that will instantiate a new SimpleObject and export it. This is demonstrated in Listing 15.13. This method must be part of an application that exists on the host that the object wants to be located. For example, if the object is exported on the server, the server becomes the host of the new object. The object may now be passed as a remote reference, and may accept remote method invocations.

This technique may be used to export an applet so that it may be available for remote callbacks. It is also useful if a particular object must subclass a specific class for specific functionality and can't extend UnicastRemoteObject.

---

**Listing 15.11  A Remote Interface for the Export Object Demonstration**

```
public interface SimpleRemoteObject extends java.rmi.Remote {
  public void test() throws java.rmi.RemoteException;
}
```

---

**Listing 15.12  An Object that Implements the Remote Interface**

```
public class SimpleObject extends Thread implements SimpleRemoteObject{
    public SimpleObject () {
    }
public void test() throws java.rmi.RemoteException {
    System.out.println ("Testing Simple Object");
    }
}
```

---

**Listing 15.13  An Example of Exporting an Object on a Remote Server**

```
public SimpleRemoteObject exportit() {
    SimpleObject so=null;
    try{
        so=new SimpleObject ();
        UnicastRemoteObject.exportObject (so);
    } catch (Exception e) {
        System.out.println ("Exception while exporting: "+e);
```

*continues*

---

**Listing 15.13    Continued**

```
    }
    return so;
}
```

---

# RMI Client-Related Classes and Interfaces

The following sections explain the client-related classes and interfaces of the Java RMI. Each class and interface serves a specific purpose in remote method invocation.

## Remote Interface

The `java.rmi.Remote` interface is the identifier for all remote objects, and must be directly or indirectly implemented for all remote objects. All remote interface subclasses must be defined as public, and include all methods that will be available for remote method invocation. In addition, all remote interface methods must throw `java.rmi.RemoteException`.

## *RemoteException* Class

The `RemoteException` class is used to handle all types of problems relating to remote objects and remote object handling. This includes I/O problems such as lost connections. `RemoteExceptions` may have nested exceptions that can provide larger detail regarding the problem encountered. Subclasses to `RemoteException` can be created and used to specify details to application specific problems:

**public RemoteException()**

creates a new `RemoteException`.

**Parameters:** None

**public RemoteException (String s)**

creates a new `RemoteException` with the specified string.

**Parameters:**

   `String s` containing the description of the problem

**public String getMessage ()**

retrieves the message of the exception.

**Parameters:** None

## *Naming* Class

The `Naming` class consists of five static methods for communicating with the Registry. The `lookup()` method returns a reference to the remote object associated with the name inside of the URL. The `bind()` method binds the remote object with the specified name into the Registry. The `rebind()` method will bind the object to the name in the Registry, overwriting any entries that already exist for the name. The `unbind()` method removes the association between the specified name and the remote server. The `list()` method returns a `String` array containing a list of the URLs bound in the Registry. The only requirement for the URL is that the host and port information and any additional information, such as a file portion, is ignored.

The `NotBoundException` is thrown if the name couldn't be found in the Registry when calling `lookup()`. An `AlreadyBoundException` is thrown if a name is already bound to an object and `bind()` is called. A `NotBoundException` will be thrown if no binding took place during `rebind()`.

To create an URL for any of these methods, a protocol, host, port, and name are included in the following format:

```
//<host>:<port>/<name>
```

For example:

```
//java.sun.com:2001/root
```

```
public static Remote lookup(String url) throws NotBoundException,
java.net.MalformedURLException, UnknownHostException, RemoteException
```

returns a reference to the remote object associated with name inside URL.

**Parameters:**

> url
>
> `String` containing the properly formatted URL to the host

```
public static void bind(String url, Remote obj) throws AlreadyBoundException,
java.net.MalformedURLException, UnknownHostException, RemoteException
```

returns nothing.

**Parameters:**

> url
>
> `String` containing the properly formatted URL to the host
>
> obj reference to the remote object to bind

```
public static void rebind(String url, Remote obj) throws RemoteException,
java.net.MalformedURLException, UnknownHostException
```

returns a reference to the remote object.

**Parameters:**

> url
>
> `String` containing the properly formatted URL to the host
>
> obj reference to the remote object to bind

```
public static void unbind(String url) throws RemoteException, NotBoundException,
java.net.MalformedURLException, UnknownHostException
```

returns nothing.

**Parameters:**

> url
>
> String containing the properly formatted URL to the host

```
public static String[] list(String url) throws RemoteException,
java.net.MalformedURLException, UnknownHostException
```

returns a String array containing a list of registered remote objects.

**Parameters:**

> url
>
> String containing the properly formatted URL to the host

# RMI Server-Related Classes and Interfaces

The following sections explain the server-related classes and interfaces of the Java RMI. Each class and interface serves a specific purpose in remote method invocation.

## *RemoteObject* Class

The RemoteObject class is an abstract class that redefines the methods of the Object class for remote object reference. The methods provided include hashCode(), equals(), and toString(). hashCode() was modified to allow remote object references to be stored in a hashtable properly. The equals() method now returns true if two remote objects are referencing the same remote object. The toString() is similar to the standard Object implementation but returns remote object specific information. Note that all other Object methods retain their original implementations and have not been altered.

```
public int hashCode()
```

determines a unique hash code for referencing the object in a hashtable and returns an int representing the hash code value determined by the algorithm.

**Parameters**: None

```
public boolean equals(Object obj)
```

determines if two object references are the same and returns true if the comparison is a match with the obj argument.

**Parameters:**

> obj: Object to compare against

```
public String toString()
```

returns a String containing class-specific information about the object.

**Parameters:** None

# *RemoteServer* Class

The RemoteServer class defines the basic behavior of a remote server object and is the super-class to all other remote server implementations. It is designed to be a framework that provides useful methods when dealing with remote objects and includes getClientHost(), setLog(), and getLog(). The getClientHost() method allows an active method to determine the originating host name that invoked the method. The ServerNotActiveException will be thrown if no remote method is active for the object. The setLog() method can be used to provide a reference to a PrintStream for logging errors encountered by the RemoteServer object. The getLog() method may be used to retrieve the stream that is being used for logging so the application may send specific information to the log for debugging or standard information reporting. This is a base class for designing remote object behavior and is not intended to be a superclass for remote objects (see UnicastRemoteObject in the next section).

```
public static String getClientHost()
```

returns a string containing the host that invoked the current running RMI method.

**Parameters:** None

```
public static void setLog (java.io.PrintStream out)
```

sets the logging PrintStream for the remote server.

**Parameters:**

> out
>
> PrintStream to send all logging messages to

```
public static java.io.PrintStream getLog()
```

returns a PrintStream reference to the logging stream.

**Parameters:** None

# *UnicastRemoteObject* Class

The only subclass of RemoteServer, the UnicastRemoteObject is designed for point-to-point active object references using the TCP protocol. The following are characteristics of UnicastRemoteObject implementations:

- The TCP protocol is the protocol that the connection transport uses.
- Invocations, parameters, and results use a stream protocol for communications between client and server.
- References are valid for a maximum of the life of the process that creates the remote object.

```
public Object clone()
```
**Parameters:** None

```
public static void exportObject (java.rmi.Remote obj)
```
exports an object that implements a remote interface but doesn't extend `UnicastRemoteServer`.

**Parameters:**

> `obj`: reference to the object to be exported

# *Unreferenced* Interface

The `Unreferenced` interface is an optional notification system that invokes the `unreferenced()` method when no more clients have a reference to the remote server. This is determined when the distributed garbage collection system, which maintains a list of references known, determines that no more references to the remote server exist. The `Unreferenced.unreferenced()` method is invoked and the remote server may modify any states or flags as appropriate. Note that the `unreferenced()` method may be called more than once as clients establish references and then drop them due to disconnection, out-of-scope issues, and so on.

```
public void unreferenced()
```
is called when remote servers no longer have references by any clients.

**Parameters:** None

# *RMISecurityManager*

`RMISecurityManager` is a sub-class of `java.lang.SecurityManager` and provides the level of security necessary when using RMI. This security manager may be used when a developer doesn't require a specific Security Manager. `RMISecurityManager` disables all functions except for those that allow class definition and access. If a security manager has not been set, Stubs will not be loaded, which ensures that some level of protection will exist for the RMI class. Table 15.1 shows the methods in `RMISecurityManager` and the effects they have on the security restrictions for an RMI application using them. This information may help to determine what methods may need to be overridden in a subclass of `RMISecurityManager` to meet the needs of an RMI application.

**Table 15.1**   *RMISecurityManager* **Method Restrictions and Allowances**

| Method | Restrictions/Allowances |
| --- | --- |
| `checkCreateClassLoader` | Disallows creating class loaders or executing `ClassLoader` methods |
| `checkAccess` | Disallows thread manipulation |
| `checkAccess` | Disallows threadgroup manipulation |

| Method | Restrictions/Allowances |
| --- | --- |
| checkExit | Disallows exiting the VM |
| checkExec | Disallows forking of processes |
| checkLink | Disallows linking dynamic linked libraries |
| checkPropertiesAccess | Disallows accessing properties except those labeled OK |
| checkPropertyAccess | Allows accessing system property key only if key.stub is true |
| checkRead | Allows/Disallows stub access to read a particular file (determines only) |
| checkRead | Disallows opening file descriptor for reading unless via socket |
| checkWrite | Allows/Disallows stub access to write a particular file (determines only) |
| checkWrite | Disallows opening file descriptor for writing unless via socket |
| checkDelete | Allows/Disallows if a specified system dependent file can be deleted (determines) |
| checkListen | Disallows listening on any port |
| checkAccept | Disallows accepting connections on any port |
| checkConnect | Disallows making connections on any port |
| checkTopLevelWindow | Allows caller/stubs to create top level windows |
| checkPackageAccess | Verifies package access |
| checkPackageDefinition | Verifies package definition access |
| checkSetFactory | Verifies stub can set a networking-related object factory |
| checkPrintJobAccess | Disallows printing from stubs |
| checkMemberAccess | Verifies if client code can access class members |
|  | Allows access to all public information |
|  | Allows non-stubs access to all default, package, and private declarations |

## RMIClassLoader Class

RMIClassLoader allows remote loading of a class via an URL. This is a separate class loader from the RMI runtime. Available local classes are always loaded first. A security manager must be set for stubs to be loaded locally or from an URL.

```
public static Class loadClass (String name) throws MalformedURLException,
ClassNotFoundException
```

loads the specified class via the URL defined in `java.rm.server.codebase` and returns the `Class` object containing the class.

**Parameters:**

`name`: The name of the class to load

```
public static synchronized Class loadClass (URL codebase, String name) throws
MalformedURLException, ClassNotFoundException
```

returns `Class` object containing the class.

**Parameters:**

codebase

the URL to attempt to load the class from

`name`: The name of the class to load

## *LoaderHandler* Interface

This interface is used by the `RMIClassLoader` class and is required to be named `LoaderHandler` in a package name specified by the property `java.rmi.loader.packagePrefix`. It contains only private methods and is for internal use.

## *RMISocketFactory* Class

`RMISocketFactory` is an abstract class that determines how the transport layer should obtain sockets. The transport layer will invoke the `createSocket()` and `createServerSocket()` methods on the `RMISocketFactory` object returned from a call to the `getSocketFactory()` method. This sequence of events happens whenever the transport needs to create sockets. The static `setSocketFactory()` method is used to set the socket factory which is used when RMI needs to get sockets. An application may invoke this method to specify a custom socket factory, but may only do it once. This technique may be used for establishing custom communications, such as secure channels, or for preprocessing. `getSocketFactory()` is static and will return the current socket factory object, or null if none is set. The `setFailureHandler()` will set the failure handler that is called by the RMI runtime should the creation of a socket handler fail. The failure handler will return `true` if a retry should occur, or `false` (default) if the attempt should not continue. The default `RMISocketFactory` implementation provides HTTP transport for firewalls by automatically attempting a connection through HTTP if a direct socket connection cannot be established. When using `createServerSocket()`, the factory will return a socket which will automatically detect if an HTTP `POST` request has been used, and will automatically produce the body of the `POST` as an HTTP response.

`public abstract java.net.Socket createSocket (String host, int port) throws IOException`

attempts to instantiate a Socket from the given host and port; used by the Transport Layer; returns a `Socket` object if the connection was successful.

**Parameters:**

> host: `String` containing the host name

> port: integer representing the port number

`public abstract java.net.ServerSocket createServerSocket (int port) throws IOException`

attempts to instantiate a `ServerSocket` for the port; used by the Transport Layer; returns `ServerSocket` object if the connection was successful.

**Parameters:**

> port: integer representing the port number

`public static void  setSocketFactory (RMISocketFactory fac) throws IOException`

used to set the socket factory from which RMI gets sockets. May be called once in an application

**Parameters:**

> fac: `RMISocketFactory` reference to use

`public static RMISocketFactory getSocketFactory()`

returns the current `RMISocketFactory` being used.

**Parameters:** none

`public static void setFailureHandler (RMIFailureHandler fh)`

establishes the handler for socket creation failures.

**Parameters:**

> h

> fh: reference to the `RMIFailureHandler` to use

`public static RMIFailureHandler getFailureHandler()`

returns the currently used `RMIFailureHandler` object.

**Parameters:** none

## *RMIFailureHandler*

The `RMIFailureHandler` class is responsible for handling any actions associated with exceptions received if a socket creation attempt fails. If a default is not set with the `RMISocketFactory` class, the creation of a Socket connection is not attempted. The `failure()` method is invoked as an exception is encountered, and returns `true` if another connection attempt should be made.

**`public boolean failure(Exception ex)`**

handles any actions when a connection attempt fails, and returns `true` if another attempt should be made, `false` if no more attempts should be made.

**Parameters:**

> ex: Exception that occurred during a connection attempt

## *LogStream* Class

The `LogStream` class is a subclass of `PrintStream` which allows various degrees of logging for debugging or general monitoring. It is called internally and logs errors associated with server calls. A call to `log()` with a new name will create a new log with the given name and use the default stream.

**`public static LogStream log(String name)`**

returns a `LogStream` reference if a log with the given name exists; if not, a log is created with the given name and uses the default stream.

**Parameters:**

> name: `String` containing the log name

**`public static void showThreadName (boolean doIt)`**

shows the name of the thread where the error occurred.

**Parameters:**

> doIt: `Boolean` indicating whether to show the thread name in the log

**`public static synchronized PrintStream getDefaultStream()`**

returns a reference to the current default `PrintStream`.

**Parameters:** none

**`public static synchronized void setDefaultStream (PrintStream newDefault)`**

sets the default stream for new logs to the given stream.

**Parameters:**

> newDefault: `PrintStream` to set as the new default stream

```
public synchronizec OutputStream getOutputStream ()
```

returns an OutputStream reference to the current output stream used for the log.

**Parameters:** none

```
public synchronized void setOutputStream (OutputStream out)
```

sets the output stream for output for which the log is sent.

**Parameters:**

out: OutputStream to use for the output of the log

```
public void write (byte b)
```

writes a byte of data to the stream by adding it to the internal buffer; if the byte is a new line, then the buffer is flushed.

**Parameters:**

b: byte of data to write

```
public void write (byte b[],int offset, int len)
```

writes an array of bytes to the stream by adding it to the internal buffer; if the byte is a new line, then the buffer is flushed.

**Parameters:**

b: byte array of data to write

offset: starting position in the array, or 0 for the first byte

len: number of bytes to write

# Stub/Skeleton Interfaces

This section describes the stub/skeleton classes that are generated by the *rmic* compiler, and also describes related classes that are referenced by the stubs/skeletons for proper RMI execution.

## *RemoteStub* Class

The superclass for all client stubs is the java.rmi.server.RemoteStub class. When the rmic compiler is used on a remote object, the generated stub file is a subclass of RemoteStub. In addition, the subclass also implements the server's remote interface. This allows remote objects to be passed to remote methods and cast to the appropriate class.

```
public abstract class RemoteStub extends java.rmi.RemoteObject() {}
```

# *RemoteCall* Interface

The `RemoteCall` interface is used to carry out a remote object call and is used by stubs and skeletons:

```
public ObjectOutput getOutputStream() throws IOException
```

returns the output stream for which a stub marshals arguments, or a skeleton marshals results.

**Parameters:** none

```
public void releaseOutputStream() throws IOException
```

manually releases the output stream connection to the transport layer.

**Parameters:** none

```
public ObjectInput getInputStream() throws IOException
```

returns the input stream for which a stub unmarshals results, or a skeleton unmarshals parameters.

**Parameters:** none

```
public void releaseInputStream() throws IOException
```

manually releases the input stream connection to the transport layer.

**Parameters:** none

```
public ObjectOutput getResultStream(boolean success) throws IOException,
StreamCorruptedException
```

returns an output stream once per remote call; if the result to be marshaled is a normal return, no exception will be thrown; otherwise, the `StreamCorruptedException` will be thrown indicating the result stream has already been obtained.

**Parameters:**

> `success`: indicates whether the call was successful and includes this result in the return header

```
public void ExecuteCall() throws Exception
```

executes the call in the correct format by calling any methods required for proper invocation.

**Parameters:** none

```
public void done() throws IOException
```

provides cleanup after the remote call has been completed.

**Parameters:** none

# *RemoteRef* Interface

Handles for remote objects are represented by the `RemoteRef` interface. Each stub has a concrete representation of a remote reference that is an instance of `RemoteRef`. The remote reference is used to properly carry out remote calls on the remote object it references.

```
public RemoteCall newCall (RemoteObject Rmtobj, Operation[] oper, int opnum, long
hash) throws RemoteException
```

creates an appropriate call object for a new remote invocation on a remote object

**Parameters:**

> `Rmtobj`: The remote object to perform the call on
>
> `oper` contains the operations available on the object
>
> `opnum`: index for the op array representing the operation to be performed this call
>
> `hash`: operation description to encode in the call

```
public void invoke (RemoteCall call) throws Exception
```

executes the remote call; passes any exceptions through the stub to the application.

**Parameters:**

> `call`: A reference to the object referencing the remote call

```
public void done (RemoteCall call) throws RemoteException
```

allows cleanup to be made after a successful call.

**Parameters:**

> `call`: A reference to the object referencing the remote call

```
public String getRefClass (java.io.ObjectOutput out)
```

returns a non-package-qualified class name of the reference type to be serialized to the out stream.

**Parameters:**

> `out`: the stream that the class will be sent to

```
public int remoteHashCode
```

returns a hash code for the remote object; two stubs referencing the same object will have the same hash code.

**Parameters:** none

```
public boolean remoteEquals(RemoteRef obj)
```

compares two remote objects for equality; test based on whether they refer to the same object; returns true if the objects are equal.

**Parameters:**

> obj: Remote reference to compare to this object

```
public String remoteToString()
```

returns a string that represents this remote object reference.

**Parameters:** none

# *ServerRef* Interface

The ServerRef interface extends the RemoteRef interface and is used to represent a server-side handle for a remote object.

```
public RemoteStub exportObject (java.rmi.Remote obj, RemoteServer server, Object
data) throws java.rmi.RemoteException
```

finds or creates a client stub object for the supplied remote object.

**Parameters:**

> obj: implementation of the remote object
>
> server: the remote server object for the implementation (may be the same as obj)
>
> data: any necessary information needed to export the object, such as port number

```
public String getClientHost()
```

returns the host name of the current client.

**Parameters:** none

# *Skeleton* Interface

The Skeleton interface is used by the skeleton implementation generated by the rmic compiler. The skeleton dispatches calls to the actual remote object implementation and is used as a server-side reference.

```
public void dispatch (Remote obj, RemoteCall call, int opnum, long hash) throws
Exception
```

unmarshals any arguments from the input stream, invokes the method, and marshals the result.

**Parameters:**

> `obj`: remote object implementation on which to invoke the method .

> `call`: `RemoteCall` object that contains the stream references.

> `opnum`: operation to perform (determines which method should be invoked); hash operation description to encrypt into the call

`public Operation[] getOperations()`

returns an array of possible operations to perform on the object.

**Parameters:** none

## *Operation* Class

The `Operation` class holds a description of a Java method that may be used when invoking a remote method on a remote object.

`public Operation (String op)`

constructor that accepts a string containing the method signature.

**Parameters:** `op`: string containing the method signature

`public String getOperation ()`

returns the description of the operation (the initialized value).

**Parameters:** none

**Returns:** string containing the operation description

`public String toString()`

returns the string representation of the object (typically the method signature).

**Parameters:** none

**Returns:** string representation of the object

# RMI Exceptions Encountered

The following tables explain the common exceptions that may be encountered during RMI applications, and some of the reasons why they occurred. Please keep in mind that these tables are very general, and may not cover all possible reasons why they occurred, but are meant to be a general troubleshooting guide.

### Table 15.2   Exceptions During Remote Object Export

| Exception | Cause |
|---|---|
| `java.rmi.StubNotFoundException` | Stub class not found, name collision, bad URL to codebase, stub not of correct class |
| `java.rmi.server.Skeleton NotFoundException` | Skeleton class not found; name collsion, bad URL, not of correct skeleton class |
| `java.rmi.server.ExportException` | The port is in use by another virtual machine |

### Table 15.3   Exceptions During RMI Calls

| Exception | Cause |
|---|---|
| `java.rmi.UnknownHostException` | Unknown host |
| `java.rmi.ConnectException` | Connection refused by host |
| `java.rmi.ConnectIOException` | I/O error when creating the connection |
| `java.rmi.MarshalException` | I/O error when marshaling the transport header, call header, or arguments |
| `java.rmi.NoSuchObjectException` | Incorrect attempt to invoke a method on an object that no longer exists |
| `java.rmi.StubNotFoundException` | Remote object not exported |

### Table 15.4   Exceptions During Returns

| Exception | Cause |
|---|---|
| `java.rmi.UnmarshalException` | Corrupted stream, return value class not found |
| `java.rmi.UnexpectedException` | An unexpected exception, not defined in the remote interface, occurred (contains the exception that occurred) |
| `java.rmi.ServerError` | An error occurred during the execution of a remote method |
| `java.rmi.ServerException` | An exception occurred during the execution of a remote method |
| `java.rmi.ServerRuntimeException` | An exception occurred during the execution of a method; may be a known exception that is defined in the remote interface |

### Table 15.5   Naming Exceptions

| Exception | Cause |
|---|---|
| java.rmi.AccessException | Attempt to bind, unbind, rebind from host other than the Registry host |
| java.rmi.AlreadyBoundException | Name is already bound to the Registry |
| java.rmi.NotBoundException | Name couldn't be found in the Registry |
| java.rmi.UnknownHostException | Registry is not running on the given host |

### Table 15.6   Other Exceptions

| Exception | Cause |
|---|---|
| java.rmi.RMISecurityException | A security exception is found and thrown by the Security Manager |
| java.rmi.server.ServerCloneException | Cloning attempt failed |
| java.rmi.server.ServerNotActiveException | Attempt was made to get the client host via the RemoteServer.getClientHost method when the remote server is not executing in a remote method |
| java.rmi.server.SocketSecurityException | Object was exported to an illegal port |

# RMI Properties

The following table presents the properties that may be modified for RMI application use. It describes the property name, typical uses, and the default value.

### Table 15.7   RMI Server Properties

| Property | Description | Default Value |
|---|---|---|
| java.rmi.server.codebase | server's URL where clients may load classes | " " |
| java.rmi.server.disableHTTP | if false, allows attempt to use HTTP for calls | false |
| java.rmi.server.hostname | specifies the hostname if getLocalHost() fails | " " |
| java.rmi.dgc.leaseValue | maximum time clients may leave remote reference | 10 min |

*continues*

**Table 15.7   Continued**

| Property | Description | Default Value |
|---|---|---|
| java.rmi.server.logCalls | sets server logging to true or false | false |
| java.rmi.server useCodebaseOnly | restricts class loading to CLASSPATH and URL in codebase property | false |

# From Here...

This chapter has provided an in-depth examination of Remote Method Invocation. The topics included in this chapter provide a developer with the knowledge required to tackle any scale enterprise development that requires distributed Java applications. In addition, it presents several advanced RMI topics that help developers build solid, easy-to-debug RMI applications.

- Chapter 12, "Introduction to Distributed Computing," will cover the basic concepts of distributed computing including DCE, RPC, and CORBA.
- Chapter 13, "Object Serialization," discusses how Java can store objects using streams for storage and persistence.
- Chapter 14, "Remote Objects," covers the basic RMI model, presents the RMI package, and demonstrates how it brings distributed computing to Java.

# PART III

# CORBA

# CHAPTER 16

# CORBA and Object Management Architecture (OMA)

In Chapter 12, "Introduction to Distributed Computing," you were introduced to Object Management Architecture (OMA) and CORBA as a mechanism to provide an object-oriented view of the distributed computing environment. In this chapter, I present an in-depth view of the OMA and CORBA architecture so that you can become familiar with their applications. In the next chapter, "WWW Applications Development Using CORBA," you take a closer look at applying IIOP-based application development for the Internet/intranet environment, using Java and JDBC. ▪

**What are CORBA and Object Management Architecture (OMA)?**

Understand what constitutes Object Management Architecture and CORBA.

**OMA standard development process**

How did the OMA standard evolve? Who controls the standard? How is the standard developed and published?

**Object Management Architecture, CORBA, IDL, and IIOP**

All the major components of the Object Management Architecture are described.

**CORBA Object Model**

Understand how the CORBA Object Model relates to the commonly understood object models (interfaces and implementation).

**CORBA application development process**

What is the CORBA application development process? Steps of the programming stages are described in detail.

**CORBA runtime environment and interoperability of ORBs**

Understand what goes on "under the hood" when a CORBA application executes.

# Using CORBA in Java Enterprise

As discussed in the section "Distributed Computing Architectures" in Chapter 12, a suitable architecture must be selected for a given application. The choice of a suitable architecture is governed by the demands of the application and the enterprise's overall technical environment. Because distributed systems, in general, are spread across multiple heterogeneous operating system environments, it is essential to choose a model of distributed computing that is open, non-restrictive, and fits elegantly with the object-oriented paradigm of application development. Object Management Architecture (OMA), of which Common Object Request Broker Architecture (CORBA) is the core transport mechanism, is such a standard model. OMA, and specifically CORBA, provide facilities to develop distributed applications using most of the legacy programming languages and operating systems. Figure 16.1 depicts the Java Enterprise architecture and the role of CORBA IIOP within the overall architecture.

**FIG. 16.1**

Java Enterprise Architecture consists of JDBC, RMI, and CORBA.

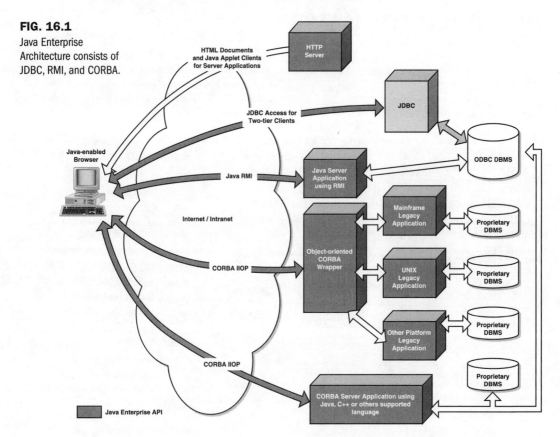

Various CORBA product vendors have already extended (or are in the process of extending) their CORBA products to work with Java in an Internet/intranet environment. Sun Microsystems, as part of Java Enterprise API, is to provide built-in CORBA support using the Java-IDL API.

---

### A Note from the Author

Various products provide support for IIOP, CORBA, or (CORBA) IDL. They all imply that the product is able to work as a CORBA-compliant client or server or both. Consult the product information to find out its level of CORBA functionality. This also assumes CORBA compliance with CORBA 2.0 level. More information on various versions of the CORBA standard appears later in this chapter in the section "History and Versions of OMA and CORBA."

---

Java Remote Method Invocation, discussed in detail in Part II of this book, "Remote Method Invocation (RMI)," provides an excellent distributed computing model for purely Java applications, where all the clients and, more importantly, all server applications are written in Java. Given that most Internet/intranet client applications are being developed using Java, there is no hurdle in using RMI from the perspective of the client programs. RMI can be used on the server end as well, if the server application also is written in Java. However, a huge amount of investment exists in the legacy server applications already being used in various organizations. Redeveloping these applications in Java is a very expensive option. Frequently, it will be necessary to leverage this existing investment by suitably interfacing Java servers to the legacy applications. CORBA and OMA provide one such mechanism. On the other hand, by developing Java servers as CORBA applications themselves, it is possible to substitute these servers with other more suitable CORBA servers, not necessarily written in Java.

# Understanding OMG and Object Management Architecture

The Object Management Group's (OMG) CORBA specification is one of the most significant standards being established in the world of distributed applications. It also has important implications for developers of object-oriented systems. CORBA extends the benefits of object-orientation across distributed heterogeneous environments, including multiple languages and multiple heterogeneous operating systems.

## Object Management Group (OMG)

Object Management Group (OMG) is a consortium of information technology vendors and academic and research institutions established in 1989. It started with fewer than a dozen members, led by Data General, Hewlett-Packard, and Sun. Starting with the objective of pooling the knowledge of Object Technology, others joined as interest in distributed computing escalated. Its current membership level exceeds 600 vendors and other organizations, including HP, IBM, AT&T, Sun/SunSoft, DEC, IONA, Expertsoft, Novell, Microsoft, BNR, Groupe Bull, ICL, Olivetti, Siemens, Objectivity, Ontos, Versant, and many others.

Object Management Architecture (OMA) is the key standard published by OMG. CORBA, Interface Definition Language (IDL), and Internet Inter-ORB Protocol (IIOP) are the centerpieces of OMA. Now that the OMA standard is approaching maturity, OMG is concentrating on how to use OMA in real-world, commercial applications.

## Object Management Architecture

CORBA, published by OMG, is a standard that provides a means for objects to interoperate with one another, regardless of vendor origin. It is the core of OMG's overall Object Management Architecture.

The pieces that make up the architecture are CORBA, CORBAservices, CORBAfacilities, and Distributed Applications, as shown in Figure 16.2.

**FIG. 16.2**
Object Management Architecture provides a complete architecture for building distributed applications.

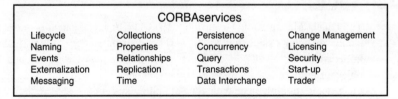

Vertical CORBAfacilities
- Application Development
- Computer Integrated Manufacturing
- Currency
- Distributed Simulation
- Financial Services
- Imagery
- Information Superhighways
- Internationalization
- Mapping
- Oil & Gas Exploration and Production
- Security
- Telecommunications

Distributed Applications

Horizontal CORBAfacilities

| • User Interface | • Information Management | • System Management | • Task Management |

CORBAservices

| Lifecycle | Collections | Persistence | Change Management |
| Naming | Properties | Concurrency | Licensing |
| Events | Relationships | Query | Security |
| Externalization | Replication | Transactions | Start-up |
| Messaging | Time | Data Interchange | Trader |

Object Request Broker (ORB)

Operating System and Network Services

■ **The Object Request Broker (ORB)** defines the CORBA object bus, which allows client objects to transparently locate server objects and invoke their methods (transfer parameters and results between them).

■ **CORBAservices, or Common Object Services**, define the system-level object frameworks that extend the bus. Some of these services are dedicated to manipulating (creating, linking, discovering, and so on) data structures (you may think of them as object hierarchies) in the distributed environment. Another set of services is dedicated to persistence data manipulation and querying such data sources. Other services, such as security and trader (yellow pages service for finding servers), provide the infrastructure on which to build applications.

■ **CORBAfacilities, or Common Facilities**, define horizontal and vertical application frameworks that are used directly by business objects. Vertical facilities are domain-specific (healthcare, finance, manufacturing, and so on) framework artifacts. Horizontal facilities are application building blocks that are not domain-specific (examples are user interface, information, system, and task management).

■ **Distributed Applications** are application interfaces that are specific to vertical industries such as financial markets, healthcare, and telecommunications and are meant to be customized by the user.

## OMG Standardization Process

One of the most unique aspects of the OMG standardization process is that OMG only publishes specifications. It does not produce implementations. Unlike other standards bodies, such as the International Standards Organization (ISO) or ANSI, OMG follows a relatively informal standardization process. Because establishing formal standards can be laborious and time-consuming, the standards developed in this manner are many times obsolete by the time they are published. OMG has been successful in establishing a process by which vendors get together and agree on a standard. Achieving this among a small number of vendors can be challenging. By achieving this with hundreds of vendors, OMG has done a remarkable job.

More information about OMG can be found at its Web site:

**http://www.omg.org**

OMG member organizations contribute technology and ideas in response to *Request for Proposals* (RFPs) issued by the OMG. Using the responses to these RFPs, the OMG adopts specifications based on commercially available technology.

## CORBAnet: The Interoperability Showcase

OMG has established a showcase to demonstrate the interoperability of CORBA products from various vendors. This is a showcase where clients running on a given operating platform can invoke methods on servers running on another platform. CORBAnet can be accessed on the Internet at:

> **http://www.corba.net/**

The Client application has been developed using the ORB product from the vendor of the client operating platform, where possible. The same applies to the Server applications, as well. Table 16.1 lists the CORBA products demonstrated by CORBAnet.

**Table 16.1    CORBA Products Demonstrated at CORBAnet**

| Vendor | CORBA Product |
| --- | --- |
| Digital | ObjectBroker |
| DNS Technologies | SmalltalkBroker |
| Expertsoft | PowerBroker CORBAplus |
| Fujitsu | ObjectDirector |
| Hewlett-Packard | HP ORB Plus |
| IBM | DSOM |
| ICL | DAIS |
| IONA | Orbix |
| Siemens Nixdorf | SORBET |
| Sun | NEO |
| Tandem | NonStop DOM |
| Visigenic | Visibroker for C++ |

CORBAnet is hosted by Distributed Systems Technology Centre in Brisbane, Australia.

# Understanding Object Management Architecture

In this section, you look at various components of Object Management Architecture (OMA). IIOP is only one of the core components of the OMA. CORBA, CORBAservices, and CORBAfacilities are the other components that provide a highly feature-rich framework for building distributed applications.

---

**Scope of CORBA Coverage in the Java Enterprise Book**

The objective of CORBA coverage in this book is limited to enabling the reader to write basic IIOP clients and servers (see the sample application in Chapter 18, "Incorporating Java, JDBC, and CORBA: A Sample Application"). Use of CORBAservices has been kept to a minimum. Issues arising from applying CORBA in the Internet are covered in detail in Chapter 17, "WWW Applications Development Using CORBA." This chapter provides a complete overview of the architecture.

---

Part
III

Ch
16

# Object Request Broker (ORB)

The Object Request Broker (ORB) is the "core object bus," connecting various objects on the distributed system. It lets objects transparently make requests to—and receive responses from—other objects located locally or remotely. It is responsible for

- providing mechanisms to find object (server) implementation for a request
- preparing object implementation (server) to receive request
- communicating request parameters to the object implementation and transferring control to it
- transmitting return values from the server and transferring control back to the client

Interface Definition Language (IDL) is the means by which definitions of various Object Implementations (servers), the methods available from each server, and the number and type of their parameters, are described to various parts of the distributed system. IDL plays the key role in configuring and reconfiguring various clients and servers.

# History and Versions of OMA and CORBA

CORBA 1.1, introduced in 1991, specified only the IDL, language bindings, and APIs for interfacing to the ORB. This provided the capability to write portable programs that could run on top of CORBA-compliant ORBs. This provided portability only at the interface level. At that time, it was left up to the vendors to provide a suitable protocol for interoperability.

CORBA 2.0, introduced in December 1994 and finally published in July 1995, specifies interoperability and collaboration across multiple CORBA-compliant ORBs. This architecture is based on General Inter-ORB Protocol (GIOP). The GIOP is a collection of message requests ORBs can make over a network. GIOP can be implemented over various network transports (for example, NetBIOS or TCP/IP). Implementation of GIOP over TCP/IP is known as the Internet Inter-ORB Protocol (IIOP). Any ORB complying with CORBA 2.0 standard must support the IIOP protocol.

# Common Object Services

CORBA Object Services are collections of system-level services, packaged as an add-on to the Object Request Broker. They augment and complement the functionality of the ORB. These are used to create a component, name it, introduce it into the environment, interrogate it, and so on. These services themselves are specified in the IDL, just like the user-written object servers (known as *implementations* in the CORBA vocabulary).

OMA includes the following common object services:

- **The Naming Service** allows components or objects connected to the ORB to locate other objects by name. It also supports federated naming contexts. The service allows objects to be bound to existing network directories or naming contexts—including ISO's X.500, OSF's DCE, and Sun's NIS. The Naming Service makes it possible to view objects that are spread over a distributed system in a neat directory structure.

- **The Life Cycle Service** defines operations for creating, copying, moving, and deleting objects. The objects can be moved from one node in the network to another, should the demands so require (for example, for load balancing).

- **The Persistence Service** provides a single interface for storing components persistently on a variety of storage servers—including Object Databases (ODBMSs), Relational Databases (RDBMSs), and simple files. Most database vendors are building interfaces to their DBMSs so that they can work as a CORBA persistence service.

- **The Event Service** allows components to dynamically register or unregister their interest in specific events. The service defines a well-known object called an event channel that collects and distributes events among components that know nothing about one another. Most of the readers will hopefully be familiar with the event-based architecture of most graphical user-interfaces (GUIs). CORBA Event Services make events accessible to the whole distributed system, thus making possible some very cool and interesting applications.

- **The Concurrency Control Service** provides a lock manager that can obtain locks on behalf of either transactions or threads.

- **The Transaction Service** provides two-phase commit coordination among recoverable components using either flat or nested transactions. With stable CORBA products already common in the marketplace, Transaction Service products will provide the next major market development. Once mature Transaction Service products are available, it will be a major step toward implementing distributed TP-Monitors. Many Transaction Service products are currently going through their pre-release stages.

- **The Relationship Service** provides a way to create dynamic associations or links between components that do not know one another. It also provides mechanisms for traversing the links that group these components. This service may be used to enforce referential integrity constraints, to track containment relationships, and for any type of linkage among components.

- **The Externalization Service** provides a standard way for getting data into and out of an object using a stream-like mechanism.

- **The Query Service** provides query operations for objects. It is a superset of SQL, based on the forthcoming SQL3 specification, and the Object Database Management Group's (ODMG) Object Query Language (OQL).

- **The Licensing Service** provides operations for metering the use of components to ensure fair compensation to the vendor for their use by the customer. The service supports any model of usage control at any point in an object's life cycle. It supports charging per session, per node, per instance creation, and per site.

- **The Properties Service** allows you to dynamically associate named values or properties with any component's state.

- **The Security Service** is essential for CORBA applications to work in the areas of business, commerce, and defense. It provides a mechanism to implement end-to-end security in multivendor object networks. Security, in general, involves confidentiality, authentication, and access control. The CORBA security service specifies mechanisms to provide these in a distributed environment. Some ORBs implementing this service are already available, and more will do so very shortly.

- **Time Service, Trader Service, Collection Service, and Change Management Service** are examples of other advanced services that are not covered in this book. You are advised to examine these services once you have become familiar with OMA, CORBA, and at least Naming, Event, and Life Cycle Services.

---

### Market Availability of CORBA Services

OMA and CORBA are very young, given that the CORBA 2.0 specification was published only in mid-1995. A large number (more than a dozen) of CORBA 2.0-compliant ORBs are already on the market. Many CORBA service standards have only been published in 1996, with standards for only the basic services (Naming, Events, and Life Cycle) announced before 1996. Most of the commercial ORBs implement essential services like Naming, Events, and Externalization. Persistence, Transaction, and Query services are being built by the database vendors or other closely related vendors. At the time of this writing, many of the key services are in beta stage. Thus, 1997 will see the general availability of more of the key CORBA services.

---

# Common Facilities

These are collections of IDL-defined components that provide services of direct use to application objects. These provide artifacts or architecture components to design applications and are of two types:

- **Horizontal Facilities (used by multiple application domains)** provide generic, application-domain-independent functionality and are further subclassified into the following four categories:

    **User Interface Facilities** similar to those provided by OO-Motif, OLE, and OpenDoc.

    **Information Management Facilities** for compound document storage and data interchange facilities.

    **System Management Facilities** to define interfaces for managing, configuring, installing, operating, and repairing distributed object components.

    **Task Management Facilities** for workflow, long transactions, agents, scripting, rules, and e-mail.

- **Vertical Facilities** will provide IDL-defined interfaces for vertical application market segments such as health, retail, telecommunications, and finance. These can be typically thought of as application frameworks.

## Application/Business Objects

Application Objects are components specific to end-user applications. These must be defined using IDL if they are to participate in ORB-mediated exchanges. Application Objects build on top of services provided by the ORB, Common Facilities, and Object Services.

# Understanding the Common Object Request Broker Architecture (CORBA)

Now look at the CORBA architecture in detail to understand how method invocation on remote objects is implemented. First, I explain how the CORBA object model differs from the conventional single-process object model. Then, you look at the Client view, the Server view, Interface Definition Language (IDL), and, finally, the steps of the method invocation.

## CORBA Object Model

Consider a common problem encountered in achieving a good understanding of CORBA. This problem is that of the inheritance of object interfaces versus the inheritance of implementations.

The elegance of CORBA architecture lies in the fact that interfaces may be dynamically mapped to one of many implementations (servers). First, consider the conventional inheritance of interfaces and implementations. Figure 16.3 shows an example of inheritance as it is generally understood.

**FIG. 16.3**

In normal inheritance in conventional object-oriented design, both interfaces and implementations are inherited.

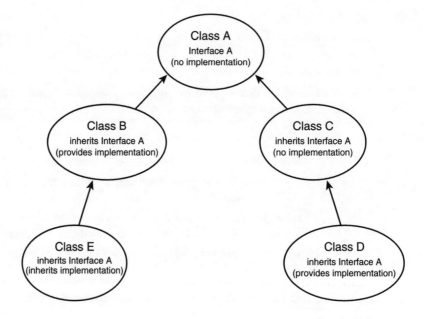

In this example, Class E inherits from Class B, which in turn inherits from Class A. Also, Class D inherits from Class C, which in turn again inherits from Class A. Class A declares only an interface. In the first example (on the left side in the diagram), Class B provides an implementation of Interface A. Class E, thus, inherits both the interface A and its implementation from B. In the second example, implementation of A is not provided until the second stage of inheritance, in class D. It is important to note that an implementation provided by a parent class (class B) must be inherited by its subclasses (class E), though it may be overridden or extended.

Now, consider inheritance of interfaces and implementations in CORBA. CORBA allows you to define interfaces that can inherit from other interfaces. Mapping of an interface to an implementation (a server) occurs at runtime, as a result of the *bind* request by the Client. Figure 16.4 illustrates two options of how three interfaces with inheritance relationships can potentially map to different implementations.

Part

III

Ch

16

**FIG. 16.4**

In CORBA, inheritance is defined for interfaces and is independent of implementation inheritance.

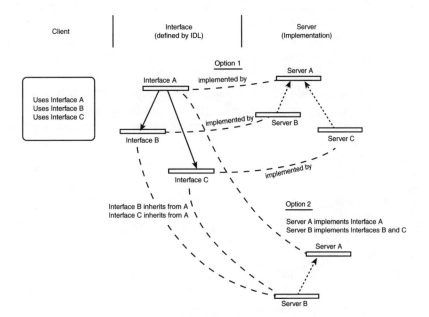

In the example shown in Figure 16.4, Interface B inherits from Interface A and Interface C also inherits from Interface A. In first option, Interfaces A, B, and C are *bound* to Implementations (servers) A, B, and C, respectively. In this case, Servers B and C also handle Interface A (because Interface B and C inherit from Interface A), and they directly invoke Server A's services as implementation.

When a CORBA server is activated, it registers the services (interfaces) it implements. At runtime, the *bind* request for a given interface picks up the appropriate server. It is possible to implement various interfaces in multiple ways in the servers. In the second option shown in Figure 16.4, Interface A is *bound* to Implementation (server) A, whereas both of Interfaces B and C are implemented (*bound* to) by Server B. Server B may still use Server A for Interface A functionality.

# Structure of a CORBA 2.0 ORB

---

### Skip This Section If...

...you are not interested in learning what internal components of the ORB are involved in making remote method invocations from the client. You can assume that "some magic" happens and the selected method gets executed on an appropriate server.

If this is the case, move to the section "Interface Definition Language (IDL)" later in the chapter.

---

CORBA 2.0 ORB provides more than just the basic messaging mechanisms needed by objects to communicate with one another across heterogeneous languages, tools, platforms, and networks. It provides the environment for managing these objects, publishing their presence through naming services, and describing their metadata. It is scalable from object interactions between objects that reside within a single process to objects that interact across distant parts of a heterogeneous network.

The ORB mechanisms described in this chapter have been available since CORBA 1.1 was introduced in 1991. CORBA 2.0 added multivendor ORB interoperability, ORB initialization services, and enhancements to the Interface Repository.

Figure 16.5 shows the client and server sides of a CORBA ORB. The areas marked by double asterisks are new to CORBA 2.0. In many CORBA discussions, the server is often referred to as the Object Implementation, where the actual object service is implemented.

**FIG. 16.5**

Common Object Request Broker Architecture consists of static and dynamic invocation interfaces on client and server ends and an ORB interface.

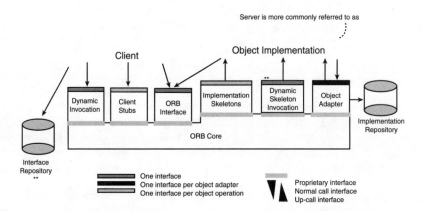

**Client Side Overview** CORBA 2.0, like SQL, provides both static and dynamic invocation of its interfaces. As shown in Figure 16.5, the components that participate from the client end are:

- **Client IDL stubs** provide the static interface to object services. These precompiled stubs define how clients invoke corresponding services on the servers. From a client's perspective, the stub acts like a local call—it is a local proxy for a remote server object. The services are defined using IDL, and both the client and the server stubs are generated by the IDL compiler. A client must have an IDL stub for each interface it uses on the server. The stub includes the code to perform marshaling of arguments.

- **Dynamic Invocation Interface (DII)** lets you discover the methods to be invoked and the number and types of their arguments at runtime. CORBA provides standard APIs for looking up the metadata that defines the server interface, generating parameters, issuing the remote call, and getting back the results.

- **Interface Repository** is a runtime database that contains machine-readable versions of the IDL-defined interfaces, thus providing the metadata repository for ORBs. The APIs allow the components to dynamically access, store, and update metadata information. **Interface Repository Interface APIs** allow you to obtain and modify the descriptions of all the registered component interfaces, the methods they support, and the parameters they require—collectively known as method signatures. Interface Repository, combined with these APIs, provides the self-documenting nature of CORBA.

- **CORBA** provides APIs to local services for use by the application. Some examples are: object to string and string to object to convert object references to strings and vice versa (to store object references and reactivate them), get_interface to provide type and metadata for an object, and get_implementation to get implementation data for an object.

**Server-Side Overview**    As shown in Figure 16.5, the server side consists of:

- **Server IDL Stubs** (implementation skeletons) which provide static interfaces to each service exported by the server. These stubs, like the ones on the client, are created using the IDL compiler.

- **Dynamic Skeleton Invocation (DSI)** provides a runtime binding mechanism for the server and is the server equivalent of a DII on the client end. The Dynamic Skeleton analyzes the parameter values in the incoming message to identify the object and object method to be invoked. In contrast, normal compiled skeletons are always defined for a particular object class and expect a method implementation for each IDL-defined method.

- **Object Adapter** sits on top of the ORB's core communication services and accepts requests on behalf of the server's objects. It provides the runtime environment for instantiating server objects, passing requests to them, and assigning them object IDs, known as object references. It also registers the classes it supports and their runtime instances with the Implementation Repository. CORBA specifies that each ORB must support a standard adapter called the Basic Object Adapter (BOA).

- **Implementation Repository** provides a runtime repository of information about the classes a server supports, the objects that are instantiated, and their IDs. It also serves as a common place to store additional administrative information of ORBs, such as trace information, audit trails, and security.

- **The Server-Side ORB Interface** is the same as the ORB Interface on the client end and provides APIs to ORB services.

# Interface Definition Language (IDL)

CORBA Interface Definition Language (IDL) is a *contractual* language, which defines a "contract" between a component or object and the rest of the distributed system (world). It defines the component's boundaries and interfaces to its potential clients. It is an entirely declarative object-oriented language, supporting multiple inheritance.

**Structure of the CORBA IDL**    CORBA IDL, also supported by the Java-IDL component of Java Development Kit 1.1, consists of modules, which further consist of interfaces. Modules provide a mechanism for bundling of interfaces, as illustrated in Listing 16.1.

---

**Listing 16.1   Structure of CORBA IDL**

```
module <identifier>
{
<type declarations>;
<constant declarations>;
<exception declarations>;

interface <identifier> [:<inheritance>]
{
<type declarations>;
<constant declarations>;
<attribute declarations>;
<exception declarations>;

[<op_type>]<identifier>(<parameters>)
[raises exception] [<context>];
.....
.....

[<op_type>]<identifier>(<parameters>)
[raises exception] [<context>];
.....
}

interface <identifier> [:<inheritance>]
.....
}
```

---

Listing 16.1 shows the structure of the CORBA IDL. The following are CORBA IDL's main components:

- **Modules** provide a namespace to group a set of class descriptions (or interface descriptions). A module adds an additional level of hierarchy in the IDL namespace.

- **Interfaces** define a set of methods (or operations) that a client can invoke on an object. An interface may be considered a class definition with an implementation section. An interface can declare one or more exceptions indicating that an operation did not perform successfully. An interface can be derived from one or more other interfaces, thus allowing multiple inheritance.

■ **Operation** is the CORBA equivalent of a method. It denotes a service provided by an object. The IDL defines the operation's signature.

■ **Data Types** define the acceptable types of values for CORBA parameters, attributes, exceptions, and return values. Basic and constructed types are supported. Basic types are short, long, unsigned short, unsigned long, float, double, char, boolean, and octet. Allowed Constructed types are enum, string, struct, array, union, sequence, and any. *Each CORBA IDL data type is mapped to a native data type using the language bindings.*

**Interface Repository**    If CORBA IDL is the metadata language for a CORBA 2.0 distributed system, the Interface Repository is the metadata database. The Interface Repository stores the compiled version of the IDL in an ORB-readable form. ORB provides a full API to inquire into and update the Interface Repository, thus providing a self-describing system.

The Interface Repository is implemented as a set of persistent objects, which represent the definitions in the IDL.

Figure 16.6 shows the class hierarchy of the Interface Repository Object Model.

**FIG. 16.6**

Interface Repository consists of modules, which consist of interfaces and which, in turn, consist of operations.

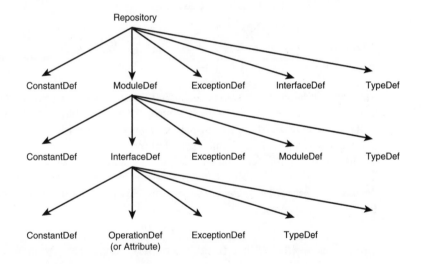

**Language Bindings to IDL**    Each CORBA IDL data type is mapped to a native data type using the language bindings. These bindings are implemented using the client stubs and server skeletons. CORBA 2.0 specifies C++, C, and Smalltalk language bindings. Standard Language Bindings for Java, Ada, Eiffel, and Object COBOL are in the process of being developed and adopted. Once the standard language bindings for a language have been adopted by OMG, they become a part of the CORBA standard.

Figure 16.7 shows how language bindings are used by the client stubs to translate language-specific object references to ORB's object references. The reverse process takes place on the server end in the Server Skeletons, where ORB's object references are translated to those of the language in which the server application is written.

**FIG. 16.7**
OMG's Standard
Language Bindings for
various programming
languages map
Interoperable Object
References (IORs) to
language-specific object
references.

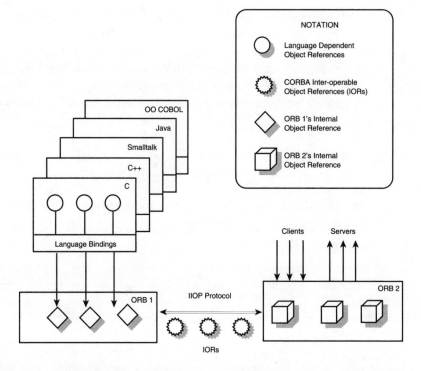

The standardizaton of Java Language bindings is currently in progress. Multiple submissions from various vendors have been made. A standard is derived from these submissions. Table 16.2 lists the CORBA IDL to Java mappings of some of the key IDL data types, as implemented in the OrbixWeb from Iona Technologies. OrbixWeb is the Java-enabled release of the leading CORBA product Orbix. The complete language binding consists of the mapping of identifiers, interfaces, attributes, operations, inheritance, and exceptions. You will need to consult the *OrbixWeb Programming Guide* (or the programming guide for the product being used by you) for the complete mapping.

**Table 16.2   CORBA IDL to Java Language Mappings (OrbixWeb)**

| OMG IDL Type | Java Data Type |
| --- | --- |
| short | short |
| long | int |
| unsigned short | int |
| unsigned long | int |
| float | float |

| OMG IDL Type | Java Data Type |
|---|---|
| double | double |
| char | char |
| boolean | boolean |
| octet | byte |

## CORBA Method Invocations

CORBA supports two types of client/server invocation: static and dynamic. Clients see the ORB object through the object interfaces, using language mappings or bindings. Static and dynamic methods of client/server invocation differ in the way and the timing of interface binding resolution.

**Static Invocation**     The static interface is generated in the form of stubs by the IDL precompiler. It is suitable for programs that know at compile-time the details of the operations they will need to invoke. The static stub interface is bound at compile-time.

**Dynamic Invocation**     Dynamic invocation method provides a flexible client/server relationship. It allows you to add new classes to the system, without requiring changes to the client code. It is suited for tools or programs that discover what services are provided at runtime. The client is coded in a generic fashion, and it dynamically interrogates at runtime what classes, interfaces, and methods are available, as well as the number and types of parameters required for the methods the client may want to use.

# Developing CORBA Applications

So far, you have looked at the OMA and CORBA architecture in detail. You also looked at static and dynamic invocation mechanisms for inter-object communication. You are now ready to consider the steps involved in developing applications using CORBA. You look at the development process for both types of invocations, static as well dynamic. Finally, you compare the pros and cons of choosing between these two invocation methods.

## Static Invocation Development Process

This section describes the development process required for the static invocation of remote methods. Figure 16.8 depicts various steps of the CORBA development process for static invocation. You will write an actual CORBA application using Java for the client as well as the server in Chapter 18, "Incorporating Java, JDBC, and CORBA: A Sample Application." Only the steps of the development process are described here.

**FIG. 16.8**

CORBA Development Process for Static Invocation starts with defining interfaces in the IDL file(s), followed by writing of client and server programs.

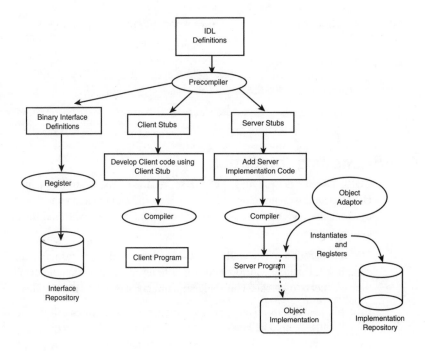

The development process consists of the following steps:

1. **Define your object classes using Interface Definition Language (IDL).** The IDL definition language defines the types of objects, their attributes, the methods they export, and the method parameters. CORBA IDL is a subset of ANSI C++ with additional constructs to support distribution. It is a *purely declarative language*. It uses the C++ syntax for constant, type, and operation definitions. It does not include any control structures or variables.

2. **Run the IDL file through a language precompiler**. A CORBA-compliant IDL pre-compiler processes the IDL files and produces *skeletons for the Implementation Server Classes.*

3. **Add the Implementation Code to the Skeletons.** The class implementor supplies the code that implements the methods in the skeletons. This constitutes the implementation of the classes.

4. **Compile the Code.** A CORBA-compliant compiler compiles the code and generates three types of output files:

    **Import Files to the Interface Repository:** These describe the objects to the Repository.

    **Client stubs for the IDL-defined methods:** These are used by the client programs wanting to invoke the remote methods.

    **Server stubs that call the methods on the server, also referred to as the up-call interfaces:** Automatic generation of stubs eliminates dependencies on a particular ORB implementation.

5. **Bind the class definitions to the Interface Repository.** Class definitions in files produced in step 4 previously are bound to specific object implementation, using a utility.

6. **Instantiate the Objects on the Server.** At startup, a server *Object Adapter* may instantiate server objects that service remote client method invocations. These runtime objects are instances of the server application classes.

7. **Register the runtime objects with the Implementation Repository.** Object Adapter records in the *Implementation Repository* the object references and type of any object it instantiates on the server. The Implementation Repository also knows which objects are supported on a particular server. The ORB uses this information to locate active objects or to request the activation of objects on a particular server.

Part
III

Ch
16

Development tools from different vendors may implement the development process differently. Increasingly, all the steps that do not require developer involvement are transparent and done automatically. Visual development tools are becoming available to facilitate the rapid development of CORBA applications.

## Dynamic Invocation Development Process

CORBA's Dynamic Invocation APIs allow a client program to dynamically build requests and invoke requests on objects. The client specifies the object to be invoked, the method to be performed, and the set of parameters through a call or a sequence of calls. This information is obtained by the client code from *Interface Repository* or similar runtime database. The dynamic invocation provides maximum flexibility by allowing new object types to be added to the distributed system at runtime.

For most applications, static invocation provides adequate functionality. Dynamic invocation is required generally for development tools, on-the-fly end-user tools, and system administration tools.

To invoke a dynamic method on an object, the client must perform the following steps:

1. **Obtain the method description from the Interface Repository.** CORBA specifies about ten calls for locating and describing objects within the repository. After an object is located, a *describe call* is used to obtain its full IDL definition.

2. **Create the argument list.** The next step is to build the argument list for the server method that the client wants to invoke. CORBA specifies a self-defining data structure for passing parameters, which it calls the NamedValueList. The list is created using the create_list operation and as many add_arg calls as it takes to add each argument to the list.

3. **Create the Request.** The request must specify the object reference, the name of the method, and the argument list. The request is created using the CORBA *create_request* call.

4. **Invoke the Request.** Finally, the request is invoked using either (1) the *invoke* API, or (2) *send followed by receive*, or (3) *unblocked send*, without expecting to receive back.

## Comparison of Static versus Dynamic Invocation

Static and dynamic invocations have very different development processes. They are used for different purposes as well. A comparison and contrast of their features appears in Table 16.3.

**Table 16.3   Static versus Dynamic Invocation**

| Criterion | Static Invocation | Dynamic Invocation |
|---|---|---|
| Flexibility | Since it is a static invocation, it needs to be changed if, say, the method required an additional parameter. Therefore, it is less flexible. | Any such change (mentioned on the left) may be accounted for by dynamic handling; it is therefore more flexible. |
| Suitability | Ideal for end-user applications where methods don't undergo a great degree of change. | Ideal for development tools, code generation, and inter-ORB utilities that must discover services and their attributes at runtime. |
| Ease of Programming | The remote method is invoked simply by invoking it by its name and passing it the parameters, using the static client IDL stubs. It is very easy to use. | Information about the remote method and its method signatures is obtained at runtime, the required parameters are assembled at runtime, and then a dynamic call to the remote method is made. It requires considerably more programming work, is harder to use, and not all programs need this level of complexity. |
| Type-Checking | Type-checking is enforced by the compiler at compile-time and is therefore robust. | Information about method signature(s) and arranging parameters to match them is done at runtime. If all possibilities are not catered to, it can result in type problems and lack of robustness. |
| Performance | A single call is made to the IDL stub, which takes it to the object implementation via the ORB and the server stub. Thus, it provides the maximum performance possible. | Multiple APIs must first be invoked to determine method signatures before the remote method may be invoked. Not ideal for performance-intensive applications. |

| Criterion | Static Invocation | Dynamic Invocation |
|---|---|---|
| Documentation | Because the code clearly shows the call being made, it is self-documenting. | The actual call to the remote procedure is not directly coded, but is intermingled with other calls. Thus, it requires specific documentation effort. |

# CORBA 2.0 Initialization

This section discusses how a client discovers an object implementation after the client is invoked or executed:

1. Obtain an object reference for your ORB, using CORBA API `ORB_Init`. This returns a reference to an ORB pseudo-object.

2. Obtain a pointer to your Object Adaptor, using method `BOA_init` on the ORB pseudo-object.

3. Discover what services are available using method `list_initial_services` on the ORB pseudo-object.

4. Decide what service you want and obtain information about them dynamically using `describe_interface` to the Interface Repository.

5. Obtain Object References for the service(s) you want, using the method `resolve_initial_references`.

An object can initialize itself in more than one ORB.

# Interoperability of ORBs

CORBA 1.1 guaranteed only portability of object implementations. It was only in CORBA 2.0 that interoperability of various ORBs was specified. It was achieved through specifying a set of common message formats and common data representations (like the XDR of Sun RPC). This specification is known as *Generic Inter-ORB Protocol (GIOP)*. CORBA 2.0 also specifies how GIOP messages are exchanged over a TCP/IP network. GIOP implementation over TCP/IP is nothing but the famous Internet Inter-ORB Protocol (IIOP).

Discover how the interoperability is achieved between various object request brokers.

## Runtime Passing of Object References

An *Object Reference* provides the information you need to uniquely specify an object within a distributed ORB system—it is a unique name or identifier.

The implementation of object references is not defined by the CORBA specification, and is therefore implementation-specific. Two CORBA-compliant ORBs may have different representations for object references.

CORBA 2.0 now defines Interoperable Object References (IOR) that vendors must use to pass object references across heterogeneous ORBs. The key to the program portability is the language-bindings, which insulate the programs from the actual representation of the object references. All ORBs must provide the same language-bindings for a particular programming language.

The client-programs obtain object references from directories, initialization services, invocations of other objects, and name services. ORB APIs, with object reference as one of the parameters, are used to obtain more information about the objects, their methods, and method signatures.

Refer to Figure 16.7, which shows how client object references are mapped to the ORB's internal object references (which can be vendor-specific) using the language bindings. In order to pass these object references to other ORBs, the ORB converts them to CORBA interoperable object references—which are converted by the receiving or server ORB to its own internal representation, and so on.

## General Inter-ORB Protocol

General Inter-ORB Protocol (GIOP) specifies a set of message formats and common data representations (CDR) for communication between ORBs. These are designed to work over any connection-oriented protocol, without any format negotiations.

Common Data Representation (CDR) maps data types defined in the OMG IDL into a flat message representation, taking into account platform specific byte-ordering and memory alignments.

Thus, IDL-level data types are first mapped to a CDR, which in turn is transmitted between ORBs as required. Transmission between various ORBs can be carried out using various transports. The approach for utilizing various communication transports is illustrated in Figure 16.9.

**FIG. 16.9**
CORBA Inter-ORB Architecture specifies general and environment-specific transports for interoperability.

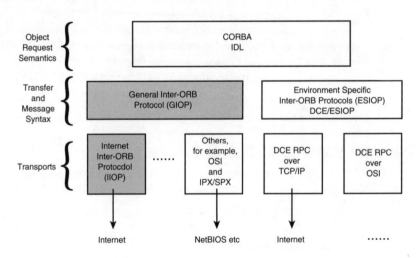

## Internet Inter-ORB Protocol

Internet Inter-ORB Protocol (IIOP) specifies how GIOP messages are exchanged over the Internet. IIOP is a compulsory component for an ORB to be CORBA 2.0-compliant. GIOP may also be transmitted over NetBIOS and other transports, but such an implementation is not considered to be CORBA 2.0-compliant, according to the OMA standard.

## Environment-Specific Inter-ORB Protocol

Part III

Ch 16

Environment-specific Inter-ORB Protocols (ESIOP) allow direct interfacing to specific existing networks, which need not be TCP/IP-based. DCE/ESIOP is one of the first ESIOPs specified for interfacing to existing DCE domains. Figure 16.9 also illustrates how IDL-level object references are mapped to DCE transports.

## ORB-to-ORB Bridging

CORBA 2.0 also provides the mechanism needed for creating generic ORB-to-ORB *stubless* bridges. In this mechanism, the Dynamic Skeleton Interface (DSI) is used to receive all outgoing messages and the Dynamic Invocation Interface (DII) is used to invoke the request on a destination ORB object. This mechanism also can be used for creating gateways to non-CORBA object brokers such as Microsoft OLE/COM. Figure 16.10 shows the logical client/server request operation using ORB-to-ORB bridging.

**FIG. 16.10**
Dynamic Skeleton
Interface and Dynamic
Invocation Interface are
combined to achieve
ORB-to-ORB bridging.

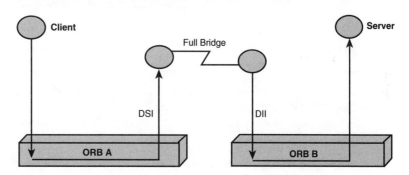

## Federated ORBs

Inter-ORB bridges and IIOP can be used to create very flexible topologies via a federation of ORBs. Figure 16.11 shows an example of an IIOP backbone with various proprietary ORBs and the DCE/ESIOP feeding into it via half-bridges. A half-bridge converts IIOP protocol into a non-IIOP protocol.

Various segments of this federated topology may be segregated on the basis of administrative needs, vendor ORB implementations, network protocols, traffic loads, types of service, and security concerns.

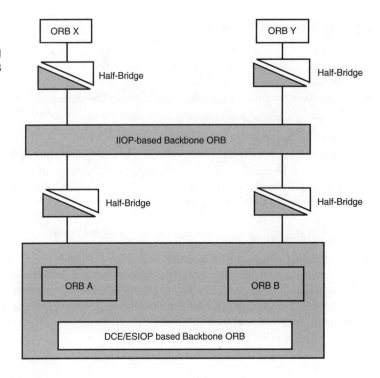

**FIG. 16.11**
IIOP, combined with DCE/ESIOP, can be used to create Federated ORB environments.

# From Here...

The following list outlines the key benefits of OMA and CORBA. They apply as equally to Java-based applications development as they do to distributed computing in general. In the next chapter, "WWW Applications Development Using CORBA," you will see how these benefits combine with the Java language's own benefits to produce a formidable force!

CORBA is the core component of OMA which provides the necessary interoperability to build distributed applications. CORBA may be used on its own without using other features of OMA.

OMA and CORBA allow servers from *heterogeneous* operating systems and languages to interoperate, making it easier to implement real-life distributed applications.

OMA and CORBA provide an Object Model, which provides *an abstract framework for developing distributed applications*. Traditional distributed applications are tied closely to underlying network protocols and mechanisms. This assists in building flexible distributed systems.

OMA and CORBA are only a specification and allow the *existing technology to be integrated*, while delivering the benefits of an abstract view of the distributed system.

CORBA and its applications are best designed using object-oriented techniques, thus *delivering all usual benefits of object-orientation*.

In this chapter, you have gained an understanding of Object Management Architecture, its core component—CORBA, and other services and facilities. You also looked at how CORBA applications using static and dynamic invocation are built. A brief overview of how federated distributed systems may be built using IIOP was also presented.

- Chapter 17, "WWW Applications Development Using CORBA," shows you how to apply CORBA in an Internet/intranet environment.
- Chapter 18, "Incorporating Java, JDBC, and CORBA: A Sample Application," presents an actual application that you can build to gain some hands-on knowledge.
- Chapter 19, "Scaling Up Web-Object Applications," provides an overview of all issues you need to consider to build Enterprise-level, large Web-Object applications. This may also be a good time to visit the Visigenic, Iona, or JavaSoft Web sites and download an evaluation copy of a CORBA product.

# CHAPTER 17

# WWW Applications Development Using CORBA

The Internet continues to capture more and more users as we go through the nineties and head for the next century. If the promise of Java and distributed object computing becomes mainstream, it will succeed in evolving the Internet to a platform. Java is an architecture-independent, object-oriented language, which supports dynamic downloading of application components in a distributed system. Java application executables (if we can call Java bytecode executables) can be distributed on demand, anywhere in a network. Because of their platform independence, they can be executed anywhere as well.

Java executables need a unified view of and access to the distributed environment. A distributed environment, in general, can consist of a variety of platforms. CORBA provides the unifying view of the distributed world. As an example of its services, it helps build a unified namespace (through the Naming Service) and eventspace (through the Event Service) in the distributed world. CORBA services are the key to making the distributed system look and feel nearly like a single operating system. Many mature products, offering full implementation of the core CORBA interoperability, are already available. Though still in early stages, sufficient CORBA services products are

## Introduction

Java and CORBA are strong on client and server ends, respectively. Together they bring multi-tier client/server applications to the Web.

## Bringing distributed objects to the World Wide Web

Understand how distributed objects offer a new level of functionality for WWW application development tools. Also understand how CORBA is an ideal choice to integrate heterogeneous servers in the Enterprise.

## CORBA application architecture for the Web

Get an overview of how CORBA architecture is applied to the WWW applications.

## WWW security for CORBA applications

Understand how Internet Inter-ORB Protocol (IIOP) fits with the current design of the HTTP protocol and Internet security implementations such as firewalls.

## CORBA products for Java applications development

Look at Visigenic's Visibroker and IONA Technologies' OrbixWeb, two of the leading tools for developing CORBA-based Web applications.

already becoming available on the market. Basic services—Naming, Event, and Lifecycle—are supported by all major CORBA products. With the arrival of the next tier of CORBA services—in the area of database processing (Persistence, Transaction, and Query services) and distributed search facilities (Trader and Property services); a unified view of the distributed system is fast becoming a reality. Because CORBA is supported by all major legacy operating system vendors, database, and system integration vendors, a very broad range of applications and tools, spread on all kinds platforms and running in organizations of all hues, will become server-level citizens of the distributed world.

Thus, Java language and its platform will provide the universal client, and Object Management Architecture (OMA) and CORBA will provide the universal server.

Before considering an actual Java-CORBA application in the next chapter, look at the limitations of the current application architecture for the Web. Then look at what is special about a Java ORB (Object Request Broker) application as compared to a non-Java ORB application. A survey of Java-enabled ORB products in the market at the time of writing follows. Take a closer look at Visigenic's Visibroker, IONA Technologies' OrbixWeb, and Sun's Java-IDL products to prepare for writing a Java-CORBA-JDBC application in the next chapter. You shall develop the example application in Chapter 18, "Incorporating Java, JDBC, and CORBA: A Sample Application," using Visigenic's Visibroker for Java. At the end of this chapter, multiple ways of implementing IIOP servers behind firewalls are discussed. You will look at two of the current options and the need for standardization. ■

# Distributed Objects for the Web

The World Wide Web started out being the universal document-browsing client. Java has made it possible for each desktop on the Internet to be the universal application client. The universal client is able to participate in a client/server interaction with any server located on the network. The network you're interested in may be an intranet or the broad Internet itself. This presents a wealth of possibilities and opportunities, provided the reliability, scalability, availability, and recoverability usually found in legacy applications can be brought to the Internet/intranet applications.

You will look at the issues of reliability, scalability, availability, and recoverability in Chapter 19, "Scaling Up Web-Object Applications." Here you look at how Java and CORBA provide the universal client/server architecture. First, a brief overview of existing architectures is provided. Second, these architectures are evaluated on the basis of defined criteria. A look at these criteria helps you appreciate why choosing between a plethora of currently available alternatives can be a confusing task.

## Client/Server Architecture Evaluation Criteria

There are a number of ways in which the core components of a client/server architecture may be implemented. You first look at the core issues of a client/server architecture, which provide a basis for evaluating various architectures.

This is by no means a complete list. Some of the advanced services, yellow pages service (known as Trader service) and Distributed Transaction Service for example, cannot fairly be included as criteria when comparing with traditional sockets-based applications, as transaction processing is implemented by using separate stand-alone products.

**Server Discovery**  Clients discover servers using one of two techniques:

- binding to a specific, predefined port on a known network node
- using name or directory services that publish the presence of servers

Most distributed architectures in practice use the former method. Standards for name and directory services are in place, but these have largely been used to implement distributed white pages applications for e-mail and file transfer. Applying these techniques to client/server interaction in a distributed environment is yet to be adopted at a large scale.

**Server Activation**  It is common to have server processes (also called daemons) waiting for a client request to arrive. In a client/server environment with a large number of clients and transactions, thousands of objects or more may be active at any given time. To properly manage the load in such circumstances, it is desirable to have some servers activated only on demand, whereas the key servers remain active, though in a *wait state* (the process is kept alive, but the operating system sets its state such that the process consumes minimum or no memory from the CPU and other machine resources) when idle. Activating the highly used servers on demand will incur the increased processing and time cost in creation of server processes. Thus, possible activation policies are:

- manual activation for permanent or persistent servers to cater to frequent requests
- on-demand activation for transient servers to service low frequency requests

**Serving Policy**  Serving policy determines how client requests are distributed across server processes and  threads. Threads are also used as servers, with the added benefit that starting and stopping threads consumes less machine resources. The simplest policy is one server process per client request, resulting in a new server process to be started for every request. In a more scalable architecture, a pool of "worker" threads actually work on a client request each. These workers may be identical, each a different one for various request types, or multiple workers available for each request type. Generally, there is only a fixed number of workers available on the server. Given that even the largest machines have limits, there will always be an upper limit on the number of workers available. If more client requests than the number of workers are received, they are either declined or asked to wait. Thus, possible options are:

- **One client per server process**—A new server process is started for every client.
- **One client per server thread**—The server carries out the role of a dispatcher and multiple worker threads are initiated or used as required.

■ **Fixed number of processes**—Only a certain number of requests can be processed at a time. Other requests are declined or asked to wait.

**Client Code Distribution**    The distribution mechanism for client-code can be:

■ **Manual**—Cases in which the client application is manually installed on all potential client machines. All legacy Internet applications such as FTP and Telnet clients are such examples.

■ **Automatic or on-demand**—This has been made possible by Java. Security design for Java has been discussed widely in the press and technical journals.

**Data Representation Externalization**    Clients and servers can exist in heterogeneous operating and programming environments. Transferring data amongst them may require marshaling and unmarshaling (conversion to and from a common data format) at the least. If an object-oriented runtime environment is used at one or both ends, conversions of data models may also be required; for example, flattening of object states on the client end before transmission and reversing the process at the server end. Data externalization is time- and resource-consuming and does not add any functionality to the infrastructure. Thus, possible values of this architecture attribute are:

■ Externalization required

■ Externalization not required

**State Representation**    A client/server interaction can go through various steps. To establish a reliable mechanism, it should be possible for a client and server to continue the interaction, even after a temporary loss of connection. This requires maintaining data about the state of the interaction. With many of the architectures supporting only stateless servers, maintaining data about the state of the interaction becomes the responsibility of the client environment. A good client/server architecture, to be scalable, should provide an elegant architecture for maintaining and recovering the state of an interaction.

**Latency**    Most client/server communication protocols, at transport or application levels of functionality as defined in OSI and TCP/IP architectures, are built upon other layers of the communication infrastructure. Some pass through more layers or incur multiple interactions as compared to others. This results in increased turnaround time to the client for satisfying a given request. You see examples of differing latencies in a comparison of various architectures in Table 17.1.

**Distributed Transactions**    A client may update the state of multiple server objects. If one of these updates cannot be committed, it should be possible to back out of the whole transaction. Some architectures make it extremely hard or impossible to implement a reliable transaction processing environment, whereas others are more adaptable to transaction processing.

# A Summary of Existing Architectures

After having outlined a set of criteria to evaluate various client/server architectures, take a look at various options available. A comparison of these features is summarized at the end of this section.

**Sockets-Based Architecture Without Java**   In this architecture, each potential client has a copy of the client code, which, when executed, establishes a connection with the server, using BSD sockets, at a specific network node and port. Server activation may be automated and managed through a monitoring process, which must be active all the time. Most Internet desktop clients, such as FTP and Telnet, are examples of this type of application. Client code distribution is manual. Latency is very much in control of the actual application, depending on the application protocol chosen.

**HyperText Transport Protocol with Common Gateway Interface**   HyperText Transport Protocol (HTTP) provides a user-friendly interface for browsing linked documents over the Internet or intranet. This interface has been made interactive by use of client-side forms and server interface to a gateway that converts character data to graphics and HTTP data. Most server logic is implemented such that it produces character or graphic output which is shipped and displayed on the client using HTTP. Server-side includes (SSI) is a form of generic HTML format, which is customized with data produced from a Common Gateway Interface (CGI) program to produce the final HTML required to be sent back to the client.

A CGI server is generally activated on demand, one server process per client request and the server is stateless, thus requiring context data to be part of the client request.

Before the keep-alive connection enhancement of HTTP in Version 1.1, HTTP was a protocol with high latency. Without a keep-alive option, browsing a document with an image (uncached) requires three round trips to the server. As shown in Figure 17.1, one trip each is required to open a TCP/IP connection, retrieve the document, and to retrieve the image.

Maintaining state of the interaction is the full responsibility of the client. There is no natural way in HTTP to maintain state, as it is a stateless protocol. The common workarounds to store state information is by passing state variables as CGI parameters or by hidden tags, which are transmitted back to the server.

Being a stateless and largely file transfer protocol, HTTP is incapable of implementing distributed transactions.

**Java-Based Sockets Architecture**   In this option, the client-side application consists of Java applets referenced in HTML (HyperText Markup Language) code. These applets are downloaded from the server on demand. Java client applets can establish connections with server processes using BSD sockets, as in the case of non-Java client applications. The server processes themselves may be Java-based or conventional servers offering listening or server sockets.

Part
III

Ch

17

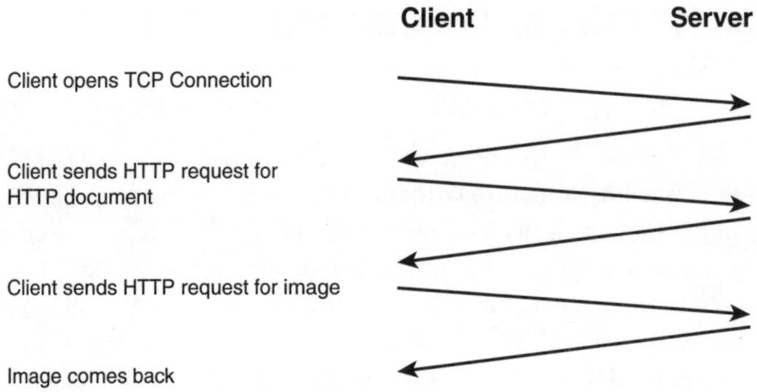

**FIG. 17.1**

Retrieving an HTML document with one uncached image requires three round trips to the HTTP server.

Client opens TCP Connection

Client sends HTTP request for HTTP document

Client sends HTTP request for image

Image comes back

The client code is distributed on demand. Server discovery is still manual or hard-coded. The full range of server activation options can be implemented, as can various serving policies. Latency with Java applications has been continuously improving. This has been achieved using the latest just-in-time compilers (JITCs) built into the Web browsers. A JITC compiles the Java bytecode to platform-specific (Windows, Solaris, and so on) binary code just before execution. In the first implementation of the Java runtime environment, the latency arose due to Java VM being an interpreter. With JITCs, the small delay of compiling the bytecode is still there, though negligible.

**Java Remote Method Invocation Architecture (RMI)**    This is relatively new architecture applicable to Java-only environments. A Java client can directly invoke methods on remote Java objects. Java objects may be moved around the network, without externalization. This is achieved by transmitting a flattened state of objects and its structure graph. Java RMI has already been covered in detail in Part II.

Java RMI overcomes the overhead of coping with heterogeneous operating and platform environments. Server discovery is based on a name service, which is a significant improvement on the hard-coded server discovery. A trader service has also been recently announced by Sun for use with Java RMI. All other benefits of Java Sockets-based architecture are still applicable.

**Java- and CORBA-Based Architecture**    CORBA is a mature architecture for developing object-oriented distributed applications. By using Java with CORBA, dynamic or on-demand downloading of the platform-independent code is combined with the scalability and versatility of CORBA architecture. Java applet or application clients are able to access and manipulate the whole distributed environment made accessible through CORBA services and applications.

# Comparison of Various Architectures

Table 17.1 summarizes the features of various client/server architectures possible for developing WWW applications.

**Table 17.1   Comparison of WWW Client/Server Architectures**

| | Server | Server Discovery | Serving Activation | Client-Policy | Data Code Distribution | Latency Marshaling or Externalization |
|---|---|---|---|---|---|---|
| Socket-based architecture without Java | Manual | Manual Automated | Flexible | Manual | Depends on middleware | Low |
| HTTP with CGI | Manual (Hard-bound) | Automated | One server process per client request | Part of HTML | Uses HTTP | High |
| Java with Sockets | Manual | Manual | Flexible | On-demand | Not required (untyped data) | Medium to Low |
| Java RMI | Using Name Service | Flexible | Flexible | On-demand | Not required even with typed data | Medium to Low |
| Java and CORBA | Automated using factory finders, Naming, and trader services | Automated using various server activation policies | Flexible (all are supported) | On-demand | Required as of now. Externalization in progress | Medium to Low |

As is evident from the comparison in Table 17.1, the Java-CORBA combination offers the most versatile set of features, but it can suffer from poor performance due to object externalization overhead. Java RMI can be a good second choice in purely Java environments. Java provides the universal client, whereas CORBA provides the universal server.

# Architecture of Java Applications Using CORBA

In Chapter 1, you looked at an overview of the Java Enterprise, consisting of JDBC, CORBA-based Java-IDL, and Java RMI. In Chapter 12, "Introduction to Distributed Computing," CORBA was introduced and discussed; Chapter 16 covered "CORBA and Object Management Architecture (OMA)." Now you look at how a CORBA client/server application is implemented in an Internet/intranet environment.

A subset of the Java Enterprise architecture, showing the use of Java and CORBA, is shown in Figure 17.2. Recall the discussion of the CORBA application development process in Chapter 16, "CORBA and Object Management Architecture (OMA)." Interface Definition Language is used to specify the client/server interface. Compiling the IDL file produces *client stubs* and *server stubs* (*skeletons* in CORBA terminology). The role of the stub and skeletons is depicted in the overall runtime architecture; shown in Figure 17.2.

**FIG. 17.2**

Java-CORBA client/
server architecture.

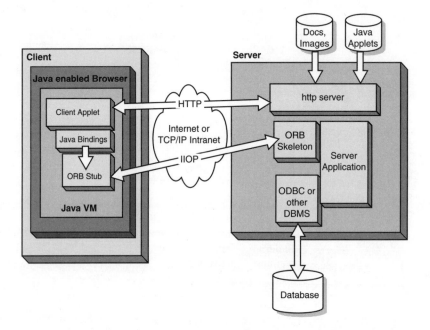

The client in Figure 17.2 is using a Java-enabled browser. The HTTP server on the server node stores HTML documents (with all the embedded images and so on) and all Java applets including the client applet for the Java-CORBA application. When the browser points to the page containing the application applet, the applet is downloaded into the browser. The client applet is built using the client-side stub generated from the IDL compiler. There is no runtime driver or process required on the client machine. The required client-side CORBA functionality is built into the client-side stubs, which do use some ORB libraries. All ORB libraries are written in Java as well and reside as class files on the codebase path on the server. These are automatically downloaded into the browser when an applet tries to use them. Netscape Navigator 4.0

will have Visibroker for Java ORB libraries bundled with it, thus eliminating the need to download them from servers.

---

### Built-In IIOP Support in Netscape Communicator 4.0

Class files for the client-side CORBA functionality, referred to previously, will be included in Netscape Navigator 4.0 as part of the Netscape Communicator. This means greatly reduced start-up times for a CORBA client. Currently, CORBA clients cannot start functioning until all these class files (quite a few) are downloaded from the server. With support of ZIPped libraries of class files in JDK 1.1, the download time would be better even for browsers without bundled IIOP class libraries.

Netscape is bundling IIOP client-side class libraries from Visigenic's Visibroker for Java products. Visibroker for Java is discussed in detail later in this chapter and also used in the development of the example application in Chapter 18, "Incorporating Java, JDBC, and CORBA: A Sample Application."

---

**Part**

**III**

**Ch**

**17**

The latest CORBA products support Java on client as well as server and are completely (or almost completely) written in Java.

In Figure 17.2, a server application and HTTP server are shown to be running on the same server machine. In real life, this need not be the case. In fact, technically it is entirely feasible for the HTTP and server applications to be located anywhere on the Internet/intranet.

The server application is written by extending the skeleton generated from the IDL compilation. The server can be activated in a number of ways. In the simplest form, it is manually started and remains active indefinitely until it is either manually terminated, or it issues a `deactivate_implementation` CORBA call.

---

 **TIP**   It is a good idea to have a copy of the CORBA 2.0 specification, which can be downloaded directly from the OMG's Web site. The exact document name and OMG's URL appears in Appendix C, "CORBA Resources."

The CORBA 2.0 specification outlines the complete API supported by any compliant CORBA product.

However, if you are inclined to know the minimal API needed to get you up and going, just carry on with the rest of this and the next chapter. The *Programming Guide and Reference Manual* for the Java ORB Product being used by you should come in handy as well.

---

CORBA also specifies various activation policies. Based on the activation policy chosen for the selected server application, or *implementation*, as CORBA calls it, one process or one thread per client request may be initiated.

Not all CORBA products implement automatic activation, as it is not part of the core-level CORBA standard compliance. However, as more CORBA products become available, you, the consumer, will win as functionality of CORBA products becomes richer and wider in features.

# Special Considerations for ORBs in an Internet/Intranet Environment

Developing CORBA IIOP applications in Java is no different from developing CORBA IIOP applications in any other language supported by the CORBA standard. However, the Internet, as well as Java, presents a few hurdles that CORBA applications must overcome. Look at two of the main problems: getting the IIOP protocol through firewalls and Java applets opening a TCP/IP port other than the HTTP host.

## TCP/IP Port Access from Java Applets

Java applets, according to the standard, should not open TCP/IP ports other than the HTTP codebase port. This is to ensure good behavior on the part of the applets that have been allowed inside a firewall through the HTTP server. If it were possible to do so, such an applet could access various TCP/IP ports inside the firewall (the sendmail port, for example) and also pass some of the information to some outside source.

This requirement, though a standard, is not enforced strictly by all browsers. Hot Java comes with the default behavior set according to the standard, but it is possible to configure it to allow applet connections to any port. Internet Explorer also allows you to bypass the restriction. Only Netscape Navigator enforces this restriction, without the option of changing it. Given Navigator's popularity, any client/server application, to work over the Internet, will need to work with this restriction. This poses an interesting problem for implementing IIOP clients that need to talk to a CORBA server listening on a TCP/IP port other than the HTTP port.

Visibroker has solved this issue by providing a combined HTTP and IIOP server stack that can serve both HTML documents and IIOP protocol connections. Visigenic's solution also addresses the firewall problem, as discussed in the following section.

## Firewalls and IIOP

Firewalls are a common part of the security implementation in an Internet environment. They work like a sentry at the door, allowing only the permitted visitors into a network (or a machine) hosting various Internet servers. A CORBA-based application server is a new kind of server being put behind the firewall. It is important to understand how IIOP works with firewalls.

**The Problem**   Firewalls filter all traffic to and from a given server node on the Internet. These are generally implemented using a dedicated machine, many times called the *bastion host*, running firewall and proxy services for various services offered by the host. Each of these proxies can allow and disallow certain clients or content. Figure 17.3 depicts an example of a firewall through which HTTP and FTP traffic is allowed. Telnet and any unknown protocols are denied access.

**FIG. 17.3**
Present firewalls will block IIOP from getting through.

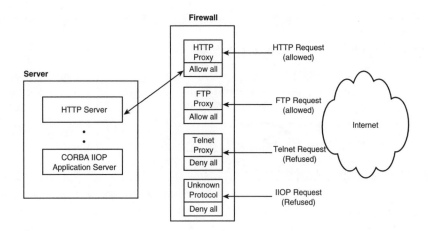

As a result, IIOP traffic in this case will not be allowed to get through, since IIOP protocol is currently unknown to the firewalls.

This problem has been resolved by CORBA IIOP vendors in their own different ways. A standard solution is hoped to emerge soon, when the options available in the industry are presented to OMG for standardization and a chosen approach agreed upon. Visigenic's Visibroker was one of the earliest ORBs for Java applications (first announced in December, 1995). Ireland's IONA Technologies offers the Orbix product, which is already the market leader in the non-Java ORB market. Their complete Java offering (including both client- and server-side Java support), OrbixWeb, was released in November, 1996. Now look at the approaches adopted by Visibroker and OrbixWeb for getting IIOP through the firewalls.

**Visibroker for Java Solution**   Visibroker for Java implements IIOP by disguising it as HTTP. IIOP packets are formatted according to HTTP protocol. The client runtime classes do the necessary conversion.

Figure 17.4 illustrates the handling of IIOP and HTTP on the server side. Both HTTP and IIOP requests are passed through the HTTP proxy, since IIOP requests appear as HTTP requests. Visigenic has a thin protocol demultiplexer called "GateKeeper." GateKeeper is capable of working as an HTTP daemon. While doing so, it can filter the IIOP requests from HTTP requests and direct them to appropriate object implementations (servers), through the OSAgent (not shown in the diagram), which is Visigenic's Name Service for locating object implementations.

Part
**III**

Ch
**17**

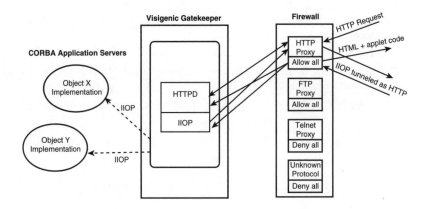

**FIG. 17.4**
Visibroker uses HTTP tunneling to get IIOP past the firewall.

**OrbixWeb Solution**   The OrbixWeb solution is based on the approach of extending the firewall mechanism to include IIOP proxies. It is based on the belief that the additional site administration effort required is worth the security benefits achievable. Its success depends on achieving an industry consensus (through OMG). This is a very recent development. The actual IIOP firewall product, known as Wonderwall, is currently available in beta and can be downloaded from **http://www-usa.iona.com/Orbix/Wonderwall/index.html**.

Figure 17.5 illustrates IONA's approach to implementing IIOP proxies.

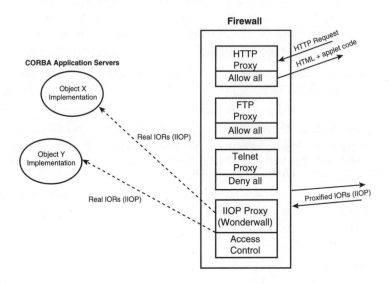

**FIG. 17.5**
OrbixWeb adds IIOP Proxies to firewall to get IIOP through and to provide a security architecture for IIOP.

As discussed in Chapter 16, "CORBA and Object Management Architecture (OMA)," Interoperable Object References (IOR) constitute the standard format for passing object reference on the wire. The real IORs for the objects behind the firewall are copied into the configuration data for the proxy and a "proxified" version is created by replacing the server's host and port in the IOR with the proxy's host and port. The client invokes methods on this proxified version of the IOR. When the proxy receives the request, it checks security definitions, which are defined through an access control list (ACL), to determine if the request should be passed on to the server. If the request should be passed on, IIOP proxy obtains the actual IOR, based on the object key in the request, and passes the request to actual implementation.

Wonderwall's approach is definitely more elegant than HTTP tunneling, with less performance overhead. Being a very recent development, there is considerable debate currently in the press regarding which of the two is the better approach. You should hope to see either a standard emerging, or both tunneling and IIOP proxies being used.

Part
III

Ch
17

# Choosing a Suitable Language for the Server Application

Starting with C and C++, CORBA specifies standard language mappings from IDL to Ada and Smalltalk as well. Language mappings for a large number of other languages are at various stages of standardization. CORBA IDL mappings for many languages have already been implemented by their vendors, even though a standardization effort on these may not have yet been completed or even started. CORBA Products for language mappings to Java, Eiffel, and Visual Basic are around. Object COBOL mapping is in progress.

Consider the issues in choosing a suitable language for the server side. Assume that the client-side will consist of Java applications or applets accessing a CORBA server.

## A Completely Java-Based Application

Increasingly wide acceptance of Java, combined with the availability of industrial-strength development tools, is making Java a good candidate for developing server applications. Nearly all major database vendors have already provided, or are in the process of providing, a way of embedding SQL or similar data manipulation statements in Java programs. At the time of this writing, development tools such as Asymetrix's SuperCede allow direct binary compilation of Java on Intel platforms.

Wider acceptance of Java for writing heavy duty server applications is still to come. 1997 could be a critical year to see some major Java projects take shape. Developing new projects using a single language offers substantial developer training and software maintenance savings. When making a decision to base a project fully on Java (for both client- and server-side), it may still be good to use CORBA for client/server communication. This will provide maximum flexibility; it will allow you to replace one CORBA-compliant server with another CORBA server supporting the same IDL interfaces. With standardization of business objects, also in progress at OMG, this will be quite easy. It will be possible to switch servers without any changes to the client code.

## Integrating Legacy Applications

Java API specifies JavaBeans as a mechanism for integrating to legacy applications. In its most current usage, Java is implementing business functionality (as opposed to jumping only text and animated applets). To build application functionality, the initial approach is to leverage the existing investment in the legacy systems. This will provide the organizations with excellent return on their existing information assets. Use of CORBA in integrating Java to legacy servers provides an excellent solution. If the legacy application to be integrated is object-oriented, its distributed interfaces are exposed using IDL. On the other hand, if the legacy application is procedural, first an object-oriented wrapper code is developed before making the application interfaces accessible through IDL.

In an environment of many platforms and languages, CORBA provides the necessary glue to make legacy applications accessible on the Internet using Java applets. In such an environment, the decision to write the server application in one language or another should be purely driven by the needs of the server application.

## Status of the OMG Mapping of IDL to Java

The current version of CORBA 2.0 specification does not include an IDL-to-Java mapping. A number of IDL-to-Java mappings are available in various products. Due to Java inheriting a large number of its features from C, C++, and Smalltalk (which already have standard CORBA mappings), the mappings from various vendors are very similar, though not identical, to one another.

OMG has put out a Request for Proposal (RFP) for Java mapping. A large number of vendors have already made submissions, often working together to submit a joint proposal. An official IDL-to-Java mapping should be forthcoming from OMG, hopefully by mid-1997.

# Object Request Brokers for Java

Many CORBA products were around even before Java came along. These CORBA products have been enhanced to support Java clients, and sometimes Java servers as well. The core implementation of these products has continued unchanged. On the other hand, new CORBA products, such as Visibroker for Java, have been entirely written in Java and are designed to work in the Internet and Java environment from the ground up.

## Survey of Java ORB Products

Table 17.2 presents a summary of CORBA products with Java support. Some of these may change between the time of this writing and publication, as new releases are announced by vendors.

**Table 17.2   CORBA Products with Java Support**

| Vendor | Product | Client/Server/Both | Native IIOP? |
|--------|---------|-------------------|--------------|
| Visigenic | Visibroker for Java | Both | Yes |
| Sun | Joe (NEO) | Client only | In Beta |
| IONA | OrbixWeb | Both | Yes |
| APM | Jade | Both | Yes |

A number of other products are available which, though providing Java mapping, are subsets of the CORBA implementation or are restricted in some other way. Please refer to the LANL Web page, **http://www.acl.lanl.gov/CORBA/**, to find out more about these products. For a complete listing of all resources for CORBA or similar products, please refer to Appendix C, "CORBA Resources."

Part

**III**

Ch

**17**

Now take a closer look at some of the CORBA products you may want to consider for your first WWW client/server application using Java. You are also provided with information to get your environment ready for developing the sample application in Chapter 18, "Incorporating Java, JDBC, and CORBA: A Sample Application."

# Visibroker for Java

Visibroker for Java is one of the earliest, if not the earliest, Java CORBA products. It was announced in December, 1995. Visigenic Corporation, the current vendor, acquired Post-Modern Computing, the original developer of CORBA products ORBeLine for C++ and Black Widow for Java, during 1996. ORBeLine and Black Widow have since been renamed to Visibroker for C++ and Visibroker for Java, respectively.

With the first release of Black Widow appearing in April of 1996, the current version (1.2) was released in November of 1996. Nearly at the time of Visigenic's purchase of Post-Modern Computing, Netscape announced that would be bundling IIOP support in its browser using Black Widow or Visibroker products. This will be available in Navigator version 4.0, which is included in the Netscape Communicator. The expected general availability of Netscape Communicator is sometime in the first half of 1997.

**About Visigenic Corporation**   Visigenic was founded in February, 1993, by Roger Sippl, founder of Informix Software, which is based in San Mateo, California. Visigenic started out providing database connectivity tools. The company obtained exclusive agreement with Microsoft to license ODBC on all non-Windows platforms. Its products include ODBC drivers for more than half a dozen enterprise databases, available on about a dozen platforms. It also provides JDBC connectivity, ODBC Software Development Kits, and ODBC Test Suites. With the acquisition of CORBA products from Post-Modern Computing, its presence in the middleware market has expanded.

**Product Data Sheet**   Visibroker for Java is available on Sun OS 4.1.x, Solaris 2.x, Digital UNIX 3.2, AIX 4.1, HP UX 10.01, Windows 95, and Windows NT 3.51 and 4.0.

Hard disk space required is about 15M.

The Java Development Kit (JDK), 1.01 or later, is required.

Visibroker for Java can be obtained from any of Visigenic's resellers or purchased online from Visigenic's Web site: **http://www.visigenic.com**. A demo version can also be downloaded from the Visigenic Online Store.  Following are the key features of Visibroker for Java:

**ORB Smart Agent**   Visibroker's key daemon is its ORB Smart Agent, known as OSAgent. Multiple instances of OSAgent may run on a network, dynamically partitioning the object namespace. In an environment where server objects are replicated, a crash of any object implementation automatically routes the requests to the other server object replicas, eliminating any interruption to service. OSAgent also dynamically performs load balancing for replicated servers.

**Native IIOP**   The only transport protocol supported by Visibroker is IIOP, thus making the product lighter in footprint and easy for beginners to understand and to work with. Many other CORBA products have proprietary transports, inherited from versions implemented before adoption of the CORBA 2.0 standard.

**IDL-to-Java Code Generator**   IDL-to-Java Code Generator creates Java stubs and skeletons, as well as the code needed to do data marshalling and unmarshalling (data conversion in heterogeneous environments). From release 1.2, example code for a client and server is also generated.

**Multithreading**   Multiple object requests can be handled by a single process, thus providing efficient use of operating system resources.

**Automatic Configuration**   Visibroker does not require tedious configuration files. Multiple OSAgents send periodic broadcast messages within the subnetwork to synchronize amongst one another and automatically reconfigure, if required.

**Smart Binding**   Direct function calls, shared memory, or remote CORBA methods are chosen for communicating between client and server. This depends, respectively, on whether the server object is in the same process as the client, in a different process but on the same node, or residing on a remote node.

**Installation**   These installation instructions are for downloading and installing from the Visigenic Web site. A shrinkwrap version includes detailed installation instructions. Complete installation instructions can also be found at **http://www.visigenic.com/techpubs/vbjava.htm**.

The main steps of the installation process are:

1.  Go to the Visigenic Web site (**http://www.visigenic.com**).
2.  Go to the Visigenic Store and complete the registration form and order form.

3. Follow the instructions for downloading.

4. Uncompress the downloaded file and run SETUP.EXE.

5. For demo versions, a license file is e-mailed automatically. Install the license file per instructions in the e-mail.

6. Modify PATH environment variable to include bin subdirectory in the installation directory.

7. Set ORBELINE environment variable to the installation directory.

8. Modify CLASSPATH environment variable to include classes subdirectory in the installation directory.

**Using Visibroker**    Excellent debugging and troubleshooting guidelines, along with the latest bugs and workarounds, are listed on the Visigenic's Web site. It is a good idea to print and read all of them before embarking on your first application. This will help you gain an understanding of the issues, the dos and don'ts of the development process. If your project involves integrating with multiple CORBA products and the ORBs do not seem to interoperate correctly, Visigenic also makes available the program IORparser to analyze the IIOP packets as they are sent on the wire. A look at the documentation for IORparser will provide some insight into the IORs and IIOP.

**Future Direction**    Inclusion in Netscape Navigator 4.0 will provide Visibroker a very large installed base, making it a nearly de facto reference CORBA implementation.

An interesting development to look forward to is the release of Object Transaction Service, based on Visigenic's Visibroker, from Hitachi. This transaction processing monitor, named TP Broker, is available for Solaris and the Windows NT version is currently in beta testing.

# OrbixWeb

OrbixWeb is the Java-enabled CORBA product from IONA Technologies, based in Dublin, Ireland. IONA is the maker of the market-leading Orbix. The history of Orbix closely follows the evolution of CORBA. Before Java, which has excellent support for developing Internet applications, and CORBA 2.0 with its interoperability specification, Orbix had implemented interoperability in a scalable fashion, though using its own proprietary protocol. Having evolved through years of industrial use, it provides a rich and full set of features, along with customization filters.

Orbix provides C++, Ada95, and Java language bindings. Orbix is definitely the CORBA product available on the largest number of platforms. It is supported on more than 10 UNIX platforms, Windows 3.1, Windows NT, OS/2, Macintosh OS, Vax VMS, QNX, and embedded real-time systems such as VxWorks. Orbix for MVS is currently in the evaluation phase. Once available, Orbix/Enterprise (product name for Orbix on MVS) will enable access to the platform which holds more than 70 percent of data in the information technology industry.

Part
III

Ch

17

IONA was also one of the early CORBA products to implement COM/CORBA interoperability.

OrbixWeb 1.0 provided only client-side support for Java. Using OrbixWeb 1.0, Java clients could communicate with Orbix servers. OrbixWeb 2.0, released in late November, 1996, provides full Java support for both the client and the server.

**N O T E**   Given that OrbixWeb 2.0 was released after commencement of this book's writing, it has not been possible to complete the example application in the next chapter by using OrbixWeb. We shall make an attempt to do so and make it available on Que's Web site (**www.quecorp.com**). ■

**Product Data Sheet**   Given the wide number of platforms on which Orbix is available, you need to contact IONA to obtain detailed information about requirements and features supported on your target platform. Initially, visit IONA's Web site to obtain more information about Iona's product range (**http://www.iona.com**).

**Product Features and Architecture**   Orbix provides all the functionality required in the OMG CORBA-specification, consisting of:

1. An IDL Compiler, which generates all the necessary code to enable transparent client interactions with potentially remote objects
2. A Dynamic Invocation Interface
3. A Basic Object Adaptor interface, with all the activation policies in the CORBA specification, is supported.
4. Interface Repository query and update interfaces

There are a number of useful extensions to CORBA provided by Orbix:

1. Implementation repository and administration tools are used to locate the executable files for a server when a request arrives for its objects. This is necessary when there is no currently active server. This repository can also be accessed through an IDL interface.
2. Programmer control over surrogates and proxies is provided, so that performance enhancement strategies such as state caching and server-side callbacks can be used. This is in contrast to inheritance, which has a high performance cost.
3. Process- and object-level filtering of incoming and outgoing messages is provided for both clients and servers. This facilitates integration of facilities such as monitoring, debugging, auditing, authentication, authorization, encryption, and groups of objects collectively responding to a request.
4. For servers with large numbers of objects, object caching is implemented.

Orbix's integration with OLE 2.0 Integration means that a CORBA server can be made to appear like an OLE control. Figure 17.6 illustrates how Orbix achieves this.

**FIG. 17.6**
Orbix server as an OLE
server in Orbix.

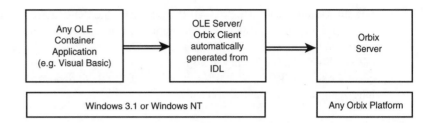

An OLE automation server is automatically generated from the CORBA IDL. This automation server acts as a client to the CORBA server (an Orbix Server in this case), whereas for a Windows-based OLE container application, like any Visual Basic application, it appears as an OLE server.

**Using OrbixWeb**    OrbixWeb extends the feature-rich, sophisticated CORBA implementation provided by Orbix into the Java domain. Given that both IIOP and IONA's proprietary Orbix protocol are supported, along with the full range of activation policies and filters, OrbixWeb can be a somewhat intimidating product for a newcomer to CORBA. Comparatively, Visibroker provides a gentler introduction from the point of view of the Java programmer.

With availability on a wide range of platforms (at least for Orbix), the corporate integrator of information systems cannot ignore Orbix and therefore, OrbixWeb.

**Future Direction**    IONA has teamed with Transarc to announce an integration between Orbix and Transarc's Encina Object Transaction Service (OTS). Once available, Object Transaction Service will enable access to the "virtual mainframe" for all OrbixWeb clients. A public beta is available for Solaris, with the final product expected to be available on Solaris, HP-UX, AIX, and Windows NT.

## Java-IDL

Sun's leadership in networking and distributed solutions needs no introduction. The company which has given NFS and Java to the I.T. industry has been working on a revolutionary operating system known as Spring. Objects, based on OMG IDL, are its core data types.

As discussed in Chapter 12, "Introduction to Distributed Computing," Sun has announced Java-IDL would be a part of the Java Enterprise API from JDK 1.1. The JDK 1.1 has since been released without Java-IDL, as the Java-IDL project seems to be running a bit late. Java-IDL is now expected to be released in the first quarter of 1997. Currently, Java-IDL is at alpha2 release. A brief overview of Java-IDL is provided, as implemented by Sun in its alpha2 release published in late December.

**Java-IDL Architecture**   The Door ORB Transport is the CORBA Product at the heart of Java-IDL alpha2; it was originally used in the Spring operating system. It uses a portable ORB core, which can be adapted to work with multiple ORB protocols. Figure 17.7 shows how the portable ORB core has been adapted from the Spring system into the Java-IDL. Though it does not currently support IIOP, the final release of Java-IDL will. It provides an elegant structure for interfacing to multiple ORBs' protocols.

**FIG. 17.7**

Java-IDL is built on a Portable ORB Core, which can support multiple transports.

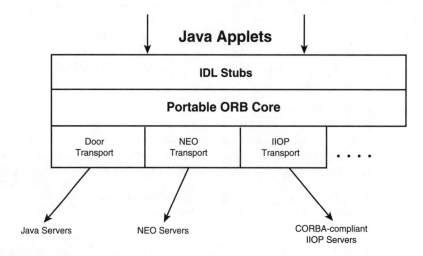

The IDL stub generator `idlgen` produces stubs which carry out the following steps for any method invocation on a remote object:

1. First call into the object reference to get a `Representation` object that is implemented by an ORB-specific transport module.

2. Use that `Representation` object to get an ORB-specific `MarshallBuffer` object.

3. Use that `MarshallBuffer` object to marshal the arguments.

4. Call the `Representation` to execute the desired method.

5. Use the `MarshallBuffer` object to unmarshal the results.

As is clear from the previous discussion, `Representation` is equivalent to Object Implementation (server) in CORBA. A generalization class has been introduced for data externalization functions, which implements marshaling and unmarshaling for the specific protocol.

**Using Java-IDL**   Java-IDL's latest release can be downloaded from the JavaSoft Java-IDL Web page at

**http://splash.javasoft.com/JavaIDL/pages/index.html**.

You may download for Sun Solaris or Win32/i86 platforms. Follow the installation instructions accessible from the previously mentioned Web page.

Examples using Java-IDL have not been implemented for the following reasons:

1. Despite CORBA standard IDL being supported, the ORB API seems to be different from that of CORBA API (for example, CORBA suggests `impl_is_ready` for a server to start waiting for client requests; whereas Java-IDL's DOOR ORB seems to use its own `publish` method). This is likely to confuse a beginner.

2. Because Java-IDL is still in alpha release, it is likely to change substantially.

3. IIOP is not yet supported, though it does not affect stand-alone applications.

The Voting Booth demo from Java-IDL was successfully run. Please refer to the Release Notes available on the previously mentioned URL on how to run the demos. Screen shots of the server log and two applet clients which access the server follow later in this chapter.

In the Voting Booth Application, a voting booth is set up by the server, for various people to come and vote on a "burning question of the day." Figure 17.8 displays the server console.

**FIG. 17.8**
Voting Booth Server is
a demo application
in Java-IDL.

As various "Citizen" clients come and vote, a log message is displayed on the server console. Duplicate attempts from the same citizen are ignored.

Voting is done using an applet that lets you see the question being voted on and registers your vote. The voting applet is shown in Figure 17.9.

Voting results are shown in another applet on the same page in a graphical manner. A view of this applet is shown in Figure 17.10.

**FIG. 17.9**

Voting Applet: demo in
Java-IDL.

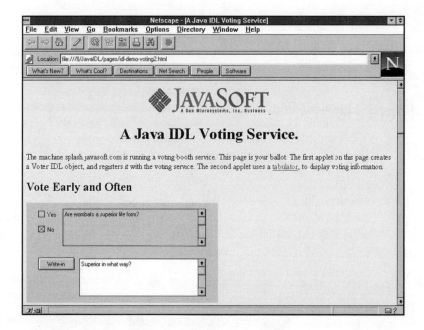

**FIG. 17.10**

Voting Results Applet:
demo in Java-IDL.

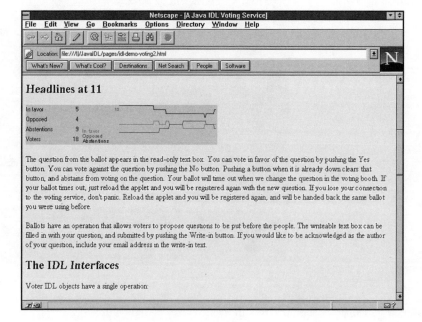

**Future Direction**   It will be interesting to see how close the ORB API supplied with the final release of Java-IDL is to that specified in the CORBA architecture specification. Currently, the difference is significant. Being an alpha release, it is hard to assess Java-IDL for serious Java-CORBA application development.

# From Here...

In this chapter, you have seen how Java and CORBA combine to bring a universal client and universal server to every Internet desktop. You also saw how the security offered by firewalls and Java applets affects Java-CORBA applications. Finally, you took a close look at three key Java-CORBA implementations: Visibroker for Java, OrbixWeb, and the official Java IIOP implementation, Java-IDL from Sun. A visit to some of the Web sites referenced here is suggested; you should also download an evaluation copy of a Java-CORBA product to build the sample application in Chapter 18, "Incorporating Java, JDBC, and CORBA: A Sample Application."

■ To develop your first Java-CORBA Application, go to Chapter 18, "Incorporating Java, JDBC, and CORBA: A Sample Application."

■ In order to understand issues in scaling Web-Object applications, go to Chapter 19, "Scaling Up Web-Object Applications."

Part
III

Ch
17

# Incorporating Java, JDBC, and CORBA: A Sample Application

It is time to roll up your sleeves and write a couple of simple CORBA object implementations, available to service requests from client programs or Java applets using IIOP. You are led through the various steps here. Starting with volatile objects that are erased from memory once the server shuts down, you go on to use JDBC to store the state of these objects in an ODBC database.

Once you have done that, you are truly a member of the "Java Enterprise Club," the application example provided in this book. The example will sign up new members and remember their contact details.

Before you start your journey through the distributed object space, check your seat belts and supplies. ■

## Getting ready

Start with a checklist of development tools that you need to obtain and install, before taking off into the Web object-space.

## Definition of the Example Application

Find out the functionality of the CORBA server and client you will be building.

## Getting your feet wet

Check out the development tools and test your understanding of IIOP application development by way of trying a basic example.

## The main course

You make the server more sophisticated by supporting persistent objects, stored in a JDBC database, and multiple applets talking to the CORBA server.

## Some basics about Object Factories

Understand the importance of Object Factories in CORBA implementations.

# Getting Ready

The secret to a good finish is a well-planned start. Now is the time to check what software you need and make sure it is installed and configured correctly. Identify what you already have, what you need to acquire (either buying or downloading an evaluation or free copy), taking the time to set it up and check that it is installed correctly, and, preferably, using the examples or demo samples supplied with the software. Read any FAQs, FEHs (Frequently Encountered Hurdles), or troubleshooting guides and, if you are keen, browse through known bugs. This not only prepares you for the use of the actual software, but a look at the FAQ and any other product reports (known bugs, and so on) also gives you an insight into issues when considering your design and coding. Remember, forewarned is forearmed. By reading FAQs, and so on, you also confirm your understanding of the techniques you are about to use.

CORBA is a conceptually rich framework. Web application development will use and test the correctness of a number of your environment's configurations. To begin with, your TCP/IP network configuration should be working properly. Finally, correct design of your object interfaces and implementations will get tested. If you are building a complete environment from scratch, you will be better off testing one tool at a time followed by *string testing* the tools (one tool correctly interfacing with another). This is one of the key factors for success with developing distributed applications.

## Operating System

You need Windows 95 or Windows NT Workstation or Server 3.51 or later. Make sure the TCP/IP networking and Dial-up Networking option is installed for Windows 95 and that Remote Access Service (RAS) is installed for Windows NT. You can also use a UNIX Workstation, running Solaris. The ORB product, Visibroker for Java, also runs on Sun OS 4.1x, Solaris 2.x, Digital UNIX 3.2, AIX 4.1, and HP UX 10.01.

The two examples discussed in this chapter were done on Windows NT Workstation Version 3.51.

## Network Setup

If you have been using Java for network applications, you probably already have a ready development environment. In that case, you can feel safe simply scanning this section quickly and moving on.

If you are part of a LAN intranet setup, make sure it is working smoothly (that there are no IP address conflicts, for example). Trying to debug distributed Java applications, and specifically CORBA applications, is next to impossible with network problems. If you experience long delays or timeouts during the testing of applets or servers, go back and check that it is not because of network problems. The way to do so is to have a small HTTP or other TCP/IP server (other than the one you are trying to test) running. If the problem (long delay or timeout) is experienced with this server as well, first make sure that the network works correctly.

Any of the following options are acceptable:

1. Machine configured with an Internet IP address and registered on DNS with a unique name
2. Machine configured just as 'localhost' on IP address **127.0.0.1**
3. If on a LAN, your machine may or may not have a name. Its IP address may be fixed or dynamically assigned upon sign-on. In all applications where a hostname is required, you can generally use an IP address instead.

   - If your machine has a name, you can use it wherever it is required to refer to various servers (assuming HTTP and IIOP servers will run on your machine).
   - If your machine has a fixed IP address, but no name, you can create a HOSTS file as required by your operating system. It is better to approach your LAN administrator to find out the best way to assign a name for your machine.
   - If your machine is assigned a new IP address dynamically, you may need to find out what it is each time you log on to the network and use the actual IP address. Consult your LAN administrator to find out how your environment is set up.

The example applications were developed on a two-node development network, running Windows 95 and Windows NT Workstation 3.51.

 **T I P** Although it is possible to test Java-CORBA applications on a single node, their behavior is different in a network environment. On a single node, communication between client and server is generally optimized to bypass some of the ORB functionality.

It is useful to have a network to test the behavior of your application in a network environment. Performance is generally slower and security checking of Java applet code is different in a network environment.

Part
**III**

Ch
**18**

# Java Development Environment

You need Symantec Café, Microsoft Visual J++, or at least Sun's JDK 1.01 or later.

CLASSPATH will need to include the ORB product and JDBC class library paths. The method to set the value of CLASSPATH is different for Café (version 1.02 and later), J++, and JDK.

Integrated development environments (IDEs) of these mentioned tools are equally helpful in developing and debugging Java-CORBA applications as they are for other Java applications.

> **CAUTION**
>
> Symantec Café (1.0 through 1.51) was used for developing the example applications. There have been reports (mostly on the CORBA newsgroup) of some CORBA applications not working well under Visual J++ or Microsoft Java VM (though OrbixWeb claims to run fine under Visual J++). If you are already using Microsoft J++, you may want to try developing CORBA applications there and consider alternatives only if that does not work.

## Database with ODBC and JDBC Drivers

To build the second example, you need ODBC and JDBC access to a database.

For Windows 95 and Windows NT, you need the 32-bit ODBC drivers. The example database has been set up using Microsoft Access. If you're using older 16-bit versions (Versions 2.x) of Access, make sure to download and install 32-bit ODBC drivers from Microsoft's Web site, **http://www.microsoft.com/**.

There are a number of JDBC drivers available. Examples in the JDBC section of this book use JetConnect, from XDB Systems, which can be used for writing Java-CORBA server programs, as well.

Once you have installed the example database from the CD-ROM to your disk, you need to add it to the list of ODBC databases installed on your machine. This is done by using the 32-bit ODBC icon in the Control Panel.

**TIP**  The Java Enterprise Club Database example applications shipped on the CD-ROM expect to find an ODBC database called JECLUB.

Also, do not forget to change the user ID and password, in the Server program for the second example application, to the values that you want the server to use to connect to the ODBC server.

## WWW Browser

You need to have access to a Java-enabled browser, ideally a 3.x version or later (3.x because of the JIT compiler for the extensive Java work involved) of Navigator or Explorer. Between the two browsers, there are some odd reports of CORBA and DCOM having the occasional "argument" (not working together) in Internet Explorer. To stay out of trouble (of the browser's making), go with Navigator. You have enough complexity on your hands to manage anyway.

## Java-CORBA Development Product

Finally, you need a CORBA Development Product for developing Java applications that work with IIOP. In Chapter 17, "WWW Applications Development Using CORBA," three products are discussed: Visibroker for Java, OrbixWeb, and Java IDL.

The example applications discussed in this chapter, and included on the CD-ROM, were developed using Visibroker for Java from Visigenic Corporation. Download and install Visibroker for Java, as explained in the section "Object Request Brokers for Java" in Chapter 17.

**NOTE**  It is recommended that you use Visibroker for Java for your first Java CORBA application. As of now, the code developed using one ORB is not directly portable to another ORB product. However, clients written in one ORB product can communicate to a server written using another product because both support IIOP on the wire and can therefore *interoperate*.

Therefore, the example code will run directly with Visibroker for Java. If you use OrbixWeb, you will find the OrbixWeb syntax is very parallel to that of Visibroker. Java IDL syntax (and even protocol interaction with ORB) is quite different. They can all interoperate (after Java IDL has an IIOP driver included) because of IIOP. ■

---

**Stop the Press**

The Java-CORBA product market is very fluid at the moment and is moving quite fast. A major product release or enhancement is coming nearly every quarter, if not more often. Freeware and academic versions are approaching fuller functionality and often include the original source code.

A free Java-CORBA product, not fully CORBA-compliant but with sufficient basic functionality, was announced in January 1997. JacORB, written entirely in Java, has been developed by Gerald Brose of Freie Universitat Berlin, Germany. It comes with IDL compiler, stub generator, Java-only programming support using static invocation only, full IIOP interoperability, and support for COSS naming service, with examples and original source code.

JacORB can be downloaded from **http://www.inf.fu-berlin.de/~brose/jacorb/**.

---

# Example Application: Java Enterprise Club

Welcome to the Java Enterprise Club. You develop the application in two stages, first without a database and second with a database. Static invocation approach is used for both stages of the example application.

## Application Overview

Java Enterprise Club has members who are interested in using Java for developing client/ server Internet or intranet applications for the corporate enterprise. They are represented by the Member object. As we shall see in the design of the IDL for the application, a Member object makes some of its methods distributed by publishing them in the IDL (you do it, in fact). The Club has a Secretary object, which keeps track of the Club's membership records. Its responsibilities include admitting new members and locating information about existing members.

Figure 18.1 depicts the overall structure of both our examples. Let us examine in detail some design decisions already made in this example. We shall also look at the alternatives available for each of these decisions in a general CORBA environment.

## Interfaces

Let us look at the definition of interfaces for Example 1. These interfaces are specified using the CORBA Interface Definition Language (IDL), as shown in Listing 18.1. All the interfaces are listed in a module called JEClub. A module provides a mechanism for bundling interfaces.

**FIG. 18.1**

Objects in Java
Enterprise Club Server.

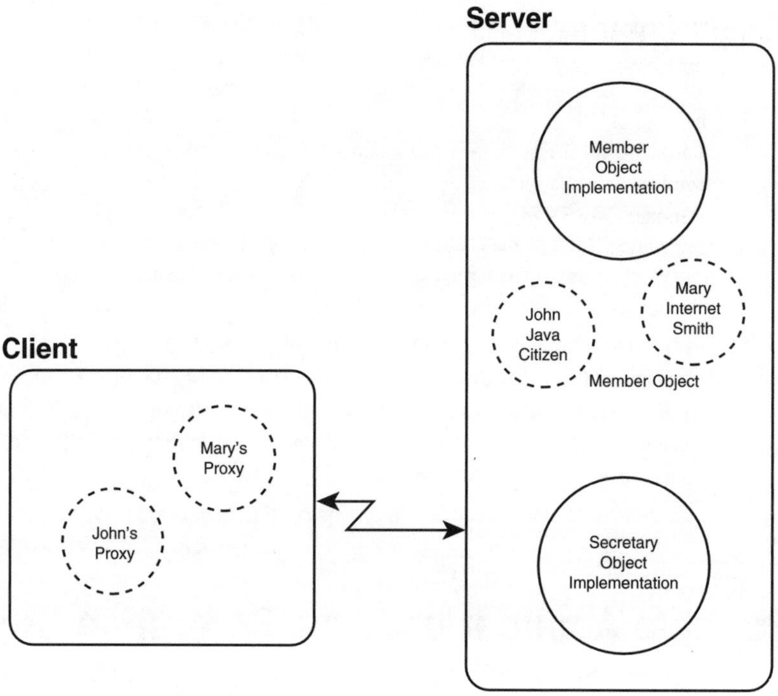

**JEClubSecretary**   The only method (interface) provided by the JEClubSecretary is admit, which returns a Member. It either creates a new Member object or finds an existing Member object and returns an object reference to it. It accepts member's name as a parameter.

**Member**   The only method (interface) provided by the Member implementation is tell_age, which is used to return member's age. Member's age is its private state.

---

**Listing 18.1   Interfaces in Java Enterprise Club Application**

```
// Java Enterprise Club :
//
// JEClub.idl

module JEClub {

  interface Member {
      long tell_age();
  };

  interface JEClubSecretary {
    Member admit(in string mbrname);
  };

};
```

# Design Choices

The design decisions we are about to discuss apply to both the examples, since Figure 18.1 depicts the structure of both examples.

**Locating an Object Implementation in a Server**    In our examples, both the Member object implementation and the Secretary object implementation are within the same executable. In a generic CORBA environment, this need not be the case. In general, the following combinations are possible:

- Multiple objects and all their methods within the same server executable
- Only one object and all its methods in a given server executable
- One object method in one server executable

The decision to choose a given approach depends on the size and class hierarchy of the object model on the server end.

**Server Activation**    In our examples, we will always be starting the Server manually, known as the *persistent server*. CORBA supports automatic server activation. A component known as Basic Object Adapter (BOA), on the server end, examines the request for an object and identifies the server implementing the object from Implementation Repository. Multiple activation policies are possible.

- **Persistent Server**—The server is manually initiated. Load-balancing and timeout policies are the responsibility of the server.
- **Shared Server**—A server with multiple object implementations is started when the request for any of the implemented objects is received.
- **Server-per-method**—The server process runs only for the duration of the particular method call.

The full range of activation policies are not supported by all CORBA products. OrbixWeb and Orbix, for instance, provide a full range of activation policies.

**Object Factories in CORBA**    In normal object-oriented programming, a class provides a constructor to build object instances. Since IDL interfaces contain methods which map to object methods in the implementation, constructor interfaces are needed to create objects. These interfaces have to be accessible before the object itself is accessible by the client. These are commonly referred to as object factories in design patterns and in CORBA as well.

In our example, we are going to use `JEClubSecretary` as a factory for instantiating `Member` objects. One of the uses of the `admit` method is to manufacture member objects and return object references to them. We shall see its other use very shortly.

**Naming Service**    Naming service in CORBA is like a file allocation table (FAT) on a hard disk. A given file's descriptor will be a number, derived from its start point on a given sector and track. A FAT associates the file descriptor to a file name, by which we know the file. Similarly, an object naming service in CORBA associates an object reference to a conveniently memorable and useful name. It even provides a directory structure to object names.

Part

III

Ch

18

To keep the examples simple, we have not used the naming service. Instead, the JEClubSecretary keeps an internal hashtable, mapping member names to their object references. When an admit request is received with a member's name, it first checks to see if it already has an object for that name. If yes, it locates its object reference and returns it in the result. If no, it invokes the constructor method from Member to make a new member object. Thus, JEClubSecretary plays a dual role of a factory and a very rudimentary and localized (to this application) naming service.

Figure 18.2 shows the Java Enterprise Club examples menu.

**FIG. 18.2**

The Java Enterprise Club examples menu.

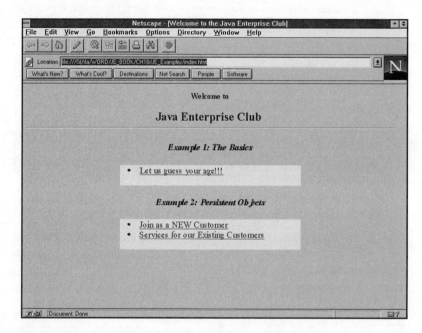

## Scope of Example One

In the first example, you gain some experience defining interfaces, implementing them, and creating and locating objects. Objects simply reside in the server memory and are lost when the server is shut down.

You first build a console (command line) client application and then convert it to an applet. This client applet will demonstrate the use of an IIOP proxy server, running at the same host as the HTTP server. This is to work around the network security restrictions on Java applets.

## Scope of Example Two

In the second example, you enhance the first example application to a more substantial application in the following ways:

■ Instead of assigning a random age, you store member contact information (such as street address and phone numbers), using a Java applet form. When you join as a new member, you get a member number and a password. Next time, you use these to enter the Java Enterprise Club. A set of services may be offered to members of Java Enterprise Club. The only service you will see in the book is to change the contact details (address, phone numbers, and so on).

■ Member object offers two interfaces: Get Member Information (get_mbr_info) and Set Member Information (set_mbr_info). Member object also offers an enhanced constructor which inserts the new member's information in an MS Access database, using JDBC. get_mbr_info and set_mbr_info retrieve and update the state of the member object (and the database), respectively.

■ JEClubSecretary offers two separate interfaces for new members (create_member) and for finding existing members (find_member).

■ You see the use of CORBA exceptions for exception handling.

# Example 1: Java Enterprise Club Without Database

Now look at your first example. It is very basic in functionality. The client gives the name of a person wanting to join the Java Enterprise Club. The server checks to see if a member object for that person exists. If it does, the server returns the object reference to the member object. If no, it creates a new member object for that person, assigning it a random age between 20 and 50 (that is the fun part). The client then invokes a remote method tell_age, declared in the IDL, on this member object. Results of the remote method invocation are displayed by the client.

You shall see two types of client: first, a Java console application that accepts the member's name from the command line argument, and second, the same functionality implemented in a Java applet. Both clients use the same server.

## IDL Interfaces and Application Structure

Listing 18.1 shows the definition of Member and JEClubSecretary interfaces and their methods. You have also seen the structure of the application in Figure 18.1.

You use the idl2java compiler to compile the IDL. As explained in Chapter 16, "CORBA and Object Management Architecture (OMA)," it generates Java source code for the server-side skeletons and client-side stubs, which are used for developing the server and client programs. These have the names _sk_<interface-name>.java and _st_<interface-name>.java, respectively. Visibroker's idl2java compiler also generates example server implementation for each interface, which can be customized to build the server. Table 18.1 summarizes the files produced from idl2java compiler and their contents. The <module name> is specified in the IDL file.

Part
III

Ch
18

**Table 18.1   Java Code Generated from *IDL2JAVA* Compiler**

| Directory | File Name | Purpose |
| --- | --- | --- |
| <module name> | <interface name>.java | Declares the interface |
| <module name> | <interface name>Operations.java | Declares methods in the interface |
| <module name> | <interface name>_var.java | Code to bind object references, and so on |
| <module name> | _sk_<interface name>.java | Server skeleton from which the server inherits |
| <module name> | _st_<interface name>.java | Client stub used by the client program |
| <module name> | _example_<interface name>.java | Example interface implementation |

# Writing the Server

You will now build the for this example. Take the time to look at the _example_Member. java and _example_JEClubSecretary.java files generated from the idl2java compiler. They appear in the JE_Examples directory structure on the Que Web site (**http://www.quecorp.com**), or you can look at those you generated.

Now look at the actual Java Enterprise Club Server, described in Listing 18.2.

**Listing 18.2   Java Enterprise Club Server for Example 1**

```
// JEClubServer.java

import java.util.*;

class Member extends JEClub._sk_Member {

  Member(int mbr_age) {
    my_age = mbr_age;
  }

  public int tell_age() throws CORBA.SystemException {
    return my_age;
  }

  private int my_age;
}
```

```
class JEClubSecretary extends JEClub._sk_JEClubSecretary {

  // Private attributes of JEClubSecretary
  private Dictionary my_members = new Hashtable();
  private Random age_random = new Random();

  // Constructor for JEClubSecretary

  JEClubSecretary(String name) {
    super(name);
  }  // end JEClubSecretary Constructor


  // Member Factory :  A class to manufacture Members

  public JEClub.Member admit(String name) throws CORBA.SystemException {

    // Lookup the member in the member list.
    JEClub.Member member = (JEClub.Member) my_members.get(name);

    if (member == null) {              // Not found. Welcome a new member

      // Create new member's random age, between 20 and 50
      int the_age = Math.abs(age_random.nextInt()) % 30 + 20;

      member = new Member(the_age);
      System.out.println(" ");
      Date date = new Date();
      System.out.println(date.toString() + " Welcoming " + name +
                       " as member.  He/she is " + the_age);

      // Export the new object reference.
      _boa().obj_is_ready(member);

      // Save the member in the member list.
      my_members.put(name, member);
    }
    else {
      Date date = new Date();
      System.out.println(" ");
      System.out.println(date.toString() + " " + name
                       + "'s been around since he/she was "
                       + member.tell_age());
    }

    // Return the member.
    return member;
  }

}

public class JEClubServer {
  public static void main(String[] args) {
    try {
```

*continues*

**Listing 18.2  Continued**

```
        // Initialize the ORB.
        CORBA.ORB orb = CORBA.ORB.init();

        // Initialize the BOA.
        CORBA.BOA boa = orb.BOA_init();

        // Create the secretary object.
        JEClubSecretary secretary =
         new JEClubSecretary("Java Enterprise Club");

        // Export the newly create object.
        boa.obj_is_ready(secretary);

        System.out.println(secretary + " is ready.");

        // Wait for incoming requests
        boa.impl_is_ready();
      }
    catch(CORBA.SystemException e) {
      System.err.println(e);
      }
    }
  }
}
```

# Understanding the Server

The Java Enterprise Club Server consists of three main parts: implementations of each of the
Member and JEClubSecretary classes, which inherit from their skeletons, and the main
JEClubServer class. You will look at each of these components and their functions in detail.

**Member Class**    Member class, on the server side, extends the member skeleton class, which is
automatically generated by the IDL compiler. Significance and use of skeletons is explained
later. The Member class has a simple constructor, which stores member's age as a private attribute. Member class also implements a trivial method, tell_age, to return the integer attribute.

Note that age is declared in the IDL to be a long, whereas it is an integer in Java. This is based
on the mapping from IDL to Java as implemented by Visibroker.

**JEClubSecretary Class**    JEClubSecretary is the class that does most of the work on the
server side. It maintains an internal hashtable that maps member names to object references to
member objects (thus serving as an internal name service). Other than a simple constructor
for the class itself, it implements a method admit to locate members in the hashtable or to construct new member objects (thus serving as a member object factory).

**Inheriting from Skeletons**    Notice the following two lines in the Member and JEClubSecretary
classes, respectively:

```
class Member extends JEClub._sk_Member { ......
```

and

```
class JEClubSecretary extends JEClub._sk_JEClubSecretary { .....
```

They both show that `Member` and `JEClubSecretary` are implemented by extending their respective skeleton classes.

Skeletons are generated as part of the IDL compilation. They provide the mechanism to receive requests from the client programs and pass them to the actual objects. Visibroker uses a number of other internal classes to map from the generic remote object provided by CORBA to the actual remote objects, which in this case are `Member` and `JEClubSecretary`.

***JEClubServer* Class**    Let us now look at the `JEClubServer`, the actual Java class that implements the server. You will examine its method `main` to understand various steps that take place in the server. Once again, please refer to Listing 18.2.

***Initializing the ORB Connection***    The very first statement within the `main` method of the server initializes a connection to the ORB as follows:

```
CORBA.ORB orb = CORBA.ORB.init();
```

This call interacts with the ORB interface. It returns a reference to the ORB itself, so that the server may use ORB facilities.

***Initializing the BOA***    The next step for a server, within a static invocation client/server setup, is to initialize the basic object adapter (BOA). The following are the BOA responsibilities to be carried out on the server end: to activate the server (if not already active and if activation is supported by the ORB); activate the object; and pass the method invocation to the object. When, in the first step, the server is activated, it carries out its initialization and notifies the BOA that it is ready by an `impl_is_ready` call. Next, as in the second step, when the object is activated, it notifies the BOA that it is ready by an `obj_is_ready(<obj.ref>)` call.

The call to initialize the BOA is:

```
CORBA.BOA boa = orb.BOA_init();
```

where `orb` is an ORB object reference.

***Notifying the BOA that an Object Is Ready***    As previously discussed, the server notifies the BOA when a given object is ready to receive requests from ORB clients. It notifies the BOA as follows:

```
boa.obj_is_ready(<object reference>);
```

where `boa` is an object reference to the basic object adapter and `<object reference>` points to the object that is ready to serve its clients.

***Notifying the BOA that the Server Is Ready***    Initialization of a server may require starting or initializing a number of objects. When all the necessary objects have been readied, the server is ready as a whole. Once this is done, the server notifies BOA that requests for any of the objects implemented by the server may be passed to the server now. This is done by:

```
boa.impl_is_ready();
```

where boa is an object reference to the basic object adapter.

**Stringified Object References**    Notice the line of code to display the secretary object reference:

```
System.out.println(secretary + " is ready.");
```

Attempting to print the object reference secretary invokes its toString() method, which is mapped to the object_to_string() function supplied by the ORB API. This will convert ORB's object references to what is known as *stringified object reference*. Stringified object references are not interoperable, but can be used for storing in cases of subsequent retrieval. Various forms of object references can be confusing for a beginner. If you are interested in more details about object references, refer to CORBA Architecture Specification from OMG, or one of the books listed in the CORBA resources at the end of Chapter 16, "CORBA and Object Management Architecture (OMA)."

That completes the discussion of the simple JEClubServer for your first implementation of the Java Enterprise Club. Now you will write a text-based console application to work as a client, which you will subsequently convert to an applet.

You will notice you have inserted a few lines of code in the server to display a message, as a new member object is created. This will help you understand what is happening inside the server when you execute the client program.

# Console Client

The console client you are writing is simply called JEClubClient, as it is a Java Enterprise Club Client. It accepts an existing or potential member's name (consisting of a maximum of two words) as command-line arguments. As output, it tells you the member's age, as guessed by the server (Java Enterprise Club Secretary class, if you want to be specific). Given that most people trying to do this example are likely to be in the age group of 20 to 50, we have asked our secretary to keep that in mind. Find out if you are in the ripe twenties or the seasoned forties, and have fun.

Listing 18.3 shows the console client for your Java Enterprise Club Server (JEClubServer).

**Listing 18.3    Java Enterprise Club Client (Console)**

```
// Java Enterprise
//
// JEClubClient.java
//
```

```
public class JEClubClient {

  public static void main(String args[]) {

    try {
        String  name_arg;

        // Initialize the ORB.
        CORBA.ORB orb = CORBA.ORB.init();

        // Bind to the club secretary object.
        JEClub.JEClubSecretary secretary =
           JEClub.JEClubSecretary_var.bind("Java Enterprise Club");

        // Obtain member name from command line arguments
        if (args.length > 1) {
           name_arg = args[0] + " " + args[1];
        }
        else if (args.length > 0)  {
           name_arg = args[0];
        }
        else {
           System.out.println ("Usage: java JEClubClient <your name>");
           return;
        }

        String name = args.length > 0 ? name_arg : "Jeff Riley";

        // Request the secretary to admit a new member
        JEClub.Member member = secretary.admit(name);

        // invoke tell_age to get member's age
        int mbr_age = member.tell_age();

        // Time for amusement.
        System.out.println (name + " is only " + mbr_age);

    } // end of try
    catch(CORBA.SystemException e) {
      System.err.println(e);
    }

  } // end of main

}
```

As you can see, it consists of only six statements and one error (exception) handling statement. This is a simple illustration of how CORBA simplifies distributed object programming. A remote object is located or created with one call and its method is invoked with another.

> **CAUTION**
>
> Make sure the IDL, the Server code, and the Client code are in the same directory.
>
> IDL compilation creates a subdirectory with the same name as the module name listed in the IDL. All generated Java code lives in this subdirectory, thus creating a Java package with the same name as the module name. Client code and Server stubs make use of this package.
>
> It is possible to move this package to somewhere on your CLASSPATH, and import the package. Do this as a part of deploying the final application.

**Initializing the ORB Connection**  As with the server, any interaction with the ORB has to start with establishing a connection to the ORB. This is done using the `CORBA.ORB.init()` call, as used by the server as well.

**Binding to a Named Object**  IDL compilation generates a file `<interface name>_var.java` (see Table 18.1), which contains the generated code for clients to be able to bind to the object of a given name. This binding takes place using Visibroker's Naming and Directory Service OSAgent.

As a programmer, all you need to do is enter the following line of code:

```
JEClub.JEClubSecretary secretary =
        JEClub.JEClubSecretary_var.bind("Java Enterprise Club");
```

This uses the `JEClubSecretary` declaration, contained in `JEClubSecretary.java` in sub-directory `JEClub`, to create an object "Java Enterprise Club" of the class `JEClubSecretary`. The reference to the remote object is obtained by using the `bind` method provided by `<interface name>_var` stub generated by IDL compilation, again in the `JEClub` subdirectory (package).

This enables you to invoke methods on the `JEClubSecretary` object named Java Enterprise Club.

**Using the *Member* Stub**  The statement to bind the secretary to the Java Enterprise Club object implementation has also used the `secretary` stub, generated from IDL compilation. The line

```
JEClub.Member member = secretary.admit(name);
```

similarly uses the `Member` stub in the `JEClub` package to declare a `member` object reference.

**Invoking Methods on Proxy**  The lines preceding the declaration of the `member` object reference build the `member` name from the command-line arguments. The line

```
JEClub.Member member = secretary.admit(name);
```

also invokes the method `admit` (with `name` as parameter) on the remote object `proxy` pointed to by `secretary`.

Another example of remote method invocation from the client is the line

```
int mbr_age = member.tell_age();
```

It invokes the method `tell_age` on the remote `member` object referenced by `member`.

**Handling Exceptions**   If you are familiar with `try` and `catch` statements in Java or C++, you do not need a substantial introduction to CORBA exceptions.

CORBA provides two categories of exceptions: System and User. Most System exceptions arise from the failure of communication between any of the client, ORB, BOA, servers, or the implementation. System exceptions can also arise from mismatched parameters and signatures. User exceptions are declared in IDL as part of the interfaces. User exceptions common to a number of interfaces can be declared at the module level within an IDL file.

As a general rule, any method invocations to ORB or remote methods must at least catch the generic CORBA System Exception. If the remote method can raise user exceptions, those should be caught as well.

## Running the Java Enterprise Club Application

Our client, as well as the server programs, are now ready; it is time to see them in action. A command-line compilation is adequate. If you are interested in using an IDE (Symantec Café, Microsoft J++, or similar), you will need to define a project for each client and server and add the client and server files to the project. Once the client and the server programs have been compiled, you are ready to run them.

The directions for running the Java Enterprise Club application described here refer to the Visibroker for Java from Visigenic. For other products, you need to follow equivalent steps for the product you're using.

**Start the *OSAgent***   `OSAgent` is the distributed directory and name service for Visibroker. Start `OSAgent` from the Visibroker for the Java program group. It starts as a minimized icon. If you maximize it, you see a blank window, which is perfectly normal.

`OSAgent` must be running first before any server can come around and register itself or its implementations.

There is a common misunderstanding by beginners to CORBA that a client-side driver is required on every potential client desktop. This may be a requirement for some non-Java ORB products, but no Java ORB product requires this.

The client component of the ORB is written in Java and the class libraries are downloaded to the client browser on demand. With support for zipped class libraries from JDK 1.1 and Netscape Navigator Version 4's bundling of Visigenic's client libraries, this download process will become even faster.

**Start the Server**   From the command line, in the work directory, run the command

```
java JEClubServer
```

If all goes as planned, and your configuration is right, you will see a message of the form

```
<stringified object reference for Java Enterprise Club> is ready.
```

as coded in the last line of the server's main method.

Listing 18.4 shows the Server Console window from our execution, as it looked after a few client invocations.

**Listing 18.4   Java Enterprise Club Server Console**

```
Symantec Java! ByteCode Compiler Version 1.02e
Copyright (C) 1996 Symantec Corporation
JEClubSecretary[Server,oid=PersistentId[interfaceName=JEClub::JEClubSecretary,ob
jectName=Java Enterprise Club]] is ready.

Tue Jan 28 22:22:33  1997 Welcoming John Citizen as member.  He/she is 23

Tue Jan 28 22:22:46  1997 Welcoming Mary Smith as member.  He/she is 35

Tue Jan 28 22:23:08  1997 Welcoming Bill Clinton as member.  He/she is 25

Tue Jan 28 22:23:23  1997 Welcoming Rajeev Arora as member.  He/she is 36

Tue Jan 28 22:23:46  1997 Welcoming Jeff Schneider as member.  He/she is 40
```

**Invite Members to Java Enterprise Club**   Now run the client and see if the ORB setup, the server, and the client are all working as intended.

Open another command window, change to your development directory, and enter the command

```
java JEClubClient <Member's Name>
```

where <Member's Name> is the member who wants to join the Java Enterprise Club (and whose age you want the club secretary to guess). Listing 18.5 shows the client console wherein you have introduced a few members to the Java Enterprise Club. Their names are entirely fictitious and any resemblance to persons living or dead is entirely coincidental.

## Listing 18.5  Java Enterprise Club Client Console

```
I:\rla\JE_Examples\example1>java JEClubClient John Citizen
Symantec Java! ByteCode Compiler Version 1.02e
Copyright (C) 1996 Symantec Corporation
John Citizen is only 23

I:\rla\JE_Examples\example1>java JEClubClient Mary Smith
Symantec Java! ByteCode Compiler Version 1.02e
Copyright (C) 1996 Symantec Corporation
Mary Smith is only 35

I:\rla\JE_Examples\example1>java JEClubClient Bill Clinton
Symantec Java! ByteCode Compiler Version 1.02e
Copyright (C) 1996 Symantec Corporation
Bill Clinton is only 25

I:\rla\JE_Examples\example1>java JEClubClient Rajeev Arora
Symantec Java! ByteCode Compiler Version 1.02e
Copyright (C) 1996 Symantec Corporation
Rajeev Arora is only 36

I:\rla\JE_Examples\example1>java JEClubClient Jeff Schneider
Symantec Java! ByteCode Compiler Version 1.02e
Copyright (C) 1996 Symantec Corporation
Jeff Schneider is only 40

I:\rla\JE_Examples\example1>
```

Part
III

Ch
18

The preceding console shows only the new members joining the club. Try repeating the same name. The response on the client end is not different from when the name was entered the first time, but if you have a look at the server console, the server displays a message of the form `<member> has been around since he/she was <age>`. It shows that it found an existing member from its internal hashtable.

### Running the Console Client from a Different Network Node

You may want to run the client from a node other than the one where the server is running. This is done as follows:

```
java -DOSAGENT_ADDR=<domain name of machine running OSAagent> JEClubClient
<Member Name>
```

You need to manually install the JEClubClient.class (and all classes in the JEClub package) and ORB runtime classes in the CLASSPATH of the machine from where you will run the command- line client.

**Using SmartFinder**   Visibroker provides an object namespace browser, called the Smart-Finder. It locates all copies of the OSAgent running within a subnetwork and lets you see what implementations are registered with them. Figure 18.3 shows the list of all manually started interfaces. The first entry is our `JEClubSecretary`, whereas the `AliasManager` entry is from the GateKeeper. You learned about GateKeeper's use for tunneling IIOP through HTTP and as a proxy in Chapter 17, "WWW Applications Development Using CORBA." We will see its use here in the applet version of the client.

**FIG. 18.3**
Browsing manually started interfaces using SmartFinder.

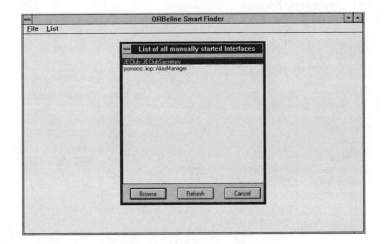

You can select an interface and press the `Browse` button to see the object implementations within that interface. Figure 18.4 shows the Java Enterprise Club object implementation registered by our interface.

**FIG. 18.4**
Browsing object implementations of an interface using SmartFinder.

# Applet Client

Now add the three Ws (WWW) to your client application. The client developed is very simple. All you need to do is as follows:

1. Design an applet with a field to enter the member name, and with a pushbutton, you will invoke the `remote` method. Figure 18.5 displays the applet.

2. Distribute the 6–7 lines of code in the console version of the Client program to the appropriate parts of the applet code. For example, initialization code is moved to the `init()` method and processing of the command line is moved to the `pushbutton-click` event handler function.

3. Compile the applet code and set up an HTML page to carry the applet to the browser.

**FIG. 18.5**

Age Guessing Applet.

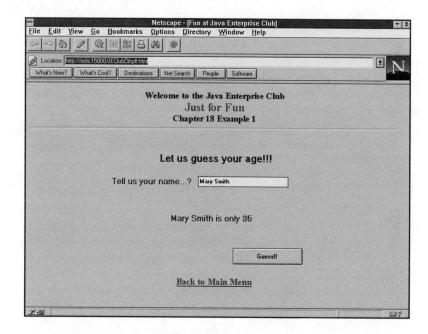

Part
III

Ch
18

Please refer to Listing 18.3 for the code for the console client. The following is a summary of the code changes made to build the applet code:

- Moved variables `orb`, `secretary`, `member`, and `mbr_age` to applet level private attributes so they can be accessed from all methods within the applet.

- The `ORB.init()` and the `Bind` to the remote `secretary` object were moved to the `init()` method inside a `try ¦ catch` statement to trap any CORBA exceptions resulting from remote invocation.

- For the `pushbutton-click` event, included the code to read the member name from the input text field. This is followed by getting a remote `member` object by invoking `secretary.admit(name)`. Finally, the member's age is retrieved from the remote `member` object by invoking `member.tell_age()` and is shown as a message on the applet.

## Running the Java Enterprise Club Applet

Running the Java applet is quite simple. There is no change required to the server. You can even leave the same server running. Make sure the class file for the applet is in the same directory as the HTML file and open the HTML file from the browser of your choice.

In order to test the applet from another node within the network, you will need to run GateKeeper from your development directory as follows (assuming the CLASSPATH and PATH were set up correctly during Visibroker installation):

```
java pomoco.iiop.GateKeeper
```

This starts GateKeeper, which is a development quality HTTP server, at the same time providing IIOP tunneling to the nearest OSAgent, Visibroker's directory and name service. Thus, HTTP and IIOP packets come bundled together while working with Visibroker for Java (see Chapter 17, "WWW Applications Development Using CORBA," for a description of IIOP tunneling). GateKeeper separates IIOP packets, directing them to OSAgent, while serving HTTP from its built-in HTTP server.

 **TIP** Make a note of the fact that GateKeeper runs on port 15,000. You need to include the port number with the domain name or IP address of your workstation for accessing HTML pages in your development directory. This will be done as follows in your Web browser:

**http://your-development-machine:15000/your-html-page.html**

## Optimization of Client/Server Communication by Visibroker

We discussed Visibroker's architecture in Chapter 17, "WWW Applications Development Using CORBA," how the inter-process communication between client and the server is optimized, depending on their location. If they are on the same machine, shared memory or queues are used to communicate between the client and the server. If they are on different machines, various ORB facilities and architecture (to marshal and unmarshal the request and handle exceptions, and so on) come into action.

A look at the GateKeeper console provides an insight into this optimization. We executed our client applet first locally (on the same machine as the server) and then on a remote node. GateKeeper shows all the HTML files and Java classes as it ships them to the client. Listing 18.6 shows the GateKeeper console when the client applet is on the same machine as the server. Only the HTML files and the basic client, server, stub, and skeleton classes are shipped.

### Listing 18.6   GateKeeper Console for a Local Applet Execution

```
Symantec Java! ByteCode Compiler Version 1.02e
Copyright (C) 1996 Symantec Corporation
VisiBroker for Java Release 1.2 (Oct 20, 1996) IIOP GateKeeper started: Tue Jan
28 22:21:42  1997
```

```
Java: Version 102 from Sun Microsystems Inc.
OS:   Windows NT version 3.51; CPU: x86
Adding search path: .
Adding search path: I:\ORB20\CLASSES
Adding search path: I:\JETCONNECT\CLASSES
rishi   826     826     0       0       1       JEClubClAplt.html
rishi   3330    4156    8432    8432    2       JEClubClAplt.class
rishi   1954    6110    581     9013    3       JEClub/JEClubSecretary_var.class

rishi   1312    7422    2263    11276   4       JEClub/_st_JEClubSecretary.class

rishi   300     7722    1082    12358   5       JEClub/JEClubSecretary.class
rishi   1059    8781    18416   30774   6       JEClub/_st_Member.class
rishi   253     9034    701     31475   7       JEClub/Member.class
```

Listing 18.7 shows the GateKeeper console when the applet is executed from a remote node. You can see a whole range of Java classes being shipped across the network. These are ORB runtime classes. Netscape Navigator 4.0 will have ORB runtime classes bundled with each client, so IIOP-enabled Java applets will be able to start executing much faster.

### Listing 18.7  GateKeeper Console for Remote Applet Execution

```
muni    1327    117949  440     58213   50      pomoco/CORBA/Locator.class
muni    390     118339  381     58594   51      CORBA/BindOptions.class
muni    7957    126296  390     58984   52      pomoco/ds/DSUser.class
muni    855     127151  711     59695   53      pomoco/ds/DatagramThread.class
muni    310     127461  371     60066   54      pomoco/ds/DSResource.class
muni    2437    129898  320     60386   55      pomoco/ds/DSMessage.class
muni    2377    132275  231     60617   56      pomoco/ds/DSRequest.class
muni    3268    135543  320     60937   57      pomoco/ds/DSAMessage.class
muni    2519    138062  231     61168   58      pomoco/ds/DSAReply.class
muni    1026    139088  480     61648   59      pomoco/ds/AreYouAliveThread.class
muni    2742    141830  591     62239   60      pomoco/ds/DSAddr.class
muni    1054    142884  721     62960   61      pomoco/ds/DSString.class
muni    1905    144789  841     63801   62      pomoco/ds/DSLogin.class
muni    3865    148654  311     64112   63      pomoco/ds/DSReply.class
muni    3488    152142  121044  185156  64      pomoco/ds/OStream.class
muni    3929    156071  741     185897  65      pomoco/ds/IStream.class
muni    826     156897  30414   216311  66      JEClubClAplt.html
muni    2070    158967  10475   226786  67      pomoco/ds/DSName.class
muni    2003    160970  1362    228148  68      pomoco/ds/DSProvider.class
muni    11843   172813  450     228598  69      pomoco/CORBA/Proxy.class
muni    17088   189901  541     229139  70      pomoco/CORBA/Stream.class
muni    5578    195479  391     229530  71      pomoco/CORBA/IiopStream.class
muni    700     196179  671     230201  72      CORBA/Request.class
```

# Example Two: Java Enterprise Club with JDBC Database of Members

The first example of the Java Enterprise Club, though simple, was important to illustrate the basic functioning of a Java-CORBA application. It had, however, very elementary functionality. In the second example, we bring the earlier application a level closer to real life applications.

## Key Improvement

The key change to the application is in the constructor for the Member class on the server end. Instead of a random integer containing age, Member constructor accepts a structure containing a member's number, password, first and last name, various address fields, and phone number. If invoked with a zero membership number, it inserts the structure supplied on the JECLUB ODBC database (accessed through JDBC/ODBC bridge from XDB Systems), assigning the member a new membership number. If invoked with a non-zero membership number, it retrieves a member with the supplied membership number from the JECLUB database; it then builds and returns a member object.

## Other Improvements

In addition to adding persistence to the Member class, we have made the following improvements:

- Member class supports both a get and set method, to retrieve and update member information in the database, respectively.
- Our friendly JEClubSecretary class (which still doubles as a localized name service and a member object factory) has separate find_member and create_member methods.
- The client application for existing members follows a sequence of authentication using membership number and password. A menu of available facilities is presented; the only facility implemented is "Change Personal Details." You are invited to build additional menu options and extend the server functionality as required.
- The client for new members allows them to enter their personal details (name, address, and so on) and get a membership number and a default password (PASSWORD).

## Changes to IDL Interfaces

Listing 18.8 shows the IDL for the second incarnation of the Java Enterprise Club. Let us examine all the enhancements one by one.

---

**Listing 18.8   Java Enterprise Club Example 2 IDL File**

```
// Java Enterprise Club:  Example Application
//
//
// Interface Definition File
```

```
//
//    JEClub.idl

module JEClub {

  // --------------------------------------------------------------------------
  -------
  //                 G L O B A L   T Y P E   D E C L A R A T I O N S
  // --------------------------------------------------------------------------
  -------

  // Member ------------------------------
  typedef long    MemberID;
  typedef string  Password;
  typedef string  FirstName;
  typedef string  LastName;
  typedef string  AddressLine1;
  typedef string  AddressLine2;
  typedef string  City;
  typedef string  State;
  typedef string  Postcode;
  typedef string  BusPhone;
  typedef string  ResPhone;

  typedef struct MemberDataDefn {
      MemberID mbr_id;
       Password    mbr_pw;
      FirstName first_name;
      LastName  last_name;
      AddressLine1 addr_line1;
      AddressLine2 addr_line2;
      City      city;
      State     state;
      Postcode  postcode;
      BusPhone  busphone;
      ResPhone  resphone;
              } MemberData;

  // --------------------------------------------------------------------------
  -------
  //                          I N T E R F A C E S
  // --------------------------------------------------------------------------
  -------

  interface Member {

      MemberDataDefn get_mbr_info();

      boolean set_mbr_info(in MemberDataDefn mbr_data);
  };

  interface JEClubSecretary {
      exception   Member_Already_Exists {MemberID  mbr_id;};
      exception   Member_Not_Found{MemberID mbr_id;};
```

*continues*

---

**Listing 18.8   Continued**

```
    Member    create_member(in MemberData mbr_data)
                   raises (Member_Already_Exists);

    Member    find_member(in MemberData mbr_data);

  };

};
```

---

**User-Defined Types**   As is common in C and C++, IDL lets you define your own elementary and compound (structure) types. Listing 18.8 shows the special types for declaring member information. These are MemberID, Password, FirstName, and so on. MemberDataDefn is the type for a structure containing one set of member information. MemberDataDefn is used as an input parameter to set_mbr_info and is the returned type for method get_mbr_info for the Member interface.

**User-Defined Exceptions**   Notice the exception definitions Member_Already_Exists and Member_Not_Found for the interface JEClubSecretary in Listing 18.8. These are the user-defined exceptions to designate application-specific exceptions that may be raised by the remote interface object. Any invocations of the related methods must provide code to handle these exceptions.

# Changes to the Server

Let us now see how the server has been enhanced to provide database functionality. Begin by looking at it one class at a time. You may want to print the file JEClubServer.java from Example2 directory on the Web site (**http://www.quecorp.com**).

**Member**   Changes to the Member class are: an improved constructor with database access, get_mbr_info now returns the member information structure, and set_mbr_info updates the member attributes in memory and the database. Let us look at the constructor in detail, as the other changes are self-explanatory.

The constructor for the Member class now builds a new member object for a given member ID by retrieving the database row for that member. For a new member, the member's information is passed to the constructor with member ID set to 0. The constructor assigns the next available member ID, stores the row in the database, and returns an object with all attributes correctly initialized:

```
if member ID = 0
        Get the next unused member ID
        Insert a new record with this member ID
        Commit database update
```

```
else
     Retrieve the database record for the specified member ID
If not found
     throw Member_Not_Found exception
else
     Return member data in the member structure
end if
     end if
```

***JEClubSecretary* Class**   The structure of the JEClubSecretary class is the same as the first example. Its name service functionality and factory functionality have been put in separate methods—find_member and create_member, respectively. The rest of the code is identical or parallel to the first example.

***JEClubServer* Class**   The following points summarize the changes to the JEClubServer, your server's main class:

1.  Notice the ODBC variables for the database environment, connector, and statement are declared static and public, so that they can be accessed by all classes in the server.
2.  All database operations handle exceptions using try-catch statements. This is adhered to in this class as well as in other classes.
3.  A final exception catcher is declared using the finally statement to catch any exceptions not handled elsewhere and close the database connection neatly.

# Client Applets' Menu Structure

Most of the complexity of the second example lies in the server, which accesses the database to retrieve and store information. We have extended the client functionality to increase its usefulness.

Example 2 has two entry points, as shown on the menu in Figure 18.6: one to join new members and one for existing members. In fact, the same applet (JEClubMbrAplt) is used with a parameter MODE (with value of NEW or EDIT) to indicate which mode we want to use. New members are taken directly to the entry of personal details, using applet PersDtl, where they are issued a new member number.

Figure 18.6 displays the overall structure of the Example 2 applets.

One of the key points demonstrated in this example is how the ORB connection and global data is passed down from the top applet to subsequent applets to build a conversation flow and to maintain context information.

A common applet, PersDtl, is used to edit personal details for new as well as existing members. Based on the mode switch passed to it, its appearance changes slightly for each case. The Personal Details applet, in its new and existing members mode, is shown in Figures 18.7 and 18.10.

**FIG. 18.6**

Example 2 applets
structure.

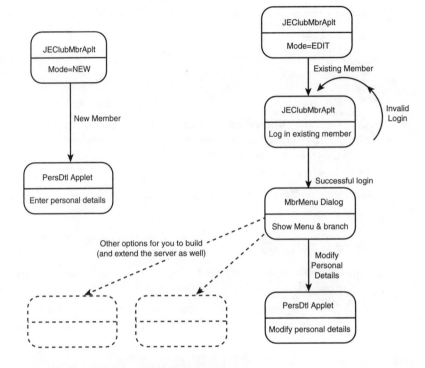

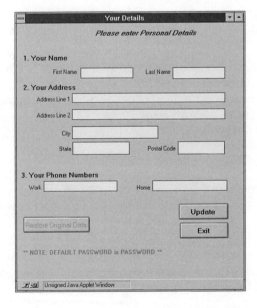

**FIG. 18.7**

Personal Details
applet (`PersDtl`) for
new members.

Existing members (see Figure 18.8) key in their member ID and password to get into the Java
Enterprise Club. Upon successful login, they get a menu of services available, which is shown

in Figure 18.9. The only menu option implemented is `Change Personal Details`. You are invited to build the other options and dream up some server functions to expand the application.

All these applets make use of `get_mbr_info` and `set_mbr_info` methods of the `member` interface and `find_member` and `create_member` methods of the `JEClubSecretary` interface, as required. If you fully understood the functioning of the first example, understanding the functioning of these applets should be straightforward.

**FIG. 18.8**

Login applet (for existing members).

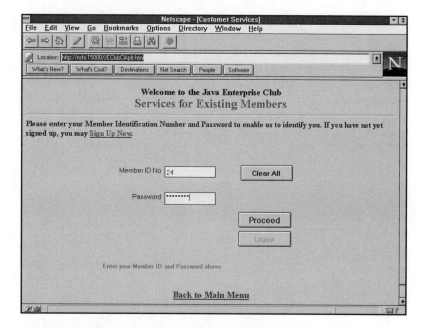

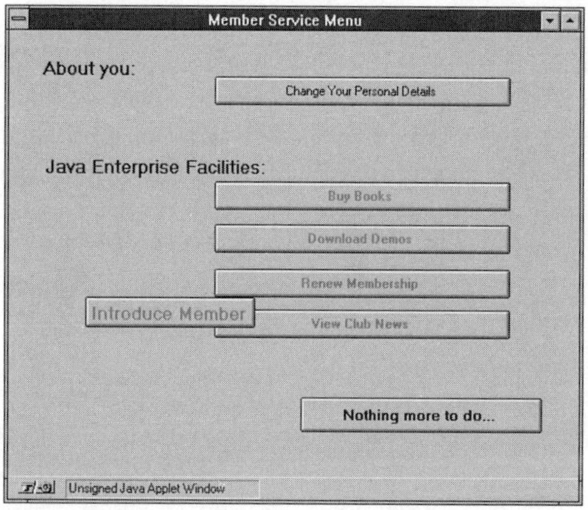

**FIG. 18.9**

Member Services Menu (MbrMenu) applet.

**FIG. 18.10**

Personal Details applet (`PersDtl`) for existing members.

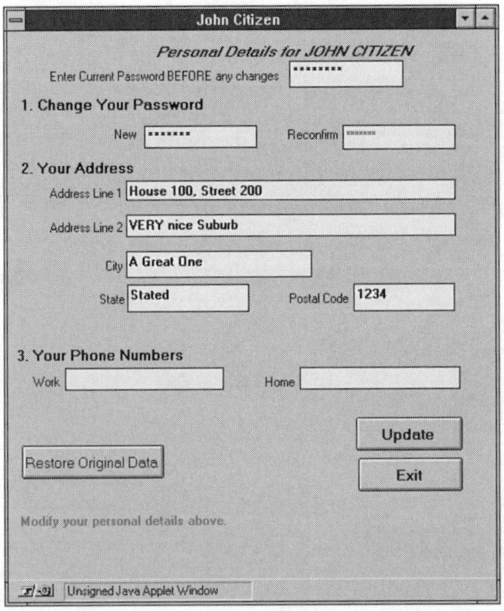

# Challenges Ahead

Example 2 showed you the basic ORB connectivity and database connectivity issues in a simple update application. In a mission-critical distributed application, transaction processing and security issues are very important. A complete discussion on building large Web-object applications appears in Chapter 19, "Scaling Up Web-Object Applications." A brief summary of transaction processing and security issues is presented here.

## Distributed Transactions

Imagine multiple servers updated by a single client. What if one of the updates failed, while all the preceding updates succeeded? You need to roll back updates on all servers other than the one on which failure occurred. This is a complex area, and you have just landed on the planet of *distributed transaction processing*. Distributed transaction processing has a number of issues, which would require a few chapters to explain, if not an entire book. Distributed transaction processing will be outlined in Chapter 19, "Scaling Up Web-Object Applications." In the meantime, you should avoid complexity if you have no mechanism with which to handle that complexity.

## Security

How does a server know that a client applet really comes from the source it claims to come from? How does a client applet ensure that the server it is talking to is the "real server," and not an impostor? These are some of the problems addressed by the design of security for distributed systems. You will be introduced to distributed security design in Chapter 19.

Distributed transaction processing and security are only two examples of challenges that lie in the design of medium- to large-sized, robust distributed applications. Chapter 19 gives an overview of these challenges. We hope to write a sequel to *Enterprise Java* to cover these challenges in greater detail. In the meantime, have fun writing distributed client applets and servers that, for the time being, live in a *trusted* world (a world not requiring extensive security) and where complexity of distributed transaction processing is avoided.

# From Here...

In this chapter, two examples were used to show you how to write your own Web-Object applications. The first example illustrated the use of CORBA for invoking methods on remote objects in an Internet/intranet environment. The second example showed you how to handle persistent (stored) objects on the server end.

To understand the challenges of large Web-Object applications, check out Chapter 19, "Scaling Up Web-Object Applications."

Part

**III**

Ch

**18**

# Scaling Up Web-Object Applications

The last three chapters provided you with an insight into the CORBA and IIOP architecture and its use in intranet/Internet client/server applications. Starting with a "Hello World!"-level application, and then considering a simple database update application, this chapter will help you think big. Scaling up a technology to the Enterprise level requires planning at the organizational and technical levels. This chapter provides a perspective of the technology, standards, and the marketplace and also gives you an overview of how to plan, build, and manage corporate distributed-object applications.

CORBA, as an architecture, has matured only during the last two years, with an interoperability standard published in 1995 and a number of interoperable CORBA products being announced in 1996. With interoperability, CORBA products are now at a level where large distributed systems may use this technology. But a recollection of the overall Object Management Architecture (OMA) will show you that it is a substantial infrastructure, which will take some time to grow. We look at a number of improvements to the CORBA infrastructure currently being considered by the Object Management Group (OMG). More importantly for the readers of this book, 1997 is likely to see the standardization of Java-CORBA binding. We introduce you to what lies ahead on the CORBA and OMA front in general, and how that will impact Web-object applications written in Java. ∎

**Introducing distributed-object applications to the Enterprise**

Find hints on how to make a business case, handle training needs, and manage the risks of introducing distributed-object technology.

**Technical architecture**

Building a distributed technical architecture requires more than an ORB or RMI. An overview is provided of the essential components of the distributed architecture, with a set of key tasks in building the architecture. Look in detail at distributed databases and distributed security.

**Software engineering for distributed-object applications**

As large distributed-object application development projects are undertaken, the software engineering methodologies and processes will have to be enhanced to cater to new challenges.

**Evolution of technology, standards, and the marketplace**

Take a sneak preview of the products currently on their way to the market, and what still lies ahead. Look at how Java, CORBA, and the WWW are likely to evolve in the short- and mid-term.

Java and CORBA on their own do not deliver the whole technical infrastructure for building distributed-object applications. Managing the scope of distributed databases and successfully implementing a distributed security policy are crucial to a distributed architecture. A brief overview of these two technologies will show you the issues requiring consideration.

Successful implementation of large-scale software systems requires a methodological approach to its full life cycle. Traditional object-oriented and structured software life-cycle methodologies need to be extended to the distributed environment. This chapter introduces you to the work already being done in an area that can be termed "distributed software engineering."

You may find the coverage of some of the topics brief—this chapter is designed to provide a checklist of the issues and steps in scaling up object applications in an Internet/intranet environment. Some of these issues are not necessarily unique to the distributed applications for the Web, but are still a critical factor in successful completion of a distributed system project.

# Introducing Distributed-Object Applications to the Enterprise

Introducing new technology to an organization is always a difficult task. Assessing its appropriateness for a given business solution, managing the change at the organizational level, and successfully deploying the technology are crucial to the final success. Without well-informed advice for each of these tasks, the risk of failure is highly increased.

## Defining the Scope of Distribution

This is one of the very first steps in any distributed application, including the Web-object applications. For newcomers to distributed-object computing, there is a temptation to convert the previously non-distributed design to a fully distributed design at a very low level of functionality.

It is important to decide, starting from top-level functionality, which aspects of the functionality need to be "published" over the network and which aspects should be kept local within a server. This choice will be dictated by business as well as technical reasons.

Making a conscious effort to define the level of distribution will help eliminate a large number of problems during the project life cycle.

## Making a Business Case

In Chapter 12, "Introduction to Distributed Computing," we looked at the advantages of distributed computing. Identify how many of these can apply to the business problem that you want to solve by using distributed technology. You will need to quantify, in dollar terms, as many of these benefits as possible. Unquantifiable benefits will need to be explained and new opportunities highlighted.

# Interacting with the Organization

Distributed systems involve integration of business processes and technologies. Each business and technical stakeholder in the proposed project must participate in the planned project.

Business stakeholders must agree, among other traditional requirements, to the degree and kind of benefits to be derived from the distributed nature of the application. This is in addition to the business functionality. It is important to provide the business a simple, modular view of the distributed system. Technical complexity of distributed systems can be overwhelming for a non-technical person.

Your distributed system may span across multiple technical platforms, or may be deployed on a technically uniform platform. If multiple organizational units are responsible for different parts of the network, it may be necessary to liaison with some or all of them to gain understanding of their specific requirements and identify the potential impact of the distributed system in their territory.

A distributed system may eventually be used in geographically disparate parts of a state, country, and very likely, even the world. Business practices within the same organization may be different in its geographically remote parts. Legal and tax regulations can have significant local nuances in different parts of the world as well as in different states of the same country.

# Training and Knowledge Transfer

Deployment of distributed systems involves requirement analysis, technical architecture design, development, and testing. A skill base to develop distributed systems may exist within an organization, it may be inadequate, or it may not exist at all. Specific training goals for different roles involved in a distributed system will need to be set, and the necessary training undertaken. Where the gap between current skill levels and target skill levels is large for a large number of roles, implementing a distributed system can be risky. In such a situation, it is common for an external consulting organization to develop the system on a turnkey basis, including training and mentoring of the employees, finalizing with a complete technology and knowledge transfer.

**Part III**

**Ch 19**

# Choosing a Pilot

Organizations with a high technical skill base may be able to develop a first, large, distributed system in a single attempt. In most cases, a pilot is undertaken to prove the technical and application architecture before attempting a large mission-critical implementation.

A pilot should be chosen in such a manner that it tests as many facets and features of the architecture as possible. Its scale should be small only in quantitative terms. It is best, if it is possible, to choose a high-use, but simple business application. Such a pilot application can even test the scalability of the chosen approach.

# Managing the Risks

Most projects involving substantial efforts, with the potential of providing substantial gains, carry organizational, financial, and technical risks. We look at some of the typical risks in developing distributed systems and present key approaches to minimizing that risk.

**Financial**   One of the key hurdles being faced by the middleware vendors is that middleware does not make a lot of money on its own. They are able to achieve revenue growth by partnerships with application and tool vendors. Since middleware is only an enabling technology, its value is delivered only by a business application that uses it. It can be just like having a computer with the most advanced hardware and operating system, but with no applications available to run on it.

From a buyer's perspective, significant investment in middleware is justified for organizations with large in-house development shops. For organizations depending on the purchase of packaged software, it is best to buy business applications with built-in CORBA interfaces (or other open distributed interfaces). In one significant development, SAP has announced that it will make the functionality of all its business applications available as CORBA 2.0 IDL interfaces, available for multi-tier client/server and intranet/Internet applications using IIOP.

Excessive investment in distributed application infrastructure does not add business functionality, and must therefore be kept in perspective of the overall financial picture. A number of hardware or operating system vendors (for example, IBM) have announced bundling of CORBA 2.0-compliant ORBs with their operating systems. These kinds of platforms, with business application packages and open interfaces, are financially the most prudent investments on behalf of the buying organizations.

**Complexity**   Excessively complex distributed applications are a distinct technical risk. Most real-life distributed systems for large business organizations can be large but not too complex, if properly designed. On the other hand, some engineering applications (for example, distributed telecommunications or real-time switching applications) are inherently much more complex.

In a business application, if the scope and granularity of distributed functionality is correctly designed, it is generally possible to keep the complexity at a manageable level.

Another approach for organizations attempting large-scale Web application development is to aim for the intranet first. This will allow the organization to learn from its own mistakes internally, before the application is released on a much wider basis on the Internet. An application over the Internet has to implement a much stronger security regime as well. An intranet, living within the organization firewall, provides the ideal protection and nurturing ground for evolving applications.

As noted earlier, limiting the scope and granularity of distribution of functionality is one of the key techniques of managing complexity. Chapter 12, "Introduction to Distributed Computing," lists a large number of benefits of distribution. It may be very practical to initially aim for only certain distribution features. Advanced features, like distributed event services, may be built in subsequent stages of the system evolution.

# Technical Architecture

One of the key challenges of designing distributed systems is building a technical architecture that can support the requirements of distributed transaction processing.

To be acceptable, a candidate architecture must possess a whole range of attributes with a certain level of guarantees. Here, we discuss some of the key attributes required of the distributed architecture. These requirements are different for different scenarios of transaction processing. The typical scenarios considered are:

- Simple Read Application
- Simple Update Application
- Complex Read Application
- Complex Update Application

We will not discuss in detail the transaction-processing requirements for each of the aforementioned scenarios. Instead, a full list of attributes is presented. Each of these will need to be examined to determine the requirements for the application being considered.

## Objectives of Distributed Technical Architecture

Conventional single- and two-tier architectures have provided mechanisms to build a huge variety of applications. We give the following wide-ranging list of mechanisms that will need to be provided for in a potential distributed architecture. A technical architect must customize the architecture based on requirements of a specific application within the organization.

**User Mode of Interaction**    A user may interact with a system in a synchronous or asynchronous manner. In a synchronous interaction, the user waits for a response to his or her transaction before proceeding with the next one. In an asynchronous interaction, the user may submit transactions and retrieve responses at a later time. Both these modes find their uses in different circumstances.

A technical architect may need to provide mechanisms to implement both modes of user interaction. An application designer is then able to apply the most appropriate method for the application design.

**System Mode of Interaction**    Components of a distributed system act as clients and servers to each other. Their interactions can again be synchronous or asynchronous. Message queuing and transaction batching may be used to implement asynchronous client/server interactions. Synchronous interaction is the most commonly used, where the client waits for the server to respond before it proceeds further.

**Transaction Logging**    Transaction logging is used by auditors and system administrators for analyzing past transactions to derive a number of statistics and to carry out specific investigations. Since a single distributed transaction may be serviced in multiple parts of the network, a suitable point and manner for logging of transactions will be required.

**Security**    Security implementation in a distributed environment acquires greater complexity because a consistent set of policies and rules need to be enforced across the whole network. We list the main facets of a complete security implementation; a detailed discussion of mechanisms to implement these is not possible here. This list is provided as a checklist for the security architecture.

Authentication consists of validating a claim by any client, server, user, or for that matter, any "resource" of the distributed system, that it is who it claims to be. User ID and password have traditionally provided the basis of authenticating users. With the progress of computing technology, much stronger security techniques have become necessary. Kerberos-based authentication servers and certificate servers are increasingly being used, on the Internet as well as intranets, for generic distributed authentication.

Once a client or user has been allowed entry to a system, he, she, or it is not allowed all types of access to all the resources. An authorization database, commonly implemented using some variation of access control lists, is implemented to define the rights of all users. All services, or servers, within the network should validate the user requests to check if the user is authorized to use the resources his or her request requires.

Implementing a consistent authorization mechanism in a distributed system requires careful planning. It is hard to build consistent authorization mechanisms on-the-fly in a distributed system. DCE Security Service is an excellent example of a distributed security product. Many CORBA products have implemented their security implementation on top of DCE security.

Key resources of the system must be protected from their integrity being compromised by client updates. These resources can be databases or even the programs and executables which form the services provided by the system. It should not be possible for a client or a user to maliciously or unintentionally interfere with the critical system components.

Non-repudiation implies that a client or user should not be able to disclaim ownership of a transaction initiated by it. Use of digital signatures has become widespread to implement non-repudiation schemes. Digital signature mechanisms may need to be implemented for all those components of the system, which must accept legal (and financial) responsibility for their transactions.

The system must ensure confidentiality of all interactions and any data held on behalf of the clients. This is implemented using a variety of encryption mechanisms. Public key encryption schemes based on large keys are state-of-the-art mechanisms for implementing encryption. Kerberos-based authentication mechanisms can provide built-in support for refreshing encryption keys.

**Performance**    Performance design of system components should match the requirements of the application. Performance can be classified along the following parameters.

Each server, and the connection infrastructure (network and middleware), should be able to support the transaction rate generated in the application. Transaction rates should be determined at each entry point to the system. This is then translated to a split as per distribution logic within the network. Finally, a combined target transaction rate for a given server is determined by cumulative assessment of all origins of transactions.

Throughput rate specifies performance in number of transactions per unit of time, whereas response time is the response time to the user. An appropriate combination of synchronous and asynchronous processing may be used to overcome response time problems. Response time criterion does not include any time required by the server between transactions for any housekeeping and so on.

Availability of the distributed system forms critical input to planning redundancy or duplicate servers. Mission-critical applications cannot afford to be unavailable where downtime can directly lead to loss of revenue.

In spite of all precautions and preventive measures, an appropriate recovery mechanism should be implemented for all resources of the system. For some services, it may be mandatory to recover from a failure very quickly (for example, in minutes) whereas for others, disruption of a few hours, while the system recovers to a usable state, may be acceptable.

**User Interface**    For simple read and update applications, HTML forms may be adequate user interfaces. For complex reads and updates, a more feature-rich interface consisting of Java applets and Javascript may be unavoidable. A combination of these can be specified as the organization standard for different categories of applications.

**Recovery of Dialog State**    All conventional transaction-processing monitors allow the implementation of pseudo-conversational transactions. In real life, a given business interaction maps to a sequence of user-interactions with the computer. In transaction processing, each of these interactions is implemented as a transaction. The complete set of interactions that forms a business transaction is generally called a dialog or conversation.

To handle a potential loss of connection between the client and the server in the middle of a dialog or conversation, TP-monitors maintain the state of the dialog for a given user and/or terminal. A similar mechanism is required for intranet/Internet transaction-processing architecture.

**Data Distribution and Access**    Data is the key resource of information systems. Integrity, scalability, and flexibility of data access and storage facilities are crucial in distributed as well as non-distributed systems. We look at data replication and data update characteristics of the data resources.

For information delivery and update, data can spend some time in the "distribution channel" itself, which connects its source and final destination. For reading of data by clients, it may be possible to access some replicas of the central database, which may be synchronized with the central database only on a periodic basis. Similarly, data updates may take time to reach the central database. The need for currency of data differs between applications. An analysis of the application requirements and cost-benefit analysis of the available mechanisms should be used to select an appropriate strategy.

Whenever a client can update two independent (from the recoverability standpoint) servers, the need to support distributed transactions arises. Two-phase commit protocol is the most common mechanism of implementing distributed transactions used by database vendors.

Many organizations with first-generation distributed systems are using remote procedure calls and other distributed computing techniques without support for distributed transactions. This has the risk of producing an inconsistent database and wrongly or incompletely serviced user requests—requiring manual recovery for each transaction.

While planning database configuration for a distributed application, care must be taken to ensure that the candidate DBMSs, if multiple, support two-phase commit protocol and can participate in a collaboration with other DBMSs.

**Information Delivery**   Most Internet mechanisms deliver information using the pull model, where the client has the responsibility of requesting information. A generic distribution architecture should implement both the pull and push models of information delivery.

The client browses an URL or sends a request to some other general application or specific server. This model works well for all situations where the client is the true originator of the transaction.

This mechanism, however, is expensive to use for notification architectures, where a server must notify all interested clients about a certain event or data change. Some notification implementations use regular polling of the server by clients to check for change in status. This generates a lot of unproductive network traffic.

The push model addresses the notification problem in an elegant fashion. All clients interested in being notified of an event or data change register their interest in a "channel" published by a server. They need not periodically poll the server to check for change of status. Instead, the server, when a change of status is detected, generates a push event for them.

The push model is ideal for stock price update services, weather and news updates services, and even distribution-of-software updates. The recent rise of companies such as PointCast and Marimba represents the well overdue, mature use of the wide area network (WAN) infrastructure.

CORBA Event Service, already implemented by a number of ORB vendors, including IONA (Orbix) and Sun (Neo), provides an elegant implementation of the push model. GUI event-loops on the desktop can be integrated with distributed event services, along with any other event-generating services, to build unprecedented levels of interactiveness in a WAN, such as the Internet or intranet.

**Workflow or Groupware Functionality**   Automation of the collaboration among participants in a business process has been the key benefit of groupware products like Lotus Notes. Increasingly, this functionality will be provided by the intranet infrastructure of the organization. A unified approach across the organization will eliminate duplication and other inefficiencies in implementing groupware functionality.

# Tasks for Building Distributed Architecture

There are certain components of a distributed architecture which need to be built from scratch, even though the majority of the building blocks may be supplied by operating system and business application vendors. The components we are talking about are what can be termed the "glue" for making the building blocks work together. Once again, a very high-level view for various integration tasks is presented.

**Integration with Existing Infrastructure**     In a large corporation, all kinds of operating platforms and business applications can be found. Each of these may run on different operating systems, network protocols, database management systems, transaction processing monitors, security schemes, and different categories of middleware. Integrating an organization where all hues of products have found a niche can be a complex, time-consuming, and expensive task. For this reason, a preemptive approach to evolving a distributed environment is critical.

As a huge variety of products can exist in each of the categories listed in the previous paragraph, there is no recommended general approach. The integration approach will be different for each organization. We, however, present a few common techniques used in the integration of distributed systems.

**Mapping of Protocols and Middleware**     Mapping of network protocols is never a strategic option but always a tactical one. Protocol conversion always carries a performance and cost overhead, without providing additional functionality. Increasingly, even the IBM mainframes running various variations of MVS and SNA have been integrated into the enterprise using TCP/IP, which has become the protocol of the enterprise, as all open systems fully support it.

A variety of middleware may also exist within an enterprise. A number of proprietary middleware solutions were already in use in the industry before the arrival of open middleware standards like CORBA, DCE, and RM-ODP (Reference Model for Open Distributed Processing). Object-oriented adoptions of DCE (for example, Hewlett-Packard's OODCE) exist. Organizations who have experimented with RPC on a significant level are discovering the need of messaging middleware, such as IBM's MQ Series and Microsoft's recently announced Messaging Service (product name not known), to implement loosely coupled distributed systems. OMG is also considering a proposal to provide a standard messaging API in CORBA. In an organization with a multitude of existing middleware products (it is not rare in large organizations), an effort has to be made to integrate or rationalize the middleware products in use. A number of commercial CORBA products do interoperate with DCE (for example, Hewlett-Packard's and Digital's ORB products).

**Wrapping of Existing Applications**     CORBA, DCE, and messaging middleware are the most likely middleware options for an organization developing a fresh middleware strategy. One of the key interfaces that has to be developed while working with CORBA and any other middleware is an object-oriented interface to and from the procedural programming domain.

In their book, *The Essential CORBA*, Thomas Mowbray and Ron Zahavi have described a number of object-wrapping techniques. The key wrapping techniques described by them are:

Wrapping with remote procedure calls

Wrapping with files

Wrapping with sockets

Wrapping with a C-API

Wrapping with scripts

Wrapping with events

Wrapping with shared memory

Wrapping with dynamic queries

Wrapping with Inter-Program Communication (IPC)

Wrapping with macros

Wrapping with header files

# Distributed Systems Software Engineering

Use of structured, disciplined project management and software development processes is critical to the success of software development projects. Various methods have been used to maximize reusability and overall life-cycle costs.

Object-oriented analysis and design have become mainstream over the last ten years. Methods for analysis, design, testing, and project management have matured and de facto standards have emerged. OMG is also currently examining analysis and design standards, submitted by the world's leading methodologists, to agree on an adopted industry standard. This activity is set to provide a second generation of analysis and design standards for the object-oriented community.

Large-scale distributed systems development, until about a couple of decades ago, was constrained by the limitations of the communication technology. Large-scale distributed software projects had been few and very specialized for their problem domain. The development of embedded software systems during the eighties using Ada has contributed substantially to modern distributed software engineering. It is only with the arrival of multi-tier client/server systems, and open standards such as OMA and DCE to support them, that developing substantial distributed software systems can be more widely contemplated.

Extending object-oriented analysis, design, and testing methods (with substantial input from distributed systems development) for multi-tier client/server development for business applications is a recent activity. This section will highlight what is special about the distributed systems' software life cycle and how various phases of the conventional SDLC life cycle are enhanced to support distributed systems development.

MOSES, one of the leading OO methodologies recently enhanced for distributed systems, is based on the work of Dr. Brian Hendersen-Sellers, Dr. Julian Edwards, G. Rasmussen, and G.C. Low. Dr. Hendersen-Sellers is the originator of MOSES and OPEN object-oriented methodologies, the latter of which was submitted in January of 1997 to OMG as a proposed object-oriented analysis and design methodology. A number of papers supporting extension of MOSES methodology to cater to distributed systems have been published in the *Journal of Object-Oriented Programming* (JOOP) and other journals during 1996 by these three authors.

# How Distributed Systems Differ

Development of distributed applications requires specific steps and considerations in the SDLC processes. We provide only a summary of how distributed systems are different to prepare you for the kind of challenges that you may face. Please refer to one of the specified references for more details. Requirement gathering and physical system design and testing all have specific considerations in distributed systems.

**Requirement Analysis**    The need for a distributed system is first seen in the requirements. Concurrence in the business environment and the different locations of the users and information resources are the two key contributing factors requiring a distributed system.

**Physical System Design**    Physical system design poses the maximum amount of challenges, since this is where all the technological difference lies.

***Partitioning and Allocation***    Partitioning is one of the key issues of designing distributed systems. Partitioning consists of deciding how the overall system will be split into a set of servers. Allocation consists of assigning these servers to various processors in the system. During development, all servers may run on a single machine before being tested and deployed in a true distributed environment. On the opposite extreme, a distributed system may be developed by a virtual team, spread in geographically different parts of the world, working on different components of system.

***Coupling and Cohesion***    Coupling and cohesion are two measures which have been used for problem analysis and modular program design.

As a system is modeled and designed, some parts of its structure exchange a lot of information with other parts. The set of parts that exchange a lot of information is said to be tightly coupled or has strong cohesion. These are generally implemented in the same physical subsystem or component so that the information exchange between them is efficient. A group of such subsystems or components provides the intermediate level of system structure (between the lowest level and the system as a whole). Subsystems also exchange information between each other, but not to the same degree as the parts within a single subsystem. An attempt is made to minimize the information exchange between subsystems since subsystems are physically different components and intercommunication between them is resource-intensive. The dependency between subsystems is also termed *coupling*. A good system design is one where an optimum level of coupling has been achieved.

Structured systems analysis, design, and programming, as well as the object-oriented approach, are built on the foundation of minimizing coupling and maximizing cohesion between various parts of a system. Parts of the system with maximum coupling are assigned to the same closely knit module (in structured programming), object (in an object-oriented approach), or server (in distributed system design).

Achieving the optimum balance of coupling and cohesion can involve many design tradeoffs.

***Granularity of Distribution***    For processes running under a single operating system, any process can call another process. Thus, all processes are visible to other processes (if permitted by security and other operating system considerations). In a distributed system, only the processes with potential clients, processes on other nodes of the network, or processes needing the services of servers on other nodes of the network should be developed with distributed functionality.

***Network Design***   Requirements of each user or "citizen" of the network contribute to the overall network utilization. Transaction volumes at all entry points in the distributed system are translated to the network traffic generated at different times of the day, week, month, and year. All such requirements of all applications and users on the network is summed up (and more) to arrive at desired network capacity for various components of the network. Network design is a complete area in itself, involving selection of appropriate topology, hardware, network operating system, and network management software.

# Distributed Software Design

There are a few steps which, if taken, will help you avoid some of the problems of handling a substantial distributed system. If they will not provide the answer, they will at least let you define a process that can be used to seek answers to problems as they arise and a process to apply solutions across the whole of the system in a team environment.

Like all large software development, standards play an important role in improving a team's productivity and in helping reduce the defects in the final product.

Distributed system development standards should be established to provide preferred solutions to the frequently occurring design problems and dos and don'ts at the design and coding levels. A consistent naming convention of all components across the network can be very useful as well.

Design patterns for distributed applications are also emerging. These provide a good design toolchest, which stores valuable experiences of other people who have already encountered and solved the same problems.

# Developing Distributed Applications

CASE tools for managing the SDLC have been continuously improving. Currently, very good development tools exist for developing and debugging non-distributed applications. Many of these are already being enhanced to record the additional information at various SDLC stages for distributed, multi-tier, client/server applications. Analysis and design notations have been enhanced. CORBA IDL is directly generated from object models. Generic facilities for debugging CORBA object implementations are becoming an integral part of the debugging tools.

In a real-life distributed system, the order of events is highly unpredictable, which makes dynamic testing of distributed applications nearly impossible. Components of a distributed system can operate and fail autonomously and independently. Some controlled methods of submitting events to the distributed system may be used for testing.

# Evolution of Technology, Standards, and the Marketplace

We will now look at how Java, OMA, and CORBA, and their supporting technology, standards, and marketplace are emerging.

## CORBA Marketplace

Compared to other industry standards, CORBA is a very young standard. Its adoption by a large body of vendors is the reason for its success. A large number of products, with CORBA 2.0 IIOP standard interoperability, are already available for nearly every major operating system on the market. The following milestones lie ahead for the CORBA marketplace during 1997 and beyond:

**General Milestones**    First, let us look at the CORBA products in the pipeline or on the horizon. These are general CORBA products that will be useful for both Java and non-Java applications.

- Availability of TP-Monitors, complying with the OMG standard Transaction Service. This will provide the commit and rollback reliability of transaction processing to the distributed environment. At the time of writing, at least two such major products are in beta, and a third one has been announced.

- More OMG standard services will be supported by ORB vendors and utility vendors. Some of the more feature-rich OMA services, already available with some ORBs, are:

  - Distributed Event Service, to make your mouse-click (and other such events) visible to the whole distributed application
  - Security Service to enforce multi-tier security
  - Trader Service to locate suitable object implementations
  - Persistence Service for database access

- ORBs will increasingly be freely given away or will form an integral part of the operating system or business application product. IBM is bundling its SOM with a number of its operating systems. All major database vendors have their own ORBs or are developing their database services with other vendors' ORBs.

- A large number of business application packages will start to provide CORBA IDL interfaces, so these packages can be used as a server from any client in the distributed system. One such major announcement is by SAP to make all its business applications available as CORBA and ActiveX distributed-object servers.

- Increased proofs of interoperability between different ORBs. Some of the current ORB product offerings do not interoperate with IIOP.

Part III
Ch 19

**Java-Specific Milestones**   All the functionality of CORBA products, with no Java support, will still be accessible by CORBA 2.0 client Java applets. The following CORBA-related market developments will help the use of CORBA in Java applications and vice versa.

- IIOP interoperable Java IDL is part of the core Java API announced by Sun. It was meant to be available as part of JDK 1.1, but is now delayed, possibly until mid-1997.

- Netscape Navigator 4.0 will be bundled with the client component of a CORBA 2.0-compliant ORB, Visigenic's Visibroker for Java. You have already used Visibroker for Java while developing the example application in the previous chapter. This will eliminate the need for a large download of ORB client at runtime, thus providing a faster initialization of ORB applets.

- Nearly all commercial ORB products will, at least, allow Java-clients to be written, if not server as well (server support requires developing IDL-to-Java bindings; more on the IDL-to-Java bindings is provided in the following section on standards).

- A number of freeware ORB products already available on the Internet will become more credible in regard to performance and interoperability. Some of these have been written entirely in Java. Some are already approaching IIOP interoperability, whereas others sacrifice interoperability to provide some other benefits.

- Support for zipped class libraries from JDK 1.1 will provide faster download for distributed ORB applets and their support classes.

## OMA and CORBA Standards

CORBA 2.0 provides a standard for interoperability across heterogeneous programming languages and operating platforms. There are a number of improvements and enhancements to the standard, currently at various stages of the standardization process, within OMG. A complete list of OMG's "work in progress" can be found at **http://www.omg.org/library/schedule.htm**.

Some of the key improvements are:

- IDL-to-Java Mapping
- Application Portability across ORB products
- Objects by Value
- Financial Facilities
- Business Objects
- IDL-to-COBOL Mapping

## WWW Standards

It does not take a very experienced Internet user to be aware of the existence of multiple HTML standards. HTML is a very new and rapidly evolving standard. Compliance to HTML 1.0 is considered adequate for basic use, but the latest version of the HTML standard is already at 3.2, and there are always more enhancements in the pipeline.

One reason for this evolution is the initial inefficiencies of the HTTP protocol. Various vendors, including significant impact by Netscape and Microsoft, have contributed to the evolution of the standard. The World Wide Web Consortium (**http://www.w3.org/**) and OMG have come together to discuss the active document standard, represented by Web-object applications. HTML is evolving to nothing but a set of objects, some of which can be CORBA objects (uncertainty about ActiveX). More details of their joint efforts can be found at the W3 home page.

# Managing Distributed Applications

Managing the software life cycle and runtime antics of distributed applications will provide a number of challenges in the coming years. OMG's licensing and administration standard services, when implemented as commercial products, may evolve into facilities which will lighten the complexity burdens of distributed applications. Research into distributed databases will provide some valuable lessons for distributed systems design and engineering. Current interest in intranets and the Internet will continue to drive the interest in multi-tier, client/server transaction processing, already acquiring significant momentum in organizations of medium to large size.

# From Here...

Successfully developing large distributed applications, be they Java RMI, Java CORBA, or plain CORBA without Java, will require new challenges for business and information systems executives, requirement models, technical designers, application developers, and network designers (to name a few). Evolving Java, CORBA, and WWW standards are rapidly addressing many of these challenges. The hardest lessons will be learned in the practical application of the technology to real-life applications. Prepare your organization to deliver the benefits of distributed Java, RMI, and CORBA applications to its customers and use these technologies to improve business financially and operationally.

- To review benefits and complexities of Distributed Computing, go to Chapter 12, "Introduction to Distributed Computing."
- To understand CORBA and Object Management Architecture, go to Chapter 16, "CORBA and Object Management Architecture (OMA)."
- To understand how Web applications can be built using CORBA, go to Chapter 17, "WWW Applications Development Using CORBA."

Part
III

Ch
19

# Appendixes

# OMG IDL Grammar

This appendix is to assist in your understanding of OMG IDL grammar. Additional information can be found in the Object Management Group's document, "The Common Object Request Broker: Architecture and Specification" or at its Web site **http://www.omg.org/library/**. ■

# The Common Object Request Broker

The following information has been extracted from Object Management Group's document, "The Common Object Request Broker: Architecture and Specification," revision 2.0, dated July 1995.

```
(1) <specification> ::= <definition>+
(2) <definition> ::= <type_dcl> ";"
                 | <const_dcl> ";"
                 | <except_dcl> ";"
                 | <interface> ";"
                 | <module> ";"
(3) <module> ::= "module" <identifier> "{" <definition> + "}"
(4) <interface> ::= <interface_dcl>
                 | <forward_dcl>
(5) <interface_dcl> ::= <interface_header> "{" <interface_body> "}"
(6) <forward_dcl> ::= "interface" <identifier>
(7) <interface_header>::= "interface" <identifier> [ <inheritance_spec> ]
(8) <interface_body> ::= <export> *
(9) <export> ::= <type_dcl> ";"
            | <const_dcl> ";"
            | <except_dcl> ";"
            | <attr_dcl> ";"
            | <op_dcl> ";"
(10) <inheritance_spec>::= ":" <scoped_name> { "," <scoped_name> } *
(11) <scoped_name> ::= <identifier>
                   | "::" <identifier>
                   | <scoped_name> "::" <identifier>
(12) <const_dcl> ::= "const" <const_type> <identifier> "=" <const_exp>
(13) <const_type> ::= <integer_type>
                  | <char_type>
                  | <boolean_type>
                  | <floating_pt_type>
                  | <string_type>
                  | <scoped_name>
(14) <const_exp> ::= <or_expr>
(15) <or_expr> ::= <xor_expr>
               | <or_expr> "|" <xor_expr>
(16) <xor_expr> ::= <and_expr>
                | <xor_expr> "^" <and_expr>
(17) <and_expr> ::= <shift_expr>
                | <and_expr> "&" <shift_expr>
(18) <shift_expr> ::= <add_expr>
             | <shift_expr> ">>" <add_expr>
             | <shift_expr> "<<" <add_expr>
(19) <add_expr> ::= <mult_expr>
             | <add_expr> "+" <mult_expr>
             | <add_expr> "-" <mult_expr>
(20) <mult_expr> ::= <unary_expr>
             | <mult_expr> "*" <unary_expr>
             | <mult_expr> "/" <unary_expr>
             | <mult_expr> "%" <unary_expr>
(21) <unary_expr> ::= <unary_operator> <primary_expr>
             | <primary_expr>
```

```
(22) <unary_operator> ::= "-"
            ¦ "+"
            ¦ "~"
(23) <primary_expr> ::= <scoped_name>
            ¦ <literal>
            ¦ "(" <const_exp> ")"
(24) <literal> ::= <integer_literal>
            ¦ <string_literal>
            ¦ <character_literal>
            ¦ <floating_pt_literal>
            ¦ <boolean_literal>
(25) <boolean_literal> ::= "TRUE"
            ¦ "FALSE"
(26) <positive_int_const>::=<const_exp>
(27) <type_dcl> ::= "typedef" <type_declarator>
            ¦ <struct_type>
            ¦ <union_type>
            ¦ <enum_type>
(28) <type_declarator> ::= <type_spec> <declarators>
(29) <type_spec> ::= <simple_type_spec>
            ¦ <constr_type_spec>
(30) <simple_type_spec>::=<base_type_spec>
            ¦ <template_type_spec>
            ¦ <scoped_name>
(31) <base_type_spec>::= <floating_pt_type>
            ¦ <integer_type>
            ¦ <char_type>
            ¦ <boolean_type>
            ¦ <octet_type>
            ¦ <any_type>
(32) <template_type_spec>::=<sequence_type>
            ¦ <string_type>
(33) <constr_type_spec>::=<struct_type>
            ¦ <union_type>
            ¦ <enum_type>
(34) <declarators> ::= <declarator> { "," <declarator> } *
(35) <declarator> ::= <simple_declarator>
            ¦ <complex_declarator>
(36) <simple_declarator>::=<identifier>
(37) <complex_declarator>::=<array_declarator>
(38) <floating_pt_type>::= "float"
                      ¦ "double"
(39) <integer_type> ::= <signed_int>
                      ¦ <unsigned_int>
(40) <signed_int> ::= <signed_long_int>
               ¦ <signed_short_int>
(41) <signed_long_int> ::= "long"
(42) <signed_short_int>::= "short"
(43) <unsigned_int> ::= <unsigned_long_int>
               ¦ <unsigned_short_int>
(44) <unsigned_long_int>::="unsigned" "long"
(45) <unsigned_short_int>::="unsigned" "short"
(46) <char_type> ::= "char"
(47) <boolean_type> ::= "boolean"
(48) <octet_type> ::= "octet"
(49) <any_type> ::= "any"
```

```
(50) <struct_type> ::= "struct" <identifier> "{" <member_list> "}"
(51) <member_list> ::= <member>+
(52) <member> ::= <type_spec> <declarators> ";"
(53) <union_type> ::= "union" <identifier> "switch" "(" <switch_type_spec> ")"
               "{" <switch_body> "}"
(54) <switch_type_spec>::=<integer_type>
             ¦ <char_type>
             ¦ <boolean_type>
             ¦ <enum_type>
             ¦ <scoped_name>
(55) <switch_body> ::= <case>+
(56) <case> ::= <case_label>+ <element_spec> ";"
(57) <case_label> ::= "case" <const_exp> ":"
             ¦ "default" ":"
(58) <element_spec> ::= <type_spec> <declarator>
(59) <enum_type> ::= "enum" <identifier> "{" <enumerator> { ","
➥<enumerator> } * "}"
(60) <enumerator> ::= <identifier>
(61) <sequence_type> ::= "sequence" "<" <simple_type_spec>
➥","<positive_int_const>">"
             ¦ "sequence" "<" <simple_type_spec> ">"
(62) <string_type> ::= "string" "<" <positive_int_const> ">"
             ¦ "string"
(63) <array_declarator>::= <identifier> <fixed_array_size>+
(64) <fixed_array_size>::= "[" <positive_int_const> "]"
(65) <attr_dcl> ::= [ "readonly" ] "attribute" <param_type_spec>
             <simple_declarator> { "," <simple_declarator> }*
(66) <except_dcl> ::= "exception" <identifier> "{" <member>* "}"
(67) <op_dcl> ::= [ <op_attribute> ] <op_type_spec> <identifier>
➥<parameter_dcls>
             [ <raises_expr> ] [ <context_expr> ]
(68) <op_attribute> ::= "oneway"
(69) <op_type_spec> ::= <param_type_spec>
             ¦ "void"
(70) <parameter_dcls> ::= "(" <param_dcl> { "," <param_dcl> } * ")"
             ¦ "(" ")"
(71) <param_dcl> ::= <param_attribute> <param_type_spec> <simple_declarator>
(72) <param_attribute> ::= "in"
             ¦ "out"
             ¦ "inout"
(73) <raises_expr> ::= "raises" "(" <scoped_name> { "," <scoped_name> } * ")"
(74) <context_expr> ::= "context" "(" <string_literal> { "," <string_literal>
➥} *")"
(75) <param_type_spec>::=<base_type_spec>
             ¦ <string_type>
             ¦ <scoped_name>
```

# Common CORBA Exceptions

This section highlights the common CORBA exceptions encountered while developing ORB applications. A brief explanation of the exception is provided, followed by possible causes and suggested remedial action. The exceptions covered here are only the basic level, common to most ORBs. For a detailed explanation, it is best to refer to the programming guide and reference for the ORB product in use.

# CORBA_COMMS_FAILURE

The following is an explanation of the CORBA_COMMS_FAILURE exception.

**Description**   A communication operation internal to the ORB could not be completed success-fully. Generally, additional information is provided.

**Cause**   Can be any reason which can cause any network operation to fail. A most common reason is an overloaded network or processor, resulting in a timeout on the communication operation.

**Suggested Remedy**   Generally, a retry at a time of lower network load will suffice. If network load is a persistent problem, it needs to be addressed by the network administrator as a separate task.

# CORBA_NO_IMPLEMENTATION

The following is an explanation of the CORBA_NO_IMPLEMENTATION exception.

**Description**   ORB could not bind the client to an implementation (server) with the parameters specified.

**Possible Causes**   Implementation selection criteria (including implementation or server name) are mistyped or wrongly formulated.

Implementation is unreachable due to being not active (for a manually started implementation).

**Suggested Remedy**   Check that implementation is active (if manually started) or registered properly in the implementation repository (if automatically started).

Check that the implementation name (and other parameters if supported by ORB and used for the request) are correct.

# Java/JDBC Resources

**W**hen developing Java applications with the Enterprise Java API, situations may be encountered that cannot be covered or predicted by this book. To assist in trouble-shooting problems, or simply to extend the knowledge presented within this tome, this appendix presents a number of available resources that exist online. These resources include developer e-mail addresses, e-mail list servers, Web pages, Web sites, and newsgroups. These resources contain vast amounts of information ranging from JavaSoft developer specifications to third-party developer insights. Enjoy! ■

# Developer E-Mail Addresses

The following is a list of e-mail addresses currently being monitored by JavaSoft. These e-mail addresses allow JavaSoft developers to receive feedback such as bug reports and suggestions. Although messages are not often acknowledged with responses, JavaSoft will monitor these addresses for comments and suggestions (see Table B.1).

**Table B.1   Developer E-Mail Addresses**

| Technology | E-Mail Address |
| --- | --- |
| JDK | jdk-comments@java.sun.com |
| Security | java-security@java.sun.com |
| RMI | rmi-support@java.sun.com |
| JDBC | jdbc@wombat.eng.sun.com |
| JDBC-ODBC | jdbc-odbc@wombat.eng.sun.com |
| Java IDL | idl-support@java.sun.com |

# Mailing Lists

Mailing lists, often called ListServs (named after the server software), offer subscriptions to topics related to specific Java technology API groups. Mailing lists tend to be concentrated on specific technologies and often do not offer or tolerate other subjects. Once subscribed, all messages sent to the mailing list are transmitted to each subscribed user. This allows users interested in similar topics to have a Q & A forum for discussing new or future technologies. Note that some of these mailing lists tend to traffic large numbers of messages per day. Consider using an e-mail client that offers features, such as filtering and custom mailboxes, to separate the incoming messages. This is highly recommended when subscribing to multiple lists simultaneously, since each list may send between five and a hundred messages per day. To subscribe, simply send an e-mail message to **listserv@java.sun.com** with the text described in Table B.2 as the body of the message.

**Table B.2   JavaSoft Mailing Lists**

| Technology | Subscribe Command |
| --- | --- |
| RMI/Object Serialization | subscribe rmi-users |
| IDL | subscribe idl-users |

# Mailing List Archives

Extending mailing list services is the mailing list archive. As messages are shared with a specific group, such as the RMI mailing list group, the messages are archived into an HTML file. This prevents questions being repeatedly asked by newcomers to the list. By retrieving the HTML document and using a browser's search capabilities, questions and answers related to specific topics can be located. Always refer to these archives before issuing a question to a mailing list to prevent harsh responses from veterans to the mailing list (see Table B.3).

**Table B.3    Mailing List Archives**

| Technology | Archive URL |
| --- | --- |
| RMI/Object Serialization | **http://chatsubo.javasoft.com/email/rmi-users/ subject.html** |
| IDL | **http://splash.javasoft.com/mail/idl-users/date.html** |
| Security | **http://jeeves.javasoft.com/hypermail/java-security-archive/index.html** |

# World Wide Web Resources

What would a resources guide be without the World Wide Web resource list? The links provided were gathered from search engine queries, other resource pages, and the JavaSoft site. Keep in mind that less-traveled links tend to expire or disappear, and highly traveled sites can be moved to new locations for higher bandwidth requirements. Please check with these sites often to keep up with any scheduled changes (see Table B.4).

**Table B.4    World Wide Web Resources**

| Company | Address | Notes |
| --- | --- | --- |
| JavaSoft | **www.javasoft.com** | Home page for all Java development |
| Sun | **java.sun.com** | Backup home page for JavaSoft. This page is usually more responsive than the JavaSoft home page, especially when new releases of the software are released. |
| | **www.javasoft.com/products/ jdk/1.1/** | JDK 1.1 API |
| | **www.javasoft.com/nav/ download/** | List of all available libraries/JDK ports |

*continues*

| Table B.4 | Continued | |
|-----------|-----------|---|
| **Company** | **Address** | **Notes** |
| Sun | www.javasoft.com/dpd/whitepapers.html | JavaSoft Whitepapers on new technologies |
| | splash.javasoft.com/jdbc/JDBCSpecifications0 | API |
| | chatsubo.javasoft.com/current/ | RMI and Distributed Systems Group |
| JavaWorld | www.javaworld.com | E-zine containing hints, tips, articles |
| Earthweb | www.gamelan.com | Applet/Application directory |
| XDB | www.xdb.com | Jet Connect JDBC Drivers |
| WebLogic | www.weblogic.com | webKona JDBC Drivers |

# Newsgroups

Newsgroups offer the easiest forum for communicating with fellow Java developers on any topic. They are grouped by general topics, and are read by many developers on a daily or weekly basis. Often, large companies, such as Symantec and JavaSoft, provide representatives to answer specific software questions and to provide input on new technologies. Newsgroups require a news client, which may be found throughout the Internet by using a search engine (see Table B.5).

| Table B.5 | Java Newsgroups |
|-----------|-----------------|
| **Newsgroup** | **General Topics/Guidelines** |
| comp.lang.java.advocacy | Discussion of why or why not to use Java and related technologies |
| comp.lang.java.api | Discussion of the Java API |
| comp.lang.java.misc | Discussion of everything else, including new books, tools, and so on |
| comp.lang.java.programmer | Discussion of the language, including design issues |
| comp.lang.java.security | Discussion of Java security aspects, including security managers and the new security API |
| comp.lang.java.setup | Discussion for end-users of the Java systems, including specific platform port information and browser compatibilities |
| comp.lang.java.tech | Discussion of technical issues, including file formats, bytecode, virtual machines, and optimization |

# CORBA Resources

Situations may occur, when developing CORBA applications with the Enterprise Java API, that have not been anticipated or covered in this book. To assist in troubleshooting these problems, or simply to extend your knowledge, this appendix presents additional resources that are available online. ■

# OMG Publications

*Object Management Architecture Overview*

*CORBA 1.1 Architecture and Specifications* (91-12-01)

*CORBA 2.0 Architecture and Specifications* (96-03-04)

*Common Services Specifications (COSS)*

# Journal Papers and Books

Steve Vinoski, "Distributed Object Computing with CORBA," *C++ Report*. July/August 1993.

D.C. Schmidt and S. Vinoski, "Introduction to Distributed Object Computing," *C++ Report*. SIGS. Vol. 7, No. 1, January 1995.

D.C. Schmidt and S. Vinoski, "Modeling Distributed Object Applications," *C++ Report*. SIGS. Vol. 7, No. 2, February 1995.

D.C. Schmidt and S. Vinoski, "Comparing Alternative Client Distributed Programming Techniques," *C++ Report*. SIGS. Vol. 7, No. 4, May 1995.

Orfali, Harkley, Edwards. *The Essential Distributed Objects Survival Guide*, Wiley. 1996.

Jon Siegel. *CORBA Fundamentals and Programming*, Wiley. 1996.

Thomas J. Mowbray and Ron Zahavi. *The Essential CORBA—Systems Integration Using Distributed Objects*, Wiley. 1995.

"Comparing DCE and CORBA," *Object Magazine*. March 1996.

# Internet Resources

As CORBA products, the market, and Information Technology industry's interest in CORBA have grown substantially, a vast number of resources are available on the Internet. A list of key Web sites, vendors' home pages, and some of the popular mailing lists on Java-CORBA appears as follows:

## Web Pages

Object Management Group
**http://www.omg.org**

Los Alamitos National Laboratory (LANL)—Advanced Computing Laboratory
**http://www.acl.lanl.gov/CORBA/**

Distributed Systems Technology Centre, Brisbane
**http://www.dstc.edu.au**

Doug Schmidt's CORBA Page
**http://www.cs.wustl.edu/~schmidt/corba.html**

Java API Overview (Java IDL)
**http://www.javasoft.com/products/apiOverview.html**

# Vendors

The following is not a complete list. Please refer to the OMG or LANL pages listed previously for a complete listing.

Digital (ObjectBroker)
**http://www.digital.com/info/objectbroker/**

Expersoft (PowerBroker)
**http://www.expersoft.com/prod_ser/index.htm**

Hewlett-Packard (ORB Plus)
**http://www.hp.com/gsy/orbplus.html**

IBM (SOM and OpenDoc)
**http://www.software.ibm.com/objects/somobjects/**

IONA Technologies (OrbixWeb for Java and Orbix)
**http://www.iona.com**

Sun Microsystems (NEO and Joe for Java)
**http://www.sun.com/solaris/neo/**

Visigenic Corporation (Visibroker for Java and C++, previously known as Blackwidow and ORBeLine, respectively) (Previously Post-Modern Computing)
**http://www.visigenic.com**

Xerox (Inter-Language Unification, or ILU)
**ftp://ftp.parc.xerox.com/pub/ilu/ilu.html**

App
C

# Newsgroups

**comp.object.corba**

**comp.object**

**comp.lang.java.programmer**

# Mailing Lists

CORBA-Dev Mailing List
**http://www.netsurf.org/~ripoutea/list/corba/maillist.html**

Java IDL-Users Maling List
Send "subscribe IDL-USERS" to **listserv@javasoft.com**

Java CORBA Mailing List
Send a message with subject "subscribe" to **JavaCORBA@luke.org**

# Third-Party Resources

The list of third-party tools and utilities is growing at a rapid pace. This appendix captures many of the common sites that have information about Enterprise Java tools. In addition to this list, it is always a good idea to stay tuned to the Java newsgroups and occasionally to perform keyword searches on the Web.

The JavaSoft newsgroups are archived at the DejaNews Web site. To search for a topic, go to the DejaNews home page, located at **http://www.dejanews.com**.

Enter Keywords:

`comp.lang.java` + (*your keywords*)

Typically, it is best to use terms that are specific to your topic: JDBC, RMI, Object Serialization, IDL, CORBA, JavaBeans, and so on. ■

| JDBC Drivers | Web Site |
| --- | --- |
| Borland International, Inc. | http://www.borland.com |
| Connect, Inc. | http://www.connectsw.com |
| DataRamp | http://www.dataramp.com |
| IBM's Database 2 (DB2) | http://www.software.ibm.com/data/db2/jdbc |
| Imaginary (mSQL) | http://www.imaginary.com |
| Intersolv | http://www.inter-soft.com |
| OpenLink Software | http://www.openlinksw.com |
| Oracle Corporation | http://www.oracle.com |
| SAS Institute, Inc.™ | http://www.sas.com/rnd/web/jdbc.html |
| SCO | http://www.vision.sco.com/brochure/sqlretriever.html |
| Sybase, Inc. | http://www.sybase.com |
| Symantec | http://www.symantec.com/dba/dbawpr1.html |
| Visigenic Software, Inc. | http://www.visigenic.com |
| WebLogic, Inc. | http://www.weblogic.com |
| XDB Systems | http://www.xdb.com |

| Java Relational Database Solutions | Web Site |
| --- | --- |
| Bulletproof | http://www.bulletproof.com |
| Informix Software, Inc. | http://www.informix.com |
| Net Dynamics | http://www.netdynamics.com |
| O2 Technology | http://www.o2tech.com |
| Open Horizon | http://www.openhorizon.com |
| Persistence Software | http://www.openhorizon.com |
| RogueWave Software, Inc. | http://www.roguewave.com |
| Sanga | http://www.sangacorp.com |

| ODBMS Vendors | Web Site |
| --- | --- |
| Fujitsu Software Corporation | http://www.fsc.fujitsu.com |
| GemStone Systems, Inc. | http://www.gemstone.com |
| Hewlett-Packard Company | http://www.hp.com |
| IBEX Corporation, S.A. | http://www.iprolink.ch/ibexcom |
| Informix (Illustra) | http://www.informix.com |
| MATISSE Software, Inc. | http://www.adb.com |

| | |
|---|---|
| O2 Technology, Inc. | **http://www.o2tech.com** |
| Object Design, Inc. | **http://www.odi.com** |
| Objectivity, Inc. | **http://www.objy.com** |
| Omniscience Object Technology, Inc. | **http://www.oracle.com** |
| ONTOS, Inc. | **http://www.ontos.com** |
| Persistence Software, Inc. | **http://www.persistence.com** |
| POET Software, Inc. | **http://www.poet.com** |
| Unisys Corporation | **http://www.osmos.com** |
| UniSQL, Inc. | **http://www.unisql.com** |
| Versant Object Technology | **http://www.versant.com** |

| **Security** | **Web Site** |
|---|---|
| Phaos | **http://www.phaos.com/** |
| RSA | **http://www.rsa.com** |
| JavaSoft | **http://www.javasoft.com/security** |

| **Integrated Development Environments** | **Web Site** |
|---|---|
| Metrowerks | **http://www.metrowerks.com** |
| Symantec | **http://www.symantec.com** |
| Microsoft | **http://www.microsoft.com** |
| IBM | **http://www.ibm.com** |
| ObjectShare | **http://www.objectshare.com** |
| Asymetrix | **http://www.asymetrix.com** |
| PowerSoft | **http://www.powersoft.com** |
| Borland | **http://www.borland.com** |
| Net Dynamics | **http://www.netdynamics.com** |
| JavaSoft | **http://www.javasoft.com** |

| **CORBA & Distributed Solutions** | **Web Site** |
|---|---|
| Visigenic | **http://www.visigenic.com/prod/vbjpd.html** |
| IONA Technologies | **http://www.iona.com** |
| WebLogic | **http://www.weblogic.com** |
| Sun | **http://www.javasoft.com** |
| Hewlett-Packard | **http://www.hp.com** |
| Digital | **http://www.digital.com/info/objectbroker** |
| Gemstone | **http://www.gemstone.com/Products/gorb.htm** |

App
D

# The JDBC API

The purpose of this appendix is to supply a complete reference guide to the JDBC classes provided in the `java.sql` package. It is divided into Interfaces, Classes, and Exceptions; each section provides method syntax and any variables, including constants. ■

# Interfaces

The following sections illustrate the methods and variables of the interfaces included in the `java.sql` package.

## *Callable* Statement

Methods:

- ▣ abstract void registerOutParameter(int parameterIndex,int sqlType) throws SQLException

- ▣ abstract void registerOutParameter(int parameterIndex, int sqlType,int scale) throws SQLException

- ▣ abstract boolean wasNull() throws SQLException

- ▣ abstract String getString(int parameterIndex) throws SQLException

- ▣ abstract boolean getBoolean(int parameterIndex) throws SQLException

- ▣ abstract byte getByte(int parameterIndex) throws SQLException

- ▣ abstract short getShort(int parameterIndex) throws SQLException

- ▣ abstract int getInt(int parameterIndex) throws SQLException

- ▣ abstract long getLong(int parameterIndex) throws SQLException

- ▣ abstract float getFloat(int parameterIndex) throws SQLException

- ▣ abstract double getDouble(int parameterIndex) throws SQLException

- ▣ abstract BigDecimal getBigDecimal(int parameterIndex, int scale) throws SQLException

- ▣ abstract byte[] getBytes(int parameterIndex) throws SQLException

- ▣ abstract Date getDate(int parameterIndex) throws SQLException

- ▣ abstract Time getTime(int parameterIndex) throws SQLException

- ▣ abstract Timestamp getTimestamp(int parameterIndex) throws SQLException

- ▣ abstract Object getObject(int parameterIndex) throws SQLException

## *Connection*

Variables:

- ▣ TRANSACTION_NONE

- ▣ TRANSACTION_READ_COMMITTED

- ▣ TRANSACTION_READ_UNCOMMITTED

- ▣ TRANSACTION_REPEATABLE_READ

- ▣ TRANSACTION_SERIALIZABLE

Methods:

■ abstract Statement createStatement() throws SQLException

■ abstract PreparedStatement prepareStatement(String sql) throws SQLException

■ abstract CallableStatement prepareCall(String sql) throws SQLException

■ abstract String nativeSQL(String sql) throws SQLException

■ abstract void setAutoCommit(boolean autoCommit) throws SQLException

■ abstract boolean getAutoCommit() throws SQLException

■ abstract void commit() throws SQLException

■ abstract void rollback() throws SQLException

■ abstract void close() throws SQLException

■ abstract boolean isClosed() throws SQLException

■ abstract DatabaseMetaData getMetaData() throws SQLException

■ abstract void setReadOnly(boolean readOnly) throws SQLException

■ abstract void setCatalog(String catalog) throws SQLException

■ abstract String getCatalog() throws SQLException

■ abstract void setTransactionIsolation(int level) throws SQLException

■ abstract int getTransactionIsolation() throws SQLException

■ abstract SQLWarning getWarnings() throws SQLException

■ abstract void clearWarnings() throws SQLException

## *DatabaseMetaData*

Variables:

■ procedureResultUnknown

■ procedureNoResult

■ procedureReturnsResult

■ procedureColumnUnknown

■ procedureColumnIn

■ procedureColumnInOut

■ procedureColumnOut

■ procedureColumnReturn

■ procedureColumnResult

■ procedureNoNulls

■ procedureNullable

■ procedureNullableUnknown

- columnNoNulls
- columnNullable
- columnNullableUnknown
- bestRowTemporary
- bestRowTransaction
- bestRowSession
- bestRowUnknown
- bestRowNotPseudo
- bestRowPseudo
- versionColumnUnknown
- versionColumnNotPseudo
- versionColumnPseudo
- importedKeyCascade
- importedKeyRestrict
- importedKeySetNull
- importedKeyNoAction
- importedKeySetDefault
- importedKeyInitiallyDeferred
- importedKeyInitiallyImmediate
- importedKeyNotDeferrable
- typeNoNulls
- typeNullable
- typeNullableUnknown
- typePredNone
- typePredChar
- typePredBasic
- typeSearchable
- tableIndexStatistic
- tableIndexClustered
- tableIndexHashed
- tableIndexOther

## Methods:

- abstract boolean allProceduresAreCallable() throws SQLException
- abstract boolean allTablesAreSelectable() throws SQLException
- abstract String getURL() throws SQLException

- abstract String getUserName() throws SQLException
- abstract boolean isReadOnly() throws SQLException
- abstract boolean nullsAreSortedHigh() throws SQLException
- abstract boolean nullsAreSortedLow() throws SQLException
- abstract boolean nullsAreSortedAtStart() throws SQLException
- abstract boolean nullsAreSortedAtEnd() throws SQLException
- abstract String getDatabaseProductName() throws SQLException
- abstract String getDatabaseProductVersion() throws SQLException
- abstract String getDriverName() throws SQLException
- abstract String getDriverVersion() throws SQLException
- abstract int getDriverMajorVersion()
- abstract int getDriverMinorVersion()
- abstract boolean usesLocalFiles() throws SQLException
- abstract boolean usesLocalFilePerTable() throws SQLException
- abstract boolean supportsMixedCaseIdentifiers() throws SQLException
- abstract boolean storesUpperCaseIdentifiers() throws SQLException
- abstract boolean storesLowerCaseIdentifiers() throws SQLException
- abstract boolean storesMixedCaseIdentifiers() throws SQLException
- abstract boolean supportsMixedCaseQuotedIdentifiers() throws SQLException
- abstract boolean storesUpperCaseQuotedIdentifiers() throws SQLException
- abstract boolean storesLowerCaseQuotedIdentifiers() throws SQLException
- abstract boolean storesMixedCaseQuotedIdentifiers() throws SQLException
- abstract String getIdentifierQuoteString() throws SQLException
- abstract String getSQLKeywords() throws SQLException
- abstract String getNumericFunctions() throws SQLException
- abstract String getStringFunctions() throws SQLException
- abstract String getSystemFunctions() throws SQLException
- abstract String getTimeDateFunctions() throws SQLException
- abstract String getSearchStringEscape() throws SQLException
- abstract String getExtraNameCharacters() throws SQLException
- abstract boolean supportsAlterTableWithAddColumn() throws SQLException
- abstract boolean supportsAlterTableWithDropColumn() throws SQLException
- abstract boolean supportsColumnAliasing() throws SQLException
- abstract boolean nullPlusNonNullIsNull() throws SQLException
- abstract boolean supportsConvert() throws SQLException

App
E

- abstract boolean supportsConvert(int fromType, int toType) throws SQLException
- abstract boolean supportsTableCorrelationNames() throws SQLException
- abstract boolean supportsDifferentTableCorrelationNames() throws SQLException
- abstract boolean supportsExpressionsInOrderBy() throws SQLException
- abstract boolean supportsOrderByUnrelated() throws SQLException
- abstract boolean supportsGroupBy() throws SQLException
- abstract boolean supportsGroupByUnrelated() throws SQLException
- abstract boolean supportsGroupByBeyondSelect() throws SQLException
- abstract boolean supportsLikeEscapeClause() throws SQLException
- abstract boolean supportsMultipleResultSets() throws SQLException
- abstract boolean supportsMultipleTransactions() throws SQLException
- abstract boolean supportsNonNullableColumns() throws SQLException
- abstract boolean supportsMinimumSQLGrammar() throws SQLException
- abstract boolean supportsCoreSQLGrammar() throws SQLException
- abstract boolean supportsExtendedSQLGrammar() throws SQLException
- abstract boolean supportsANSI92EntryLevelSQL() throws SQLException
- abstract boolean supportsANSI92IntermediateSQL() throws SQLException
- abstract boolean supportsANSI92FullSQL() throws SQLException
- abstract boolean supportsIntegrityEnhancementFacility() throws SQLException
- abstract boolean supportsOuterJoins() throws SQLException
- abstract boolean supportsFullOuterJoins() throws SQLException
- abstract boolean supportsLimitedOuterJoins() throws SQLException
- abstract String getSchemaTerm() throws SQLException
- abstract String getProcedureTerm() throws SQLException
- abstract String getCatalogTerm() throws SQLException
- abstract boolean isCatalogAtStart() throws SQLException
- abstract String getCatalogSeparator() throws SQLException
- abstract boolean supportsSchemasInDataManipulation() throws SQLException
- abstract boolean supportsSchemasInProcedureCalls() throws SQLException
- abstract boolean supportsSchemasInTableDefinitions() throws SQLException
- abstract boolean supportsSchemasInIndexDefinitions() throws SQLException
- abstract boolean supportsSchemasInPrivilegeDefinitions() throws SQLException
- abstract boolean supportsCatalogsInDataManipulation() throws SQLException
- abstract boolean supportsCatalogsInProcedureCalls() throws SQLException

- abstract boolean supportsCatalogsInTableDefinitions() throws SQLException
- abstract boolean supportsCatalogsInIndexDefinitions() throws SQLException
- abstract boolean supportsCatalogsInPrivilegeDefinitions() throws SQLException
- abstract boolean supportsPositionedDelete() throws SQLException
- abstract boolean supportsPositionedUpdate() throws SQLException
- abstract boolean supportsSelectForUpdate() throws SQLException
- abstract boolean supportsStoredProcedures() throws SQLException
- abstract boolean supportsSubqueriesInComparisons() throws SQLException
- abstract boolean supportsSubqueriesInExists() throws SQLException
- abstract boolean supportsSubqueriesInIns() throws SQLException
- abstract boolean supportsSubqueriesInQuantifieds() throws SQLException
- abstract boolean supportsCorrelatedSubqueries() throws SQLException
- abstract boolean supportsUnion() throws SQLException
- abstract boolean supportsUnionAll() throws SQLException
- abstract boolean supportsOpenCursorsAcrossCommit() throws SQLException
- abstract boolean supportsOpenCursorsAcrossRollback() throws SQLException
- abstract boolean supportsOpenStatementsAcrossCommit() throws SQLException
- abstract boolean supportsOpenStatementsAcrossRollback() throws SQLException
- abstract int getMaxBinaryLiteralLength() throws SQLException
- abstract int getMaxCharLiteralLength() throws SQLException
- abstract int getMaxColumnNameLength() throws SQLException
- abstract int getMaxColumnsInGroupBy() throws SQLException
- abstract int getMaxColumnsInIndex() throws SQLException
- abstract int getMaxColumnsInOrderBy() throws SQLException
- abstract int getMaxColumnsInSelect() throws SQLException
- abstract int getMaxColumnsInTable() throws SQLException
- abstract int getMaxConnections() throws SQLException
- abstract int getMaxCursorNameLength() throws SQLException
- abstract int getMaxIndexLength() throws SQLException
- abstract int getMaxSchemaNameLength() throws SQLException
- abstract int getMaxProcedureNameLength() throws SQLException
- abstract int getMaxCatalogNameLength() throws SQLException
- abstract int getMaxRowSize() throws SQLException
- abstract boolean doesMaxRowSizeIncludeBlobs() throws SQLException
- abstract int getMaxStatementLength() throws SQLException

App
E

■ abstract int getMaxStatements() throws SQLException

■ abstract int getMaxTableNameLength() throws SQLException

■ abstract int getMaxTablesInSelect() throws SQLException

■ abstract int getMaxUserNameLength() throws SQLException

■ abstract int getDefaultTransactionIsolation() throws SQLException

■ abstract boolean supportsTransactions() throws SQLException

■ abstract boolean supportsTransactionIsolationLevel(int level) throws SQLException

■ abstract boolean supportsDataDefinitionAndDataManipulationTransactions() throws SQLException

■ abstract boolean supportsDataManipulationTransactionsOnly() throws SQLException

■ abstract boolean dataDefinitionCausesTransactionCommit() throws SQLException

■ abstract boolean dataDefinitionIgnoredInTransactions() throws SQLException

## Driver

Methods:

■ abstract Connection connect(String url, Properties info) throws SQLException

■ abstract boolean acceptsURL(String url) throws SQLException

■ abstract DriverPropertyInfo[] getPropertyInfo(String url, Properties info) throws SQLException

■ abstract int getMajorVersion()

■ abstract int getMinorVersion()

■ abstract boolean jdbcCompliant()

## PreparedStatement

Methods:

■ abstract ResultSet executeQuery() throws SQLException

■ abstract int executeUpdate() throws SQLException

■ abstract void setNull(int parameterIndex, int sqlType) throws SQLException

■ abstract void setBoolean(int parameterIndex, boolean x) throws SQLException

■ abstract void setByte(int parameterIndex, byte x) throws SQLException

■ abstract void setShort(int parameterIndex, short x) throws SQLException

■ abstract void setInt(int parameterIndex, int x) throws SQLException

■ abstract void setLong(int parameterIndex, long x) throws SQLException

■ abstract void setFloat(int parameterIndex, float x) throws SQLException

- abstract void setDouble(int parameterIndex, double x) throws SQLException

- abstract void setBigDecimal(int parameterIndex, BigDecimal x) throws SQLException

- abstract void setString(int parameterIndex, String x) throws SQLException

- abstract void setBytes(int parameterIndex, byte x[]) throws SQLException

- abstract void setDate(int parameterIndex, Date x) throws SQLException

- abstract void setTime(int parameterIndex, Time x) throws SQLException

- abstract void setTimestamp(int parameterIndex, Timestamp x) throws SQLException

- abstract void setAsciiStream(int parameterIndex, InputStream x, int length) throws SQLException

- abstract void setUnicodeStream(int parameterIndex, InputStream x, int length) throws SQLException

- abstract void setBinaryStream(int parameterIndex, InputStream x, int length) throws SQLException

- abstract void clearParameters() throws SQLException

- abstract void setObject(int parameterIndex, Object x, int targetSqlType, int scale) throws SQLException

- abstract void setObject(int parameterIndex, Object x, int targetSqlType) throws SQLException

- abstract void setObject(int parameterIndex, Object x) throws SQLException

- abstract boolean execute() throws SQLException

## *ResultSet*

Methods:

- abstract boolean next() throws SQLException

- abstract void close() throws SQLException

- abstract boolean wasNull() throws SQLException

- abstract String getString(int columnIndex) throws SQLException

- abstract boolean getBoolean(int columnIndex) throws SQLException

- abstract byte getByte(int columnIndex) throws SQLException

- abstract short getShort(int columnIndex) throws SQLException

- abstract int getInt(int columnIndex) throws SQLException

- abstract long getLong(int columnIndex) throws SQLException

- abstract float getFloat(int columnIndex) throws SQLException

- abstract double getDouble(int columnIndex) throws SQLException

- abstract BigDecimal getBigDecimal(int columnIndex, int scale) throws SQLException

App

E

■ abstract byte[] getBytes(int columnIndex) throws SQLException

■ abstract Date getDate(int columnIndex) throws SQLException

■ abstract Time getTime(int columnIndex) throws SQLException

■ abstract Timestamp getTimestamp(int columnIndex) throws SQLException

■ abstract InputStream getAsciiStream(int columnIndex) throws SQLException

■ abstract InputStream getUnicodeStream(int columnIndex) throws SQLException

■ abstract InputStream getBinaryStream(int columnIndex) throws SQLException

■ abstract String getString(String columnName) throws SQLException

■ abstract boolean getBoolean(String columnName) throws SQLException

■ abstract byte getByte(String columnName) throws SQLException

■ abstract short getShort(String columnName) throws SQLException

■ abstract int getInt(String columnName) throws SQLException

■ abstract long getLong(String columnName) throws SQLException

■ abstract float getFloat(String columnName) throws SQLException

■ abstract double getDouble(String columnName) throws SQLException

■ abstract BigDecimal getBigDecimal(String columnName, int scale) throws SQLException

■ abstract byte[] getBytes(String columnName) throws SQLException

■ abstract Date getDate(String columnName) throws SQLException

■ abstract Time getTime(String columnName) throws SQLException

■ abstract Timestamp getTimestamp(String columnName) throws SQLException

■ abstract InputStream getAsciiStream(String columnName) throws SQLException

■ abstract InputStream getUnicodeStream(String columnName) throws SQLException

■ abstract InputStream getBinaryStream(String columnName) throws SQLException

■ abstract SQLWarning getWarnings() throws SQLException

■ abstract void clearWarnings() throws SQLException

■ abstract String getCursorName() throws SQLException

■ abstract ResultSetMetaData getMetaData() throws SQLException

■ abstract Object getObject(int columnIndex) throws SQLException

■ abstract Object getObject(String columnName) throws SQLException

■ abstract int findColumn(String columnName) throws SQLException

## *ResultSetMetaData*

Variables:

- columnNoNulls
- columnNullable
- columnNullableUnknown

Methods:

- abstract int getColumnCount() throws SQLException
- abstract boolean isAutoIncrement(int column) throws SQLException
- abstract boolean isCaseSensitive(int column) throws SQLException
- abstract boolean isSearchable(int column) throws SQLException
- abstract boolean isCurrency(int column) throws SQLException
- abstract int isNullable(int column) throws SQLException
- abstract boolean isSigned(int column) throws SQLException
- abstract int getColumnDisplaySize(int column) throws SQLException
- abstract String getColumnLabel(int column) throws SQLException
- abstract String getColumnName(int column) throws SQLException
- abstract String getSchemaName(int column) throws SQLException
- abstract int getPrecision(int column) throws SQLException
- abstract int getScale(int column) throws SQLException
- abstract String getTableName(int column) throws SQLException
- abstract String getCatalogName(int column) throws SQLException
- abstract int getColumnType(int column) throws SQLException
- abstract String getColumnTypeName(int column) throws SQLException
- abstract boolean isReadOnly(int column) throws SQLException
- abstract boolean isWritable(int column) throws SQLException
- abstract boolean isDefinitelyWritable(int column) throws SQLException

## *Statement*

Methods:

- abstract ResultSet executeQuery(String sql) throws SQLException
- abstract int executeUpdate(String sql) throws SQLException
- abstract void close() throws SQLException

App
E

- abstract int getMaxFieldSize() throws SQLException

- abstract void setMaxFieldSize(int max) throws SQLException

- abstract int getMaxRows() throws SQLException

- abstract void setMaxRows(int max) throws SQLException

- abstract void setEscapeProcessing(boolean enable) throws SQLException

- abstract int getQueryTimeout() throws SQLException

- abstract void setQueryTimeout(int seconds) throws SQLException

- abstract void cancel() throws SQLException

- abstract SQLWarning getWarnings() throws SQLException

- abstract void clearWarnings() throws SQLException

- abstract void setCursorName(String name) throws SQLException

- abstract boolean execute(String sql) throws SQLException

- abstract ResultSet getResultSet() throws SQLException

- abstract int getUpdateCount() throws SQLException

- abstract boolean getMoreResults() throws SQLException

# Classes

The following sections illustrate the methods and variables of the classes included in the java.sql package.

## *Date*

Methods:

- Date(int year, int month, int day)

- Date(long date)

- void setTime(long date)

- static Date valueOf(String s)

- String toString()

- int getHours()

- int getMinutes()

- int getSeconds()

- void setHours(int i)

- void setMinutes(int i)

- void setSeconds(int i)

# DriverManager

Methods:

- static synchronized Connection getConnection(String url, Properties info) throws SQLException
- static synchronized Connection getConnection(String url, String user, String password) throws SQLException
- static synchronized Connection getConnection(String url) throws SQLException
- static Driver getDriver(String url) throws SQLException
- static synchronized void registerDriver(Driver driver) throws SQLException
- static void deregisterDriver(Driver driver) throws SQLException
- static Enumeration getDrivers()
- static void setLoginTimeout(int seconds)
- static int getLoginTimeout()
- static void setLogStream(PrintStream out)
- static PrintStream getLogStream()
- static void println(String message)

# DriverPropertyInfo

Variables:

- name
- description
- required
- value
- choices

Methods:

- DriverPropertyInfo(String name, String value)

# Time

Methods:

- Time(int hour, int minute, int second)
- Time(long time)
- void setTime(long time)
- static Time valueOf(String s)

- String toString()
- int getYear()
- int getMonth()
- int getDay()
- int getDate()
- void setYear(int i)
- void setMonth(int i)
- void setDate(int i)

## *Timestamp*

Methods:

- Timestamp(int year, int month, int date, int hour, int minute, int second, int nano)
- Timestamp(long time)
- static Timestamp valueOf(String s)
- String toString()
- int getNanos()
- void setNanos(int n)
- boolean equals(Timestamp ts)
- boolean before(Timestamp ts)
- boolean after(Timestamp ts)

## Types

Variables:

- BIT
- TINYINT
- SMALLINT
- INTEGER
- BIGINT
- FLOAT
- REAL
- DOUBLE
- NUMERIC
- DECIMAL
- CHAR

- VARCHAR
- LONGVARCHAR
- DATE
- TIME
- TIMESTAMP
- BINARY
- VARBINARY
- LONGVARBINARY
- NULL
- OTHER

# Exceptions

The following sections illustrate the methods and variables of the exceptions included in the java.sql package.

## *DataTruncation*

Methods:

- `DataTruncation(int index, boolean parameter, boolean read, int dataSize, int transferSize)`
- `int getIndex()`
- `boolean getParameter()`
- `boolean getRead()`
- `int getDataSize()`
- `int getTransferSize()`

## *SQLException*

Methods:

- `SQLException(String reason, String SQLState, int vendorCode)`
- `SQLException(String reason, String SQLState)`
- `SQLException(String reason)`
- `SQLException()`
- `String getSQLState()`
- `int getErrorCode()`
- `SQLException getNextException()`
- `synchronized void setNextException(SQLException ex)`

## *SQLWarning*

Methods:

- SQLWarning(String reason, String SQLstate, int vendorCode)
- SQLWarning(String reason, String SQLstate)
- SQLWarning(String reason)
- SQLWarning()
- SQLWarning getNextWarning()
- void setNextWarning(SQLWarning w)

# Index

# S

**scaling up WWW applications, 423-424**
distributed systems software engineering, 432-434
introducing distributed-object applications, 424-426
managing distributed application, 437
technical architecture, 427-432
data distribution/access, 429-430
groupware functionality, 430
information delivery, 430
integration with existing infrastructure, 431
mapping protocols/middleware, 431
performance, 428-429
recovery of dialog state, 429
security, 428
system interaction mode, 427-428
transaction logging, 427-428
user interaction mode, 427
user interface, 429
wrapping existing applications, 431-432

**schemas**
creation methods, 185
getSchemaName(int) method, 77
querying, 99-100

**scrambling code,** *see* **obfuscation**

**security, 8, 209, 420**
applets, 210-215
CAs (certificate authorities), 215
certificates, 211
creating digital signatures (Javakey utility), 213-215
Crema, 216
digital signatures, 212-215
Mocha, 216-217
obfuscation, 217-219
public/private keys, 211-212
distributed computing, 234-235
architecture, 428
e-mail address, 448
hidden HTML pages, 189
mailing list archive, 449
Mocha, 216-217
obfuscation, 217-219
object serialization, 261-262
privileges
columns, 119-122
tables, 105-108

RMI, 291-293
class loading, 291-292
firewalls, 292-293
RMISecurityManager class, 326-327
Security API family, 10
Virtual Machine byte code checks, 195

**security managers (RMI)**
creating remote clients, 288
implementing remote servers, 287

**SELECT statement, manipulating text/image data, 27**

**sendMessage() method, remote client implementation, 302**

**Serializable interface, RMI model, 279-285**

**serialization,** *see* **object serialization**

**serialver utility (JDK 1.1), 259-260**

**Server API family, 11**

**server-side includes (SSI), 371**

**ServerRef interface, 334**

**servers**
CORBA ORBs, 353
CORBA WWW applications, 369-370
file servers, code storage, 189-190
Java Enterprise Club example application, 397
example 2 changes, 416-417
JEClubSecretary class, 402-403
JEClubServer class, 417
Member class, 402, 416-417
starting, 408
writing, 400-402
languages (CORBA WWW applications), 379-380
push/pull, 430
RMI (server components), 273, 283
client/server applications, 275-277
implementing, 296-300, 310-314
implementing servers, 286-287
peer-to-peer applications, 277-278
properties, 337-338
remote server interfaces, 294, 309-310

RemoteServer class, 325
server-related classes/interfaces, 324-331
Web servers, code storage, 188-189

**services**
CORBA, 243-244
CORBA object services, 347-349

**Set collection, ODBMS, 178**

**setAutoClose() method, connection class, 50**

**setAutoCommit() method, connection class, 49**

**setCursorName() method, 75**

**setFailureHandler() method, 328-329**

**setLog() method, RMI applications, 320, 325**

**setLoginTimeout() method, DriverManager, 57-58**

**setLogStream() method, DriverManager, 56**

**setMaxRows() method, 74**

**setPriority() method, 156**

**setQueryTimeout method, 72**

**setQueryTimeout() method, 71-72**

**setReadOnly() method, connection class, 49**

**setSocketFactory() method, 328-329**

**sharing files, .jar files, 201**

**signatures, applets,** *see* **applets, signing**

**SimpleObject class, 321**
new version, 260-261
ObjectOutputStream class, 251-252

**skeleton class,** *see* **stub/skeleton classes**

**Skeleton interface, 334-335**

**skeleton/stub classes, generating (RMI applications), 289**

**skeletons, Java Enterprise Club example application, 402-403**

**sleep() method**
Thread class, Runnable interface, 154
threads, blocked threads, 157

**smallint data type, 22**
mapping to Java types, 24

# Complete and Return this Card
# for a *FREE* Computer Book Catalog

Thank you for purchasing this book! You have purchased a superior computer book written expressly for your needs. To continue to provide the kind of up-to-date, pertinent coverage you've come to expect from us, we need to hear from you. Please take a minute to complete and return this self-addressed, postage-paid form. In return, we'll send you a free catalog of all our computer books on topics ranging from word processing to programming and the Internet.

Mr. ☐  Mrs. ☐  Ms. ☐  Dr. ☐

Name (first) ☐☐☐☐☐☐☐☐☐☐☐  (M.I.) ☐  (last) ☐☐☐☐☐☐☐☐☐☐☐☐☐☐☐☐☐

Address ☐☐☐☐☐☐☐☐☐☐☐☐☐☐☐☐☐☐☐☐☐☐☐☐☐☐☐☐☐☐☐☐☐☐☐

City ☐☐☐☐☐☐☐☐☐☐☐☐☐☐  State ☐☐  Zip ☐☐☐☐☐ ☐☐☐☐

Phone ☐☐☐ ☐☐☐ ☐☐☐☐  Fax ☐☐☐ ☐☐☐ ☐☐☐☐

Company Name ☐☐☐☐☐☐☐☐☐☐☐☐☐☐☐☐☐☐☐☐☐☐☐☐☐☐☐☐☐

E-mail address ☐☐☐☐☐☐☐☐☐☐☐☐☐☐☐☐☐☐☐☐☐☐☐☐☐☐☐☐☐

## 1. Please check at least (3) influencing factors for purchasing this book.

Front or back cover information on book ........................ ☐
Special approach to the content ................................ ☐
Completeness of content ...................................... ☐
Author's reputation .......................................... ☐
Publisher's reputation ....................................... ☐
Book cover design or layout .................................. ☐
Index or table of contents of book ........................... ☐
Price of book ................................................ ☐
Special effects, graphics, illustrations ..................... ☐
Other (Please specify): _____

## 2. How did you first learn about this book?

Saw in Macmillan Computer Publishing catalog .......... ☐
Recommended by store personnel ................................ ☐
Saw the book on bookshelf at store ............................ ☐
Recommended by a friend ....................................... ☐
Received advertisement in the mail ............................ ☐
Saw an advertisement in: _____ ☐
Read book review in: _____ ☐
Other (Please specify): _____ ☐

## 3. How many computer books have you purchased in the last six months?

This book only ....... ☐     3 to 5 books ..................... ☐
2 books .................. ☐     More than 5 ..................... ☐

## 4. Where did you purchase this book?

Bookstore ................................................... ☐
Computer Store .............................................. ☐
Consumer Electronics Store .................................. ☐
Department Store ............................................ ☐
Office Club ................................................. ☐
Warehouse Club .............................................. ☐
Mail Order .................................................. ☐
Direct from Publisher ....................................... ☐
Internet site ............................................... ☐
Other (Please specify): _____ ☐

## 5. How long have you been using a computer?

☐ Less than 6 months      ☐ 6 months to a year
☐ 1 to 3 years            ☐ More than 3 years

## 6. What is your level of experience with personal computers and with the subject of this book?

|              | With PCs | With subject of book |
|--------------|----------|----------------------|
| New          | ☐        | ☐                    |
| Casual       | ☐        | ☐                    |
| Accomplished | ☐        | ☐                    |
| Expert       | ☐        | ☐                    |

Source Code ISBN: 0-7897-0887-6

**7. Which of the following best describes your job title?**

Administrative Assistant .................................. ☐
Coordinator .................................................... ☐
Manager/Supervisor ....................................... ☐
Director .......................................................... ☐
Vice President ................................................ ☐
President/CEO/COO ...................................... ☐
Lawyer/Doctor/Medical Professional ............ ☐
Teacher/Educator/Trainer .............................. ☐
Engineer/Technician ...................................... ☐
Consultant ...................................................... ☐
Not employed/Student/Retired ...................... ☐
Other (Please specify): _____ ☐

**8. Which of the following best describes the area of the company your job title falls under?**

Accounting ..................................................... ☐
Engineering .................................................... ☐
Manufacturing ............................................... ☐
Operations ..................................................... ☐
Marketing ...................................................... ☐
Sales .............................................................. ☐
Other (Please specify): _____ ☐

**9. What is your age?**

Under 20 ........................................................ ☐
21-29 .............................................................. ☐
30-39 .............................................................. ☐
40-49 .............................................................. ☐
50-59 .............................................................. ☐
60-over ........................................................... ☐

**10. Are you:**

Male ............................................................... ☐
Female ............................................................ ☐

**11. Which computer publications do you read regularly? (Please list)**

_____
_____
_____
_____
_____
_____
_____
_____

*Comments*: _____
_____
_____

Fold here and scotch-tape to mail.

# Check out Que® Books
# on the World Wide Web
# http://www.quecorp.com

As the biggest software release in computer history, Windows 95 continues to redefine the computer industry. Click here for the latest info on our Windows 95 books

Make computing quick and easy with these products designed exclusively for new and casual users

Examine the latest releases in word processing, spreadsheets, operating systems, and suites

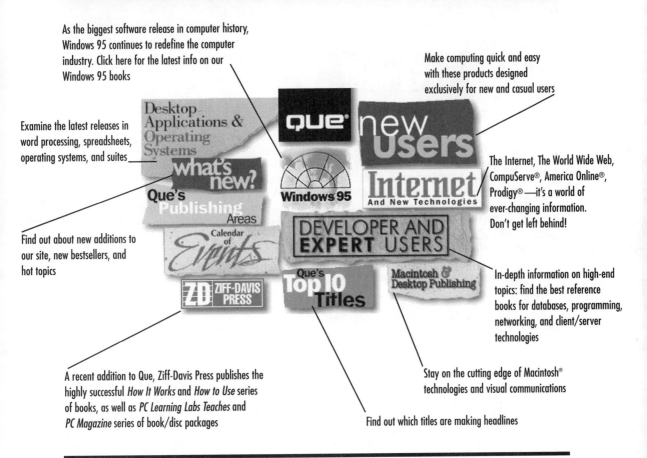

The Internet, The World Wide Web, CompuServe®, America Online®, Prodigy®—it's a world of ever-changing information. Don't get left behind!

Find out about new additions to our site, new bestsellers, and hot topics

In-depth information on high-end topics: find the best reference books for databases, programming, networking, and client/server technologies

A recent addition to Que, Ziff-Davis Press publishes the highly successful *How It Works* and *How to Use* series of books, as well as *PC Learning Labs Teaches* and *PC Magazine* series of book/disc packages

Stay on the cutting edge of Macintosh® technologies and visual communications

Find out which titles are making headlines

---

With 6 separate publishing groups, Que develops products for many specific market segments and areas of computer technology. Explore our Web Site and you'll find information on best-selling titles, newly published titles, upcoming products, authors, and much more.

- Stay informed on the latest industry trends and products available
- Visit our online bookstore for the latest information and editions
- Download software from Que's library of the best shareware and freeware

MACMILLAN COMPUTER PUBLISHING USA

A VIACOM COMPANY

## Technical ----- Support:

If you need assistance with the information in this book or with a CD/Disk accompanying the book, please access the Knowledge Base on our Web site at **http://www.superlibrary.com/general/support**. Our most Frequently Asked Questions are answered there. If you do not find the answer to your questions on our Web site, you may contact Macmillan Technical Support **(317) 581-3833** or e-mail us at **support@mcp.com**.

Please check out additional information regarding the code listings found in this book and other helpful Enterprise Java tips at the Que Web site at **www.quecorp.com/enterprise/**.